SO-AZX-860

iStockphoto.com_pixelfit

Love the Great Outdoors?

When getting away means getting off the beaten path, visit **AAA.com/campgrounds** or **AAA.com/maps** for:

⚠ Thousands of places to camp across the U.S. and Canada

⚠ Complete mapping and travel information to plan your adventure

iStockphoto.com_welcomia

Look for locations with the trusted mark of approval.

Inspected & Approved

Make the Connction

For trip planning and local activities, AAA guidebooks are just the beginning.

Open the door to a whole lot more on AAA.com. Get extra travel insight, more information and online booking.

Find this symbol for places to look, book and save on AAA.com.

Maine, New Hampshire & Vermont

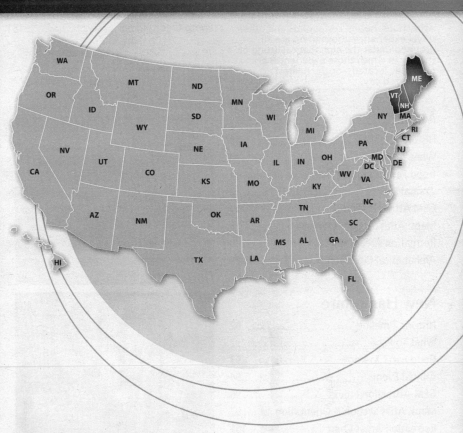

Published by AAA Publishing
1000 AAA Drive, Heathrow, FL 32746-5063
Copyright AAA 2019, All rights reserved

The publisher has made every effort to provide accurate, up-to-date information but accepts no responsibility for loss or injury sustained by any person using this book. TourBook® guides are published for the exclusive use of AAA members. Not for sale.

Advertising Rate and Circulation Information: (407) 444-8280

Printed in the USA by Quad/Graphics

This book is printed on paper certified by third-party standards for sustainably managed forestry and production.

 Printed on recyclable paper.
Please recycle whenever possible.

Stock #4615

CONTENTS

Get more travel information at AAA.com/travelguides and AAA.com/traveltips

Attractions, hotels, restaurants and other travel experience information are all grouped under the alphabetical listing of the city in which those experiences are physically located—or the nearest recognized city.

Featured Information

Maine

New Hampshire

Vermont

free to
rock the boat

TripAssist travel insurance allows you to go with the flow. It can free you up to make the most of your vacation. Nothing will hold you back knowing that you and your travel plans are safe.

Talk to your AAA Travel Agent today for more information.

Using Your Guide

AAA TourBook guides are packed with travel insights, maps and listings of places to stay, play, eat and save. For more listings, more details and online booking, visit **AAA.com/travelguides**.

Helping You Make the Connection
Look for this symbol 🔗 throughout the guides for direct links to related content.

A to Z City Listings
Cities and places are listed alphabetically within each state or province. Attractions, hotels and restaurants are listed once — under the city in which they are physically located.

Cities that are considered part of a larger destination city or area have an expanded city header. The header identifies the larger region and cross-references pages that contain shared trip planning resources:

- Destination map – outline map of the cities that comprise a destination city or area
- Attraction spotting map – regional street map marked with attraction locations
- Hotel/restaurant spotting map and index – regional street map numbered with hotel and restaurant locations identified in an accompanying index

Cities that are not considered part of a larger destination city or area but have a significant number of listings may have these resources within the individual city section:

- Attraction spotting map
- Hotel/restaurant spotting map and index

Location Abbreviations
Directions are from the center of town unless otherwise specified, using these highway abbreviations:

Bus. Rte.=business route
CR=county road
FM=farm to market
FR=forest road
Hwy.=Canadian highway
I=interstate highway
LR=legislative route
R.R.=rural route
SR/PR=state or provincial route
US=federal highway

About Listed Establishments
AAA/CAA Inspected & Approved hotels and restaurants are listed on the basis of merit alone after careful evaluation and approval by full-time, professionally trained AAA inspectors. An establishment's decision to advertise in the TourBook guide has no bearing on its evaluation or rating; nor does inclusion of advertising imply AAA endorsement of products and services.

Information in this guide was believed accurate at the time of publication. However, since changes inevitably occur between annual editions, please contact your AAA travel professional, visit **AAA.com/travelguides** or download the free AAA Mobile app to confirm prices and schedules.

Attraction Listing Icons
- SAVE AAA Discounts & Rewards® member discount
- Electric vehicle charging station on premises. Domestic station information provided by the U.S. Department of Energy. Canadian station information provided by Plug'n Drive Ontario.
- GT Guided Tours available
- Camping facilities
- Food on premises
- Recreational activities
- Pet friendly (Call for restrictions/fees.)
- Picnicking allowed

In select cities only:
- Mass transit station within 1 mile. Icon is followed by station name and AAA/CAA designated station number within listing.

GEM AAA/CAA travel experts may designate an attraction of exceptional interest and quality as a AAA GEM — a *Great Experience for Members®*. See GEM Attraction Index (listed on CONTENTS page) for a complete list of locations.

Consult the online travel guides at **AAA.com/travelguides** or visit AAA Mobile for additional things to do if you have time.

Hotel Listing Icons
May be preceded by CALL and/or SOME UNITS.

Member Information:
- SAVE Member rates: discounted standard room rate or lowest public rate available at time of booking for dates of stay.

ECO Eco-certified by government or private organization.

[charging icon] Electric vehicle charging station on premises. Domestic station information provided by the U.S. Department of Energy. Canadian station information provided by Plug'n Drive Ontario.

[X] Smoke-free premises

In select cities only:

[transit icon] Mass transit station within 1 mile. Icon is followed by station name and AAA/CAA designated station number within listing.

Services:

[+] Airport transportation

[pet icon] Pet friendly (Call for restrictions/fees.)

[restaurant icon] Restaurant on premises

[restaurant icon]+ Restaurant off premises

[room service icon] Room service for 2 or more meals

[bar icon] Full bar

[child care icon] Child care

BIZ Business center

[accessible icon] Accessible features (Call property for available services and amenities.)

Activities:

[casino icon] Full-service casino

[pool icon] Pool

[health club icon] Health club or exercise room on premises

In-Room Amenities:

HS High-speed Internet service

$HS High-speed Internet service (Call property for fees.)

[wireless icon] Wireless Internet service

$[wireless icon] Wireless Internet service (Call property for fees.)

[no wireless icon] No wireless Internet service

[movie icon] Pay movies

[refrigerator icon] Refrigerator

[microwave icon] Microwave

[coffeemaker icon] Coffeemaker

[no A/C icon] No air conditioning

[no TV icon] No TV

[no phone icon] No telephones

Restaurant Listing Icons

SAVE AAA Discounts & Rewards® member discount

ECO Eco-certified by government or private organization.

[charging icon] Electric vehicle charging station on premises. Domestic station information provided by the U.S. Department of Energy. Canadian station information provided by Plug'n Drive Ontario.

[no A/C icon] No air conditioning

[accessible icon] Accessible features (Call property for available services and amenities.)

[smoking icon] Designated smoking section

B Breakfast

L Lunch

D Dinner

24 Open 24 hours

LATE Open after 11 p.m.

[pet icon] Pet friendly (Call for restrictions/fees.)

In select cities only:

[transit icon] Mass transit station within 1 mile. Icon is followed by station name and AAA/CAA designated station number within listing.

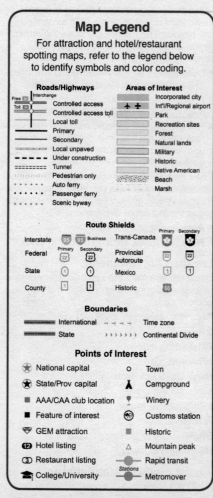

Map Legend

For attraction and hotel/restaurant spotting maps, refer to the legend below to identify symbols and color coding.

Roads/Highways
Interchange
Free
Toll
Controlled access
Controlled access toll
Local toll
Primary
Secondary
Local unpaved
Under construction
Tunnel
Pedestrian only
Auto ferry
Passenger ferry
Scenic byway

Areas of Interest
Incorporated city
Int'l/Regional airport
Park
Recreation sites
Forest
Natural lands
Military
Historic
Native American
Beach
Marsh

Route Shields
Interstate   95   95 Business   Trans-Canada   Primary Secondary
Federal   Primary 22   Secondary 22   Provincial Autoroute   22   22
State   (1)   (1)   Mexico   1   1
County   1   1   Historic   66

Boundaries
International   Time zone
State   Continental Divide

Points of Interest
National capital   o Town
State/Prov capital   A Campground
AAA/CAA club location   Winery
Feature of interest   Customs station
GEM attraction   Historic
12 Hotel listing   △ Mountain peak
3 Restaurant listing   Rapid transit
College/University   Stations Metromover

Understanding the Diamond Ratings

Hotel and restaurant evaluations are unscheduled to ensure our professionally trained inspectors encounter the same experience members do.

- When an establishment is Diamond Rated, it means members can expect a good fit with their needs. The inspector assigns a rating that indicates the type of experience to expect.
- While establishments at high levels must offer increasingly complex personalized services, establishments at every level are subject to the same basic requirements for cleanliness, comfort and hospitality. Learn more at **AAA.com/diamonds**.

Hotels	Restaurants
Budget-oriented, offering basic comfort and hospitality.	Simple, economical food, often quick-serve, in a functional environment.
Affordable, with modestly enhanced facilities, décor and amenities.	Familiar food, often cooked to order, served in casual surroundings.
Distinguished, multifaceted with enhanced physical attributes, amenities and guest comforts.	Trendy cuisine, skillfully prepared and served, with expanded beverage options, in an enhanced setting.
Refined, stylish with upscale physical attributes, extensive amenities and high degree of hospitality, service and attention to detail.	Distinctive fine-dining. Creative preparations, skillfully served, often with wine steward, amid upscale ambience.

Ultimate luxury, sophistication and comfort with extraordinary physical attributes, meticulous personalized service, extensive amenities and impeccable standards of excellence.	Leading-edge cuisine of the finest ingredients, uniquely prepared by an acclaimed chef, served by expert service staff led by maître d' in extraordinary surroundings.

Guest Safety

Inspectors view a sampling of rooms during evaluations and, therefore, AAA/CAA cannot guarantee the presence of working locks and operational fire safety equipment in every guest unit.

Contacting AAA/CAA About the TourBook Guide

Tell us what you think about the content and format of the TourBook guide or about your experience at a listed hotel, restaurant or attraction. If your visit to an attraction, hotel or restaurant listed by AAA/CAA doesn't meet your expectations, please tell us about it **during your visit or within 30 days.** Be sure to save your receipts and other documentation for reference. Or, maybe you'd like to recommend a place you visited and would like AAA inspectors to consider.

Use the easy online form at **AAA.com/MemberFeedback** to send us the details.

Alternatively, you can email your comments to: memberrelations@national.aaa.com or submit them via postal mail to: AAA Member Comments, 1000 AAA Dr., Box 61, Heathrow, FL 32746.

Cadillac Mountain

Maine

Maine is a love affair between earth and water. Here, the two meet in an embrace to create some of the most beautiful coastal scenery in America. And like any relationship, the encounter between unlike partners can be stormy; whipped by marine winds and pounded by white-capped breakers, the rugged shore is a sight to behold.

No visit to Maine would be complete without an excursion to the crown jewel of its scenic coast: Acadia National Park. Consisting mostly of Mount Desert Island, Acadia is the second most visited national park in the country. The reason? An array of stunning landscapes range from sandy beaches—a rare sight along Maine's rocky northern coast—to Cadillac Mountain, the highest point on the eastern coastline of North America.

From a distance, the rounded granite

Pemaquid Point Lighthouse

humps of Acadia's mountains seem to materialize out of the ocean. Two of the island's top draws: Thunder Hole, a cleft in the Otter Cliffs that produces a rumbling boom when the surf crashes through it, and Bar Harbor, a resort village of fine mansions, quaint inns and fishing wharves.

Think of Maine and you'll likely picture a lighthouse looming over a rock-strewn, wave-washed shore. There's a reason: More than 60 towers dot the coast here, including Pemaquid Point Lighthouse, one of the state's most picturesque. During storms, raging surf often engulfs the lighthouse's base, which is 79 feet above water. In Portland's Fort Williams Park stands the Portland Head Light, one of the nation's most historic; it was constructed in 1791 under the authorization of George Washington.

More than 90 percent of Maine's land area is forested, hence its official nickname: The "Pine Tree State." Vast areas of virtually uninhabited woodland offer plenty of room for vacationers to get away from it all. And there's no better time to make your escape than during Maine's fall foliage season, when the hills catch fire with autumn hues.

The Appalachian Trail is always a good bet for gorgeous alpine scenery; the footpath follows the crest of the Appalachian Mountains from Mount Springer in Georgia to the foot of Mount Katahdin. A huge granite monolith rising 5,259 feet, this peak—Maine's highest—is just a stone's throw away from Moosehead Lake, an outdoor recreation magnet attracting campers, boaters and water skiers.

Authors and Artists

For more than a century artists of all kinds have sought refuge and inspiration along the state's craggy shores and wooded hillsides.

One of the first to do so was poet Henry Wadsworth Longfellow, who referred to his childhood home of Portland as "the beautiful town that is seated by the sea." To explore the town, stop by the brick 1786 Longfellow House, where the poet lived as a boy; to experience the sea, hop aboard one of the tour boats that cruise into Casco Bay among the picturesque Calendar Islands.

Maine has recharged the creative batteries of other authors as well. Harriet Beecher Stowe penned Uncle Tom's Cabin while living in Brunswick. Edna St. Vincent Millay was born in Rockland and began her career in Camden, where she is honored by a statue at the harbor's head. And various state locations have served as backdrops in the horror novels of Bangor resident Stephen King.

The dramatic, wind-swept coastline and hardy Down East fishermen kept painter Winslow Homer busy for many years of his career, while the town of Cushing inspired several of Andrew Wyeth's paintings.

Recreation

Warm weather brings a migration of visitors to the powder-soft sand of southern Maine's shoreline. Despite the summer crowds, there still are some quiet beaches where you can enjoy the rush of water between your toes. But getting wet isn't necessary to enjoy the water; windjammer cruises in Penobscot Bay pass by historic lighthouses and nature preserves filled with dolphins, seals and bald eagles.

Swimmers will find the water somewhat warm July through August. Ogunquit, a historic seaside village, was named after the Abenaki Indian word for "the beautiful place by the sea." Its beach is a wide sandbar between the Ogunquit River and the Atlantic.

Old Orchard Beach, with its amusement park, pier and arcades, is a center for summer fun. As a result, the beach around the pier can be a bit crowded late June through Labor Day. Try heading north up the shore if you need room for sand castles or sunning.

Other water adventures lead you inland. The Forks—where two churning rivers meet to form the Kennebec—offers a 12-mile rafting run through a deep, tree-lined gorge. High water combines with few obstacles, creating raging foam and class IV drops.

The rafting season starts with the spring runoff and continues through October.

Acadia National Park, Maine's premier outdoor destination, is a breathtaking combination of cobblestone beaches and glacier-carved mountains. More than 125 miles of hiking trails range from short beach walks to the steep Precipice Trail. Forty-five miles of broken-stone carriage roads are populated with hikers and cyclists in summer; they are groomed for cross-country skiers and snowshoers soon after the first snowfall.

Nearly all of Acadia is contained on Mount Desert Island. Park Loop Road, which passes jagged bluffs, glassy lakes and Cadillac Mountain, is wide enough to offer a safe, scenic route for cyclists. In summer the road is full, but you'll have the island practically to yourself during the spring and fall.

Baxter State Park in north-central Maine is the northern terminus of the Appalachian Trail. Maine's highest peak, Mount Katahdin, is the main attraction here.

Downhill skiing takes on a new twist at Camden Snow Bowl. There's nowhere else in the East where you can sail down slopes while enjoying spectacular views of the Atlantic Ocean. The Snow Bowl also has Maine's only public toboggan chute. Other major ski areas include Sunday River, renowned for its snowmaking ability, and Sugarloaf Mountain Resort.

Old Orchard Beach pier

Historic Timeline

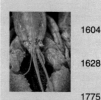

1604	Samuel de Champlain sights Mount Desert Island, now the location of Acadia National Park.
1628	A trading post is begun by the Plymouth Colony at the present-day site of Augusta.
1775	The first naval battle of the Revolutionary War is fought in Machias Bay.
1820	Maine enters the Union as a free state as part of the Missouri Compromise.
1827	Augusta is named state capital.
1842	Maine's northeastern boundary with New Brunswick is finally settled by the Webster-Ashburton Treaty.
1868	The University of Maine opens with 12 students and two teachers.
1947	The first Maine Lobster Fest is held in Rockland, known as the "Lobster Capital of the World."
1962	The main ground station for the nation's first communications satellite is installed in Andover.
1968	Maine native Edmund Muskie is the Democratic nominee for vice president of the United States.
1997	Senator William Cohen is chosen by President Clinton to be Secretary of Defense.

What To Pack

Temperature Averages Maximum/Minimum	JANUARY	FEBRUARY	MARCH	APRIL	MAY	JUNE	JULY	AUGUST	SEPTEMBER	OCTOBER	NOVEMBER	DECEMBER
Augusta	28/11	32/15	40/23	53/35	65/45	74/54	79/60	78/59	70/51	57/40	45/31	34/19
Bangor	27/7	31/10	40/21	53/32	65/42	74/52	79/58	78/56	70/48	58/37	45/29	34/15
Bar Harbor	31/14	35/17	42/25	53/35	65/45	74/54	79/59	78/59	71/52	59/42	48/33	37/21
Caribou	20/1	24/4	34/15	48/30	63/41	72/50	76/55	74/53	65/45	52/35	38/25	26/10
Greenville	22/-1	26/1	35/11	48/26	61/38	71/49	76/54	74/52	66/45	53/34	40/25	28/11
Portland	31/13	35/17	42/25	53/35	64/44	73/54	79/59	78/58	70/50	59/39	48/31	37/20

From the records of The Weather Channel Interactive, Inc.

Good Facts To Know

ABOUT THE STATE

POPULATION: 1,328,361.

AREA: 35,380 square miles; ranks 39th.

CAPITAL: Augusta.

HIGHEST POINT: 5,259 ft., Mount Katahdin.

LOWEST POINT: Sea level, Atlantic Ocean.

TIME ZONE(S): Eastern. DST.

GAMBLING

MINIMUM AGE FOR GAMBLING: 21.

REGULATIONS

TEEN DRIVING LAWS: No passengers other than family members are permitted for 270 days after a driver's license is obtained unless supervised by a licensed driver over 20 years old with 2 consecutive years of full licensure. Driving is not permitted midnight-5 a.m. The minimum age for an unrestricted driver's license is 16 years and 9 months. For more information about Maine driver's license regulations phone (207) 624-9000.

SEAT BELT/CHILD RESTRAINT LAWS: Seat belts are required for driver and all passengers ages 18 and over. Children ages 8-18 and at least 57 inches tall are required to use a seat belt. Booster seats are required for children under 8 and weighing 40-80 pounds; child safety seats are required for those under 40 pounds. Children under age 12 and less than 100 pounds are required to be in the rear seat, if available. AAA recommends the use of seat belts and appropriate child restraints for the driver and all passengers.

CELLPHONE RESTRICTIONS: Text messaging is prohibited for all drivers. Instruction permit holders and persons under 18 are banned from using cellphones while driving. State law also prohibits distracted driving, defined as any activity unrelated to the actual operation of a motor vehicle and interfering with the vehicle's safe operation.

HELMETS FOR MOTORCYCLISTS: Required for drivers under 18, drivers with a learner's permit, drivers in their first year of licensure, and all passengers if the driver is required to wear one.

RADAR DETECTORS: Permitted. Prohibited for use by commercial vehicles.

MOVE OVER LAW: Driver is required to slow down and vacate the lane nearest stopped police, fire, utility and rescue vehicles using audible or flashing signals. Law also requires driver to move over for tow truck drivers assisting motorists.

FIREARMS LAWS: Vary by state and/or county. Contact Maine State Police Special Investigations Unit, State House Station #164, Augusta, ME 04333; phone (207) 624-7210.

HOLIDAYS

HOLIDAYS: Jan. 1 ▪ Martin Luther King Jr. Day, Jan. (3rd Mon.) ▪ Washington's Birthday/Presidents Day, Feb. (3rd Mon.) ▪ Patriot's Day, Apr. (3rd Mon.) ▪ Memorial Day, May (4th Mon.) ▪ July 4 ▪ Labor Day, Sept. (1st Mon.) ▪ Columbus Day, Oct. (2nd Mon.) ▪ Veterans Day, Nov. 11 ▪ Thanksgiving, Nov. (4th Thurs.) ▪ day after Thanksgiving, Nov. (4th Fri.) ▪ Christmas, Dec. 25.

MONEY

TAXES: Maine's general sales tax is 5.5 percent. There is a 9 percent tax for lodging and prepared food and a 10 percent tax for short-term automobile rentals.

VISITOR INFORMATION

INFORMATION CENTERS: State welcome centers are at 499 US 1 in Kittery, (207) 439-1319 ▪ at I-295 exit 17 and 1100 US 1 in Yarmouth, (207) 846-0833 ▪ at 97 Main St. in Fryeburg, (207) 935-3639 ▪ at 39 Union St., Suite B in Calais, (207) 454-2211 ▪ in Hampden North at Milepost 175 on I-95N, (207) 862-6628 ▪ in Hampden South at Milepost 179 on I-95S, (207) 862-6638 ▪ and at 28 Ludlow Rd. in Houlton, (207) 532-6346. The Hampden North, Hampden South, Calais, Kittery, Yarmouth and Houlton offices are open daily 8-6, Memorial Day-Columbus Day, and daily 9-5, rest of year. The Fryeburg office is open Wed.-Mon. 8-6, mid-July through Labor Day, and Wed.-Mon. 9-5, rest of year. The Kittery office is closed Thanksgiving and Christmas, and the Hampden offices are closed Jan. 1, Easter, Thanksgiving and Christmas.

FURTHER INFORMATION FOR VISITORS:

Maine Office of Tourism
59 State House Station
Augusta, ME 04330
(888) 624-6345

Maine Tourism Association
327 Water St.
Hallowell, ME 04347
(800) 767-8709

FISHING AND HUNTING REGULATIONS:

Department of Inland Fisheries and Wildlife
284 State St.
Augusta, ME 04333-0041
(207) 287-8000
(800) 452-4664

Maine Annual Events
Please call ahead to confirm event details.

 Visit **AAA.com/travelguides/events** to find AAA-listed events for every day of the year

WINTER

Dec.
- Christmas Prelude / Kennebunkport 207-967-0857
- Holiday Stroll / Skowhegan 207-612-2571
- Freeport Sparkle Weekend / Freeport 207-865-1212

Jan.
- Snodeo / Rangeley / 207-497-6153
- Lobster Dip / Old Orchard Beach / 207-879-0489

Feb.
- U.S. National Toboggan Championships / Camden 207-236-3438
- Winterfest / Camden / 207-236-9656

SPRING

Mar.
- Bath Antique Sales / Bath 207-832-7798
- Maine Boatbuilders Show / Portland 207-774-1067

Apr.
- Portland Home Show / Portland 800-237-6024
- Bath Antique Sale / Bath 207-832-7798
- Patriots Day Celebration / Ogunquit 207-646-2939

May
- May Day Celebration / Kennebunk 207-985-2102

SUMMER

June
- The Whatever Family Festival Augusta / 207-623-4559
- Greek Heritage Festival / Portland 207-774-0281
- Windjammer Days / Boothbay Harbor / 207-633-2353

July
- Bath Heritage Days / Bath 207-442-7291

Aug.
- Skowhegan State Fair / Skowhegan 207-474-2947
- Maine Lobster Festival / Rockland 800-576-7512
- American Folk Festival / Bangor 207-262-7765

FALL

Sept.
- Capriccio / Ogunquit / 207-646-6170
- Trail's End Festival / Millinocket 207-723-4443

Oct.
- York Harvestfest and Kidsfest / York 207-363-4422

Nov.
- Rockland Festival of Lights Celebration / Rockland 207-593-6093

White Columns, Kennebunkport

Coastal Maine Botanical
Gardens, Boothbay

Bass Harbor Head Light,
Southwest Harbor

Mount Desert Island

Augusta

Index: Great Experience for Members

AAA editor's picks of exceptional note

Acadia National Park

Portland Museum of
Art

Coastal Maine
Botanical Gardens

Victoria Mansion

See Orientation map on p. 24 for corresponding grid coordinates, if applicable.
*Indicates the GEM is temporarily closed.

Acadia National Park (I-6)
Acadia National Park *(See p. 28.)*

Augusta (I-4)
Maine State Museum *(See p. 32.)*

Bangor (H-5)
Cole Land Transportation Museum
(See p. 34.)

Bath (J-4)
Maine Maritime Museum *(See p. 46.)*

Boothbay (J-4)
Coastal Maine Botanical Gardens *(See p. 47.)*

Campobello Island, New Brunswick
Roosevelt Campobello International Park
(See p. 66.)

Ogunquit (L-2)
Ogunquit Museum of American Art
(See p. 68.)

Portland (K-3)
Longfellow House *(See p. 71.)*

Portland Museum of Art *(See p. 73.)*

Victoria Mansion *(See p. 74.)*

STAY CONNECTED

TO ALL THE THINGS
MEMBERSHIP CAN DO FOR YOU

- member discounts around you
- cheapest gas nearby
- Diamond Rated hotels and restaurants
- travel information and reservations
- roadside assistance

Download today. Connect every day.
AAA.com/mobile | CAA.ca/mobile

Maine

Atlas Section

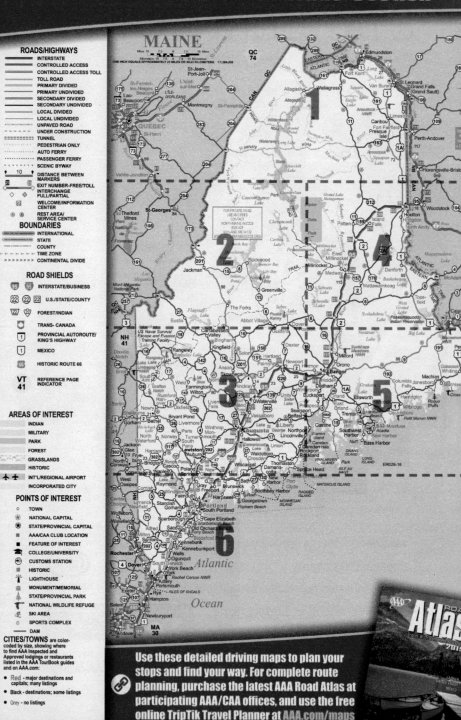

Use these detailed driving maps to plan your stops and find your way. For complete route planning, purchase the latest AAA Road Atlas at participating AAA/CAA offices, and use the free online TripTik Travel Planner at AAA.com/maps

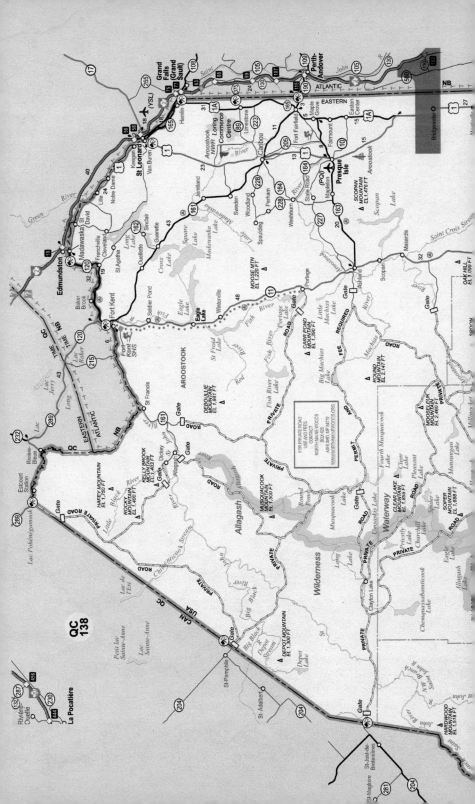

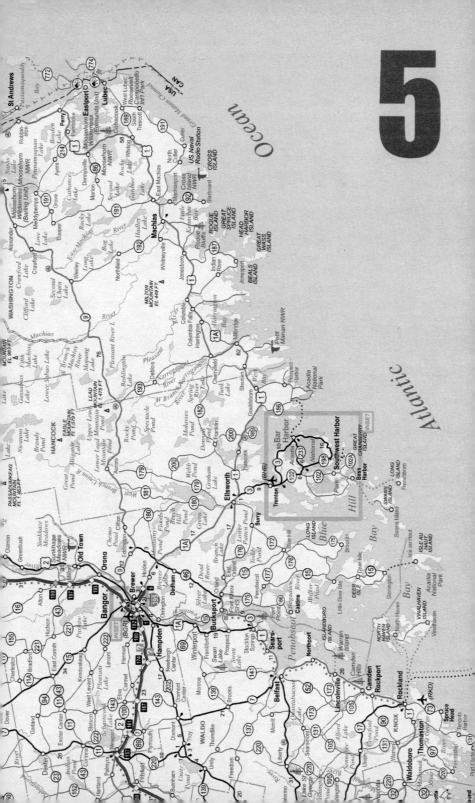

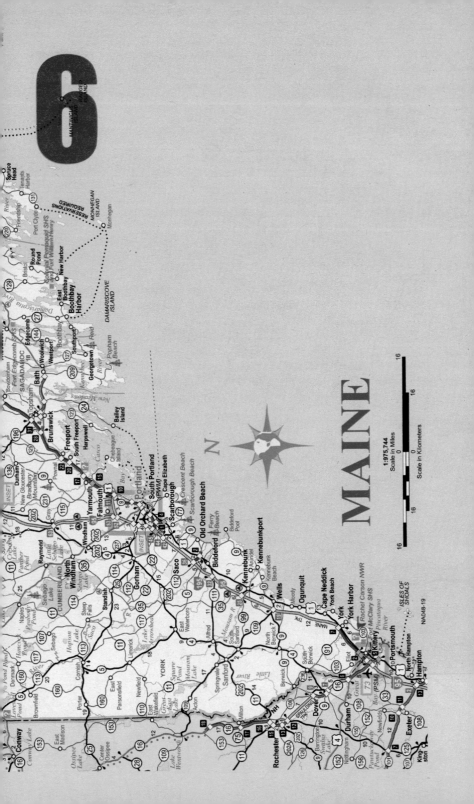

GET YOUR DRIVE TRIP BACK ON TRACK

When a drive trip takes an unexpected turn, use the **MOBILE APP** or go **ONLINE** to quickly request roadside service.

- New, more intuitive user interface
- Easier service request submissions
- Frequent status updates
- Service Tracker feature to follow service vehicle en route to your location

AAA.com/mobile
CAA.ca/mobile

Download on the
App Store

GET IT ON
Google play

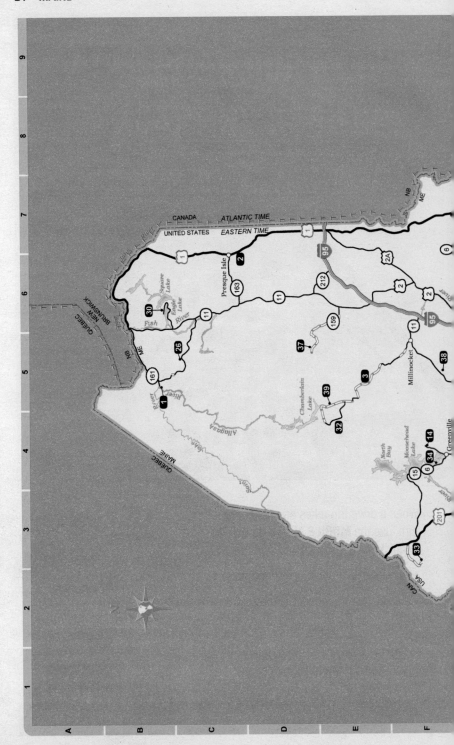

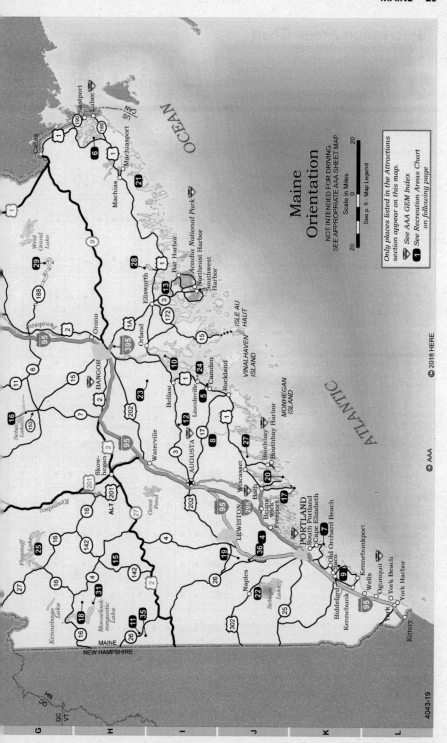

Maine Orientation

NOT INTENDED FOR DRIVING.
SEE APPROPRIATE AAA SHEET MAP.

Only places listed in the Attractions
section appear on this map.

Scale in Miles

20   0   20

See p. 6 - Map Legend

See AAA GEM Index

See Recreation Areas Chart
on following page

© 2018 HERE

© AAA

4043-19

Recreation Areas Chart

The map location numerals in column 2 show an area's location on the preceding map.

Find thousands of places to camp at AAA.com/campgrounds

	MAP LOCATION	CAMPING	PICNICKING	HIKING TRAILS	BOATING	BOAT RAMP	BOAT RENTAL	FISHING	SWIMMING	PET FRIENDLY	BICYCLE TRAILS	WINTER SPORTS	VISITOR CENTER	LODGE/CABINS	FOOD SERVICE
NATIONAL PARKS *(See place listings.)*															
Acadia (I-6) 47,748 acres. Bird-watching, cross-country skiing, horseback riding, ice fishing, mountain climbing, snowmobiling, snowshoeing, whale watching.			•	•	•	•	•	•	•	•	•	•	•		•
STATE															
Allagash Wilderness Waterway (B-5) River and lakes in northwestern Maine. Canoeing, cross-country skiing, hunting, ice fishing, snowmobiling, snowshoeing.	**1**	•		•	•			•		•		•			
Aroostook (C-6) 800 acres 4 mi. s. of Presque Isle on US 1, then w. and s. via a park road. Scenic. Bird-watching, canoeing, cross-country skiing, snowmobiling, snowshoeing; nature trails, playground.	**2**	•	•	•	•	•	•	•	•	•		•			
Baxter (E-5) 209,501 acres (10 separate areas) n. of Millinocket and w. of Patten in north-central Maine off SR 159. Boating (non-motorized only), camping (primitive), hunting, rock-climbing, snowmobiling.	**3**	•	•	•	•			•	•	•		•	•	•	
Bradbury Mountain (J-3) 800 acres w. of Freeport off US 95 on SR 136, then n. on SR 9. Bird-watching, cross-country skiing, horseback riding, hunting, snowmobiling, snowshoeing; nature trails, playground.	**4**	•	•	•						•	•	•			
Camden Hills (I-5) 5,474 acres 2 mi. n. of Camden on US 1. Scenic. Bird-watching, cross-country skiing, horseback riding, hunting, snowmobiling, snowshoeing.	**5**	•	•	•						•	•	•			
Cobscook Bay (H-8) 888 acres 2 mi. s.e. of Dennysville off US 1. Beachcombing, bird-watching, canoeing, kayaking; nature trails, playground.	**6**	•	•	•	•	•	•			•		•			
Crescent Beach (K-3) 243 acres 8 mi. s. of Portland off CR 77 in Cape Elizabeth. Beachcombing, bird-watching, cross-country skiing, sea kayaking.	**7**		•	•	•			•	•						•
Damariscotta Lake (I-4) 17 acres in Jefferson off SR 32. Canoeing; beach, playground.	**8**		•		•	•		•	•						
Ferry Beach (K-2) 117 acres in Saco on SR 9. Beachcombing; beach, nature center, trails. Note: Seasonal restrictions apply to leashed pets.	**9**		•	•					•						
Fort Point (I-5) 120 acres 7 mi. n.e. of Searsport off US 1. Historic. Bird-watching, cross-country skiing; fort ruins, lighthouse, pier.	**10**		•	•	•			•		•	•	•	•	•	
Grafton Notch (H-2) 3,000 acres 14 mi. n. of Bethel on SR 26 between Upton and Newry. Bird-watching, cross-country skiing, hunting, snowmobiling, snowshoeing, wildlife viewing.	**11**		•	•				•		•		•			
Lake St. George (I-4) 1,017 acres 2 mi. w. of Liberty on SR 3. Canoeing, cross-country skiing, hunting, snowmobiling; playground.	**12**	•	•	•	•	•	•	•	•	•		•			
Lamoine (I-6) 55 acres 6.5 mi. s.e. of Ellsworth on SR 184. Cross-country skiing, hunting, sea kayaking, wildlife viewing; playground.	**13**	•	•		•	•		•		•		•			
Lily Bay (F-4) 925 acres 8 mi. n.e. of Greenville on Lily Bay Rd. Bird-watching, canoeing, cross-country skiing, hunting, ice fishing, kayaking, snowmobiling, snowshoeing; playground.	**14**	•	•	•	•	•	•	•	•	•		•			
Mt. Blue (H-3) 8,000 acres (two areas) n. of Weld on a gravel road. Bird-watching, canoeing, cross-country skiing, horseback riding, hunting, snowmobiling, snowshoeing; motorized-vehicle trails, nature center, playground.	**15**	•	•	•	•	•	•	•	•	•		•	•		
Peaks-Kenny (G-4) 839 acres 6 mi. n. of Dover-Foxcroft on SR 153. Canoeing, hunting; beach, playground.	**16**	•	•	•				•	•	•		•			
Popham Beach (J-3) 529 acres w. of Popham Beach via SR 209. Beachcombing, bird-watching, hunting, sea kayaking, surfing, windsurfing. Note: Seasonal pet restrictions apply.	**17**		•		•			•	•	•					
Rangeley Lake (H-2) 869 acres s.w. of Rangeley via SR 17 on the s. shore of Rangeley Lake. Bird-watching, canoeing, snowmobiling; playground.	**18**	•	•	•	•	•	•	•	•	•		•			

Recreation Areas Chart

The map location numerals in column 2 show an area's location on the preceding map.

Find thousands of places to camp at AAA.com/campgrounds

	MAP LOCATION	CAMPING	PICNICKING	HIKING TRAILS	BOATING	BOAT RAMP	BOAT RENTAL	FISHING	SWIMMING	PET FRIENDLY	BICYCLE TRAILS	WINTER SPORTS	VISITOR CENTER	LODGE/CABINS	FOOD SERVICE
Range Pond (J-3) 750 acres in Poland off SR 122. Canoeing, cross-country skiing, hunting, kayaking, snowmobiling, snowshoeing, wildlife viewing, windsurfing; nature trails, playground.	19		•	•	•	•			•	•	•				
Reid (J-4) 768 acres 2 mi. e. of Georgetown on SR 127. Beachcombing, bird-watching, cross-country skiing, surfing.	20		•	•				•	•	•			•		•
Roque Bluffs (H-7) 275 acres 7 mi. s. of Machias off US 1 on Roque Bluffs Rd. Bird-watching, canoeing, cross-country skiing, sea kayaking, snowshoeing; beach, playground.	21		•	•	•	•		•	•	•			•		
Sebago Lake (J-2) 1,300 acres 3 mi. s. of Naples off US 302. Nature programs. Canoeing, cross-country skiing, snowshoeing; beach, playground.	22	•	•	•	•	•	•	•	•				•		•
Swan Lake (H-5) 67 acres n. of Swanville off SR 141. Canoeing, hunting; beach, playground.	23		•		•			•	•	•					
Warren Island (I-5) 70 acres in Penobscot Bay. Accessible by private boat only. Sea kayaking, wildlife viewing.	24	•	•						•						
OTHER															
Bigelow Preserve (G-3) 36,000 acres n. of New Portland off SR 27. Bird-watching, canoeing, cross-country skiing, hunting, kayaking, snowmobiling, snowshoeing.	25	•	•	•				•	•	•	•	•	•		
Deboullie (C-5) 21,871 acres 41 mi. s.w. of Fort Kent. Canoeing, cross-country skiing, hunting, snowmobiling, snowshoeing, wildlife viewing.	26	•	•	•				•	•				•		
Dodge Point (J-4) 521 acres 3.5 mi. s.w. of Newcastle off River Road. Scenic. Beachcombing, cross-country skiing, hunting, wildlife viewing; interpretive trails.	27			•				•	•						
Donnell Pond (H-6) 14,000 acres 15 mi. n.e. of Ellsworth off SR 182 and Donnell Pond Road. Scenic. Canoeing, cross-country skiing, hunting, snowshoeing, wildlife viewing.	28	•	•	•	•			•	•				•		
Duck Lake (G-6) 27,000 acres 59 mi. n.e. of Old Town. Canoeing, cross-country skiing, hunting, snowmobiling, snowshoeing; all-terrain vehicle trails.	29	•			•	•		•	•						
Eagle Lake (B-6) 23,000 acres 16 mi. s. of Fort Kent off CR 11. Cross-country skiing, hunting, snowmobiling, snowshoeing, wildlife viewing; all-terrain vehicle trails.	30	•	•	•				•	•				•		
Four Ponds (H-2) 6,000 acres 20 mi. s.w. of Rangeley off SR 17. Canoeing, cross-country skiing, hunting, snowmobiling, snowshoeing, wildlife viewing.	31	•	•	•	•			•					•		
Gero Island (E-4) 3,845 acres n.w. of Millinocket off SR 11. Canoeing, hunting, wildlife viewing.	32	•	•	•	•			•		•					
Holeb (F-3) 20,000 acres 44 mi. n.w. of The Forks off US 201 and Holeb Road. Canoeing, hunting.	33	•	•		•	•		•	•						
Little Moose (F-4) 15,000 acres 7.5 mi. w. of Greenville. Bird-watching, canoeing, cross-country skiing, hunting, snowmobiling, snowshoeing; all-terrain vehicle trails.	34	•		•	•			•	•			•	•		
Mahoosuc (H-2) 27,000 acres near Bethel off SR 26. Hunting, snowmobiling, snowshoeing, wildlife viewing; all-terrain vehicle trails.	35	•	•			•	•	•	•	•	•	•	•		
Outlet Beach (J-3) on Outlet Rd. 1 mi. e. of SR 26 on shore of Sabbathday Lake near Poland Spring. Canoeing, kayaking, paddleboating.	36		•		•	•	•	•	•						•
Scraggly Lake (D-5) 9,092 acres off Grand Lake Rd. n.w. of Mount Chase. Bird-watching, canoeing, cross-country skiing, hunting, snowmobiling, snowshoeing; all-terrain vehicle trails.	37	•	•	•				•	•	•			•		
Seboeis Lake (F-5) 15,628 acres 20 mi. s.w. of Millinocket off SR 11. Canoeing, hunting, snowmobiling, wildlife viewing; all-terrain vehicle trails.	38	•	•		•	•		•	•						
Telos Lake (E-5) 23,000 acres 48 mi. n.w. of Millinocket off Telos Road. Canoeing, cross-country skiing, hunting, snowmobiling, snowshoeing, wildlife viewing.	39	•	•		•	•		•					•		

ACADIA NATIONAL PARK (I-6)
• Attractions map p. 31

Elevations in the park range from sea level at Sand Beach to 1,530 ft. at Cadillac Mountain. Refer to AAA maps for additional elevation information.

Southeast of Bangor, Acadia National Park possesses an unusual combination of ocean and mountain scenery and is a popular vacation destination. The park includes more than 54 square miles of Mount Desert Island, the largest rock-based island on the Atlantic coast.

Dominating the park are the ancient, rounded peaks of the Mount Desert Mountains, worn down by countless centuries of erosion. Great granite cliffs, undermined by the pounding surf at their bases, rise from the ocean. Nowhere along the Atlantic seaboard is the "stern and rockbound coast" more picturesque.

Twenty-six peaks, mostly bare at their summits, are forested with spruce, fir, pine and northern hardwood trees. Some 500 types of wildflowers, including many Arctic species, grow in the park, and the area is a sanctuary for a variety of birds and other animals.

Samuel de Champlain sighted Mount Desert Island in 1604 and named it "L'Isle des Monts Deserts," which means island of bare mountains. It was the site of a short-lived settlement by French Jesuits in 1613, and for many years was part of the French province of Acadia, from which the park derives its name.

General Information and Activities

The park is accessible all year and is the perfect spot for those who love adventure travel. However, except for two short sections, the 27-mile Park Loop Road is typically closed from December to mid-April by snow, sleet or ice; state and town roads are kept open. Cadillac Mountain Road extends to the

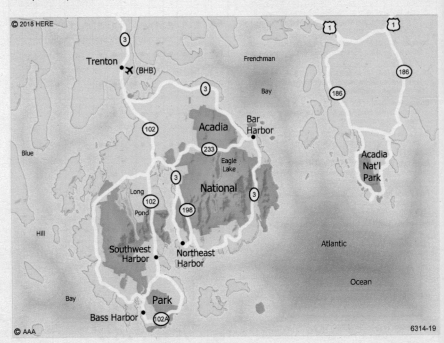

© 2018 HERE
© AAA
6314-19

This map shows cities in Acadia National Park where you will find attractions, hotels and restaurants. Cities are listed alphabetically in this book on the following pages.

AAA Life Insurance Company

MAKE LIFE
A PRIORITY

PUT A PLAN IN PLACE FOR
THE FUTURE WITH LIFE INSURANCE

You insure your automobile, your home, and your most valuable possessions.

But have you taken the steps to help protect your most precious asset:
Your life and the lives of those most important to you?

AAA Life Insurance Company offers you additional peace of mind.

▸ **Term Life**　　　▸ **Permanent Life**　　　▸ **Annuities**

Get a FREE Quote Today! Visit AAALife.com

summit of 1,530-foot Cadillac Mountain *(see attraction listing this page)*, offering a spectacular view of the coast.

Some 125 miles of hiking trails reach every mountain summit and valley; detailed hiking trail maps are available for purchase. There also are 45 miles of graded carriage roads suitable for walking, bicycling, cross-country skiing and jogging. *See Recreation Areas Chart.*

Park ranger programs are usually offered mid-May to mid-October. Programs include mountain hikes, campground programs and natural history walks, all fun things to do with friends. Check the park's program schedule for details. Park rangers also explain the area's geology, history, marine life and wildlife on three cruises around Frenchman Bay and the Cranberry Islands. Check at the visitor center for a current listing of programs.

Park information may be obtained at Hulls Cove Visitor Center *(see attraction listing this page)*, open daily 8:30-4:30, mid-April through October (8-6 in July and August). From November to mid-April, park information may be obtained at park headquarters (which serves as the winter visitor center).

Private operators are available during the season to conduct daily sightseeing, deep-sea fishing, whale-watching and lobster-fishing cruises from Bar Harbor as well as from Northeast, Southwest and Bass harbors.

Audio tours, available at the Hulls Cove Visitor Center through Eastern National Bookstore, describe the geological origin, ecology and history of the park and contain instructions for making the drive around Acadia, beginning at Hulls Cove; phone (207) 288-4988 for the bookstore.

ADMISSION to the park May-Oct. is by 7-day pass, which costs $25 per private vehicle, $20 per motorcycle. Admission per person arriving on foot or bicycle is $12; free (ages 0-15). Admission rest of year is free. Annual passes cost $50. A camping fee is charged.

PETS are permitted in the park if they are attended and physically restricted at all times; leashes may be up to 6 feet in length. Pets are not permitted on the swimming beaches in season or on the ladder hiking trails on mountain cliffs; they also are not permitted in public buildings, some campgrounds and most lakes.

ADDRESS inquiries to Acadia National Park Information, P.O. Box 177, Bar Harbor, ME 04609; phone (207) 288-3338.

CADILLAC MOUNTAIN is accessible by way of 3.5-mi. Cadillac Mountain Rd., which is off Park Loop Rd. about 1 mi. s. of the park's Cadillac Mountain entrance. Visitors can drive all the way to the rocky summit of 1,530-foot Cadillac Mountain, the highest point on the U.S. Atlantic seaboard. From a .4-mile loop trail at the top, the panorama encompasses Bar Harbor, almost the whole of Mount Desert Island and the wooded islands in Frenchman Bay.

Hikers also can reach the summit via the moderately difficult 2.2 mi. (one way) North Ridge Trail and the strenuous 3.7 mi. (one way) Cadillac Mountain South Ridge Trail from Blackwoods Campground. **Note:** Cadillac Mountain Road is closed in winter (typically Dec. 1-Apr. 14).

Cost: Included in Acadia National Park admission, valid for 7 days, May-Oct. $30 (per private vehicle); $25(per motorcycle); $15 (per person arriving on foot or bicycle). Admission rest of year free. **Phone:** (207) 288-3338.

CARRIAGES OF ACADIA, departing from Wildwood Stables, off SR 3 at Acadia National Park's Stanley Brook entrance, offers horse-drawn carriage rides along the carriage roads. Tour options include the 1-hour Day Mountain Tour, the 2-hour Mr. Rockefeller Bridge Tour and the 2-hour Day Mountain Summit ride.

Hours: Day Mountain Tour departs daily at 9 and 1, late May to mid-Oct. Mr. Rockefeller's Bridge Tour departs daily at 9:45 and 1:45, late May to mid-Oct. Day Mountain Summit ride departs daily at 4, late May-Aug. 31. Phone ahead to confirm schedule. **Cost:** $24-$40; $14-$16 (ages 6-12); $9-$11 (ages 2-5). Reservations are recommended. **Phone:** (207) 276-5721 or (877) 276-3622.

GREAT HEAD TRAIL is accessible from the Sand Beach parking lot off Park Loop Rd., 4 mi. s. of Bar Harbor. The 1.5-mile loop trail atop the sea cliffs of the Great Head Peninsula offers wonderful views of the ocean, Sand Beach, Otter Point and a steep granite dome known as the Beehive. Because the route from the beach is steep, this trail is considered moderately difficult. **Phone:** (207) 288-3338.

HULLS COVE VISITOR CENTER is 2.75 mi. n. of Bar Harbor on SR 3 at Hulls Cove. A 12-minute film about the island is shown on the half-hour. **Hours:** Daily 8-6, July-Aug.; 8:30-4:30, mid-Apr. through June 30 and Sept.-Oct. **Cost:** Free. **Phone:** (207) 288-3338.

ISLESFORD HISTORICAL MUSEUM is accessible via mail boat or tour boat from Northeast or Southwest Harbor to Little Cranberry Island. The exhibits focus on 19th-century living on the Cranberry Islands. **Time:** Allow 30 minutes minimum. **Hours:** Daily 11-4, third Mon. in June-day before Labor Day; Mon.-Sat. 9-3, Sun. 11-4, Labor Day-Sept. 30. Phone ahead to confirm schedule. **Cost:** Free. **Phone:** (207) 288-3338.

PARK LOOP ROAD begins near the Hulls Cove Visitor Center and runs s. in a loop, connecting Mount Desert Island's mountains and seashore. It provides access to a number of interesting features: Sand Beach, partially formed of shell fragments; Great Head, one of the highest sheer Atlantic headlands in the United States; Thunder Hole, a wave-cut chasm producing loud reverberations

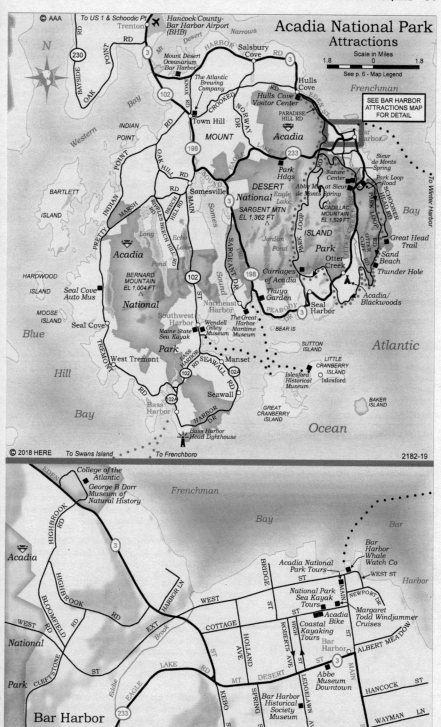

Acadia National Park
Attractions

Scale in Miles

1.8   0   1.8

See p. 6 - Map Legend

© AAA

N

To US 1 & Schoodic Pt.
Trenton

Hancock County-
Bar Harbor Airport
(BHB)

Mt
Desert
Narrows

HARBOR

Salsbury
Cove

RD

Mount Desert
Oceanarium
Bar Harbor

The Atlantic
Brewing
Company

Hulls
Cove

Hulls Cove
Visitor Center

PARADISE
HILL RD

Frenchman

SEE BAR HARBOR
ATTRACTIONS MAP
FOR DETAIL

BAYSIDE

OAK

POINT

RD

230

KNOX

RD

102

CROOKED

NORWAY

RD

Bar
Harbor

EDEN

ST

Town Hill

Acadia

Sieur
de Monts
Spring

Western

Bay

INDIAN

POINT

OAK HILL

RD

MOUNT

198

DR

EAGLE

LAKE

233

Park
Hdqs

Nature
Center

Abbe Mus at Sieur
de Monts Spring

Park Loop
Road

To Winter Harbor

BARTLETT

ISLAND

MARSH

PRETTY

INDIAN

POINT

RIPPLES BEACH HILL RD

BEECH HILL RD

Somesville

Long

Pond

Echo
Lake

MAIN

RD

3

DESERT

National

Eagle
Lake

SARGENT MTN
EL 1,362 FT

CADILLAC
MOUNTAIN
EL 1,529 FT

ISLAND

Great Head
Trail

SCHOONER HEAD RD

Bay

HARDWOOD

ISLAND

Seal Cove
Auto Mus

Acadia

BERNARD
MOUNTAIN
EL 1,004 FT

National

SARGENT DR

Jordan
Pond

PARK

LOOP

Park

OTTER

CLIFF

RD

Sand
Beach

Thunder Hole

MOOSE
ISLAND

Seal Cove

Southwest
Harbor

102

Northeast
Harbor

Wendell
Gilley
Museum

198

Carriages
of Acadia

Thuya
Garden

PEABODY

DR

Otter
Creek

Seal
Harbor

3

Acadia/
Blackwoods

Blue

Hill

West Tremont

TREMONT

RD

Park

BASS

HARBOR

RD

SEAWALL

Manset

102A

The Great
Harbor
Maritime
Museum

Maine State
Sea Kayak

BEAR IS

SUTTON
ISLAND

Atlantic

Bay

102

Seawall

102A

HARBOR

DR

Bass
Harbor

Bass Harbor
Head Lighthouse

Islesford
Historical
Museum

LITTLE
CRANBERRY
ISLAND

Islesford

GREAT
CRANBERRY
ISLAND

BAKER
ISLAND

Ocean

© 2018 HERE

To Swans Island

To Frenchboro

2182-19

College of the
Atlantic

George B Dorr
Museum of
Natural History

Frenchman

EDEN

ST

HIGHBROOK

RD

Acadia

3

HIGHBROOK

RD

BLOOMFIELD

RD

WEST

ST

National

CLEFTSTONE

ST

Park

Bar Harbor

233

Eddie

EAGLE

LAKE

RD

Eagle

KEBO

ST

SPRING

ST

MT

DESERT

ST

HARBOR LN

EXT

Brook

WEST

COTTAGE

ST

HOLLAND

AVE

ROBERTS

AVE

HIGH

ST

BRIDGE

ST

MAIN

ST

Acadia National
Park Tours

National Park
Sea Kayak
Tours

Acadia
Bike

Coastal
Kayaking
Tours

Bar
Harbor

3

Abbe
Museum
Downtown

Bar Harbor
Historical
Society
Museum

LEDGELAWN

AVE

Bar Harbor
Whale Watch Co

WEST ST

NEWPORT DR

Harbor

Margaret
Todd Windjammer
Cruises

ALBERT MEADOW

HANCOCK

ST

WAYMAN

LN

Bay

when waves and tide are right; Otter Cliff and Otter Point, with a dense forest that extends to the edge of the sea; and Cadillac Mountain, with its stunning views. **Time:** Allow 3 hours, 30 minutes minimum. **Phone:** (207) 288-3338.

SCHOODIC POINT is at the tip of Schoodic Peninsula on the eastern side of Frenchman Bay—about an hour's drive from Bar Harbor. Beside the point, Schoodic Head rises more than 400 feet, commanding a sweeping view eastward toward the Bay of Fundy and westward toward the Mount Desert Mountains. A park road from SR 186 follows the coast of the peninsula. **Phone:** (207) 288-3338.

SIEUR DE MONTS SPRING, near Bar Harbor, is a memorial to George B. Dorr, a co-founder of Acadia National Park. The area includes the Abbe Museum at Sieur de Monts Spring, the Nature Center and the Wild Gardens of Acadia.

Abbe Museum at Sieur de Monts Spring, off Sieur de Monts near the spring, contains regional artifacts of Native American culture. **Hours:** Daily 10-5, late May to mid-Oct. **Cost:** $3; $1 (ages 11-17). Combination ticket with Abbe Museum Downtown $8; $4 (ages 11-17). **Phone:** (207) 288-2179.

Nature Center, near Sieur de Monts Spring, houses a climate change exhibit. The Wild Gardens of Acadia, a living field guide to flowers and trees found within the park, is next to the center. **Hours:** Nature center daily 9-5, June 1-Columbus Day; Sat.-Sun. 9-5, in May. Gardens daily 24 hours, year-round. **Cost:** Free. **Phone:** (207) 288-3338.

AUBURN pop. 23,055, elev. 183'

HILTON GARDEN INN AUBURN RIVERWATCH
(207)784-4433

Hotel
$123-$442

AAA Benefit:
Members save 5% or more!

Address: 14 Great Falls Plaza 04210 **Location:** SR 4, just e on Hampshire St; center. **Facility:** 138 units. 6 stories, interior corridors. **Terms:** 1-7 night minimum stay, cancellation fee imposed. **Pool:** heated indoor. **Activities:** hot tub, exercise room. **Guest Services:** valet and coin laundry.

⊘ For exclusive
AAA member savings and
benefits: AAA.com/hertz

RESIDENCE INN BY MARRIOTT AUBURN
(207)777-3400

Extended Stay Hotel
$98-$424

Residence INN.

AAA Benefit:
Members save 5% or more!

Address: 670 Turner St 04210 **Location:** I-95 exit 80 southbound; exit 75 northbound; from SR 100, just w. **Facility:** 100 units, some two bedrooms, efficiencies and kitchens. 4 stories, interior corridors. **Terms:** cancellation fee imposed. **Amenities:** safes. **Pool:** heated indoor. **Activities:** hot tub, exercise room. **Guest Services:** valet and coin laundry. **Featured Amenity:** breakfast buffet.

SLEEPY TIME MOTEL   (207)783-1435
Motel. **Address:** 46 Danville Corner Rd 04210

WHERE TO EAT

AMATO'S   207/786-3726
Pizza Sandwiches. Quick Serve. **Address:** 1813 Washington St S 04210

MAC'S GRILL   207/783-6885
American. Casual Dining. **Address:** 1052 Minot Ave 04210

AUGUSTA (I-4) pop. 19,136, elev. 47'

A trading post was founded in 1628 by the Plymouth Colony. John Alden and Capt. Miles Standish, immortalized by Henry Wadsworth Longfellow, were among the original settlers. In 1754 Fort Western was erected on the east bank of the Kennebec River. In 1797 the community chose Augusta as its name, presumably to honor the daughter of Gen. Henry Dearborn.

Capital of the state since 1827, Augusta is at the head of navigation on the Kennebec River. The city differs from most Maine communities that occupy both sides of a river in that it did not grow into twin cities. Augusta is the seat of many of Maine's governmental agencies and offices.

Kennebec Valley Chamber of Commerce: 269 Western Ave., Augusta, ME 04330. **Phone:** (207) 623-4559.

MAINE STATE MUSEUM, in the Cultural Building in the State House Complex, contains exhibits depicting Maine's natural environment, prehistory and social history. Back to Nature features natural history scenes and a display of gems and minerals found in Maine, while 12,000 Years in Maine presents an extensive view of the state's prehistoric cultures with stone tools, weapons and clay pottery on display.

Made In Maine is the museum's exhibit of 19th-century manufacturing technologies and products and features a three-story water-powered woodworking mill. **Time:** Allow 1 hour minimum. **Hours:**

Tues.-Fri. 9-5, Sat. 10-4. Closed major holidays. **Cost:** $3; $2 (ages 6-18 and 62+); $10 (family, two adults and all accompanying children ages 6-18). **Phone:** (207) 287-2301.

BEST WESTERN PLUS CIVIC CENTER INN
(207)622-4751

Hotel
$90-$200

Best Western PLUS

AAA Benefit: Members save up to 15% and earn bonus points!

Address: 110 Community Dr 04330 **Location:** I-95 exit 112A northbound; exit 112 southbound, just s on SR 8, 11 and 27. Adjacent to Augusta Civic Center. **Facility:** 100 units. 2 stories, interior corridors. **Pool:** outdoor. **Activities:** exercise room. **Guest Services:** valet and coin laundry. **Featured Amenity:** continental breakfast.

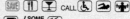

FAIRFIELD INN & SUITES BY MARRIOTT AUGUSTA
(207)623-2200

Hotel. **Address:** 14 Anthony Ave 04330

AAA Benefit: Members save 5% or more!

HAMPTON INN AUGUSTA
(207)622-4077

Hotel. **Address:** 388 Western Ave 04330

AAA Benefit: Members save 5% or more!

HOMEWOOD SUITES BY HILTON AUGUSTA
(207)480-2050

Extended Stay Hotel
$134-$446

HOMEWOOD SUITES BY HILTON

AAA Benefit: Members save 5% or more!

Address: 377 Western Ave 04330 **Location:** I-95 exit 109 northbound; exit 109B southbound, just w on US 202. **Facility:** 121 efficiencies. 4 stories, interior corridors. **Terms:** 1-7 night minimum stay, cancellation fee imposed. **Pool:** heated indoor. **Activities:** picnic facilities, exercise room. **Guest Services:** valet and coin laundry. **Featured Amenity:** breakfast buffet.

QUALITY INN & SUITES MAINE EVERGREEN HOTEL AUGUSTA
(207)622-3776

Hotel
$81-$259

Address: 65 Whitten Rd 04330 **Location:** I-95 exit 109 northbound; exit 109A southbound, off US 202, SR 11 and 100. Located in a commercial area. **Facility:** 76 units. 3 stories, interior/exterior corridors. **Pool:** heated outdoor. **Activities:** exercise room. **Guest Services:** coin laundry. **Featured Amenity:** full hot breakfast.

SENATOR INN & SPA
207/622-5804

Hotel
Rates not provided

Address: 284 Western Ave 04330 **Location:** I-95 exit 109 northbound; exit 109A southbound, on US 202, SR 11 and 100. **Facility:** 125 units. 2 stories, interior/exterior corridors. **Dining:** Cloud 9, see separate listing. **Pool:** heated outdoor, heated indoor. **Activities:** sauna, hot tub, steamroom, exercise room, spa. **Guest Services:** valet laundry. **Featured Amenity:** breakfast buffet.

WHERE TO EAT

CLOUD 9
207/622-0320

American Casual Dining
$10-$29

AAA Inspector Notes: Don't let the formal décor fool you into thinking the atmosphere is stuffy. The menu features fresh Maine seafood as well as pasta and vegetarian items. Be sure to ask for the dessert cart as it looks good enough to add calories at a glance. **Features:** full bar, Sunday brunch, happy hour. **Reservations:** suggested, weekends. **Address:** 284 Western Ave 04330 **Location:** I-95 exit 109 northbound; exit 109A southbound, on US 202, SR 11 and 100; in Senator Inn & Spa. B L D

FAT CATS CAFE
207/213-4045

Sandwiches Soup. Quick Serve. **Address:** 256 State St 04330

RIVERFRONT BARBEQUE & GRILLE
207/622-8899

Barbecue. Casual Dining. **Address:** 300 Water St 04330

BANGOR (H-5) pop. 33,039, elev. 21'
• Hotels p. 34 • Restaurants p. 35

Bangor, at the head of tidewater and navigation on the Penobscot River, is the principal retail, cultural and commercial center for eastern and northern Maine. Bangor area industries are based on papermaking, timber products, electronics, shoes and tourism. Several notable public and private colleges and universities are located here.

Bangor's survival was threatened by the War of 1812; blockade running and privateering became essential to maintain solvency. A resurgence in the timber trade following the war tripled Bangor's population during the 1830s. Within a few decades, the city became the leading lumber port of the world. Bangor's harbor became known as the Devil's Half-Acre due to the proliferation of drinking and gambling.

Of interest is the Paul Bunyan statue on Main Street, which is an appropriate 31 feet high and weighs about 1.5 tons. The Bangor Historical Society, in the Thomas A. Hill House at 159 Union St., contains antiques, artifacts and pictures from the 19th century. Various walking tours also are offered; phone (207) 942-1900.

Blackbeard's Family Fun Park at 339 Odlin Rd. offers miniature golf courses, bumper boats, a ropes obstacle course, waterslides, laser tag, a go-cart track and a 10-cage batting facility; phone (207) 945-0233.

Cross Insurance Center, 515 Main St., hosts national acts and conventions; phone (207) 561-8333 for ticket information. Summer heats up when Waterfront Concerts brings in first-rate entertainment such as Sting, Toby Keith and Jeff Dunham; phone (207) 358-9327. At downtown's American Folk Festival in late August, there's music aplenty; genres include bluegrass, gospel, jazz and zydeco; phone (207) 262-7765.

Bangor Region Chamber of Commerce: 2 Hammond Street #1, Bangor, ME 04401. **Phone:** (207) 947-0307.

Self-guiding tours: Aspects of the city's history can be experienced through a self-guiding walking tour; maps are available from the Bangor Historical Society at 159 Union St.; phone (207) 942-1900.

 COLE LAND TRANSPORTATION MUSEUM, off I-95 exit 182A following signs to the War Memorials at 405 Perry Rd., includes a 72-foot 1840s covered bridge and more than 200 vehicles illustrating the evolution of land transportation from wagons to automobiles to 18-wheelers. Among the items exhibited are antique recreational vehicles, motorcycles, a locomotive, a railroad station, farm equipment, horse-drawn logging sleds, farm and logging trucks, snowplows and more than 2,000 enlarged and captioned photographs of early life in Maine.

Also featured are hundreds of military artifacts from the Civil War to World War II, including uniforms, insignias, weapons and armored vehicles. The museum also is home to the Maine World War II Veterans Memorial, the Maine Vietnam Veterans Memorial, the Maine Korean Veterans Memorial and the Maine Military Order of the Purple Heart Memorial. **Time:** Allow 1 hour minimum. **Hours:** Daily 9-5, May 1-Nov. 11. **Cost:** $7; $5 (ages 62+); free (ages 0-18). **Phone:** (207) 990-3600.

MAINE DISCOVERY MUSEUM is at 74 Main St. This museum comprises three floors of hands-on exhibits and activities for children including Nature Trails and Turtle Alley; Booktown, featuring classic Maine children's books; Fit for Fun; Body Journey; Artscape; Trade Winds; and Sounds Abound, which features a karaoke studio.

Time: Allow 1 hour minimum. **Hours:** Tues.-Sat. 10-5, Sun. noon-5, with extended hours in summer. Closed Easter, July 4, Labor Day week, Thanksgiving, Christmas Eve and Christmas. **Cost:** $7.50; free (ages 0-1). **Phone:** (207) 262-7200.

BANGOR INN & SUITES　　　207/947-0355

Hotel
Rates not provided

Address: 701 Hogan Rd 04401 **Location:** I-95 exit 187 (Hogan Rd), 0.3 mi w. Across from Bangor Mall. **Facility:** 103 units. 2 stories (no elevator), interior corridors. **Parking:** winter plug-ins. **Guest Services:** valet laundry, area transportation. **Featured Amenity:** breakfast buffet.

BEST WESTERN WHITE HOUSE INN　　(207)862-3737

Hotel
$130-$350

Best Western. **AAA Benefit:** Members save up to 15% and earn bonus points!

Address: 155 Littlefield Ave 04401 **Location:** I-95 exit 180 (Coldbrook Rd), 5.5 mi s of downtown. Located by a truck stop. **Facility:** 77 units, some efficiencies. 3 stories, interior corridors. **Terms:** cancellation fee imposed. **Amenities:** safes. **Pool:** heated outdoor. **Activities:** hot tub, exercise room. **Guest Services:** valet and coin laundry. **Featured Amenity: continental breakfast.**

COMFORT INN BANGOR MALL　　(207)990-0888
Hotel. **Address:** 10 Bangor Mall Blvd 04401

COURTYARD BY MARRIOTT BANGOR　(207)262-0070
Hotel. **Address:** 236 Sylvan Rd 04401

AAA Benefit: Members save 5% or more!

FAIRFIELD INN BY MARRIOTT BANGOR　(207)990-0001

Hotel
$83-$306

Fairfield **AAA Benefit:** Members save 5% or more!

Address: 300 Odlin Rd 04401 **Location:** I-95 exit 182B, just e on US 2 and SR 100. Located in a commercial area. **Facility:** 153 units. 3 stories, interior corridors. **Terms:** cancellation fee imposed. **Pool:** heated indoor. **Activities:** sauna, hot tub, exercise room. **Guest Services:** valet and coin laundry. **Featured Amenity: breakfast buffet.**

FIRESIDE INN & SUITES　　(207)942-1234
Hotel. **Address:** 570 Main St 04401

FOUR POINTS BY SHERATON BANGOR AIRPORT
(207)947-6721

Hotel
$70-$182

FOUR POINTS BY SHERATON **AAA Benefit:** Members save 5% or more!

Address: 308 Godfrey Blvd 04401 **Location:** At Bangor International Airport. **Facility:** 111 units. 9 stories, interior corridors. **Terms:** cancellation fee imposed, resort fee. **Dining:** Godfrey's Grille & Lounge, see separate listing. **Pool:** heated indoor. **Activities:** exercise room. **Guest Services:** valet laundry.

HAMPTON INN BANGOR　　207/990-4400
Hotel. **Address:** 261 Haskell Rd 04401

AAA Benefit: Members save 5% or more!

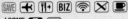

HILTON GARDEN INN BANGOR   207/262-0099
❤❤❤ Hotel. **Address:** 250 Haskell Rd 04401

AAA Benefit:
Members save 5% or more!

HOLIDAY INN-BANGOR   207/947-0101
❤❤❤ Hotel. **Address:** 404 Odlin Rd 04401

HOLLYWOOD CASINO HOTEL BANGOR   207/974-3500
❤❤❤
Hotel
Rates not provided

Address: 500 Main St 04401 **Location:** I-395 exit 3B, just n. **Facility:** Check out the action at this casino hotel on Bangor's riverfront, located across from the Cross Insurance Center. Then retire to a comfortable, spacious guest room with a king- or queen-size bed. 152 units. 7 stories, interior corridors. **Amenities:** safes. **Dining:** 2 restaurants, also, Celebrity Bar & Grill, Epic Buffet, see separate listings. **Activities:** exercise room. **Guest Services:** valet and coin laundry.

[SAVE] 🐾 ➡ ❚❙ ▭ CALL ⟨&⟩
🅷 BIZ HS 📶 ✕ ♨ ▯
/ SOME UNITS 🛗

HOWARD JOHNSON INN   (207)942-5251
❤❤ Hotel. **Address:** 336 Odlin Rd 04401

QUALITY INN BANGOR AIRPORT   (207)942-8272
❤❤ Hotel. **Address:** 250 Odlin Rd 04401

QUALITY INN BANGOR MALL   (207)942-7899
❤❤ Hotel. **Address:** 750 Hogan Rd 04401

RAMADA   (207)947-6961
❤❤ Hotel. **Address:** 357 Odlin Rd 04401

RESIDENCE INN BY MARRIOTT BANGOR
    (207)433-0800
❤❤❤❤
Extended Stay Hotel
$106-$387

Residence INN. **AAA Benefit:**
Members save 5% or more!

Address: 22 Bass Park Blvd 04401 **Location:** I-395 exit 3B, just n. **Facility:** 124 kitchen units. 5 stories, interior corridors. **Terms:** cancellation fee imposed. **Dining:** Timber Kitchen & Bar, see separate listing. **Pool:** heated indoor. **Activities:** hot tub, exercise room. **Guest Services:** valet and coin laundry, area transportation. **Featured Amenity:** breakfast buffet.

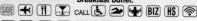

[SAVE] ➡ ❚❙ ▭ CALL ⟨&⟩ 🛥 🅷 BIZ HS 📶
✕ 🛗 🖥 ▯ / SOME UNITS 🐾

RODEWAY INN   (207)945-0111
❤ Motel. **Address:** 327 Odlin Rd 04401

SUPER 8   (207)945-5681
❤❤ Hotel. **Address:** 462 Odlin Rd 04401

TOWNEPLACE SUITES BY MARRIOTT BANGOR
    (207)262-4000
❤❤❤ Extended Stay Hotel. **Address:** 240 Sylvan Rd 04401

AAA Benefit:
Members save 5% or more!

WHERE TO EAT

BLAZE   207/922-2660
❤❤❤ American Pizza. Casual Dining. **Address:** 16 Broad St 04401

CELEBRITY BAR & GRILL   207/974-3500
❤❤ American. Casual Dining. **Address:** 500 Main St 04401

DYSART'S RESTAURANT & TRUCK STOP   207/942-4878
❤ American. Casual Dining. **Address:** 530 Coldbrook Rd 04401

EPIC BUFFET   207/974-3500
❤ American. Buffet Style. **Address:** 500 Main St 04401

THE GARDEN GRILLE & BAR   207/262-0099
❤❤ American. Casual Dining. **Address:** 250 Haskell St 04401

GODFREY'S GRILLE & LOUNGE   207/947-6721
❤❤ Traditional American. Casual Dining. **Address:** 308 Godfrey Blvd 04401

GOVERNOR'S RESTAURANT & BAKERY   207/947-3113
❤❤ American. Casual Dining. **Address:** 643 Broadway St 04401

GREEN TEA RESTAURANT   207/262-5566
❤❤ Asian Sushi. Casual Dining. **Address:** 11 Bangor Mall Blvd 04401

HAPPY CHINA BUFFET   207/990-6688
❤❤ Chinese. Buffet Style. **Address:** 753 Stillwater Ave 04401

ICHIBAN JAPANESE RESTAURANT   207/262-9308
❤❤ Japanese. Casual Dining. **Address:** 226 Union St 04401

LAS PALAPAS MEXICAN RESTAURANT   207/947-3500
❤❤ Mexican. Casual Dining. **Address:** 8 Bangor Mall Blvd 04401

MASSIMO'S CUCINA ITALIANA   207/945-5600
❤❤ Italian. Casual Dining. **Address:** 96 Hammond St 04401

MIGUEL'S MEXICAN RESTAURANT   207/942-3002
❤❤ Mexican. Casual Dining. **Address:** 697 Hogan Rd 04401

ORIENTAL JADE RESTAURANT & BAR   207/947-6969
❤❤ Chinese. Casual Dining. **Address:** 178 Bangor Mall Blvd 04401

PADDY MURPHY'S IRISH PUB   207/945-6800
❤❤ Irish. Casual Dining. **Address:** 26 Main St 04401

PEPINO'S MEXICAN RESTAURANT   207/947-1233
❤❤ Mexican. Casual Dining. **Address:** 49 N Park St 04401

SEA DOG BREWING CO   207/947-8009
❤❤ American. Casual Dining. **Address:** 26 Front St 04401

TIMBER KITCHEN & BAR   207/433-0844
❤❤❤ American. Casual Dining. **Address:** 22 Bass Park Blvd 04401

ZEN ASIAN BISTRO & LOUNGE   207/947-3030
❤❤ Asian Fusion. Casual Dining. **Address:** 128 Main St 04401

BAR HARBOR (I-6) pop. 2,552, elev. 240'
- **Hotels p. 42 • Restaurants p. 44**
- **Hotels & Restaurants map & index p. 37, 39**
- **Part of Acadia National Park area — see map p. 28**

Bar Harbor lies at the entrance to Acadia National Park on Mount Desert Island. The beauty of sea, mountain, lake and forest have made this region well-known as a resort. By the turn of the 20th century Bar Harbor had become the summer playground for America's wealthy; millionaires J.P. Morgan, Joseph Pulitzer and John D. Rockefeller were among those who owned "cottages."

(See maps & indexes p. 37, 39.)

However, newly instituted income taxes, World War I and the Great Depression nearly removed the leisure class from Bar Harbor by the 1930s. Many of the abandoned cottages, like their owners, succumbed to disaster and bad luck. Then a fire swept through Bar Harbor in 1947, ravaging 237 homes, including most of the estates, destroying more than 17,000 acres and leaving $23 million in charred ruins. The history of Bar Harbor can be seen in a collection of photographs and artifacts at the Bar Harbor Historical Society Museum, 33 Ledgelawn Ave.; phone (207) 288-0000.

A network of motor highways, carriage roads and mountain trails preserves the striking scenery for visitors. The Great Meadow Loop Trail connects downtown Bar Harbor with Acadia National Park.

One of the best ways to explore the area is to hop on the Island Explorer, a free shuttle bus operating late June through Columbus Day. Rides to Northeast Harbor, Southwest Harbor, Acadia National Park, beaches, campgrounds and other destinations originate at the Bar Harbor Village Green. Rides to Brown Mountain are offered late June through August 31. Shuttle passengers going to Acadia National Park should purchase a park entry permit at the Village Green prior to departing; phone (207) 667-5796.

Whale-watching cruises, sailing charters and working lobster boat excursions depart from Bar Harbor May through October.

Jackson Laboratory, 1.5 miles south on SR 3, is a national genetics research center. Public walking tours are offered on select Thursday mornings in summer; reservations can be made online. For information phone (800) 474-9880.

Bar Harbor Chamber of Commerce / Acadia Welcome Center: 2 Cottage St., Bar Harbor, ME 04609. **Phone:** (207) 288-5103 or (800) 288-5103.

ABBE MUSEUM DOWNTOWN is downtown at 26 Mount Desert St. Permanent and changing exhibits devoted to Maine's Native American heritage grace the galleries. Exhibits focus on the cultures, history, art and archeology of the Wabanaki people— members of the Passamaquoddy, Penobscot, Micmac and Maliseet tribes—who live in Maine today. The Wabanaki also includes several bands of the Abenaki tribe, located primarily in New Hampshire, Vermont and Québec. **Time:** Allow 1 hour minimum. **Hours:** Daily 10-5, May-Oct.; Thurs.-Sat. 10-4, rest of year. **Cost:** (includes Abbe Museum at Sieur de Monts Spring) $8; $4 (ages 11-17). **Phone:** (207) 288-3519.

ACADIA NATIONAL PARK TOURS, 53 Main St., offers narrated 2.5-hour bus tours of Bar Harbor and Acadia National Park. The tour includes the mansions of Bar Harbor, Sieur de Monts Spring, Thunder Hole and Cadillac Mountain. **Hours:** Tours depart daily at 10 and 2, mid-May to late Oct. **Cost:** $32.50; $20 (ages 0-12). **Phone:** (207) 288-0300.

THE ATLANTIC BREWING COMPANY, 7 mi. w. on SR 3 (Mt. Desert St./Eden St.), then 1.4 mi. s. to 15 Knox Rd., offers 30-minute tours during which visitors observe the entire brewing process, from fermentation to bottling. The brewery produces 60 kegs per day; samples of its ales, as well as its root beer and blueberry soda, are available. **Time:** Allow 1 hour minimum. **Hours:** Tours depart daily at 2, 3 and 4, Memorial Day weekend-Columbus Day. **Cost:** Free. **Phone:** (207) 288-2337. 🍴

MARGARET TODD **WINDJAMMER CRUISES** depart from the Bar Harbor Inn Pier. Three cruises of Frenchman's Bay are available on the 151-foot-long, four-masted schooner or the 91-foot-long wooden schooner *Bailey Louise Todd.* Bald eagles, porpoises and seals may be seen during a morning sail; on the afternoon narrated sail, passengers may picnic and help hoist the sails. The sunset sail offers live music.

Note: Passengers are advised to bring a warm jacket or sweater, particularly during cooler months. **Time:** Allow 2 hours minimum. **Hours:** Cruises depart daily at 10, 2 and dusk, May 15-Oct. 15. Phone ahead to confirm schedule. **Cost:** $42; $39 (ages 65+); $37 (retired military with ID); $32 (ages 6-11); $7 (ages 2-5); free (ages 0-1 and active military with ID). **Phone:** (207) 288-4585, (207) 546-2927 during winter, or (207) 288-2373 during summer. 🎫 🦽 🎫

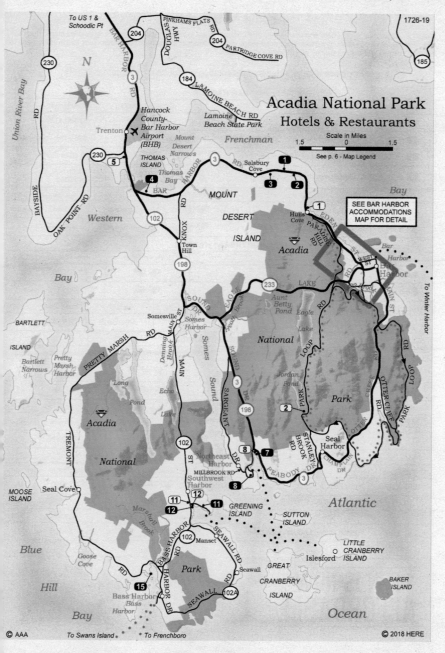

Acadia National Park
Hotels & Restaurants

Acadia National Park

This index helps you "spot" where approved hotels and restaurants are located on the corresponding detailed maps. Hotel daily rate range is for comparison only. Restaurant price range is a combination of lunch and/or dinner. Turn to the listing page for more information and consult display ads for special promotions.

 For more details, rates and reservations: AAA.com/travelguides/hotels

BAR HARBOR

Map Page	Hotels	Diamond Rated	Rate Range	Page
1 p. 37	High Seas Motel	◈◈	$70-$145	44
2 p. 37	Hutchins Mountain View Cottages	◈	$96-$152	44
3 p. 37	**Best Western Acadia Park Inn**	◈◈	$109-$349 SAVE	44
4 p. 37	Acadia Sunnyside Motel & Cottages	◈◈	Rates not provided	42

Map Page	Restaurants	Diamond Rated	Cuisine	Price Range	Page
① p. 37	**Chart Room**	◈◈	American	$11-$43	44
② p. 37	Jordan Pond House	◈◈	American	$10-$33	45

NORTHEAST HARBOR

Map Page	Hotels	Diamond Rated	Rate Range	Page
7 p. 37	Asticou Inn	◈◈	$155-$375	67
8 p. 37	**Kimball Terrace Inn**	◈◈	$75-$235 SAVE	67

Map Page	Restaurant	Diamond Rated	Cuisine	Price Range	Page
⑧ p. 37	Asticou Restaurant	◈◈◈	American	$15-$40	68

SOUTHWEST HARBOR

Map Page	Hotels	Diamond Rated	Rate Range	Page
11 p. 37	Clark Point Inn	◈◈◈	Rates not provided	85
12 p. 37	The Kingsleigh Inn	◈◈◈	$175-$325	85

Map Page	Restaurants	Diamond Rated	Cuisine	Price Range	Page
⑪ p. 37	Cafe 2 & Eat-a-Pita	◈◈	American	$6-$26	85
⑫ p. 37	Cafe Dry Dock	◈◈	American	$10-$26	85

BASS HARBOR

Map Page	Hotel	Diamond Rated	Rate Range	Page
15 p. 37	Ann's Point Inn	◈◈◈◈	$350-$390	45

TRENTON

Map Page	Restaurant	Diamond Rated	Cuisine	Price Range	Page
⑤ p. 37	Trenton Bridge Lobster Pound	◈	Seafood	$9-$25	85

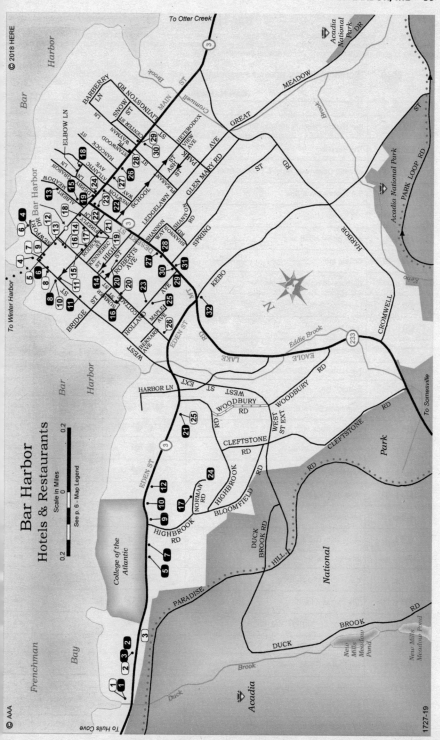

Bar Harbor
Hotels & Restaurants

Scale in Miles

0.2   0.2

See p. 6 - Map Legend

© AAA

© 2018 HERE

1727-19

Bar Harbor

This index helps you "spot" where approved hotels and restaurants are located on the corresponding detailed maps. Hotel daily rate range is for comparison only. Restaurant price range is a combination of lunch and/or dinner. Turn to the listing page for more information and consult display ads for special promotions.

 For more details, rates and reservations: AAA.com/travelguides/hotels

BAR HARBOR

Map Page	Hotels	Diamond Rated	Rate Range	Page
1 p. 39	**Bar Harbor Regency Holiday Inn**	◆◆◆	Rates not provided [SAVE]	43
2 p. 39	The Bayview	◆◆◆	Rates not provided	44
3 p. 39	**Atlantic Oceanside Hotel & Event Center**	◆◆◆	Rates not provided [SAVE]	42
4 p. 39	**Bar Harbor Inn & Spa**	◆◆◆	Rates not provided [SAVE]	42
5 p. 39	Bar Harbor Motel	◆◆	Rates not provided	43
6 p. 39	**West Street Hotel**	◆◆◆◆	Rates not provided [SAVE]	44
7 p. 39	**Acadia Inn**	◆◆◆	Rates not provided [SAVE]	42
8 p. 39	**Harborside Hotel Spa & Marina**	◆◆◆◆	Rates not provided [SAVE]	44
9 p. 39	Highbrook Motel	◆◆	Rates not provided	44
10 p. 39	Cleftstone Manor	◆◆◆	Rates not provided	44
11 p. 39	Manor House Inn	◆◆◆	Rates not provided	44
12 p. 39	Bar Harbor Hotel-Bluenose Inn	◆◆◆	$219-$509	42
13 p. 39	Seacroft Inn	◆◆	$79-$159	44
14 p. 39	Hearthside Bed & Breakfast	◆◆◆	Rates not provided	44
15 p. 39	**Balance Rock Inn**	◆◆◆◆	$255-$1055 [SAVE]	42
16 p. 39	Black Friar Inn & Pub	◆◆	Rates not provided	44
17 p. 39	Atlantic Eyrie Lodge	◆◆	Rates not provided	42
18 p. 39	Moseley Cottage Inn & Town Motel	◆◆	Rates not provided	44
19 p. 39	Ivy Manor Inn	◆◆◆	Rates not provided	44
20 p. 39	Maples Inn Bed & Breakfast	◆◆◆	Rates not provided	44
21 p. 39	Wonder View Inn	◆◆	$119-$289	44
22 p. 39	Bar Harbor Villager Motel	◆◆	Rates not provided	43
23 p. 39	The Elmhurst Inn	◆◆◆	Rates not provided	44
24 p. 39	Hampton Inn by Hilton Bar Harbor	◆◆◆	Rates not provided	44
25 p. 39	**Bar Harbor Manor** (See ad p. 43.)	◆◆◆	$79-$399 [SAVE]	42
26 p. 39	Bar Harbor Grand Hotel	◆◆◆	Rates not provided	42
27 p. 39	Anne's White Columns Inn	◆◆◆	$129-$249	42
28 p. 39	Mira Monte Inn	◆◆◆	Rates not provided	44
29 p. 39	Primrose Place	◆◆	$105-$195	44

BAR HARBOR (cont'd)

Map Page	Hotels (cont'd)		Diamond Rated	Rate Range	Page
30 p. 39	Primrose Inn		◈◈◈	$169-$310	44
31 p. 39	Holbrook House		◈◈◈	$129-$299	44
32 p. 39	Bar Harbor Quality Inn		◈◈	$147-$169	43

Map Page	Restaurants	Diamond Rated	Cuisine	Price Range	Page
1 p. 39	Stewman's at Regency	◈◈	Seafood	$13-$35	45
2 p. 39	La Bella Vita at Bar Harbor Regency	◈◈◈	Traditional Italian Seafood Pizza	$15-$30	45
3 p. 39	Jack Russell's Steakhouse & Brewery	◈◈	American	$11-$38	45
4 p. 39	Fish House Grill	◈◈	Seafood	$12-$35	45
5 p. 39	**Paddy's Irish Pub**	◈◈◈	Irish	$12-$32	45
6 p. 39	**The Reading Room Restaurant at the Bar Harbor Inn & Spa**	◈◈◈	Seafood	$29-$42	45
7 p. 39	Galyn's Restaurant	◈◈◈	American	$16-$56	45
8 p. 39	Stewman's Lobster Pound Downtown	◈◈	Seafood	$13-$35	45
9 p. 39	Geddy's Pub	◈◈	American	$9-$25	45
10 p. 39	**La Bella Vita Ristorante**	◈◈◈	Italian	$14-$40	45
11 p. 39	West Street Cafe	◈◈	American	$8-$35	45
12 p. 39	Testa's Restaurant	◈◈	American	$12-$30	45
13 p. 39	Jeannie's Great Maine Breakfast	◈◈	Breakfast	$7-$12	45
14 p. 39	Route 66 Restaurant	◈◈	American	$10-$27	45
15 p. 39	Siam Orchid Thai Restaurant	◈◈	Thai	$10-$18	45
16 p. 39	Lompoc Cafe	◈◈	American	$10-$21	45
17 p. 39	The Dog and Pony Tavern	◈◈	American	$4-$19	45
18 p. 39	Bar Harbor Beer Works	◈◈	Comfort Food	$10-$30	44
19 p. 39	Side Street Cafe	◈◈	American	$9-$28	45
20 p. 39	Jordan's Restaurant	◈◈	American	$7-$15	45
21 p. 39	Mama DiMatteo's	◈◈	Italian	$12-$27	45
22 p. 39	CherrySTONES	◈◈	American	$12-$30	45
23 p. 39	Cafe This Way	◈◈◈	American	$8-$26	44
24 p. 39	Blaze	◈◈◈	New Pizza	$10-$30	44
25 p. 39	The Looking Glass Restaurant	◈◈	American	$16-$42	45
26 p. 39	2 Cats Cafe & Inn	◈◈	Breakfast	$8-$20	44
27 p. 39	McKay's Public House	◈◈◈	American	$12-$30	45
28 p. 39	Poor Boys Gourmet Restaurant	◈◈	American	$12-$36	45
29 p. 39	**Havana Restaurant**	◈◈◈	Latin American	$21-$35	45
30 p. 39	Mache Bistro	◈◈◈	French	$18-$32	45

For complete hotel, dining and attraction listings: AAA.com/travelguides

(See maps & indexes p. 37, 39.)

ACADIA INN

207/288-3500 **7**

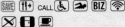
Hotel
Rates not provided

Address: 98 Eden St 04609 **Location:** 1 mi w on SR 3. **Facility:** 95 units. 3 stories, interior corridors. **Amenities:** safes. **Pool:** heated outdoor. **Activities:** hot tub, playground, lawn sports, trails. **Guest Services:** coin laundry. **Featured Amenity: continental breakfast.**

SAVE | CALL | BIZ |

ACADIA SUNNYSIDE MOTEL & COTTAGES
207/288-3602 **4**

Cottage. **Address:** 1441 State Hwy 3 04609

ANNE'S WHITE COLUMNS INN
(207)288-5357 **27**

Bed & Breakfast. **Address:** 57 Mt Desert St 04609

ATLANTIC EYRIE LODGE
207/288-9786 **17**

Hotel. **Address:** 6 Norman Rd 04609

ATLANTIC OCEANSIDE HOTEL & EVENT CENTER
207/288-5801 **3**

Hotel
Rates not provided

Address: 119 Eden St 04609 **Location:** Oceanfront. 1.8 mi w on SR 3. Adjacent to ferry landing. **Facility:** 153 units, some two bedrooms, kitchens, houses and condominiums. 2-4 stories, interior/exterior corridors. **Amenities:** safes. **Pool:** heated outdoor, heated indoor. **Activities:** hot tub, boat dock, fishing, playground, lawn sports, exercise room. **Guest Services:** coin laundry. **Featured Amenity: continental breakfast.**

SAVE | ECO | | | BIZ |

BALANCE ROCK INN
(207)288-2610 **15**

Historic Bed & Breakfast
$255-$1055

Address: 21 Albert Meadow 04609 **Location:** Oceanfront. Just s of Main St; center. Located in a residential area. **Facility:** This turn-of-the-century oceanfront mansion borders a shore path. Many guest rooms feature decks, fireplaces and jetted bathtubs. 27 units, some kitchens. 3 stories, interior/exterior corridors. **Terms:** closed 10/27-5/16, 14 day cancellation notice-fee imposed. **Amenities:** safes. **Pool:** heated outdoor. **Activities:** exercise room. **Guest Services:** valet laundry. **Featured Amenity: breakfast buffet.**

SAVE | | BIZ | / SOME UNITS |

BAR HARBOR GRAND HOTEL
207/288-5226 **26**

Hotel. **Address:** 269 Main St 04609

BAR HARBOR HOTEL-BLUENOSE INN
(207)288-3348 **12**

Hotel. **Address:** 90 Eden St 04609

BAR HARBOR INN & SPA
207/288-3351 **4**

Hotel
Rates not provided

Address: 1 Newport Dr 04609 **Location:** Oceanfront. At Main St; center. Located by Municipal Town Pier. **Facility:** 153 units, some two bedrooms. 2-3 stories, interior/exterior corridors. **Amenities:** safes. **Dining:** The Reading Room Restaurant at the Bar Harbor Inn & Spa, see separate listing. **Pool:** heated outdoor. **Activities:** sauna, hot tub, recreation programs in summer, playground, exercise room, spa. **Guest Services:** valet laundry. **Featured Amenity: full hot breakfast.**

SAVE | | | | | | BIZ |

/ SOME UNITS |

BAR HARBOR MANOR
(207)288-3829 **25**

Hotel
$79-$399

Address: 47 Holland Ave 04609 **Location:** Between Cottage and Mt Desert sts; center. **Facility:** 43 units, some two bedrooms and kitchens. 2-3 stories, interior/exterior corridors. **Terms:** closed 10/31-5/1, 10 day cancellation notice-fee imposed. **Activities:** exercise room. *(See ad p. 43.)*

SAVE | | CALL | | BIZ |

| | | / SOME UNITS |

(See maps & indexes p. 37, 39.)

BAR HARBOR MOTEL 207/288-3453 **5**
♥♥ Motel. **Address:** 100 Eden St 04609

BAR HARBOR QUALITY INN (207)288-5403 **32**
♥♥ Hotel. **Address:** 40 Kebo St 04609

🔗 **Use the free travel planning tools at AAA.com/maps**

BAR HARBOR REGENCY HOLIDAY INN
207/288-9723 **1**

Hotel
Rates not provided

Address: 123 Eden St 04609 **Location:** Oceanfront. 1 mi w on SR 3. **Facility:** 280 units. 3-4 stories, interior corridors. **Terms:** check-in 4 pm. **Amenities:** safes. **Dining:** La Bella Vita at Bar Harbor Regency, Stewman's at Regency, see separate listings. **Pool:** heated outdoor. **Activities:** hot tub, marina, tennis, game room, lawn sports, exercise room. **Guest Services:** coin laundry, area transportation.

BAR HARBOR VILLAGER MOTEL 207/288-3211 **22**
♥♥ Motel. **Address:** 207 Main St 04609

▼ See AAA listing p. 42 ▼

(See maps & indexes p. 37, 39.)

THE BAYVIEW   207/288-5861   **2**
 Hotel. **Address:** 111 Eden St 04609

BEST WESTERN ACADIA PARK INN

(207)288-5823   **3**

Hotel
$109-$349

Best Western.

AAA Benefit: Members save up to 15% and earn bonus points!

Address: 452 State Hwy 3 04609 **Location:** 4.8 mi w. Located in a rural area. **Facility:** 96 units. 1 story, exterior corridors. **Terms:** closed 10/19-4/18, cancellation fee imposed. **Amenities:** safes. **Pool:** heated outdoor. **Activities:** playground, lawn sports, picnic facilities. **Guest Services:** coin laundry.

BLACK FRIAR INN & PUB   207/288-5091   **16**
 Country Inn. **Address:** 10 Summer St 04609

CLEFTSTONE MANOR   207/288-4951   **10**
 Historic Bed & Breakfast. **Address:** 92 Eden St 04609

THE ELMHURST INN   207/288-3044   **23**
 Historic Bed & Breakfast. **Address:** 40 Holland Ave 04609

HAMPTON INN BY HILTON BAR HARBOR   207/288-3210   **24**
 Hotel. **Address:** 12 Norman Rd 04609

AAA Benefit: Members save 5% or more!

HARBORSIDE HOTEL SPA & MARINA

207/288-5033   **8**

Hotel
Rates not provided

Address: 55 West St 04609 **Location:** Oceanfront. Center. **Facility:** Located in the heart of downtown, this property sits on Frenchman Bay. Each guest room has upscale, pod coffeemakers, plush bedding and a balcony or a patio. This resort also has its own marina. 193 units, some two bedrooms, three bedrooms and efficiencies. 3 stories, interior/exterior corridors. **Terms:** check-in 4 pm. **Amenities:** safes. *Some:* video games. **Dining:** La Bella Vita Ristorante, see separate listing. **Pool:** heated outdoor. **Activities:** sauna, hot tub, steamroom, marina, tennis, recreation programs, exercise room, spa. **Guest Services:** complimentary laundry.

HEARTHSIDE BED & BREAKFAST   207/288-4533   **14**
 Bed & Breakfast. **Address:** 7 High St 04609

HIGHBROOK MOTEL   207/288-3591   **9**
 Motel. **Address:** 94 Eden St 04609

HIGH SEAS MOTEL   (207)288-5836   **1**
 Motel. **Address:** 339 State Hwy 3 04609

HOLBROOK HOUSE   (207)288-4970   **31**
 Historic Bed & Breakfast. **Address:** 74 Mt Desert St 04609

HUTCHINS MOUNTAIN VIEW COTTAGES
(207)288-4833   **2**
 Cottage. **Address:** 286 State Hwy 3 04609

IVY MANOR INN   207/288-2138   **19**
 Historic Country Inn. **Address:** 194 Main St 04609

MANOR HOUSE INN   207/288-3759   **11**
 Historic Bed & Breakfast. **Address:** 106 West St 04609

MAPLES INN BED & BREAKFAST   207/288-3443   **20**
 Historic Bed & Breakfast. **Address:** 16 Roberts Ave 04609

MIRA MONTE INN   207/288-4263   **28**
 Historic Bed & Breakfast. **Address:** 69 Mt Desert St 04609

MOSELEY COTTAGE INN & TOWN MOTEL
207/288-5548   **18**
 Hotel. **Address:** 12 Atlantic Ave 04609

PRIMROSE INN   (207)288-4031   **30**
 Historic Bed & Breakfast. **Address:** 73 Mt Desert St 04609

PRIMROSE PLACE   (207)288-3771   **29**
 Boutique Motel. **Address:** 51 Holland Ave 04609

SEACROFT INN   (207)288-4669   **13**
 Bed & Breakfast. **Address:** 18 Albert Meadow 04609

WEST STREET HOTEL

207/288-0825   **6**

Hotel
Rates not provided

Address: 50 West St 04609 **Location:** Jct Main St. **Facility:** Guest rooms are spacious and have a tasteful nautical theme; many offer beautiful views of the harbor. For a panoramic view, head up to the rooftop pool. Each floor has a complimentary pantry area. 85 units, some two bedrooms. 4 stories, interior/exterior corridors. **Terms:** check-in 4 pm. **Amenities:** safes. **Dining:** Paddy's Irish Pub, see separate listing. **Pool:** heated outdoor. **Activities:** recreation programs, kids club, exercise room. **Guest Services:** complimentary laundry.

WONDER VIEW INN   (207)288-3358   **21**
 Hotel. **Address:** 50 Eden St 04609

WHERE TO EAT

2 CATS CAFE & INN   207/288-2808   **26**
 Breakfast. Casual Dining. **Address:** 130 Cottage St 04609

BAR HARBOR BEER WORKS   207/288-2886   **18**
 Comfort Food. Casual Dining. **Address:** 119 Main St 04609

BLAZE   207/801-2755   **24**
 New Pizza. Casual Dining. **Address:** 198 Main St 04609

CAFE THIS WAY   207/288-4483   **23**
 American. Casual Dining. **Address:** 14 Mt Desert St 04609

CHART ROOM   207/288-9740   **1**

American
Casual Dining
$11-$43

AAA Inspector Notes: This popular eatery serves only the freshest seafood and Certified Angus Beef and offers lovely patio dining in season. Located at the entrance to Acadia National Park, it features a pleasant seaside setting overlooking Hulls Cove. **Features:** full bar, early bird specials. **Reservations:** suggested. **Address:** 585 Eden St 04609 **Location:** On SR 3, 2.5 mi w at Hulls Cove.

(See maps & indexes p. 37, 39.)

CHERRYSTONES 207/801-2290 ㉒
♦♦ American. Casual Dining. **Address:** 185 Main St 04609

THE DOG AND PONY TAVERN 207/288-0900 ⑰
♦♦ American. Casual Dining. **Address:** 4 Rodick Pl 04609

FISH HOUSE GRILL 207/288-3070 ④
♦♦ Seafood. Casual Dining. **Address:** 1 West St 04609

GALYN'S RESTAURANT 207/288-9706 ⑦
♦♦ American. Casual Dining. **Address:** 17 Main St 04609

GEDDY'S PUB 207/288-5077 ⑨
♦♦ American. Casual Dining. **Address:** 19 Main St 04609

HAVANA RESTAURANT 207/288-2822 ㉙
♦♦♦ **Latin American Fine Dining $21-$35** **AAA Inspector Notes:** The restaurant features creative cuisine, with a Latin touch for their innovative menu. Signature dishes include roasted mushrooms and soba noodles in a crisp spring roll wrap with soy glaze, seafood paella and Prime steak. Select a nice pairing from the large and eclectic wine list. **Features:** full bar. **Address:** 318 Main St 04609 **Location:** Center. **Parking:** street only.
Ⓓ

JACK RUSSELL'S STEAKHOUSE & BREWERY 207/288-5214 ③
♦ American. Casual Dining. **Address:** 102 Eden St 04609

JEANNIE'S GREAT MAINE BREAKFAST 207/288-4166 ⑬
♦♦ Breakfast. Casual Dining. **Address:** 15 Cottage St 04609

JORDAN POND HOUSE 207/276-3316 ②
♦♦ American. Casual Dining. **Address:** Acadia National Park 04609

JORDAN'S RESTAURANT 207/288-3586 ⑳
♦♦ American. Casual Dining. **Address:** 80 Cottage St 04609

LA BELLA VITA AT BAR HARBOR REGENCY 207/801-3979 ②
♦♦♦ Traditional Italian Seafood Pizza. Casual Dining. **Address:** 123 Eden St 04609

LA BELLA VITA RISTORANTE 207/288-5033 ⑩
♦♦♦ **Italian Casual Dining $14-$40** **AAA Inspector Notes:** This eatery features attractive Italian countryside décor and a brick pizza oven. In the summer season, enjoy great patio dining overlooking the pool and the harbor. The menu includes a fine selection of Italian dishes made with fresh, local ingredients, hot focaccia bread and a broad assortment of Italian wines. **Features:** full bar, patio dining. **Address:** 55 West St 04609 **Location:** Center; in Harborside Hotel Spa & Marina.
Ⓑ Ⓛ Ⓓ CALL ♿

LOMPOC CAFE 207/288-9392 ⑯
♦♦ American. Casual Dining. **Address:** 36 Rodick St 04609

THE LOOKING GLASS RESTAURANT 207/288-5663 ㉕
♦♦ American. Casual Dining. **Address:** 50 Eden St 04609

MACHE BISTRO 207/288-0447 ㉚
♦♦♦ French. Casual Dining. **Address:** 321 Main St 04609

MAMA DIMATTEO'S 207/288-3666 ㉑
♦♦ Italian. Casual Dining. **Address:** 34 Kennebec Pl 04609

MCKAY'S PUBLIC HOUSE 207/288-2002 ㉗
♦♦ American. Gastropub. **Address:** 231 Main St 04609

PADDY'S IRISH PUB 207/288-0825 ⑤
♦♦♦ **Irish Gastropub $12-$32** **AAA Inspector Notes:** Ideally located across from the harbor, this upbeat and friendly place offers indoor and outdoor dining. The vast menu includes selections of local fresh seafood, steaks and items cooked on the popular open rotisserie, which guests can view through the glass. **Features:** full bar. **Address:** 50 West St 04609 **Location:** Jct Main St; in West Street Hotel. **Parking:** on-site (fee).
Ⓑ Ⓛ Ⓓ CALL ♿

POOR BOYS GOURMET RESTAURANT 207/288-4148 ㉘
♦♦ American. Casual Dining. **Address:** 300 Main St 04609

THE READING ROOM RESTAURANT AT THE BAR HARBOR INN & SPA 207/288-3351 ⑥
♦♦♦ **Seafood Fine Dining $29-$42** **AAA Inspector Notes:** The popular and busy restaurant used to be an 1887 social club. The lovely oceanfront setting and outdoor terrace afford splendid harbor views. On the menu are flavorful fresh seafood and pasta dishes, which match with a good wine list. The blueberry pie is excellent. **Features:** full bar, Sunday brunch. **Reservations:** suggested. **Address:** Newport Dr 04609 **Location:** At Main St; center; in Bar Harbor Inn & Spa. Ⓑ Ⓓ

ROUTE 66 RESTAURANT 207/288-3708 ⑭
♦♦ American. Casual Dining. **Address:** 21 Cottage St 04609

SIAM ORCHID THAI RESTAURANT 207/288-9669 ⑮
♦♦ Thai. Casual Dining. **Address:** 30 Rodick St 04609

SIDE STREET CAFE 207/801-2591 ⑲
♦♦ American. Casual Dining. **Address:** 49 Rodick St 04609

STEWMAN'S AT REGENCY 207/288-9723 ①
♦♦ Seafood. Casual Dining. **Address:** 123 Eden St 04609

STEWMAN'S LOBSTER POUND DOWNTOWN 207/288-0346 ⑧
♦♦ Seafood. Casual Dining. **Address:** 35 West St 04609

TESTA'S RESTAURANT 207/288-3327 ⑫
♦♦ American. Casual Dining. **Address:** 53 Main St 04609

WEST STREET CAFE 207/288-5242 ⑪
♦♦ American. Casual Dining. **Address:** 76 West St 04609

BASS HARBOR
• Hotels & Restaurants map & index p. 37
• Part of Acadia National Park area — see map p. 28

ANN'S POINT INN (207)244-9595 ⑮
♦♦♦♦ Contemporary Bed & Breakfast. **Address:** 79 Ann's Point Rd 04653

BATH (J-4) pop. 8,514, elev. 7'
• Hotels p. 46 • Restaurants p. 46

Bath, on the west bank of the Kennebec River, has been an active center of shipbuilding since the early 1600s. Nuclear naval vessels and large merchant ships are now built at Bath Iron Works. Residential sections have a number of old mansions dating from Bath's days as a major port. The Chocolate Church Arts Center, 804 Washington St., offers year-round cultural events; phone (207) 442-8455.

In the town of Woolwich, one mile east of Bath, visitors on Sunday afternoons can tour the Woolwich Historical Society Museum, which is housed in an early 19th-century home and features quilts, rugs, fabrics, home furnishings, farm equipment and tools from the 19th and early 20th centuries; phone (207) 443-4833 during the summer, or (207) 443-5684 during the off-season.

MAINE MARITIME MUSEUM, 243 Washington St., is on a 20-acre site of a 19th-century shipyard where large wooden sailing ships were constructed and launched. In five original shipyard buildings, visitors learn about the process of building a wooden schooner. A highlight is the life-size sculpture of the *Wyoming*, reputedly the largest sailing ship built in the United States. The Maritime History Building contains paintings, ship models, displays of ship artifacts, photographs and video presentations. The lobstering exhibit describes the development of one of the state's leading economic activities.

In season, visitors can visit the Bath Iron Works to see modern U.S. Navy destroyers under construction, then take a trolley tour of historic Bath; glimpse up to 10 lighthouses on a boat cruise from the Long Reach area of the Kennebec River and surrounding waters; or peek into the Victorian-era life of the Bath family at the William T. Donnell House.

Time: Allow 2 hours minimum. **Hours:** Daily 9:30-5. Bath Iron Works Story Trolley Tour Mon.-Fri. at noon (also Mon., Wed. and Fri. at 2), Sat. at 10, early June-late Oct. Closed Jan. 1, Thanksgiving and Christmas. **Cost:** $17.50; $16 (ages 65+); $10.50 (ages 6-12). Bath Iron Works Story Trolley Tour (includes museum) $30; $20 (ages 0-11). Prices may vary; phone ahead. **Phone:** (207) 443-1316. [T]

HAMPTON INN BY HILTON BATH BRUNSWICK AREA
207/386-1310
Hotel. **Address:** 140 Commercial St 04530

AAA Benefit: Members save 5% or more!

RESIDENCE INN BY MARRIOTT-BATH BRUNSWICK AREA
(207)443-9741

Extended Stay Hotel
$95-$385

Residence INN. **AAA Benefit:** Members save 5% or more!

Address: 139 Richardson St 04530 **Location:** 0.3 mi s on US 1; at State Rd. **Facility:** 86 units, some two bedrooms, efficiencies and kitchens. 4 stories, interior corridors. **Terms:** cancellation fee imposed. **Pool:** heated indoor. **Activities:** exercise room. **Guest Services:** valet and coin laundry. **Featured Amenity:** breakfast buffet.

WHERE TO EAT

AMATO'S
207/442-9600
Pizza Sandwiches. Quick Serve. **Address:** 111 Centre St 04530

BEALE STREET BARBEQUE
207/442-9514
Barbecue. Casual Dining. **Address:** 215 Water St 04530

J. R. MAXWELL & CO.
207/443-2014
American. Casual Dining. **Address:** 122 Front St 04530

MAE'S CAFE & BAKERY
207/442-8577
Breakfast Breads/Pastries. Casual Dining. **Address:** 160 Centre St 04530

BELFAST (I-5) pop. 6,668, elev. 103'

Formerly a prosperous shipbuilding center, Belfast is a community resplendent with restored Federal and early Victorian homes built by former sea merchants. The city, located on Penobscot Bay, is becoming a cultural center with artists, writers and craftspeople adding to the economic revival of Waldo County.

The 1-mile Belfast Harbor Walk runs along the downtown waterfront from Footbridge Road to Commercial Street and offers views of the Passagassawakeag River.

Local theater groups, including Cold Comfort Theater, (207) 930-7244, and Midcoast Actors' Studio, (207) 370-7592, offer productions year-round. Local cruise and aviation companies offer summer tours by appointment.

Belfast Area Chamber of Commerce-Belfast: 14 Main St., Belfast, ME 04915. **Phone:** (207) 338-5900.

Self-guiding tours: Walking tour brochures are available from the chamber of commerce.

BELFAST BAY INN
(207)338-5600

Boutique Hotel
$259-$439

Address: 70 Main St 04915 **Location:** Just e of High St; downtown. **Facility:** Residential-style rooms feature luxurious bedding, Renaissance artwork, hardwood floors and plush area rugs. Ample closet space and stocked refrigerators will make arriving and unpacking a breeze. 8 units. 3 stories, interior corridors. **Terms:** 14 day cancellation notice-fee imposed. **Amenities:** safes. **Featured Amenity:** full hot breakfast.

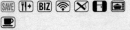

BELFAST HARBOR INN
(207)338-2740
Hotel. **Address:** 91 Searsport Ave (Rt 1) 04915

FIRESIDE INN & SUITES, OCEAN'S EDGE
207/338-2090
Hotel. **Address:** 159 Searsport Ave 04915

THE JEWELED TURRET INN
(207)338-2304
Historic Bed & Breakfast. **Address:** 40 Pearl St 04915

YANKEE CLIPPER MOTEL
(207)338-2353
Motel. **Address:** 50 Searsport Ave 04915

WHERE TO EAT

DARBY'S RESTAURANT & PUB
207/338-2339
International. Casual Dining. **Address:** 155 High St 04915

DELVINO'S GRILL & PASTA HOUSE
207/338-4565
New Italian Pizza. Gastropub. **Address:** 52 Main St 04915

DOCKSIDE FAMILY RESTAURANT   207/338-6889
♥♥ American. Casual Dining. **Address:** 30 Main St 04915

NAUTILUS SEAFOOD & GRILL   207/218-4218
♥♥ Seafood Steak. Casual Dining. **Address:** 95 Searsport Ave 04915

NEIGHBORHOOD RESTAURANT   207/505-0425
♥♥♥ New International. Casual Dining. **Address:** 132 S High St 04915

OCEAN'S EDGE RESTAURANT   207/338-2090
♥♥ American. Casual Dining. **Address:** 159 Searsport Ave 04915

SENG THAI RESTAURANT   207/338-0010
♥♥ Thai. Casual Dining. **Address:** 139 Searsport Ave 04915

YOUNG'S LOBSTER POUND   207/338-1160
♥ Seafood. Quick Serve. **Address:** 2 Fairview St 04915

BIDDEFORD (K-2) pop. 21,277, elev. 75'
• Hotels & Restaurants map & index p. 58

In 1662 one of the region's first sawmills was erected in Biddeford. The lure of waterpower gradually built the city into an important manufacturing center. Biddeford's diverse economic base relies on boatbuilding and the production of plastic, machinery, electronics and baked goods.

Biddeford is closely bound economically and culturally to Saco *(see place listing p. 82)*, its sister city across the river. This interdependency is evident in the cooperative efforts shown in the restoration of the 1895 opera house; the acoustically perfect City Theater, (207) 282-0849, is an outstanding example of late 19th-century ornamental architecture.

Both cities take advantage of the educational and cultural opportunities offered by the University College at Saco and the University of New England, 4 miles east on Pool Road overlooking the sea.

Biddeford-Saco Chamber of Commerce & Industry: 28 Water St., Suite 1, Biddeford, ME 04005. **Phone:** (207) 282-1567.

HOLIDAY INN EXPRESS   (207)294-6464 **44**
♥♥♥ Hotel. **Address:** 45 Barra Rd 04005

AMATO'S   207/286-2934
♥ Pizza Sandwiches. Quick Serve. **Address:** 458 Alfred St 04005

BOOTHBAY (J-4) elev. 127'

BOOTHBAY RAILWAY VILLAGE, 3.5 mi. n. on SR 27 to 586 Wiscasset Rd., depicts a turn-of-the-20th-century Maine village containing railroad memorabilia, antique cars and trucks and a general store as well as the 1847 Boothbay Town Hall and the Spruce Point Chapel. Visitors can ride on a narrow-gauge, coal-fired steam engine. A Christmas train runs in December.

Time: Allow 2 hours minimum. **Hours:** Village daily 10-5, Memorial Day-third Sun. in Oct. Trains depart most days hourly 11-4. Phone ahead to confirm schedule. **Cost:** $14; $12 (ages 65+); $7 (ages 3-18); free (ages 0-2 and active duty military and families with ID). **Phone:** (207) 633-4727.

COASTAL MAINE BOTANICAL GARDENS is, from Rte. 1, 9.3 mi. s. on SR 27, .25 mi. w. on Corey Ln., then 1 mi. w. on Barters Island Rd. to 132 Botanical Gardens Dr. The 275-acre botanical garden contains some 91,000 plants representing more than 1,430 species. Waterfalls, sculptures and stonework are featured, and 2 miles of trails are in waterfront and woodland settings.

Water-spraying whale sculptures welcome visitors to the 2-acre Bibby and Harold Alfond Children's Garden, which celebrates the works of E.B. White, Robert McCloskey, Barbara Cooney and other children's authors with ties to the state. Kids can listen to a storyteller, curl up with a good book in the Story Barn, explore a tree house, maneuver their way through a maze and sit in a rowboat.

In the Lerner Garden of the Five Senses visitors stimulate their bodies and minds by walking barefoot on a stone labyrinth, admiring and smelling blooming lavender, sampling fresh herbs, touching a fuzzy lamb's ear leaf and trying out a "sound stone."

Little ones will have a ball designing and constructing homes for imaginary forest dwellers in Fairy House Village. Sustainability is the theme of the LEED-certified Bosarge Family Education Center. Other must-sees include the Rhododendron, Rose, Kitchen, Hillside, Meditation and Forest Pond gardens. The site hosts workshops, art shows, concerts and events throughout the year.

Food is available seasonally. **Time:** Allow 2 hours minimum. **Hours:** Gardens daily 9-5, Apr. 15-Oct. 31 (also 5-6, July-Aug.). Closed Thanksgiving and Christmas. **Cost:** Admission Apr. 15-Oct. 31 $16; $14 (ages 65+); $8 (ages 3-17). Free rest of year. **Phone:** (207) 633-8000. **GT** **⊤**

BOOTHBAY HARBOR (J-4) pop. 1,086, elev. 20'

A picturesque seaport, Boothbay Harbor retains the atmosphere of an old New England village. Fishing craft lie alongside wharves that follow the quaint, winding village streets. Yachtsmen and artists began vacationing in the area in the early 1900s. Word soon spread of the region's natural beauty, and Boothbay Harbor began the slow transition from shipping center to resort area.

The Boothbay Harbor region's waterfront offers visitors a glimpse into seafaring history and an array of nautical activities on the Maine coast. With a strong shipbuilding and fishing heritage, the harbor shelters a wide variety of boats.

River cruises, ocean cruises, whale watches, sailing and deep-sea fishing trips leave local piers daily and vary in length from 1 hour to an entire day. The *Balmy Days II* makes day trips to Monhegan Island late May to early October; phone (207) 633-2284 or (800) 298-2284.

In late June antique boats and a parade are part of the ⛵ Windjammer Days celebration. The Fall Foliage Festival, featuring craft displays and train rides, is held early to mid-October.

Boothbay Harbor Region Chamber of Commerce: 192 Townsend Ave., Boothbay Harbor, ME 04538. **Phone:** (207) 633-2353.

CAP'N FISH'S WHALE WATCH AND SCENIC NATURE CRUISES, downtown on the waterfront at Pier 1, offers a variety of sightseeing cruises along the Maine coast, including the Puffin Nature, Whale- and Seal-Watching, Lobster Trap Hauling, Damariscove Harbor, Kennebec River-Bath and Pemaquid Point Lighthouse cruises.

Hours: Whale-watching cruise departs Mon.-Fri. at 9:30 and 1:30, Sat. at 9:30, Sun. at 12:30, July 1-early Sept.; Mon.-Fri. at noon, Sat.-Sun. at 12:30, early Sept. to mid-Oct.; Sat. at noon, Sun. at 12:30, in June. Schedule for other cruises varies. Ticket office opens at 8. Phone ahead to confirm schedule. **Cost:** Whale-watching cruise $56; $32 (ages 6-14); $20 (dogs); $19 (ages 0-5). Fares for other cruises vary; phone ahead. Reservations are recommended. **Phone:** (207) 633-3244 or (800) 636-3244. 🍴

ATLANTIC ARK INN   207/633-5690
🔷🔷 Bed & Breakfast. **Address:** 62 Atlantic Ave 04538

BEACH COVE WATERFRONT INN   207/633-0353
🔷🔷 Motel. **Address:** 48 Lakeview Rd 04538

BLUE HERON SEASIDE INN   (207)633-7020
🔷🔷🔷 Bed & Breakfast. **Address:** 65 Townsend Ave 04538

BOOTHBAY HARBOR INN   207/633-6302
🔷🔷 Hotel. **Address:** 31 Atlantic Ave 04538

BROWN'S WHARF INN   (207)633-5440

🔷🔷🔷
Hotel
$139-$239

Address: 121 Atlantic Ave 04538 **Location:** Waterfront. East side of town. **Facility:** 72 units, some kitchens and cottages. 3 stories, exterior corridors. **Terms:** closed 10/14-5/22, 2 night minimum stay, 3 day cancellation notice-fee imposed. **Amenities:** safes. **Dining:** Brown's Wharf Restaurant, see separate listing. **Activities:** marina, fishing. **Guest Services:** coin laundry.

SAVE 🍴 🍽 CALL 👤 BIZ 📶 ✕ 🛗 🖥

CAP'N FISH'S WATERFRONT INN   (207)633-6605
🔷🔷 Hotel. **Address:** 63 Atlantic Ave 04538

FISHERMAN'S WHARF INN   (207)633-5090
🔷🔷 Classic Hotel. **Address:** 22 Commercial St Pier 6 04538

FLAGSHIP INN & SUITES   207/633-5094

🔷🔷
Motel
Rates not provided

Address: 200 Townsend Ave 04538 **Location:** On SR 27, just n of jct SR 96. **Facility:** 82 units. 2 stories (no elevator), exterior corridors. **Pool:** heated outdoor. **Activities:** hot tub, playground, picnic facilities, trails. **Featured Amenity:** continental breakfast.

SAVE ECO 🍴 CALL 👤 🚐 BIZ 📶 ✕ 🛗 🖥 / SOME UNITS 🐾 🖥

HARBORAGE INN ON THE OCEANFRONT   207/633-4640
🔷🔷🔷 Classic Bed & Breakfast. **Address:** 75 Townsend Ave 04538

TUGBOAT INN   (207)633-4434
🔷🔷 Hotel. **Address:** 80 Commercial St 04538

WHERE TO EAT

BOOTHBAY LOBSTER WHARF   207/633-4900
🔷 Regional Seafood. Quick Serve. **Address:** 97 Atlantic Ave 04538

BROWN'S WHARF RESTAURANT   207/633-5440

🔷🔷
Seafood
Casual Dining
$16-$32

AAA Inspector Notes: *Classic.* An area fixture since 1944, the family-owned restaurant provides a panoramic view of Boothbay Harbor. On the menu is a good selection of fresh seafood, steak, lamb and pasta dishes, plus prime rib on the weekends. **Features:** full bar, patio dining. **Reservations:** suggested. **Address:** 121 Atlantic Ave 04538 **Location:** East side of town; in Brown's Wharf Inn.

B D CALL 👤

CHINA BY THE SEA   207/633-4449

🔷🔷
Chinese
Casual Dining
$8-$22

AAA Inspector Notes: Traditional and quite tasty, the dishes at this restaurant are made-to-order, which results in excellent quality meals. **Features:** full bar. **Address:** 96 Townsend Ave 04538 **Location:** Center. L D

KALER'S RESTAURANT   207/633-5839

Regional
Seafood
Casual Dining
$9-$26

AAA Inspector Notes: Located on the waterfront, this eatery is known for its fresh crab and lobster specialties. The menu also includes salads, chowder, and fried, baked and broiled seafood, as well as chicken, burgers, sandwiches and quesadillas. Try one of the chowders before your meal. My favorite is the lobster corn chowder, which is a bit spicy but filled with lots of lobster meat. **Features:** full bar, patio dining, happy hour. **Address:** 48 Commercial St 04538 **Location:** Center. **Parking:** street only. L D CALL

TUGBOAT RESTAURANT   207/633-4434

Seafood. Casual Dining. **Address:** 80 Commercial St 04538

BRUNSWICK (J-3) pop. 15,175, elev. 63'
• Restaurants p. 50

Industry, recreation and education are important pursuits in Brunswick, the chief city of the eastern Casco Bay area. Industry began in the 1620s when an English trader's success with exporting sturgeon and salmon from the falls of the lower Androscoggin River induced his company to establish a post. From that time until about 1730 the settlement of Pejepscot rose and fell as warring Native Americans destroyed it in 1690 and again in 1722.

Between disasters, during 1714-15, a group called the Pejepscot Proprietors bought the post, built Fort George and planned the spacious grid pattern of the streets. One thoroughfare was the Twelve Rod Road, now Maine Street; measuring 198 feet across, it is one of the widest streets in New England. By the late 1700s the settlement, renamed Brunswick, was an important lumbering, milling and shipbuilding center.

Bowdoin College, established in 1794, is the home of the Maine State Music Theater, where a professional cast performs Broadway musicals early June to late August; phone (207) 725-8769. A summer organ music series is presented on Tuesdays at noon in the summer at the First Parish Church; phone (207) 729-7331. Free open-air concerts are held on the Mall on Wednesday evenings late June through August.

Harriet Beecher Stowe's inspiration for "Uncle Tom's Cabin" supposedly came from a sermon delivered at the First Parish Church on Maine Street, open for worship since 1717. Another celebrated local was Gov. Joshua Lawrence Chamberlain, noted for his defense at Gettysburg and for being the only Union general to receive a battlefield promotion from Gen. Ulysses S. Grant.

Southern Midcoast Maine Chamber: 8 Venture Ave., Brunswick, ME 04011. **Phone:** (207) 725-8797.

JOSHUA LAWRENCE CHAMBERLAIN MUSEUM, 226 Maine St., is a partially restored Federal-style house with Victorian Gothic additions. The house once belonged to Joshua Lawrence Chamberlain, a Civil War hero, president of Bowdoin College and governor of Maine 1867-71. Guests Chamberlain

entertained at the house include Gen. Ulysses S. Grant, Helen Keller and Henry Wadsworth Longfellow.

Hours: Tues.-Sat. 10-4, Sun. 1-4, Memorial Day weekend-Columbus Day weekend; Fri.-Sat. 10-4, Sun. 1-4, day after Columbus Day-Veterans Day weekend. Guided tours depart on the hour. Last admission 1 hour before closing. **Cost:** $12; $10 (ages 65+ and active military and students with ID); $6 (ages 6-16); $30 (family, two adults and up to three children). Combination ticket with Skolfield-Whittier House $16; $10 (ages 6-16); $55 (family, two adults and up to three children). **Phone:** (207) 729-6606.
GT

BEST WESTERN PLUS BRUNSWICK BATH
           (207)725-5251

Hotel
$90-$200

 Best Western PLUS **AAA Benefit:** Members save up to 15% and earn bonus points!

Address: 71 Gurnet Rd 04011 **Location:** On SR 24, 1 mi s of US 1. **Facility:** 68 units. 3 stories, interior corridors. **Terms:** cancellation fee imposed. **Pool:** heated indoor. **Activities:** exercise room. **Guest Services:** valet and coin laundry.

SAVE CALL BIZ

/ SOME UNITS HS

COMFORT INN   (207)729-1129

Hotel. **Address:** 199 Pleasant St 04011

FAIRFIELD INN & SUITES BY MARRIOTT   (207)721-0300

Hotel. **Address:** 36 Old Portland Rd 04011

AAA Benefit: Members save 5% or more!

RELAX INN   (207)725-8761

Motel
$65-$130

Address: 133 Pleasant St 04011 **Location:** I-295 exit 28, 1 mi n on US 1. **Facility:** 52 units, some efficiencies. 2 stories (no elevator), exterior corridors. **Featured Amenity: continental breakfast.** SAVE

TRAVELERS INN   (207)729-3364

Motel
$55-$160

Address: 130 Pleasant St 04011 **Location:** I-295 exit 28, 1 mi n on US 1. **Facility:** 37 units. 2 stories (no elevator), exterior corridors. **Terms:** cancellation fee imposed. **Guest Services:** coin laundry. **Featured Amenity: continental breakfast.**

SAVE BIZ

AMATO'S   207/729-5514
♦ Pizza Sandwiches. Quick Serve. **Address:** 148 Pleasant St 04011

BOMBAY MAHAL RESTAURANT   207/729-5260
♦♦ Indian. Casual Dining. **Address:** 99 Maine St 04011

EL CAMINO   207/725-8228
♦♦ Mexican. Casual Dining. **Address:** 15 Cushing St 04011

THE GREAT IMPASTA   207/729-5858
♦♦ Italian. Casual Dining. **Address:** 42 Maine St 04011

HENRY & MARTY   207/721-9141
♦♦ American. Casual Dining. **Address:** 61 Maine St 04011

SCARLET BEGONIA'S   207/721-0403
♦♦ American. Casual Dining. **Address:** 16 Station Ave 04011

WILD OATS BAKERY & CAFE   207/725-6287
♦ Deli. Quick Serve. **Address:** 149 Maine St 04011

CALAIS (G-8) pop. 3,123, elev. 19'

Calais (KAL-is) is on the west bank of Passamaquoddy Bay at the mouth of the St. Croix River, a U.S.-Canadian boundary. Connected by the International Bridge to St. Stephen, New Brunswick, the city enjoys the distinction of being Maine's only international city.

Timber, fertile soil and an abundance of fish and game attracted the first settlers to the area in 1604. The town became an important lumbering and shipbuilding center. In 1809 the Massachusetts legislature named the settlement for the port of Calais, France, in acknowledgment of that country's assistance during the American Revolution.

The section of US 1 between Calais and Bar Harbor is a scenic drive from which visitors might see nesting eagles.

St. Croix Valley Chamber of Commerce: 39 Union St., Calais, ME 04619. **Phone:** (207) 454-2308.

Shopping: Duty Free Americas is located at 40 Main St., phone (207) 454-3476, and 97 Bering St., phone (207) 454-8905.

ST. CROIX ISLAND INTERNATIONAL HISTORIC SITE is 8 mi. s. on US 1 to 84 St. Croix Dr. The site, on the mainland shore of the St. Croix River, offers a view of 6.5-acre St. Croix Island, settled by the French in 1604. Many in the French expedition died of scurvy that winter and were buried on the island; the survivors departed and founded Port Royal in present-day Nova Scotia.

An interpretive trail leading to the viewpoint is adorned with bronze statues of French settlers and Passamaquoddy Native Americans who were present when the French arrived. A model depicting the settlement as it may have appeared in 1604 is displayed. The visitor center features interpretive panels, Native American baskets and replicas of artifacts excavated on the island. Ranger-led interpretive talks are offered daily mid-May through Columbus Day.

Note: Visits to the island are discouraged due to the island's fragile nature. Picnicking is permitted on the mainland. **Time:** Allow 30 minutes minimum. **Hours:** Grounds daily dawn-dusk. Visitor center daily 9-5, July-Aug.; Wed.-Sun. 9-5, late May-June 30 and Sept. 1-Columbus Day. The bronze statues are covered during off-season and winter months to preserve them from inclement weather. **Cost:** Free. **Phone:** (207) 454-3871.

KING CHINA RESTAURANT   207/454-1111
♥♥ Chinese. Casual Dining. **Address:** 180 North St 04619

CAMDEN (I-5) pop. 3,570, elev. 33'
• Restaurants p. 53

Camden's beauty has attracted many writers, painters and artisans, including Edna St. Vincent Millay, whose career began in this town. A statue at the head of the harbor honors the poet, and Millay memorabilia is housed in the Whitehall Inn at 52 High St. Shaded streets, white clapboard churches and flower gardens contribute to the tranquil atmosphere.

As a year-round resort the seaside town also is popular with sports enthusiasts. Bicycling is a favorite pastime and sailing, kayaking and canoeing, on either the ocean or one of many lakes, prevails in the summer; ice-skating and cross-country and downhill skiing predominate in winter. The toboggan run at the Camden Snow Bowl is open to the public; phone (207) 236-3438. Windjammer cruises and lobstering provide summer recreation, and coastal cruising via scenic US 1 is rewarding year-round.

Cultural enthusiasts can attend performances at the Camden Opera House; phone (207) 236-7963. Summer highlights include a variety of events; schooner races, antique shows, church fairs and lobster festivals are all on the agenda. Occasional concerts as well as a juried art show in July are presented at Amphitheatre and Harbor Park, on Atlantic Avenue at the waterfront.

Camden Hills State Park *(see Recreation Areas Chart)* is 2 miles north on US 1. A 1-mile road that leads to the summit of Mount Battie offers scenic views of Camden village and harbor. On a clear day, Acadia National Park and Monhegan Island can be seen.

Penobscot Bay Regional Chamber of Commerce—Camden: 2 Public Landing, Camden, ME 04843. **Phone:** (207) 236-4404 or (800) 562-2529.

Self-guiding tours: Brochures and maps are available from the chamber of commerce, which is on the public landing.

MERRYSPRING NATURE CENTER is at 30 Conway Rd. The 66-acre nature park and education center includes herb, rose and perennial gardens; the Kitty Todd Arboretum; a greenhouse; walking trails; and the Ross Center, which houses a library and visitor facilities. **Time:** Allow 1 hour, 30 minutes minimum. **Hours:** Park open daily dawn-dusk. Ross Center open Tues.-Fri. 9-2. **Cost:** Free. **Phone:** (207) 236-2239.

16 BAY VIEW   (207)706-7990

Historic Boutique Hotel
$149-$699

Address: 16 Bay View St 04843 **Location:** Just e of Main St; center. **Facility:** Each luxurious room features a balcony, a gas fireplace and upscale appointments. All bathrooms include a free-standing soaking/spa tub and a marble spa-style shower with body-massaging jets. 21 units. 3 stories, interior corridors. **Parking:** on-site and valet. **Terms:** 3 day cancellation notice-fee imposed. **Amenities:** safes. **Guest Services:** valet laundry. **Featured Amenity:** breakfast buffet.

ABIGAIL'S INN   207/236-2501
♥♥♥ Historic Bed & Breakfast. **Address:** 8 High St 04843

BIRCHWOOD   207/236-4204
♥♥ Extended Stay Motel. **Address:** 530 Belfast Rd 04843

BLUE HARBOR HOUSE INN   207/236-3196

Bed & Breakfast
Rates not provided

Address: 67 Elm St 04843 **Location:** On US 1, just s of downtown. **Facility:** This restored 1810 inn has English-style gardens and New England country décor. Each room is individually decorated with great care and comfort in mind. A full gourmet breakfast is served daily. 11 units. 2 stories (no elevator), interior/exterior corridors. **Featured Amenity:** full hot breakfast.

CAMDEN WINDWARD HOUSE   877/492-9656
♥♥♥ Historic Bed & Breakfast. **Address:** 6 High St 04843

CEDAR CREST INN   207/236-4839
♥♥ Hotel. **Address:** 115 Elm St 04843

GRAND HARBOR INN   (207)230-7177

Boutique Hotel
$159-$799

Address: 14 Bay View Landing 04843 **Location:** Just e of Main St; center. **Facility:** In the heart of Camden, this hotel offers spacious rooms and suites on the second floor overlooking the harbor and marina. All rooms have balconies, fireplaces and jetted tubs with separate showers. 11 units. 2 stories, interior corridors. **Terms:** 3 day cancellation notice-fee imposed. **Amenities:** safes. **Dining:** Peter Ott's on the Water, see separate listing. **Activities:** massage. **Guest Services:** valet laundry. **Featured Amenity:** continental breakfast.

HARTSTONE INN & HIDEAWAY   207/236-4259
♥♥♥ Country Inn. **Address:** 41 Elm St 04843

HAWTHORN INN   (207)236-8842
♥♥♥ Historic Bed & Breakfast. **Address:** 9 High St 04843

LORD CAMDEN INN

(207)236-4325

Hotel
$99-$439

Address: 24 Main St 04843 **Location:** Just n of Washington St; center. **Facility:** 36 units. 4 stories, interior corridors. **Terms:** cancellation fee imposed. **Activities:** exercise room. **Guest Services:** valet laundry. **Featured Amenity:** full hot breakfast.

RELAIS & CHATEAUX CAMDEN HARBOUR INN

(207)236-4200

Classic Historic
Country Inn
$250-$2195

Address: 83 Bayview St 04843 **Location:** Jct US 1, 0.3 mi e. **Facility:** This local landmark was built in 1874. Rooms are tastefully decorated with a modern theme and some offer a fireplace. Some guest rooms have views of Penobscot Bay, the town and the surrounding hills. 20 units. 3 stories (no elevator), interior/exterior corridors. **Terms:** 2 night minimum stay - seasonal and/or weekends, 14 day cancellation notice-fee imposed, resort fee. **Dining:** Natalie's, see separate listing. **Activities:** massage. **Guest Services:** valet laundry. **Featured Amenity:** full hot breakfast.

▼ See AAA listing p. 65 ▼

CAMDEN DELI   207-236-8343
▼ Deli. Quick Serve. **Address:** 37 Main St 04843

FRESH   207/236-7005
▼▼▼ American. Casual Dining. **Address:** 1 Bay View Landing 04843

HARTSTONE INN   207/236-4259
▼▼▼ American. Fine Dining. **Address:** 41 Elm St 04843

LONG GRAIN   207/236-9001
▼▼ Thai Fusion. Casual Dining. **Address:** 31 Elm St 04843

MARRINER'S RESTAURANT   207/236-4949
▼▼ American. Casual Dining. **Address:** 35 Main St 04843

NATALIE'S   207/236-7008

New England Fine Dining
$68-$109
AAA Inspector Notes: This restaurant offers a not-soon-to-be-forgotten dining experience. The chefs deliver the freshest ingredients available to your table by changing the menu often. The vibrant dining room and wraparound porch afford postcard-worthy views of the marina and mountains. Lobster, vegetarian and seven-course tasting menus are available, in addition to an à la carte menu, all paired with extraordinary wine selections and exclusive spirits. **Features:** full bar, patio dining. **Reservations:** suggested. **Address:** 83 Bayview St 04843 **Location:** Jct US 1, 0.3 mi e; in Relais & Chateaux Camden Harbour Inn. [D]

PETER OTT'S ON THE WATER   207/236-4032
▼ American. Casual Dining. **Address:** 16 Bayview Landing 04843

WATERFRONT RESTAURANT   207/236-3747
▼▼ American. Casual Dining. **Address:** 48 Bayview St 04843

CAPE ELIZABETH (K-3) elev. 27'

Cape Elizabeth was named by Capt. John Smith in 1615 for Princess Elizabeth, sister of Charles I of England. Early settlers managed to exist by fishing and farming. Closely associated with Portland (then Falmouth) in its earliest days, the settlement was recognized as a separate district in 1765 and finally granted status as an incorporated town during the Revolutionary unrest of 1775.

Few farms remain, as "the Cape" has become primarily a residential center for the Greater Portland area. The diverse coastal landscape includes sandy beaches, craggy cliffs and saltwater marshes and is accessible through two state parks as well as one town-owned park.

Two Lights State Park, 3 miles south on SR 77, features walking areas, scenic views from a rocky headland and picnic facilities. The park is next to Two Lights Lighthouse, which marks the entrance to Casco Bay. Crescent Beach State Park, 1 mile south on SR 77, offers recreational opportunities, picnic facilities and views of Richmond Island *(see Recreation Areas Chart)*.

PORTLAND HEAD LIGHT is at 1000 Shore Rd. in Fort Williams Park. First operated in 1791 under the authorization of President George Washington, it was the first light completed after the founding of the United States and is one of the oldest lighthouses in continuous use in the country. Highlights include a

museum, several cliffside walking paths, an arboretum and views of Casco Bay.

Hours: Park open daily dawn-dusk. Museum open daily 10-4, Memorial Day-Oct. 31; Sat.-Sun. 10-4, late Apr.-late May and Nov. 1-early Dec. **Cost:** Park admission by donation. Museum $2; $1 (ages 6-18). **Phone:** (207) 799-2661. 🎟

INN BY THE SEA   (207)799-3134

Classic Resort Hotel
$219-$2199
Address: 40 Bowery Beach Rd 04107 **Location:** Oceanfront. On SR 77, 7 mi s. **Facility:** The impressive views of the Atlantic and the gracious gardens beckon you to explore this scenic destination along Crescent Beach. 61 units, some two bedrooms, efficiencies and kitchens. 3 stories, interior/exterior corridors. **Parking:** on-site and valet. **Terms:** check-in 4 pm, 2 night minimum stay - seasonal and/or weekends, 30 day cancellation notice-fee imposed, resort fee. **Dining:** Sea Glass, see separate listing. **Pool:** heated outdoor. **Activities:** steamroom, recreation programs in season, bicycles, lawn sports, exercise room, spa. **Guest Services:** valet laundry.
🆂🅰🆅🅴 🄴🄲🄾 🍽 🔥 🍸 CALL 🔊 🏊 ⊕ BIZ 📶
✕ 🅱 💻 /SOME UNITS 🐾 ▨

THE GOOD TABLE RESTAURANT   207/799-4663
▼▼ Regional American. Casual Dining. **Address:** 527 Ocean House Rd 04107

THE LOBSTER SHACK AT TWO LIGHTS   207/799-1677
▼ Seafood. Quick Serve. **Address:** 225 Two Lights Rd 04107

SEA GLASS   207/799-3134
▼▼▼ American. Fine Dining. **Address:** 40 Bowery Beach Rd 04107

CAPE NEDDICK pop. 2,568
• Hotels & Restaurants map & index p. 58

CLIFF HOUSE MAINE   207/361-1000 [83]

Resort Hotel
Rates not provided
Address: 591 Shore Rd 03902 **Location:** Oceanfront. 2.8 mi ne of US 1 via River Rd. **Facility:** This magnificent resort sits on a cliff overlooking the rocky coastline. The guest rooms are designed with luxury in mind using plush bedding and cozy robes; many units have a private balcony. 226 units, some two bedrooms. 3-7 stories, interior corridors. **Parking:** on-site and valet. **Terms:** check-in 4 pm. **Amenities:** safes. **Dining:** 2 restaurants. **Pool:** heated outdoor, heated indoor. **Activities:** sauna, hot tub, steamroom, recreation programs, bicycles, lawn sports, exercise room, spa. **Guest Services:** valet laundry.
🆂🅰🆅🅴 🍽 🔥 🍸 CALL 🔊 🏊 ⊕ 📶 ✕

ELLSWORTH (I-6) pop. 7,741, elev. 112'
• Hotels p. 54 • Restaurants p. 54

Ellsworth began as a lumbering and shipbuilding center in 1763 and moved into the industrial era via waterpower from the Union River. Today the city is a bustling service center for the region. Lamoine State

Park *(see Recreation Areas Chart)*, 6.5 miles southeast of the southern terminus of SR 184, offers scenic views of Frenchman Bay and Mount Desert Island. Visitors can see eagles, ospreys, harbor seals and other wildlife at Ellsworth Marine Waterfront Park off Water Street.

Ellsworth also is surrounded by several lakes and streams that offer opportunities for boating, canoeing and fishing.

Ellsworth Area Chamber of Commerce: 163 High St., Ellsworth, ME 04605. **Phone:** (207) 667-5584.

DOWNEAST SCENIC RAILROAD, departing from 245 Main St., offers a scenic 10-mile round-trip excursion on the historical Calais Branch line. From railcars pulled by a 1948 diesel-powered locomotive, passengers view forests, wetlands and lakes and often spot such wildlife as beavers, deer, moose, herons and osprey. The trip lasts about 90 minutes. **Hours:** Trips depart Sat.-Sun (also Memorial Day, Labor Day and Columbus Day) at 10:30 and 1:30; schedules vary May-June. Phone ahead to confirm schedule. **Cost:** $15; $8 (ages 3-12). Reservations are recommended. **Phone:** (866) 449-7245.

[SAVE] **WOODLAWN MUSEUM/BLACK HOUSE** is on SR 172 off US 1. On a self-guiding audio tour visitors explore this Federal-style house built in the 1820s for Col. John Black, who played a major role in developing Maine's lumber industry. With elegant woodwork and an elliptical flying staircase, the home is as it appeared during occupation by three generations of the Black family. Period furnishings reflect a privileged lifestyle. On the 180-acre grounds are gardens, hiking trails, a carriage house and what is said to be the state's largest croquet court.

Time: Allow 30 minutes minimum. **Hours:** Grounds daily dawn-dusk. House Tues.-Sat. 10-5, Sun. 1-4, June-Sept.; Tues.-Sun 1-4 in May and Oct. **Cost:** Grounds free. House $12; $5 (ages 6-18). **Phone:** (207) 667-8671. [picnic symbol]

COMFORT INN ELLSWORTH-BAR HARBOR   (207)667-1345
[diamond][diamond] Hotel. **Address:** 130 High St 04605

THE EAGLES LODGE MOTEL   (207)667-3311
[diamond] Motel. **Address:** 278 High St 04605

ELLSWORTH RAMADA   (207)667-9341

Hotel
$139-$219

Address: 215 High St 04605 **Location:** Jct US 1, 1A and SR 3. Next to shopping plaza. **Facility:** 103 units. 2 stories (no elevator), interior corridors. **Amenities:** safes. **Pool:** heated indoor. **Activities:** sauna, exercise room. **Guest Services:** coin laundry. **Featured Amenity:** continental breakfast.

HAMPTON INN   207/667-2688
[diamond][diamond][diamond] Hotel. **Address:** 6 Downeast Hwy 04605

AAA Benefit: Members save 5% or more!

TWILITE MOTEL   207/667-8165
[diamond][diamond] Motel. **Address:** 147 Bucksport Rd 04605

WHERE TO EAT

HELEN'S RESTAURANT   207/667-2433
[diamond][diamond] American. Casual Dining. **Address:** 55 Downeast Hwy 04605

JORDAN'S SNACK BAR   207/667-2174
[diamond] American. Quick Serve. **Address:** 200 Downeast Hwy 04605

THE MEX   207/667-4494
[diamond][diamond] Mexican. Casual Dining. **Address:** 191 Main St 04605

THE RIVERSIDE CAFE   207/667-7220
[diamond][diamond] American. Casual Dining. **Address:** 151 Main St 04605

UNION RIVER LOBSTER POT   207/667-5077
[diamond][diamond] Seafood. Casual Dining. **Address:** 8 South St 04605

FREEPORT (J-3) pop. 1,485, elev. 126'

Founded in 1789, the town is best known as the home of the L.L. Bean sporting goods store, which is open daily 24 hours, 365 days a year. More than 170 other retail shops and name-brand outlets surround the village.

In addition to retail outlet merchandising, chief contributors to the economy are tourism and lobstering. The 40-foot Big Indian statue, 1 mile north of I-295 exit 17, is a frequently photographed local landmark.

Wolfe's Neck Woods State Park, 426 Wolfe's Neck Rd., offers several self-guiding nature trails that include views of Casco Bay and the Harraseeket River. The park, which is open year-round, also presents educational and interpretive programs.

Freeport Historical Society's Harrington House, 45 Main St., features changing exhibits relating to the history of Freeport dating from the late 18th century to the present. Pettengill Farm & Gardens, 1.5

miles east of downtown Freeport, is a 19th-century saltwater farm that includes an 1810 saltbox house and 140 acres of gardens, fields and woods; phone (207) 865-3170 for both attractions.

Visit Freeport: 23 Depot St., Freeport, ME 04032. **Phone:** (207) 865-1212.

BEST WESTERN FREEPORT INN
(207)865-3106

Hotel
$60-$300

AAA Benefit: Members save up to 15% and earn bonus points!

Address: 31 US 1 04032 **Location:** I-295 exit 17, 1 mi n. **Facility:** 80 units. 3 stories (no elevator), interior/exterior corridors. **Terms:** cancellation fee imposed. **Pool:** outdoor. **Activities:** playground.

BREWSTER HOUSE BED & BREAKFAST
(207)865-4121

Historic Bed & Breakfast. **Address:** 180 Main St 04032

CANDLEBAY INN
(207)865-1868

Historic Bed & Breakfast. **Address:** 8 Maple Ave 04032

CASCO BAY INN
207/865-4925

Hotel
Rates not provided

Address: 107 US 1 04032 **Location:** I-295 exit 17 northbound, 1 mi n; exit 20 southbound, 1.5 mi s. **Facility:** 48 units. 2 stories (no elevator), interior corridors. **Guest Services:** coin laundry. **Featured Amenity:** continental breakfast.

HAMPTON INN BY HILTON
207/865-1400

Hotel. **Address:** 194 Lower Main St 04032

AAA Benefit: Members save 5% or more!

HILTON GARDEN INN FREEPORT DOWNTOWN
207/865-1433

Hotel. **Address:** 5 Park St 04032

AAA Benefit: Members save 5% or more!

HOLIDAY INN EXPRESS HOTEL & SUITES
207/865-9020

Hotel. **Address:** 450 Blue Star Memorial Hwy 04032

THE JAMES PLACE INN
(207)865-4486

Historic Bed & Breakfast. **Address:** 11 Holbrook St 04032

KENDALL TAVERN INN BED & BREAKFAST
207/865-1338

Historic Bed & Breakfast. **Address:** 213 Main St 04032

WHITE CEDAR INN
(207)865-9099

Historic Bed & Breakfast. **Address:** 178 Main St 04032

WHERE TO EAT

AZURE CAFE
207/865-1237

Italian. Casual Dining. **Address:** 123 Main St 04032

BROAD ARROW TAVERN   207/865-9377

Regional American Casual Dining $11-$30

AAA Inspector Notes: *Classic.* This popular eatery exudes a Maine hunting lodge vibe, right down to the wood accents, hunter green painted walls and wall mounted moose head. The wood-fired oven and grill produce all the menu favorites that focuses on locally sourced ingredients. The lunch buffet displayed along the open kitchen bar is a favorite among locals and tourists. **Features:** full bar, Sunday brunch. **Address:** 162 Main St 04032 **Location:** I-295 exit 22, 0.5 mi e; in Harraseeket Inn. L D CALL

2 blocks N. of LL Bean, garden patio with stone firepit

CONUNDRUM
207/865-0303

American. Casual Dining. **Address:** 117 US Rt 1 04032

GRITTY MCDUFF'S
207/865-4321

American. Brewpub. **Address:** 187 Lower Main St 04032

LINDA BEAN'S MAINE KITCHEN & TOPSIDE TAVERN
207/865-9835

American. Casual Dining. **Address:** 88 Maine St 04032

PETRILLO'S
207/865-6055

Italian. Casual Dining. **Address:** 15 Depot St 04032

FRYEBURG pop. 1,631

MAIN STREET BED & BREAKFAST
(207)935-7171

Bed & Breakfast. **Address:** 660 Main St 04037

THE OXFORD HOUSE INN
207/935-3442

Historic Country Inn. **Address:** 548 Main St 04037

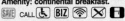

WHERE TO EAT

THE OXFORD HOUSE INN
207/935-3442

Regional American. Fine Dining. **Address:** 548 Main St 04037

GEORGETOWN

COVESIDE BED & BREAKFAST
(207)371-2807

Bed & Breakfast. **Address:** 6 Gotts Cove Ln 04548

THE MOORING B&B
(207)371-2790

Bed & Breakfast. **Address:** 132 Seguinland Rd 04548

GREENVILLE (F-4) pop. 1,257, elev. 1,034'
• Hotels p. 56 • Restaurants p. 56

Greenville, at the south end of Moosehead Lake, is in an area noted for a variety of year-round recreational activities. Swimming, fishing, canoeing, hiking, mountain climbing, horseback riding, seaplane tours and white-water rafting are pursued in summer. Hunting for deer, bears, moose and partridges is available in the fall; cross-country and downhill skiing and snowmobiling are enjoyed in winter.

Several cruises and a shuttle service are available to Mount Kineo, a historic Native American gathering place in Moosehead Lake. Visitors to the peninsula can enjoy hiking trails and a pebble beach.

Moosehead Lake Region Chamber of Commerce: 480 Moosehead Lake Rd., Greenville, ME 04441. **Phone:** (207) 695-2702.

BLAIR HILL INN (207)695-0224

ॐॐॐ ॐॐॐ
Historic Country Inn
$329-$559

Address: 351 Lily Bay Rd 04441 **Location:** 2 mi n. **Facility:** This lovely restored 1897 mansion, positioned on a hill, offers splendid views of Moosehead Lake and the surrounding hills. The upscale decorative touches and spacious guest rooms are sure to please. 10 units. 3 stories (no elevator), interior corridors. **Terms:** closed 11/1-5/15, 2 night minimum stay - weekends, 21 day cancellation notice-fee imposed. **Activities:** exercise room, spa. **Guest Services:** valet laundry. **Featured Amenity:** full hot breakfast.

[SAVE] 🍴 🍸 💺 [BIZ] 📶 ✕ ☎

CHALET MOOSEHEAD LAKEFRONT MOTEL   207/695-2950
ॐॐ Motel. **Address:** 12 N Birch St 04442

KINEO VIEW MOTOR LODGE   (207)695-4470
ॐॐ Motel. **Address:** 50 Overlook Dr 04441

THE LODGE AT MOOSEHEAD LAKE   207/695-4400

ॐॐॐ ॐॐॐ
Country Inn
Rates not provided

Address: 368 Lily Bay Rd 04441 **Location:** 2.5 mi n. **Facility:** Overlooking Moosehead Lake the lodge affords splendid lake and mountain views. The guest rooms are uniquely decorated in Maine themes with upscale appointments. 9 units, some two bedrooms and kitchens. 2 stories (no elevator), interior corridors. **Activities:** recreation programs, game room. **Guest Services:** valet laundry. **Featured Amenity:** full hot breakfast.

[SAVE] 🍴 🍸 [BIZ] 📶 ✕ ☎
🛏 🖥 /SOME UNITS 🐾 🖼

WHERE TO EAT

KELLY'S LANDING   207/695-4438
ॐॐ American. Casual Dining. **Address:** Rt 15 04442

STRESS FREE MOOSE PUB & CAFE   207/695-3100
ॐॐ American. Casual Dining. **Address:** 65 Pritham Ave 04441

KENNEBUNK (K-2) pop. 5,214, elev. 51'
• Hotels & Restaurants map & index p. 58

The Kennebunks—Kennebunk, Kennebunkport *(see place listing)* and Kennebunk Beach—constitute one of Maine's most popular coastal resort areas. Kennebunk developed between the Mousam and Kennebunk rivers about 1650 and was originally part of the town of Wells *(see place listing p. 86)*. By 1730 there were shipyards along the Mousam; these and a brisk West Indies trade supported Kennebunk until the Revolution, after which water-powered industries assumed economic leadership.

In the first half of the 19th century Kennebunk, like Kennebunkport and nearly every other tidewater Maine settlement, caught shipbuilding fever. Between 1800 and 1850 more than 1,000 wooden schooners, clippers and cargo vessels emerged from the area's 50-odd shipyards.

Legacies of this period's wealth and skill are the beautifully detailed Colonial, Federal, Greek Revival and Victorian houses that grace Kennebunk's national historic district, which includes upper Main Street, Summer Street and a portion of US 1. First Parish Church on Main Street has a bell cast by Paul Revere's foundry in its Christopher Wren steeple.

Kennebunk-Kennebunkport-Arundel Chamber of Commerce: 16 Water St., Kennebunk, ME 04043. **Phone:** (207) 967-0857.

Self-guiding tours: Guide books for a self-guiding walking tour of Kennebunk are available from the chamber of commerce or The Brick Store Museum, 117 Main St.

[SAVE] **THE BRICK STORE MUSEUM,** 117 Main St., occupies an early 19th-century commercial block in the heart of Kennebunk's National Register Historic District. Changing exhibitions showcase fine and decorative arts and artifacts pertaining to regional history. Architectural walking tours and beach tours are available seasonally. **Time:** Allow 2 hours minimum. **Hours:** Tues.-Fri. 10-5, Sat. 10-4, Sun. noon-4. Archives by appointment. Closed major holidays. **Cost:** $7; $6 (ages 60+); $3 (ages 6-16 and students with ID); $20 (family Tues.-Fri.); $10 (family Sat.). **Phone:** (207) 985-4802.

GRACE WHITE BARN INN & SPA   (207)967-2321 **51**
ॐॐॐ ॐॐॐ Historic Country Inn. **Address:** 37 Beach Ave 04043

HAMPTON INN BY HILTON KENNEBUNK/KENNEBUNKPORT
207/985-9200 **47**
ॐॐॐ Hotel. **Address:** 6 Independence Dr 04043

AAA Benefit: Members save 5% or more!

KING'S PORT INN   (207)967-4340 **50**
ॐॐॐ Hotel. **Address:** 18 Western Ave 04043

PORT INN KENNEBUNK, AN ASCEND HOTEL COLLECTION MEMBER   (207)985-6100 **49**
ॐॐॐ Motel. **Address:** 55 York St 04043

WALDO EMERSON INN   207/985-4250 **48**
ॐॐॐ Historic Bed & Breakfast. **Address:** 108 Summer St 04043

WHERE TO EAT

AMATO'S   207/985-0014
ॐ Pizza Sandwiches. Quick Serve. **Address:** 48 Portland Rd 04043

FEDERAL JACK'S RESTAURANT & BREW PUB
207/967-4322 **25**
ॐॐ American. Casual Dining. **Address:** 8 Western Ave 04043

MEKHONG THAI RESTAURANT   207/967-8827
ॐॐ Thai. Casual Dining. **Address:** 35 Western Ave 04043

ON THE MARSH BISTRO   207/967-2299 **26**
ॐॐॐ Continental. Fine Dining. **Address:** 46 Western Ave 04043

(See map & index p. 58.)

RYAN'S CORNER HOUSE IRISH PUB & RESTAURANT
207/967-3564 (24)

♥♥ Irish. Casual Dining. **Address:** 17 Western Ave 04043

WHITE BARN INN RESTAURANT   207/967-2321 (27)

♥♥♥♥♥ Regional American. Fine Dining. **Address:** 37 Beach Ave 04043

KENNEBUNKPORT (K-2) pop. 1,238, elev. 5'

• **Hotels p. 64** • **Restaurants p. 64**
• **Hotels & Restaurants map & index p. 58**

A popular summer resort, Kennebunkport has long been a favorite among artists and writers who have found both its history and quaint setting conducive to creativity. Novelist Kenneth Roberts, born in Kennebunk, used the Kennebunkport area as a setting for his "Chronicles of Arundel," and author Booth Tarkington wrote at dockside in his schooner *Regina*. Many galleries and craft shops attest to Kennebunkport's continuing affinity with the arts.

Dock Square has restored structures housing boutiques and galleries. Parson's Way, a scenic public walkway, begins at Dock Square and continues past Walker's Point. Along the docks several boats offer chartered deep-sea fishing, sailing, whale-watching or lobstering excursions. Sightseeing cruises of the Kennebunk River and coastal islands also are available.

Beyond the village Ocean Avenue follows the rocky shore of Cape Arundel to Cape Porpoise, a year-round fishing village. From Cape Porpoise pier it is possible to view the lighthouse on Goat Island. This scenic drive is lined with fine old mansions that are now restaurants or lodgings.

A waterspout, produced by water forced by the incoming tide through such formations as the spouting rock and the blowing cave, can be seen at Cape Arundel near Walker's Point—summer home of former President George H.W. Bush. Parking is not permitted along Ocean Avenue, but it is available at nearby Womby Beach. Farther "down east" via SR 9 is picturesque Goose Rocks Beach.

Self-guiding tours: Guide books for a self-guiding walking tour of Kennebunkport are available at White Columns *(see attraction listing)*.

RUGOSA LOBSTER TOURS, departing from docks behind Nonantum Resort, 95 Ocean Ave., takes visitors on a 60- to 75-minute tour of the Kennebunk River while crew explain and demonstrate the intricacies of a lobster haul. Passengers may watch crew members pulling lobster traps out of the water, extracting the catch and resetting traps for the next pull. Hands-on safe handling of lobsters also is offered.

Note: Vessel operates in open water; make sure you carry appropriate medication if you're prone to seasickness. Tours are limited to 20 passengers. **Time:** Allow 1 hour, 30 minutes minimum. **Hours:** Tours depart daily at 10:30, 1 and 3:30 (also at 5:30, July-Aug.), Memorial Day-Columbus Day (weather permitting). Phone ahead to confirm schedule. **Cost:** $35; $25 (ages 6-12). Tours are not recommended for ages 0-3. Ages 0-15 are not permitted on 3:30 tour in Aug. Reservations are required. **Phone:** (207) 468-4095.

WHITE COLUMNS is at 8 Maine St. Guided tours take visitors through this 1853 Greek Revival-style house containing original Victorian furnishings, pictures and personal belongings from four generations of Perkins and Nott families. Displays at the First Families Museum offer insight into the town's history. Of interest is the From Sea Captains to Presidents exhibit that tells the story of early seafarers and shipbuilders as well as Kennebunkport's most famous summer resident, former President George H.W. Bush. The garden offers a peaceful park-like setting.

Time: Allow 1 hour minimum. **Hours:** House tours Mon.-Sat. 10-4, Memorial Day-Columbus Day and first two weeks in Dec. Last tour departs 1 hour before closing. Closed major holidays. Phone ahead to confirm schedule. **Cost:** House and museum $10; free (ages 0-11). **Phone:** (207) 967-2751.

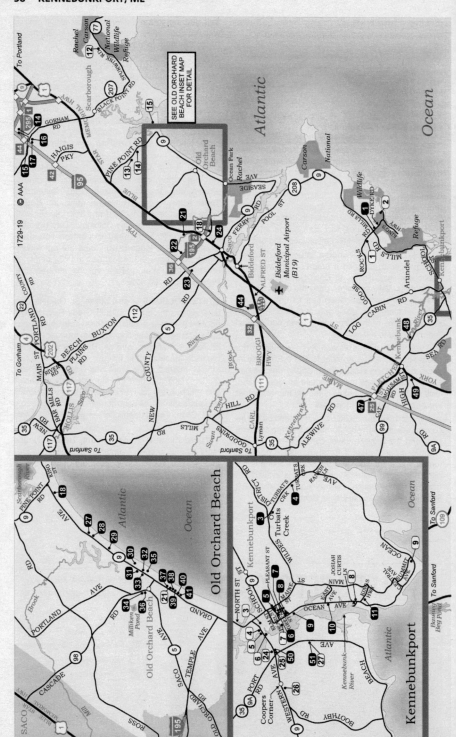

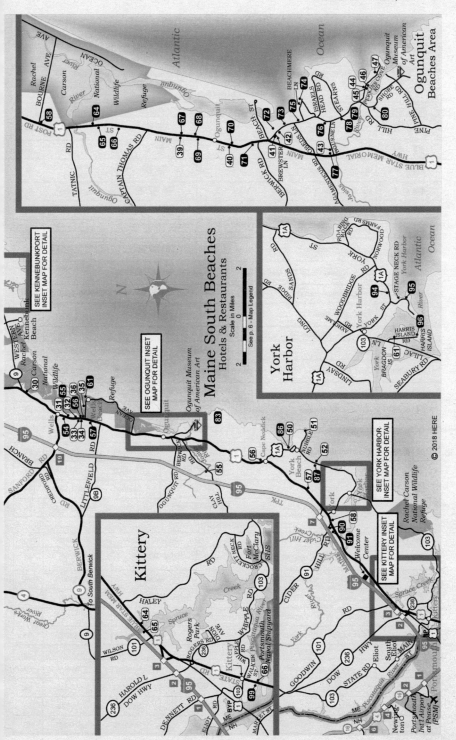

Maine South Beaches
Hotels & Restaurants

Ogunquit Beaches Area

York Harbor

Kittery

© 2018 HERE

Scale in Miles

See p. 6 - Map Legend

SEE KENNEBUNKPORT INSET MAP FOR DETAIL

SEE OGUNQUIT INSET MAP FOR DETAIL

SEE YORK HARBOR INSET MAP FOR DETAIL

SEE KITTERY INSET MAP FOR DETAIL

Maine South Beaches

This index helps you "spot" where approved hotels and restaurants are located on the corresponding detailed maps. Hotel daily rate range is for comparison only. Restaurant price range is a combination of lunch and/or dinner. Turn to the listing page for more information and consult display ads for special promotions.

 For more details, rates and reservations: AAA.com/travelguides/hotels

KENNEBUNKPORT

Map Page	Hotels	Diamond Rated	Rate Range	Page
1 p. 58	Ocean Woods Resort	♦♦	Rates not provided	64
3 p. 58	Lodge At Turbat's Creek	♦♦	$89-$199	64
4 p. 58	Rhumb Line Resort	♦♦	Rates not provided	64
5 p. 58	Maine Stay Inn & Cottages	♦♦♦	$149-$459	64
6 p. 58	The Captain Jefferds Inn	♦♦♦	$199-$449	64
7 p. 58	**Captain Lord Mansion**	♦♦♦♦	$199-$599 [SAVE]	64
8 p. 58	Captain Fairfield Inn	♦♦♦	Rates not provided	64
9 p. 58	The Yachtsman Hotel and Marina Club	♦♦♦	Rates not provided	64
10 p. 58	The Nonantum Resort	♦♦♦	$159-$549	64
11 p. 58	The Colony Hotel	♦♦♦	Rates not provided	64

Map Page	Restaurants	Diamond Rated	Cuisine	Price Range	Page
① p. 58	Earth	♦♦♦♦	New American	$18-$55	64
② p. 58	Tides Beach Club	♦♦♦	Regional American	$16-$38	64
③ p. 58	Bandaloop	♦♦♦	International	$19-$32	64
④ p. 58	Alisson's Restaurant	♦♦	Seafood	$10-$28	64
⑤ p. 58	**Hurricane Restaurant**	♦♦♦	Regional American	$12-$50	64
⑥ p. 58	The Clam Shack	♦	Seafood	$4-$29	64
⑦ p. 58	**Arundel Wharf Restaurant**	♦♦♦	Seafood	$10-$34	64
⑧ p. 58	Mabel's Lobster Claw	♦♦	Seafood	$11-$35	64
⑨ p. 58	Ocean Restaurant	♦♦♦♦	New American	$34-$44	64

SCARBOROUGH

Map Page	Hotels	Diamond Rated	Rate Range	Page
14 p. 58	Homewood Suites by Hilton Portland	♦♦♦	Rates not provided	83
15 p. 58	Fairfield Inn by Marriott Portland Maine Mall	♦♦	$64-$330	83
16 p. 58	Candlewood Suites Portland-Scarborough	♦♦	$89-$299	83
17 p. 58	Residence Inn by Marriott Portland/Scarborough	♦♦♦	$80-$355	83
18 p. 58	Sea-ward on the Oceanfront Guest House	♦♦	$98-$224	83

Map Page	Restaurants	Diamond Rated	Cuisine	Price Range	Page
⑫ p. 58	Spurwink Country Kitchen	♦♦	American	$8-$24	83
⑬ p. 58	Bayley's Seafood Restaurant	♦	Seafood	$10-$25	83
⑭ p. 58	Ken's Place	♦	Seafood	$6-$28	83
⑮ p. 58	The Bait Shed	♦♦	Seafood	$10-$31	83

SACO

Map Page	Hotels	Diamond Rated	Rate Range	Page
21 p. 58	Wagon Wheel Motel I & II	◈◈	Rates not provided	83
22 p. 58	**Hampton Inn by Hilton**	◈◈◈	$103-$321 SAVE	82
23 p. 58	**Ramada Saco Old Orchard Beach Area**	◈◈	$75-$260 SAVE	83
24 p. 58	Saco Motel	◈	Rates not provided	83

Map Page	Restaurant	Diamond Rated	Cuisine	Price Range	Page
18 p. 58	The Lobster Claw Pound & Restaurant	◈	Seafood	$12-$34	83

OLD ORCHARD BEACH

Map Page	Hotels	Diamond Rated	Rate Range	Page
27 p. 58	Royal Anchor Resort	◈◈◈	$98-$255	70
28 p. 58	Ocean Walk Hotel	◈◈	$89-$329	70
29 p. 58	Friendship Oceanfront Suites	◈◈	$89-$299	70
30 p. 58	The Beachfront Condotels	◈	Rates not provided	70
31 p. 58	Beau Rivage Motel	◈	$99-$299	70
32 p. 58	The Crest Motel	◈	$130-$299	70
33 p. 58	Executive Motel	◈	$195-$250	70
34 p. 58	Atlantic Birches Inn	◈◈◈	$117-$262	70
35 p. 58	The Aquarius Motel	◈	Rates not provided	70
36 p. 58	Old Orchard Beach Inn	◈◈◈	Rates not provided	70
37 p. 58	Kebek 3 Motel	◈◈	$110-$215	70
38 p. 58	The Edgewater	◈◈◈	Rates not provided	70
39 p. 58	Sea View Inn	◈◈	Rates not provided	70
40 p. 58	Waves Oceanfront Resort	◈◈	Rates not provided	70
41 p. 58	The Gull Motel	◈◈	Rates not provided	70

Map Page	Restaurant	Diamond Rated	Cuisine	Price Range	Page
21 p. 58	Joseph's By the Sea	◈◈◈	Continental	$10-$35	70

BIDDEFORD

Map Page	Hotel	Diamond Rated	Rate Range	Page
44 p. 58	Holiday Inn Express	◈◈◈	$89-$299	47

KENNEBUNK

Map Page	Hotels	Diamond Rated	Rate Range	Page
47 p. 58	Hampton Inn by Hilton Kennebunk/Kennebunkport	◈◈◈	Rates not provided	56
48 p. 58	Waldo Emerson Inn	◈◈◈	Rates not provided	56
49 p. 58	Port Inn Kennebunk, an Ascend Hotel Collection Member	◈◈◈	$114-$239	56
50 p. 58	King's Port Inn	◈◈◈	$99-$299	56
51 p. 58	Grace White Barn Inn & Spa	◈◈◈◈	$290-$1580	56

Map Page	Restaurants	Diamond Rated	Cuisine	Price Range	Page
24 p. 58	Ryan's Corner House Irish Pub & Restaurant	◈◈	Irish	$10-$28	57

Map Page	Restaurants (cont'd)	Diamond Rated	Cuisine	Price Range	Page
25 p. 58	Federal Jack's Restaurant & Brew Pub	❖❖❖	American	$10-$24	56
26 p. 58	On the Marsh Bistro	❖❖❖	Continental	$24-$45	56
27 p. 58	White Barn Inn Restaurant	❖❖❖❖❖	Regional American	$125-$165	57

WELLS

Map Page	Hotels	Diamond Rated	Rate Range	Page
54 p. 58	Carriage House Motel, Cottages & Suites	❖❖	$79-$179	86
55 p. 58	Elmwood Resort Hotel	❖❖❖	Rates not provided	86
56 p. 58	The Garrison	❖❖	Rates not provided	86
57 p. 58	**Hampton Inn & Suites by Hilton**	❖❖❖	$267-$380 [SAVE]	86
58 p. 58	Wells-Moody Motel	❖	Rates not provided	86

Map Page	Restaurants	Diamond Rated	Cuisine	Price Range	Page
30 p. 58	**Maine Diner**	❖❖	American	$6-$32	87
31 p. 58	Fisherman's Catch	❖	Seafood	$8-$37	86
32 p. 58	The Steakhouse	❖❖	Steak	$16-$30	87
33 p. 58	**Mike's Clam Shack**	❖❖	Regional Seafood	$9-$30	87
34 p. 58	**Congdon's Family Restaurant & Bakery**	❖❖	American	$8-$19	86
35 p. 58	Billy's Chowder House	❖❖	Seafood	$10-$30	86
36 p. 58	Varano's Italian Restaurant	❖❖	Italian	$15-$34	87

WELLS BEACH

Map Page	Hotel	Diamond Rated	Rate Range	Page
61 p. 58	Atlantic Oceanfront Motel	❖❖	$79-$369	87

OGUNQUIT

Map Page	Hotels	Diamond Rated	Rate Range	Page
64 p. 58	Mariner Resort	❖❖	$84-$259	69
65 p. 58	Ogunquit Resort Motel	❖❖	$69-$429	69
66 p. 58	**The Milestone**	❖❖	$69-$284 [SAVE]	69
67 p. 58	**The Dunes on the Waterfront**	❖❖❖	$135-$615	68
68 p. 58	Stage Run By The Sea	❖❖	$59-$289	69
69 p. 58	**Gorges Grant Hotel**	❖❖❖	$109-$389 [SAVE]	69
70 p. 58	**Juniper Hill Inn**	❖❖❖	$99-$314 [SAVE]	69
71 p. 58	Studio East Motor Inn	❖❖	Rates not provided	69
72 p. 58	**Terrace by the Sea**	❖❖	$91-$337 [SAVE]	69
73 p. 58	Sea Chambers	❖❖	Rates not provided	69
74 p. 58	The Beachmere Inn	❖❖❖	Rates not provided	68
75 p. 58	The Anchorage by the Sea	❖❖❖	$109-$415	68
76 p. 58	Sea Rose Suites	❖❖	Rates not provided	69
77 p. 58	**Meadowmere Resort**	❖❖❖	$99-$599 [SAVE]	69
78 p. 58	The Grand Hotel	❖❖❖	Rates not provided	69

OGUNQUIT (cont'd)

Map Page	Hotels (cont'd)	Diamond Rated	Rate Range	Page
79 p. 58	Hartwell House Inn	◆◆◆	$209-$459	69
80 p. 58	Yardarm Village Inn	◆◆	$105-$185	69

Map Page	Restaurants	Diamond Rated	Cuisine	Price Range	Page
39 p. 58	The Egg & I	◆	American	$4-$15	69
40 p. 58	Bintliff's Ogunquit	◆◆	American	$11-$39	69
41 p. 58	Gypsy Sweethearts	◆◆	Regional American	$14-$30	69
42 p. 58	Five-O Shore Road	◆◆◆	Mediterranean	$22-$38	69
43 p. 58	Jonathan's Restaurant	◆◆	Continental	$24-$34	69
44 p. 58	Oarweed Restaurant & Lobster Pound	◆◆	Seafood	$7-$37	69
45 p. 58	Barnacle Billy's	◆	American Seafood	$5-$40	69
46 p. 58	Barnacle Billy's Etc.	◆◆	Seafood	$11-$40	69
47 p. 58	M.C. Perkins Cove	◆◆◆	Regional American	$13-$46	69

CAPE NEDDICK

Map Page	Hotel	Diamond Rated	Rate Range	Page
83 p. 58	Cliff House Maine	◆◆◆◆	Rates not provided SAVE	53

YORK BEACH

Map Page	Hotels	Diamond Rated	Rate Range	Page
86 p. 58	The Union Bluff Hotel	◆◆◆	Rates not provided	88
87 p. 58	The Anchorage Inn	◆◆◆	Rates not provided	88

Map Page	Restaurants	Diamond Rated	Cuisine	Price Range	Page
50 p. 58	Union Bluff Pub & Grill	◆◆	American	$11-$30	88
51 p. 58	Fox's Lobster House	◆◆	Seafood	$10-$47	88
52 p. 58	Sun & Surf	◆◆	Regional Seafood	$10-$35	88

YORK

Map Page	Hotels	Diamond Rated	Rate Range	Page
90 p. 58	Microtel Inn & Suites by Wyndham	◆◆	$75-$209	87
91 p. 58	Best Western York Inn	◆◆	$69-$450 SAVE	87

Map Page	Restaurants	Diamond Rated	Cuisine	Price Range	Page
55 p. 58	Clay Hill Farm	◆◆◆	American	$24-$35	87
56 p. 58	Walkers Maine	◆◆◆◆	New American	$14-$32	87
57 p. 58	Wild Willy's Burgers	◆	Burgers	$7-$10	87
58 p. 58	Ruby's Genuine Brick Oven	◆◆	American	$8-$19	87

YORK HARBOR

Map Page	Hotels	Diamond Rated	Rate Range	Page
94 p. 58	York Harbor Inn	◆◆◆	Rates not provided	89
95 p. 58	Stage Neck Inn (See ad p. 89.)	◆◆◆◆	Rates not provided SAVE	89
96 p. 58	Dockside Guest Quarters	◆◆◆	Rates not provided	89

Map Page	Restaurant	Diamond Rated	Cuisine	Price Range	Page
61 p. 58	Dockside Restaurant on York Harbor	◆◆◆	Regional American	$10-$33	89

KITTERY

Map Page	Hotel	Diamond Rated	Rate Range	Page
99 p. 58	Water Street Inn	◈◈◈	$79-$295	65

Map Page	Restaurants	Diamond Rated	Cuisine	Price Range	Page
64 p. 58	Robert's Maine Grill	◈◈◈	Seafood	$14-$38	65
65 p. 58	Bob's Clam Hut	◈	Regional Seafood	$7-$40	65
66 p. 58	**Warren's Lobster House**	◈◈	Regional Seafood	$11-$34	65

CAPTAIN FAIRFIELD INN　　207/967-4454　**8**
◈◈◈ Historic Boutique Bed & Breakfast. **Address:** 8 Pleasant St 04046

THE CAPTAIN JEFFERDS INN　　(207)967-2311　**6**
◈◈◈ Historic Bed & Breakfast. **Address:** 5 Pearl St 04046

CAPTAIN LORD MANSION　　(207)967-3141　**7**
◈◈◈◈◈
Classic Historic Bed & Breakfast
$199-$599
Address: 6 Pleasant St 04046 **Location:** From Dock Square, 0.3 mi s on Ocean Ave, then just ne on Greene St. **Facility:** This beautifully restored 1814 Federalist-style property features classic décor to enhance the feel of the period while being mindful of up-to-date amenities and luxury comforts. 16 units. 3 stories (no elevator), interior corridors. **Terms:** 2 night minimum stay - weekends, 15 day cancellation notice-fee imposed. **Activities:** bicycles, massage. **Guest Services:** complimentary laundry. **Featured Amenity: full hot breakfast.**

(SAVE) (ECO) (⊞) (⊓⊦) (BIZ) (📶) (✕)

(☎) (🛈)

THE COLONY HOTEL　　207/967-3331　**11**
◈◈◈ Classic Historic Hotel. **Address:** 140 Ocean Ave 04046

LODGE AT TURBAT'S CREEK　　(207)967-8700　**3**
◈◈ Motel. **Address:** 7 Turbats Creek Rd 04046

MAINE STAY INN & COTTAGES　　(207)967-2117　**5**
◈◈◈ Historic Bed & Breakfast. **Address:** 34 Maine St 04046

THE NONANTUM RESORT　　(207)967-4050　**10**
◈◈◈ Historic Resort Hotel. **Address:** 95 Ocean Ave 04046

OCEAN WOODS RESORT　　207/967-1928　**1**
◈◈ Hotel. **Address:** 71 Dyke Rd 04046

RHUMB LINE RESORT　　207/967-5457　**4**
◈◈ Hotel. **Address:** 41 Turbats Creek Rd 04046

THE YACHTSMAN HOTEL AND MARINA CLUB
　　207/967-2511　**9**
◈◈◈ Boutique Vintage Hotel. **Address:** 59 Ocean Ave 04046

WHERE TO EAT

ALISSON'S RESTAURANT　　207/967-4841　**4**
◈◈ Seafood. Casual Dining. **Address:** 11 Dock Square 04046

ARUNDEL WHARF RESTAURANT　　207/967-3444　**7**
◈◈◈
Seafood
Casual Dining
$10-$34
AAA Inspector Notes: This attractive harborfront restaurant serves well-prepared fresh local seafood. Lighter fare is offered at lunch. The nautical-themed dining room feels casual and relaxed. If the weather is nice, ask for a table on the deck. **Features:** full bar, patio dining. **Reservations:** suggested. **Address:** 43 Ocean Ave 04046 **Location:** From Dock Square, just e. (L) (D)

BANDALOOP　　207/967-4994　**3**
◈◈◈ International. Casual Dining. **Address:** 2 Dock Square 04046

THE CLAM SHACK　　207/967-2560　**6**
◈ Seafood. Quick Serve. **Address:** 2 Western Ave 04043

EARTH　　207/967-6550　**1**
◈◈◈◈ New American. Fine Dining. **Address:** 354 Goose Rocks Rd 04046

HURRICANE RESTAURANT　　207/967-9111　**5**
◈◈◈
Regional American Fine Dining
$12-$50
AAA Inspector Notes: Offering lovely water views from a wall of windows, this restaurant features fresh seafood, including local lobster and oysters. Steaks and vegetarian options also are available, as is an extensive wine list to complement your selection. The lobster chowder is their signature but the five-onion soup is a real delight and may prompt other guests to ask if you ordered dessert first. The giant seafood tower and the baked stuffed lobster are the real draws here; just make sure you're hungry. **Features:** full bar. **Reservations:** suggested. **Address:** 29 Dock Square 04046 **Location:** Center; at Dock Square. **Parking:** on-site (fee) and street. (L) (D)

MABEL'S LOBSTER CLAW　　207/967-2562　**8**
◈◈ Seafood. Casual Dining. **Address:** 124 Ocean Ave 04046

OCEAN RESTAURANT　　207/967-2125　**9**
◈◈◈◈ New American. Fine Dining. **Address:** 208 Ocean Ave 04046

TIDES BEACH CLUB　　207/967-3757　**2**
◈◈◈ Regional American. Casual Dining. **Address:** 254 Kings Hwy 04046

KITTERY (L-2) pop. 4,562, elev. 34'
• Hotels & Restaurants map & index p. 58, 128

Settled in the early 1600s, Kittery was an important shipbuilding, shipping and lumbering center. One of the oldest shipyards in the nation and among the first owned by the federal government, the Portsmouth Naval Shipyard on Seavey's Island was established in 1800. The *Ranger,* the first ship to fly the Stars and Stripes, was launched at Kittery under the command of John Paul Jones on May 10, 1777. In 1917 the first American submarine, the USS *L-8,* was launched from the Portsmouth Navy Yard.

Kittery is noted for its historic sites, rocky beaches and thriving outlet trade on US 1. Fort Foster, constructed soon after the Civil War, is situated on Gerrish Island in a park setting. The remains of the fort are open to the public Memorial Day to Labor Day, and visitors can enjoy views of Portsmouth Harbor, picnicking and nature trails.

(See maps & indexes p. 58, 128.)

Shopping: More than 120 outlet shops can be found at Kittery Outlets, off N. US 1, including Calvin Klein, Banana Republic, Eddie Bauer and Reebok.

WATER STREET INN   (207)994-9735 99

◆◆◆ Country Inn. **Address:** 6 Water St 03904

WHERE TO EAT

BOB'S CLAM HUT   207/439-4233 65

◆ Regional Seafood. Quick Serve. **Address:** 315 US 1 03904

ROBERT'S MAINE GRILL   207/439-0300 64

◆◆◆ Seafood. Casual Dining. **Address:** 326 US Rt 1 03904

WARREN'S LOBSTER HOUSE   207/439-1630 66

◆◆
Regional Seafood Casual Dining $11-$34

AAA Inspector Notes: *Historic.* A landmark from the 1940s, this restaurant's knotty-pine dining room overlooking the Piscataqua River is warm and inviting. The soup and salad bar is a meal in itself and has more than 50 selections. The house specialty is lobster naturally (priced daily), but the wide menu also has several beef dishes and plenty of other seafood—so if it lives in Maine waters it will be on the menu. During the winter months hours may vary due to the weather, so call ahead before venturing out. **Features:** full bar, patio dining, Sunday brunch, happy hour. **Address:** 11 Water St 03904 **Location:** I-95 exit 2, 0.3 mi e on SR 236 to Kittery Traffic Cir, then just s on US 1; at base of Memorial Bridge. L D CALL

LEWISTON (J-3) pop. 36,592, elev. 200'

The larger of the "Twin Cities of the Androscoggin" and the second largest city in the state, Lewiston occupies the river's east bank, across from Auburn *(see place listing p. 32).* Lewiston's early years gave little hint of what it would become. The first settler erected a log cabin within the present city limits in 1770, but subsequent growth was slow.

Although a woolen mill began operation in 1819, it was not until the waterpower of the Androscoggin River was harnessed about 1850 that Lewiston began developing into a major textile center. By the 1870s cottons and woolens were issuing from the mills of several large companies.

At the same time many French Canadians were recruited to work in the mills, leaving Lewiston with a rich Franco-American heritage. The city now is experiencing economic diversification, with strong service, retail and innovative technology sectors.

Another Lewiston tradition is Bates College, founded in 1864. A highlight of the 75-acre campus is rocky 340-foot Mount David. The view from its summit encompasses Lewiston, Auburn and the Androscoggin Valley and extends 50 miles west to the Presidential Range in New Hampshire. Lewiston Falls and Dam, which provided the city's industrial impetus, is best seen from Longley Bridge on US 202.

The Franco Center, 46 Cedar St., was built in 1907 as St. Mary's Parish. The converted church features stained-glass windows and hosts dance and musical performances; phone (207) 783-1585.

Lewiston Auburn Metropolitan Chamber of Commerce: 415 Lisbon St., Suite 100, Lewiston, ME 04240. **Phone:** (207) 783-2249.

HAMPTON INN BY HILTON LEWISTON-AUBURN
(207)344-1000

◆◆◆◆
Hotel $112-$432

AAA Benefit: Members save 5% or more!

Address: 15 Lincoln St 04243 **Location:** On SR 196, just s of SR 11 and 202. **Facility:** 93 units. 4 stories, interior corridors. **Terms:** 1-7 night minimum stay, cancellation fee imposed. **Pool:** heated indoor. **Activities:** exercise room. **Guest Services:** valet and coin laundry. **Featured Amenity:** breakfast buffet.

WHERE TO EAT

DAVINCI'S EATERY   207/782-2088

◆◆ Italian. Casual Dining. **Address:** 150 Mill St 04240

GOVERNOR'S RESTAURANT & BAKERY   207/753-0173

◆◆ American. Casual Dining. **Address:** 1185 Lisbon St 04240

LINCOLNVILLE (I-5) elev. 23'

A coastal community with a beach area on Penobscot Bay, Lincolnville is the mainland terminal for ferry service to Islesboro, a small yet scenic island frequented by summer visitors. The bay, a popular launching point for sailing trips, also amuses watersports enthusiasts with paddleboarding and other pursuits. A large portion of Camden Hills State Park is within the town—the park's wooded hills are a great vantage point from which to view striking panoramas of the coast and of the fall foliage.

CEDARHOLM GARDEN BAY INN   (207)236-3886

◆◆◆ Cottage. **Address:** Eden's Inlet 04849

MOUNT BATTIE MOTEL   207/236-3870

◆◆
Motel Rates not provided

Address: 2158 Atlantic Hwy 04849 **Location:** On US 1, 1.6 mi s of jct SR 173. **Facility:** 21 units, some two bedrooms. 1 story, exterior corridors. **Parking:** winter plug-ins. **Featured Amenity:** continental breakfast. *(See ad p. 52.)*

VICTORIAN BY THE SEA   207/236-3785

◆◆◆ Historic Bed & Breakfast. **Address:** 33 Sea View Dr 04849

YOUNGTOWN INN & RESTAURANT   207/763-4290

◆◆ Historic Country Inn. **Address:** 581 Youngtown Rd 04849

WHERE TO EAT

LOBSTER POUND RESTAURANT   207/789-5550

◆◆ Seafood. Casual Dining. **Address:** 2521 Atlantic Ave 04849

YOUNGTOWN INN & RESTAURANT   207/763-4290
👑👑👑 French. Casual Dining. **Address:** 581 Youngtown Rd 04849

LUBEC (H-8) pop. 349, elev. 10'

Settled in 1780, Lubec is in the easternmost area of Maine. It holds the distinction of being the first spot where the sun rises in the continental United States. Situated on a peninsula, the community offers scenic ocean vistas and many opportunities to explore Maine's rugged coastline.

Tours of Lubec and Cobscook provides self-guiding audio tours, including an intertidal zone shore walk, a nature walk through an Arctic bog and a walk along historic Water Street. Tours may be downloaded online or rented from the Eastland Motel, 385 County Rd.

Boats may be chartered to view the coastal scenery as well as whales, seals and birds. Machias Seal Island, one of only three islands in Maine that serve as home to the Atlantic puffin, also is accessible by boat. Some of the highest tides in the United States occur at Johnson Bay.

West Quoddy Head Light Keepers Association and Visitor Center: in Quoddy Head State Park at 973 S. Lubec Rd., Lubec, ME 04652. **Phone:** (207) 733-2180.

THE EASTLAND MOTEL   207/733-5501
👑👑 Motel. **Address:** 385 County Rd 04652

THE INN ON THE WHARF   207/733-4400
👑👑 Country Inn. **Address:** 69 Johnson St 04652

PEACOCK HOUSE BED AND BREAKFAST   207/733-2403
👑👑👑 Historic Bed & Breakfast. **Address:** 27 Summer St 04652

WHERE TO EAT

FISHERMAN'S WHARF RESTAURANT & SEAFOOD
                                                                    207/733-4400
👑👑 Seafood. Casual Dining. **Address:** 69 Johnson St 04652

FRANK'S DOCKSIDE RESTAURANT & TAKE OUT
                                                                    207/733-4484
👑👑 American. Casual Dining. **Address:** 20 Water St 04652

UNCLE KIPPY'S RESTAURANT   207/733-2400
👑👑 American. Casual Dining. **Address:** 170 Main St 04652

Nearby New Brunswick

CAMPOBELLO ISLAND

For more than a century, from 1767 to 1881, Campobello Island belonged to the Owen family. The 1835 home of Adm. William F. Owen, who so loved the sea that he reputedly built a quarterdeck on which to pace in its presence, is preserved at Deer Point. A picturesque lighthouse stands at East Quoddy Head; whales and porpoises can sometimes be spotted in the offshore waters.

James Roosevelt visited Campobello in 1883 when his son, Franklin, was just a year old. From then until 1921, Franklin D. Roosevelt spent most of his summers on the island. A small collection of items relating to the Roosevelt family is among the displays at the Campobello Public Library and Museum, at 3 Welshpool St. in the village of Welshpool; phone (506) 752-7082.

ROOSEVELT CAMPOBELLO INTERNATIONAL PARK is connected to Lubec, Maine, by the Franklin D. Roosevelt Memorial Bridge, and from June through September by ferry from Deer Island. Here visitors can explore Franklin and Eleanor Roosevelt's summer home in the early years of the 20th century and find out why they and their children so loved the people and the natural beauty of their "beloved island."

The centerpiece of the 1,134-hectare (2,802-acre) memorial is the 34-room "cottage" filled with family mementos. The visitor center has an introductory film and exhibits pertaining to the Roosevelts' history and the friendship between the U.S. and Canada. A guided tour of the grounds is available. "Tea With Eleanor," the story of Eleanor Roosevelt's life, is offered daily by expert guides and includes tea and cookies.

The park's natural areas feature scenic drives and walking trails along coves, bogs, beaches and cliffs.

Note: The park is in the Atlantic time zone, 1 hour ahead of the Eastern time zone. The hours listed are in the Eastern time zone. **Hours:** Grounds and nature areas open daily dawn-dusk, year-round. Roosevelt Cottage open daily 9-5, Memorial Day weekend-Saturday after Columbus Day. Last tour is at 4:45. Visitor center open daily 9-5, Memorial Day weekend through Oct. 31. Visit the website or phone ahead for "Tea With Eleanor" times and reservation information. **Cost:** Free; donations welcome. **Phone:** (506) 752-2922 or (877) 851-6663. GT 🍴

This ends the Lubec section and resumes the alphabetical city listings for Maine.

MACHIAS (H-7) pop. 1,274, elev. 20'

Founded in 1763, Machias (ma-CHY-us) is Maine's oldest town east of the Penobscot River. The name means "bad little falls," in reference to the Machias River's plunge through a deep gorge that lies just behind Main Street. Machias is the center of commerce and government for Washington County; industries include blueberry processing, seafood harvesting and processing, and lumber and wood products. It also is a starting point for hunting and fishing trips into the interior lake country.

As the Revolution became inevitable, patriotic enthusiasm engulfed the citizens of Machias, especially the group who frequented Job Burnham's tavern. In June 1775, after learning that a British warship would arrive to requisition lumber for British barracks, Capt. Jeremiah O'Brien and his cohorts convened at the tavern to plan a Colonial response. The battle resulting from that meeting took place off

Machiasport *(see place listing)* on June 12, 1775—5 days before Bunker Hill.

Roque Bluffs State Park, 7 miles south off US 1 on Roque Bluffs Road, contains Maine's easternmost sandy beach. *See Recreation Areas Chart.*

Machias Bay Area Chamber of Commerce: 2 Kilton Lane, Machias, ME 04654. **Phone:** (207) 255-4402.

MACHIAS RIVER INN   (207)255-4861

Motel
$99-$164

Address: 103 Main St 04654 **Location:** Waterfront. 0.5 mi e on US 1. **Facility:** 39 units, some two bedrooms and kitchens. 2 stories (no elevator), interior/exterior corridors.

WHERE TO EAT

THE BLUEBIRD RANCH RESTAURANT   207/255-3351
American. Casual Dining. **Address:** 78 E Main St 04654

HELEN'S RESTAURANT   207/255-8423
American. Casual Dining. **Address:** 111 Main St 04654

HING GARDEN RESTAURANT   207/255-8882
Chinese. Casual Dining. **Address:** 46 Main St 04654

MILLINOCKET (F-5) pop. 4,466, elev. 359'

RECREATIONAL ACTIVITIES
White-water Rafting
• **New England Outdoor Center** is at 30 Twin Pines Rd. White-water rafting and other activities are offered. **Hours:** Rafting offered daily late Apr. to mid-Oct. Phone ahead to confirm schedule. **Phone:** (207) 723-5438 or (800) 766-7238.

5 LAKES LODGE   (207)723-5045
Bed & Breakfast. **Address:** 46 Marina Dr 04462

WHERE TO EAT

THE RIVER DRIVER'S RESTAURANT & PUB   207/723-5438
Regional American. Casual Dining. **Address:** Black Cat Rd 04462

SCOOTIC IN RESTAURANT   207/723-4566
American. Casual Dining. **Address:** 70 Penobscot Ave 04462

NAPLES (J-2) pop. 428, elev. 276'

On the northwestern edge of Sebago Lake, Naples is the location of the Songo Lock, opened in 1830 for transportation along the 42-mile canal system to Portland. The lock now links the north end of Long Lake and Sebago Lake. The hand-operated gate is the only remnant of the old lock system connecting western Maine with the coast.

Such recreational opportunities as boating, windsurfing, seaplane rides and mail boat runs are popular in Naples, an area characterized by rolling hills and crystal-blue lakes. The causeway offers the opportunity for striking views of Mount Washington in the White Mountains of New Hampshire.

The old-fashioned riverboat *Songo River Queen II*, berthed at the causeway in the center of town at 841 Roosevelt Tr. (US 302), offers sightseeing cruises Memorial Day weekend to early October; phone (207) 693-6861.

NEW HARBOR

SHAW'S FISH & LOBSTER WHARF RESTAURANT
                                       207/677-2200
Seafood. Quick Serve. **Address:** 129 SR 32 04554

NORTHEAST HARBOR (I-6) elev. 66'
• **Restaurants p. 68**
• **Hotels & Restaurants map & index p. 37**
• **Part of Acadia National Park area — see map p. 28**

Located on the southern end of Mount Desert Island at the mouth of Somes Sound, this bustling village is a major yachting center and popular summer vacation spot. The Great Harbor Maritime Museum, 124 Main St., features boat models, photographs and changing exhibits relating to the region's seafaring history; phone (207) 276-5262.

THUYA GARDEN is accessed via the Asticou Terraces gravel parking area, 1 mi. w. on Harborside Rd. to jct. SR 198, then 1 mi. s. on SR 3. The .25-mile Terrace Trail affords beautiful views of Northeast Harbor from several terraces and lookout points along the granite hillside. At the top, semiformal English gardens, indigenous eastern Maine woodlands, winding paths and a reflecting pool comprise Thuya Garden.

The Asticou Terraces trail is fairly steep and includes stairs. Comfortable walking shoes are recommended. A handicap entrance and accessible parking lot can be reached via Thuya Drive; parking is limited. **Time:** Allow 1 hour, 30 minutes minimum. **Hours:** Daily dawn-dusk, May-Oct. **Cost:** Donations. **Phone:** (207) 276-3727.

ASTICOU INN   (207)276-3344 **7**
Classic Hotel. **Address:** 15 Peabody Dr 04662

KIMBALL TERRACE INN   (207)276-3383 **8**

Motel
$75-$235

Address: 10 Huntington Rd 04662 **Location:** Overlooking Municipal Pier. **Facility:** 70 units. 3 stories, exterior corridors. **Terms:** closed 10/25-5/3, 7 day cancellation notice-fee imposed. **Pool:** outdoor.

(See map & index p. 37.)

ASTICOU RESTAURANT   207/276-3344   (8)
♥♥♥ American. Fine Dining. **Address:** 15 Peabody Dr 04662

NORTHPORT

POINT LOOKOUT RESORT & CONFERENCE CENTER
(207)789-2000

Resort Cabin
$119-$449

Address: 67 Atlantic Hwy 04849 **Location:** 4 mi s on US 1; at Lincolnville town line. **Facility:** These well-appointed one-, two- and three-bedroom pine log cabins are set on the side of a mountain among acres of beautiful wooded terrain. Each cabin has a screened porch with Adirondack chairs. 106 cabins, some kitchens. 1 story, exterior corridors. *Bath:* shower only. **Parking:** winter plug-ins. **Terms:** check-in 4 pm, 2 night minimum stay - seasonal and/or weekends, cancellation fee imposed. **Activities:** fishing, tennis, recreation programs in season, playground, game room, picnic facilities, trails, health club.

[SAVE] [ECO] [¶¶] [🛏] [BIZ] [📶] [✕] [📱] [📷] [📄]
/ SOME UNITS [🐕]

OGUNQUIT (L-2) elev. 20'
• Hotels & Restaurants map & index p. 58

Ogunquit was called "beautiful place by the sea" by the Abenaki Indians, who were early inhabitants of this region. The town is 15 miles north of the New Hampshire border, with a 3-mile sandy beach stretching northward and more than a mile of picturesque rocky shore to the south. The Ogunquit River, a 2-mile tidewater river, parallels the beach and is separated from it by sand dunes.

Shore Road leads to Perkins Cove, a quaint working harbor with a footbridge spanning its entrance. Perkins Cove offers specialty shops, waterfront restaurants and art galleries as well as fishing, lobstering and whale-watching opportunities. The "Marginal Way" is a mile-long scenic footpath along the granite shoreline leading from Perkins Cove to Ogunquit's village and beach.

Ogunquit is a popular summer resort, especially among artists. The Village Center has shops, theaters and parks lining its streets. The Ogunquit Playhouse, a half-mile south of town on US 1, has presented exceptional summer theater since the 1930s; phone (207) 646-5511. Art exhibits are held throughout the summer months at the Ogunquit Museum of American Art *(see attraction listing)* and the Barn Gallery. Trolleys offer transportation around town from June to October.

Ogunquit Chamber of Commerce: 36 Main St., Ogunquit, ME 03907. **Phone:** (207) 646-2939.

OGUNQUIT HERITAGE MUSEUM is at 86 Obeds Ln. Housed in the circa 1780 Captain Winn House, the museum offers changing exhibits about the history of the town, its inhabitants and houses as well as a pictorial history of the art, fishing and shipbuilding communities. The house features original architectural details and is surrounded by gardens and a park. **Time:** Allow 30 minutes minimum. **Hours:** Tues.-Sat. 1-5, June-Oct. **Cost:** Donations. **Phone:** (207) 646-0296.

OGUNQUIT MUSEUM OF AMERICAN ART is s.e. of Perkins Cove at 543 Shore Rd. The museum showcases approximately 3,000 works of such renowned American artists as Charles Burchfield, Marsden Hartley, Robert Henri, Rockwell Kent, Walt Kuhn, Gaston Lachaise, Reginald Marsh and William Zorach.

Highlights include a comprehensive American Modernism collection featuring pieces by artists who were part of the Ogunquit Art Colony, which was established in the 1890s. Special exhibits that change two or three times during the season spotlight other nationally known American artists. The main gallery's glass wall offers stunning views of the Atlantic Ocean. Lush gardens, alluring coastline, a reflection pond, sculptures and sheltered benches allow visitors an opportunity to unwind on the 3-acre grounds. **Time:** Allow 1 hour minimum. **Hours:** Daily 10-5, May-Oct. Phone ahead to confirm schedule. **Cost:** $10; $9 (ages 60+ and students with ID); free (ages 0-11). **Phone:** (207) 646-4909.

THE ANCHORAGE BY THE SEA   (207)646-9384   (75)
♥♥♥ Hotel. **Address:** 125 Shore Rd 03907

THE BEACHMERE INN   207/646-2021   (74)
♥♥♥ Hotel. **Address:** 62 Beachmere Pl 03907

(See map & index p. 58.)

GORGES GRANT HOTEL   (207)646-7003 69

Hotel
$109-$389

Address: 449 Main St 03907 **Location:** 0.6 mi n on US 1. **Facility:** 81 units. 2 stories (no elevator), interior corridors. **Pool:** heated outdoor, heated indoor. **Activities:** hot tub, exercise room. **Guest Services:** coin laundry.

THE GRAND HOTEL   207/646-1231 78
Hotel. **Address:** 276 Shore Rd 03907

HARTWELL HOUSE INN   (207)646-7210 79
Bed & Breakfast. **Address:** 312 Shore Rd 03907

JUNIPER HILL INN   (207)646-4501 70

Hotel
$99-$314

Address: 336 Main St 03907 **Location:** 0.3 mi n on US 1. **Facility:** 101 units. 2 stories (no elevator), interior/exterior corridors. **Pool:** heated outdoor, heated indoor. **Activities:** hot tub, game room, limited exercise equipment. **Guest Services:** coin laundry. **Featured Amenity:** continental breakfast.

MARINER RESORT   (207)646-5931 64
Hotel. **Address:** 734 Main St 03907

MEADOWMERE RESORT   (207)646-9661 77

Hotel
$99-$599

Address: 74 Main St 03907 **Location:** 0.5 mi s on US 1. **Facility:** 144 units. 2-3 stories, interior/exterior corridors. **Terms:** 1-3 night minimum stay - weekends, 7 day cancellation notice-fee imposed. **Pool:** heated outdoor, heated indoor. **Activities:** sauna, hot tub, steamroom, game room, picnic facilities, health club, spa. **Guest Services:** coin laundry. **Featured Amenity:** continental breakfast.

THE MILESTONE   (207)646-4562 66

Hotel
$69-$284

Address: 687 Main St 03907 **Location:** On US 1, 1 mi n. **Facility:** 84 units. 1-2 stories (no elevator), exterior corridors. **Terms:** closed 10/17-4/18, cancellation fee imposed. **Pool:** heated outdoor. **Activities:** hot tub, exercise room. **Guest Services:** coin laundry. **Featured Amenity:** continental breakfast.

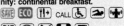

OGUNQUIT RESORT MOTEL   (207)646-8336 65
Hotel. **Address:** 719 Main St 03907

SEA CHAMBERS   207/646-9311 73
Motel. **Address:** 67 Shore Rd 03907

SEA ROSE SUITES   207/646-7300 76
Hotel. **Address:** 214 Shore Rd 03907

STAGE RUN BY THE SEA   (207)646-4823 68
Motel. **Address:** 2 Kingfield Ave 03907

STUDIO EAST MOTOR INN   207/646-7297 71
Motel. **Address:** 267 Main St 03907

TERRACE BY THE SEA   (207)646-3232 72

Motel
$91-$337

Address: 23 Wharf Ln 03907 **Location:** Oceanfront. Jct US 1, just se on Shore Rd, then just ne. **Facility:** 61 units, some two bedrooms, efficiencies and kitchens. 2 stories (no elevator), interior/exterior corridors. **Terms:** closed 12/10-3/28, 2-4 night minimum stay - seasonal and/or weekends, 14 day cancellation notice-fee imposed. **Amenities:** safes. **Pool:** heated outdoor. **Featured Amenity:** continental breakfast.

YARDARM VILLAGE INN   (207)646-7006 80
Historic Bed & Breakfast. **Address:** 406 Shore Rd 03907

WHERE TO EAT

BARNACLE BILLY'S   207/646-5575 45
American Seafood. Quick Serve. **Address:** 50-70 Perkins Cove Rd 03907

BARNACLE BILLY'S ETC.   207/646-4711 46
Seafood. Casual Dining. **Address:** 50 Perkins Cove Rd 03907

BINTLIFF'S OGUNQUIT   207/646-3111 40
American. Casual Dining. **Address:** 335 Main St 03907

THE EGG & I   207/646-8777 39
American. Casual Dining. **Address:** 501 Main St 03907

FIVE-O SHORE ROAD   207/646-5001 42
Mediterranean. Fine Dining. **Address:** 50 Shore Rd 03907

GYPSY SWEETHEARTS   207/646-7021 41
Regional American. Casual Dining. **Address:** 30 Shore Rd 03907

JONATHAN'S RESTAURANT   207/646-4777 43

Continental Fine Dining
$24-$34

AAA Inspector Notes: Amid attractive surroundings, this restaurant's specialties include caramelized, pan-seared salmon dusted with sugar and dill and lobster ravioli. Contributing to the atmosphere is a fine collection of American paintings and lovely gardens. **Features:** full bar. **Reservations:** suggested. **Address:** 92 Bourne Ln 03907 **Location:** 0.5 mi s on US 1, just e.

M.C. PERKINS COVE   207/646-6263 47
Regional American. Fine Dining. **Address:** 111 Perkins Cove Rd 03907

OARWEED RESTAURANT & LOBSTER POUND
          207/646-4022 44
Seafood. Casual Dining. **Address:** 65 Perkins Cove Rd 03907

OLD ORCHARD BEACH (K-3) pop. 8,624, elev. 15'

- Hotels p. 70 • Restaurants p. 70
- Hotels & Restaurants map & index p. 58

Old Orchard Beach, one of the oldest seashore resorts in Maine, boasts a 7-mile strip of white sand coastline. The low surf makes the area a favorite spot for swimming. Recreational pastimes include

(See map & index p. 58.)

golf, tennis and deep-sea fishing. There are amusement parks and arcades in town. Automobile races take place May through September at nearby Beech Ridge Motor Speedway; phone (207) 885-5800. In summer there's harness racing at Scarborough Downs, 7 miles north of town; phone (207) 883-4331.

Note: Policies concerning admittance of children to pari-mutuel betting facilities vary. Phone for information.

Old Orchard Beach Chamber of Commerce: 11 First St., Old Orchard Beach, ME 04064. **Phone:** (207) 934-2500.

SAVE **PALACE PLAYLAND AMUSEMENT PARK** is at 1 Old Orchard St. Established in 1902, the 4-acre oceanfront park offers 28 rides and a 24,000-square-foot arcade featuring more than 250 electronic games. Among the rides are two roller coasters, the Galaxi and the Orient Express; the Chance Menagerie carousel; the Electra Wheel, a Ferris wheel more than 70 feet tall; and many rides for children, including Dizzy Dragon and Winky the Whale. Games of skill and free entertainment are available.

Note: Height restrictions apply to certain rides. **Time:** Allow 1 hour minimum. **Hours:** Rides open Mon.-Fri. at noon, Sat.-Sun. at 11, mid-June to late Aug.; schedule varies late Aug.-Labor Day. Closing times vary. Arcade open mid-Apr. through Columbus Day; phone for days and hours. Ride and arcade schedules vary; phone ahead. Fireworks display Thurs. at 9:45, late June-late Aug. **Cost:** Single tickets $1.45 (two to four tickets required per ride). Twenty-four tickets $33.50. Fifty tickets $64.50. One-day unlimited rides pass $36.95; $30.95 (for all two-ticket rides, under 48 inches tall). Prices may vary; phone ahead. A two-day unlimited rides pass also is available. **Phone:** (207) 934-2001. 🍴

THE AQUARIUS MOTEL   207/934-2626 **35**
💎 Motel. **Address:** 1 Brown St 04064

ATLANTIC BIRCHES INN   (207)934-5295 **34**
💎💎💎 Historic Bed & Breakfast. **Address:** 20 Portland Ave 04064

THE BEACHFRONT CONDOTELS   207/934-7434 **30**
💎 Motel. **Address:** 1 Walnut St 04064

BEAU RIVAGE MOTEL   (207)934-4668 **31**
💎 Motel. **Address:** 54 E Grand Ave 04064

THE CREST MOTEL   (207)934-4060 **32**
💎 Motel. **Address:** 35 E Grand Ave 04064

THE EDGEWATER   207/934-2221 **38**
💎💎💎 Boutique Motel. **Address:** 57 W Grand Ave 04064

EXECUTIVE MOTEL   (207)934-4637 **33**
💎 Classic Motel. **Address:** 38 E Grand Ave 04064

FRIENDSHIP OCEANFRONT SUITES   (207)934-4644 **29**
💎💎 Motel. **Address:** 167 E Grand Ave 04064

THE GULL MOTEL   207/934-4321 **41**
💎💎 Motel. **Address:** 89 W Grand Ave 04064

KEBEK 3 MOTEL   (207)934-5253 **37**
💎 Motel. **Address:** 53 W Grand Ave 04064

OCEAN WALK HOTEL   (207)934-1716 **28**
💎💎 Motel. **Address:** 197 E Grand Ave 04064

OLD ORCHARD BEACH INN   207/934-5834 **36**
💎💎💎 Historic Bed & Breakfast. **Address:** 6 Portland Ave 04064

ROYAL ANCHOR RESORT   (207)934-4521 **27**
💎💎💎 Classic Motel. **Address:** 203 E Grand Ave 04064

SEA VIEW INN   207/934-4180 **39**
💎💎 Motel. **Address:** 65 W Grand Ave 04064

WAVES OCEANFRONT RESORT   207/934-4949 **40**
💎💎 Motel. **Address:** 87 W Grand Ave 04064

WHERE TO EAT

JOSEPH'S BY THE SEA   207/934-5044 **21**
💎💎💎 Continental. Fine Dining. **Address:** 55 W Grand Ave 04064

ORLAND (H-5) elev. 190'

Traditional handcrafting became a major industry in Orland with the 1970 establishment of H.O.M.E. (Home-workers Organized for More Employment). The cooperative, which began as an outlet for locally made products, has since expanded to include a chapel, a museum, a lumber mill, pottery and weaving shops and an extensive rural education program.

Various craft demonstrations can be seen at the H.O.M.E. compound, which is at the corner of US 1 and School House Road; for further information phone (207) 469-7961.

The town's many lakes and streams as well as the Narramissic River are popular with swimmers, canoeists and kayakers.

ORONO (H-5) pop. 9,474, elev. 80'

Although small industries and farming contribute to Orono's economy, the main focus of this Penobscot Valley town is the University of Maine. Since its opening in 1868 with 12 students and two teachers, the land-grant institution has grown to an enrollment of more than 11,000. The university is a center for teaching, research, public service and cultural activity.

The Collins Center for the Arts houses the 1,435-seat Hutchins Concert Hall; phone (207) 581-1755. The Maynard F. Jordan Planetarium and Observatory offers multimedia astronomy programs and views of the heavens; phone (207) 581-1341. Other university highlights are the ornamental gardens, anthropological museum, dairy and sheep barns, modern athletic facilities and the largest library in the state. Brochures for a self-guiding walking tour are available at the visitor center near the Munson Road entrance. Phone (207) 581-3740 for general information.

BLACK BEAR INN CONFERENCE CENTER   (207)866-7120
▼▼▼ Hotel. **Address:** 4 Godfrey Dr 04473

UNIVERSITY INN ACADEMIC SUITES   (207)866-4921
▼▼ Hotel. **Address:** 5 College Ave (US 2) 04473

WHERE TO EAT

WOODMAN'S BAR & GRILL   207/866-4040
▼▼ American. Casual Dining. **Address:** 31 Main St 04473

OXFORD pop. 1,263

HAMPTON INN BY HILTON OXFORD   207/539-6055
▼▼▼ Hotel. **Address:** 151 Main St   **AAA Benefit:**
04270   Members save 5%
                                      or more!

OXFORD CASINO HOTEL   207/539-6777
▼▼▼ Hotel. **Address:** 777 Casino Way 04270

PORTLAND (K-3) pop. 66,194, elev. 34'
- **Hotels p. 78** • **Restaurants p. 79**
- **Hotels & Restaurants map & index p. 75**

"The beautiful town that is seated by the sea," wrote poet Henry Wadsworth Longfellow of his birthplace, Portland. Longfellow's town has become the largest city in Maine and a major industrial and manufacturing center for northern New England. Attractively restored 19th-century buildings, tree-lined streets and a fringe of parks readily evoke the grace that inspired the poet's tribute.

The Old Port on the waterfront was the heart of Portland's busy 19th-century commercial activities. After fire leveled the heart of the city in 1866, the district was reconstructed in a classic Victorian style. The architecture, cobblestone streets and old street lamps recapture the flavor of the city's early seaport days. Many of the warehouses, ship chandleries and merchant exchanges now serve as boutiques, restaurants, bars and bookshops. At the Maine State Pier on Commercial Street is the "Whaling Wall," a 950-foot mural depicting sea life found in the Gulf of Maine.

Culturally, Portland is Maine's showplace. Dozens of galleries and museums on Congress Street offer free admission during Portland's First Friday Artwalk, held the first Friday of the month. Founded in 1974, Portland Stage Company, 25A Forest Ave., produces seven to nine shows each season; phone (207) 774-0465. Three centuries of art and architecture are on display at the Portland Museum of Art (see attraction listing p. 73). The Merrill Auditorium, 20 Myrtle St., is home to the Portland Symphony Orchestra and hosts a variety of musical acts throughout the year; phone (207) 842-0800 for tickets.

Baseball fans can cheer on the Portland Sea Dogs, the AA affiliate of the Boston Red Sox, at Hadlock Field; phone (207) 879-9500 for information.

At the northeasternmost end of the peninsula is the Eastern Promenade, a 68-acre recreation area with grassy slopes and magnificent views of Casco Bay and the surrounding Calendar Islands. The 2.1-mile Eastern Promenade Trail runs along the waterfront and connects with Back Cove Trail. Maps are available from the ranger station at East End Beach (off Cutter Street).

The Calendar Islands, so called because their number was thought to be 365 (they actually number closer to 220), are east of Portland in Casco Bay. Capt. John Smith first explored these islands in 1614. Crescent Beach (see Recreation Areas Chart) and Two Lights state parks are nearby in Cape Elizabeth.

The city has a network of more than 30 trails for hiking, biking and cross-country skiing; phone (207) 775-2411. Excursions and charters for whale watching, deep-sea fishing, fall foliage viewing and tours to lighthouses and the Casco Bay islands are available. For information contact AAA Northern New England, 68 Marginal Way, Portland, ME 04101; phone (207) 780-6800 or (800) 222-3760.

Greater Portland Convention and Visitors Bureau: 14 Ocean Gateway Pier, Portland, ME 04101. **Phone:** (207) 772-5800.

Self-guiding tours: Brochures for a walking tour of the city's architectural highlights are available daily for $1.25 at the convention and visitors bureau. Each map outlines tours through the Old Port, Congress Street, State Street and the Western Promenade.

The Portland Freedom Trail walking tour identifies 16 former Underground Railroad sites; phone (207) 591-9980 for information.

Shopping: Gift shops and restaurants are housed in quaint 19th-century brick buildings in downtown's Old Port, between Congress and Commercial streets near Exchange Street. The Portland Farmers' Market is held on the Park Avenue side of Deering Oaks Park Sat. 7-1, late Apr.-late Nov. and at Monument Square on Congress Street Wed. 7-1, Apr.-Dec.; the market moves to 84 Cove St. Sat. 9-1, rest of year.

LONGFELLOW HOUSE, 489 Congress St., was built 1785-86 by Gen. Peleg Wadsworth, maternal grandfather of Henry Wadsworth Longfellow. It was here that the curious blue-eyed boy turned celebrated poet spent his childhood years. Situated on about 1.5 acres on the back side of town, it was the first all-brick home in Portland, constructed in the neoclassical style with bricks barged from Philadelphia. The residence was originally a two-story structure; in 1815 a third story with seven rooms was added after an 1814 fire ruined the gable roof.

The brass knocker that greets you at the front door is the original. Upon crossing the threshold, you'll find a lovely blend of fixtures and décor from three different generations. An impressive collection of furniture, including a circa 1805 leather side chair and an 1808 high-post bed; portraits; records; and

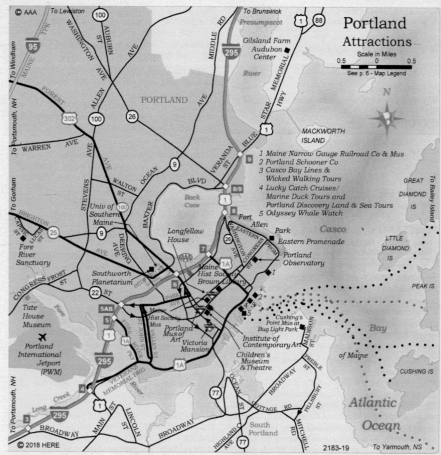

Portland Attractions

1 Maine Narrow Gauge Railroad Co & Mus
2 Portland Schooner Co
3 Casco Bay Lines & Wicked Walking Tours
4 Lucky Catch Cruises/ Marine Duck Tours and Portland Discovery Land & Sea Tours
5 Odyssey Whale Watch

(See map & index p. 75.)

other personal possessions of the Longfellow and Wadsworth families have been preserved.

The last family member to reside in the house was Anne Longfellow Pierce, who died in 1901 and deeded the property to the Maine Historical Society. During an extensive 2.5-year restoration project that concluded in 2002, experts analyzed family photographs and letters as well as paint shades and wallpaper scraps in an attempt to reproduce the woodwork hues, wall coverings, drapery, carpets and upholstery that adorned the interior in the 1850s. Today the Longfellow House is the one remaining private residence in the now urbanized eastern section of Congress Street.

Time: Allow 1 hour minimum. **Hours:** Mon.-Sat. 10-5, Sun. noon-5, June-Oct.; daily noon-5, in May. Last tour departs 1 hour before closing. Closed major holidays. Phone ahead to confirm schedule. **Cost:** (includes Maine Historical Society Museum) $15; $13 (ages 65+ and students with ID); $4 (ages 6-17). **Phone:** (207) 774-1822. [GT]

Maine Historical Society Brown Library, at the rear of the Longfellow House grounds, is a research library containing a collection of more than 125,000 books and two million manuscript pages. **Hours:** Wed.-Sat. 10-4 (also Tues. 10-4, May-Oct.). Closed major holidays. **Cost:** $10; free (students). **Phone:** (207) 774-1822.

MARINE DUCK TOURS departs from 177 Commercial St. An amphibious vehicle transports visitors on a 1-hour narrated land and sea tour of Portland. The land cruise covers historical and scenic landmarks of the city. The sea cruise navigates the waters of Casco Bay with lighthouses, historic forts and the Calendar Islands on view.

Note: Visitors arriving in an RV may have difficulty finding a parking spot. **Time:** Allow 1 hour, 30 minutes minimum. **Hours:** Trips depart daily 10-5, Apr.-Oct. **Cost:** $30; $27 (ages 65+); $22 (ages 4-15); free (ages 0-3; limit two per group). Reservations are recommended. **Phone:** (207) 774-3825.

LUCKY CATCH CRUISES is .3 mi. s.e. on Franklin Arterial/US 1A, then .2 mi. s.w. on Commercial

(See map & index p. 75.)
St./US 1A to 170 Commercial St. (at Long Wharf).
The intricacies of a lobster haul are demonstrated
during 80- to 90-minute cruises on the 37-foot-long
Lucky Catch. Willing passengers may don aprons
and gloves and participate in setting an assortment
of lobster traps. An overview of lobsters discusses
their biology, conservation, humane treatment and a
variety of methods for cooking.

Time: Allow 1 hour, 30 minutes minimum. **Hours:**
Cruises depart daily starting at 10:30, early May-late
Oct. Phone ahead to confirm schedule. **Cost:** $35;
$33 (ages 65+); $30 (ages 13-18); $20 (ages 3-12).
Reservations are recommended. **Phone:** (207)
761-0941.

**MAINE NARROW GAUGE RAILROAD CO. AND
MUSEUM,** off I-295 exit 7, .8 mi. s.e. on Franklin St.,
then .3 mi. e. to 58 Fore St. following signs, is dedicated to preserving Maine's narrow gauge railroad
equipment. Highlights of the museum include a two-
foot gauge parlor car, coaches, locomotives and railroad artifacts. Thirty-minute train rides on two-foot
gauge track run along Casco Bay and the Portland
Waterfront.

Time: Allow 1 hour minimum. **Hours:** Museum
Sat.-Thurs. 9:30-4, Fri. 11:30-4, mid-May to late Oct.
Trains depart Sat.-Thurs. on the hour 10-3, Fri. on
the hour noon-3. Phone ahead to confirm schedule.
Cost: Museum $3; $2 (ages 3-12 and 62+). Combination museum and train ride $10; $9 (ages 62+);
$6 (ages 3-12). Additional fees may be charged for
special events. **Phone:** (207) 828-0814.

PORTLAND DISCOVERY LAND & SEA TOURS,
departing from Long Wharf at 170 Commercial St.,
offers 1-hour and 1.75-hour narrated trolley tours of
Portland. The 1-hour Peek at Portland tour covers
local history and architecture with views of the
Eastern Promenade, Victoria Mansion, the Longfellow House and the Old Port district. The 1.75-hour
Portland City and Lighthouse Tour includes a stop at
Portland Head Light.

A 1.5-hour Lighthouse Lovers Cruise affords passengers views of lighthouses, forts and wildlife in
Casco Bay. A 1.75-hour combination Land & Sea
tour includes the trolley tour and a harbor cruise. A
sunset cruise also is available seasonally.

Hours: The 1-hour trolley tour departs daily on
the hour 11-4, mid-June to early Sept. The 1.75-hour
trolley tour departs daily at 11:30, 1:30 and 3:30
(also at 9:30 a.m., late May to mid-Oct.), late Apr.-
late Oct. Trolley schedule is expanded when cruise
ships are in port. The 1.5-hour lighthouse cruise departs daily at 10:30, 12:30, 2:30 and 4:30, mid-June
to late Aug; 11:30, 1:30 and 3:30, early May to mid-
June and late Aug.-late Oct. Phone for combination
tour and sunset cruise departure times.

Cost: The 1-hour trolley tour $16; $10 (ages
3-12). The 1.75-hour trolley tour or lighthouse cruise
$24; $17 (ages 3-12). Sunset cruise $28; $19 (ages
3-12). Land & Sea tours $48; $30 (ages 3-12).
Phone: (207) 774-0808.

PORTLAND HEAD LIGHT—see Cape Elizabeth
p. 53.

PORTLAND MUSEUM OF ART, 7
Congress Sq., houses an extensive
collection of American, European and contemporary
art, as well as iconic works from Maine artists. Displays include works by American artists Rockwell
Kent, Winslow Homer and Andrew Wyeth. The museum's European collection includes works by
Edgar Degas, Claude Monet and Pablo Picasso.
Sculpture and decorative objects also are
showcased.

Guided 2.5-hour tours of the restored Winslow
Homer Studio, where the renowned artist lived and
worked from 1883 until his death in 1910, depart
from the museum; reservations are required.

Time: Allow 1 hour minimum. **Hours:** Daily 11-6
(also Thurs.-Fri. 6-8 p.m.), Memorial Day-Columbus
Day; Wed.-Sun. 11-6 (also Thurs.-Fri. 6-8 p.m.), rest
of year. Winslow Homer Studio tours offered Thurs.-
Sun. at 11:30 and 2, mid-Apr. through late June and
early Sept.-Oct. 30; Mon. and Fri. at 11:30 and 2,
late June-early Sept. Closed Jan. 1, July 4, Thanksgiving and Christmas. **Cost:** $15; $13 (ages 65+);
$10 (students with ID); free (ages 0-14 and to all Fri.
4-8). Winslow Homer Studio tour $55; $25 (students
with ID). **Phone:** (207) 775-6148.

PORTLAND SCHOONER CO. departs from Maine
State Pier, 56 Commercial St., beyond Casco Bay
Lines Gate 5. Launched in 1912 and 1924 respec-
tively, the 88-foot and 72-foot wooden schooners
Wendameen and *Bagheera* are elegantly decorated
in period detail with mahogany trim and brass oil
lamps. The 2-hour trip on Casco Bay affords visitors
an opportunity to experience the sounds of the
ocean and the sights along the Maine coast.

Time: Allow 2 hours minimum. **Hours:** Departures daily at 10:30, 1, 3:30 and 6, May 1-Labor
Day; at noon, 2:30 and 5, day after Labor Day-Oct.
31. Phone ahead to confirm schedule. **Cost:** $46;
$30 (ages 3-12). **Phone:** (207) 766-2500 or (877)
246-6637.

SOUTHWORTH PLANETARIUM is in the science building on the University of Southern
Maine campus; take I-295 exit 6B, go 1 blk. w. on
Forest Ave., then .5 blk. s. to 70 Falmouth St. Regularly changing astronomy shows, classes, movies
and concerts are offered. Planetarium programs are
projected onto a 30-foot dome. Seating capacity is
65. Featured in the exhibit area is Heaven on Earth,
a permanent exhibit of the solar system.

Time: Allow 1 hour minimum. **Hours:** Astronomy
shows Mon. and Wed. at 1, Fri. at 7 and 8:30, Sat.
at 3 (also Sun. at 3, Sept.-May). Phone ahead to
confirm exhibit area schedule. **Cost:** One evening
show $6.50; $6 (ages 5-17 and 65+). Matinee $5.50;
$5 (ages 5-17 and 65+). Combination ticket for two
evening shows $11; $10 (ages 5-17 and 65+). Exhibit area free. **Phone:** (207) 780-4249.

(See map & index p. 75.)

VICTORIA MANSION, 109 Danforth St. between State and High sts., is a stunning Italianate-style house designed by distinguished New Haven architect Henry Austin. Built 1858-60 as an opulent summer home for hotelier Ruggles Sylvester Morse and his wife, the brownstone mansion boasts a four-story tower, several porches and such conveniences as running water, a gas lighting system and central heating.

An extensive collection of furniture by interior designer Gustave Herter complements the original painted *trompe l'oeil* walls and ceilings. Elaborate wood carvings and drapery; carpets; glassware; porcelain; and silver are some of the other treasures within. A whopping 90 percent of the home's original furnishings have been preserved.

The Turkish smoking room (believed to have been the first smoking room incorporated into a private American residence), the billiard room and the master bedroom's attached washroom are frills characteristic of mid-19th-century luxury hotels. Also noteworthy are the spectacular displays of stained glass, including the three-story stair hall's dazzling 6-by-25-foot skylight. From late November to early January holiday festivities showcase the house in Christmas splendor.

Time: Allow 1 hour minimum. **Hours:** Mon.-Sat. 10-4, Sun. 1-5, May-Oct. Additional hours are available day after Thanksgiving-first Sun. in Jan.; phone ahead to confirm schedule. Last tour begins 15 minutes before closing. Closed Jan. 1, Memorial Day, July 4, Labor Day and Christmas. **Cost:** $16; $14 (ages 62+); $7 (college students with ID); $5 (ages 6-17); $35 (family, two adults and up to five children in same household); free (active military with ID). **Phone:** (207) 772-4841. GT

WICKED WALKING TOURS depart from Bell Buoy Park, 72 Commercial St. On a walking tour through the Old Port, participants discover Portland's darker side as theatrical guides relate a blend of eerie legends, comedic tales and historical oddities. **Time:** Allow 1 hour minimum. **Hours:** Departures various days at 8 p.m. Phone ahead to confirm schedule. **Cost:** $19.99; $17.99 (ages 65+ and active military and veterans with ID); $14.99 (ages 0-12). Advance ticket purchase is required. **Phone:** (207) 730-0490 after hours, or (888) 718-4253 for ticket reservations Mon.-Fri. 9-9.

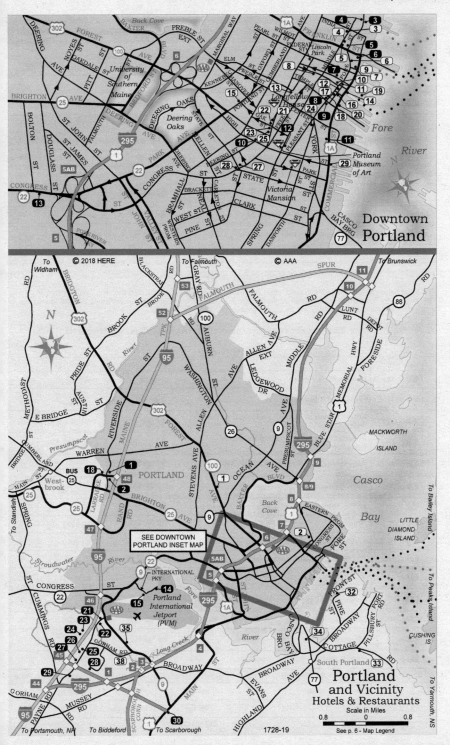

Downtown Portland

Portland and Vicinity
Hotels & Restaurants

Scale in Miles
0.8   0.8

See p. 6 - Map Legend

© 2018 HERE   © AAA

1728-19

✈ Airport Hotels

Map Page	PORTLAND INTERNATIONAL JETPORT (Maximum driving distance from airport: 2.8 mi)	Diamond Rated	Rate Range	Page
13 p. 75	Clarion Hotel Portland, 2.5 mi	◆◆◆	$89-$230	78
14 p. 75	Embassy Suites by Hilton Hotel, 0.3 mi	◆◆◆	Rates not provided	78
15 p. 75	Hilton Garden Inn Portland Airport, 0.5 mi	◆◆◆	$133-$390	78
22 p. 75	Comfort Inn Airport, 1.7 mi	◆◆	$85-$174	84
27 p. 75	Days Inn Airport/Maine Mall, 2.6 mi	◆◆	$53-$200	84
25 p. 75	**DoubleTree by Hilton, 2.4 mi**	◆◆◆	$89-$399 SAVE	84
28 p. 75	Hampton by Hilton Portland Airport, 2.8 mi	◆◆◆	Rates not provided	84
23 p. 75	**Holiday Inn Express & Suites, 2.5 mi**	◆◆◆	$94-$359 SAVE	84
21 p. 75	Home2 Suites by Hilton Portland Airport, 1.3 mi	◆◆◆	Rates not provided	84
24 p. 75	**Portland Marriott at Sable Oaks, 2.5 mi**	◆◆◆	$101-$342 SAVE	84

Portland and Vicinity

This index helps you "spot" where approved hotels and restaurants are located on the corresponding detailed maps. Hotel daily rate range is for comparison only. Restaurant price range is a combination of lunch and/or dinner. Turn to the listing page for more information and consult display ads for special promotions.

 For more details, rates and reservations: AAA.com/travelguides/hotels

PORTLAND

Map Page	Hotels	Diamond Rated	Rate Range	Page
1 p. 75	Ramada Plaza Portland	◆◆	$72-$215	79
2 p. 75	Fireside Inn & Suites	◆◆	Rates not provided	78
3 p. 75	**Residence Inn by Marriott Portland Downtown/ Waterfront**	◆◆◆	$94-$629 SAVE	79
4 p. 75	**AC Hotel by Marriott Portland Downtown Waterfront**	◆◆◆	$100-$527 SAVE	78
5 p. 75	Hampton Inn Portland Downtown-Waterfront	◆◆◆	Rates not provided	78
6 p. 75	Hilton Garden Inn Portland Downtown Waterfront	◆◆◆	Rates not provided	78
7 p. 75	**Portland Regency Hotel & Spa**	◆◆◆	$129-$509 SAVE	79
8 p. 75	**Hyatt Place Portland Old Port**	◆◆◆	$119-$999 SAVE	78
9 p. 75	**Portland Harbor Hotel**	◆◆◆◆	$169-$650 SAVE	79
10 p. 75	**The Westin Portland Harborview**	◆◆◆◆	$73-$286 SAVE	79
11 p. 75	Courtyard by Marriott Portland Downtown/Waterfront	◆◆◆	$103-$593	78
12 p. 75	**Holiday Inn by the Bay**	◆◆◆	Rates not provided SAVE	78
13 p. 75	Clarion Hotel Portland	◆◆◆	$89-$230	78
14 p. 75	Embassy Suites by Hilton Hotel	◆◆◆	Rates not provided	78
15 p. 75	Hilton Garden Inn Portland Airport	◆◆◆	$133-$390	78

Map Page	Restaurants	Diamond Rated	Cuisine	Price Range	Page
1 p. 75	Mekong Asian Bistro	◆◆	Thai	$8-$17	80
2 p. 75	Silly's	◆◆	American	$8-$16	80
3 p. 75	Ribollita	◆◆◆	Regional Italian	$13-$20	80

Map Page	Restaurants (cont'd)	Diamond Rated	Cuisine	Price Range	Page
④ p. 75	Eventide Oyster Co.	🔷🔷🔷	Seafood	$10-$19	80
⑤ p. 75	**Hugo's Restaurant**	🔷🔷🔷🔷	Regional American	$24-$90	80
⑥ p. 75	Fore Street Restaurant	🔷🔷🔷🔷	New American	$32-$60	80
⑦ p. 75	Old Port Sea Grill and Raw Bar	🔷🔷🔷	Seafood	$11-$32	80
⑧ p. 75	Tandoor	🔷🔷	Indian	$8-$16	80
⑨ p. 75	Scales	🔷🔷🔷	New Seafood	$16-$39	80
⑩ p. 75	The Holy Donut	🔷🔷	Breads/Pastries Coffee/Tea	$3-$6	80
⑪ p. 75	The Old Port Tavern	🔷🔷	American	$9-$25	80
⑫ p. 75	Gritty McDuff's	🔷🔷	American	$9-$18	80
⑬ p. 75	**David's Restaurant**	🔷🔷🔷	American	$13-$32	79
⑭ p. 75	Portland Lobster Co	🔷	Seafood	$8-$23	80
⑮ p. 75	**Back Bay Grill**	🔷🔷🔷	Regional American	$26-$38	79
⑯ p. 75	Vignola Cinque Terre	🔷🔷🔷	Italian	$14-$35	80
⑰ p. 75	Street & Company	🔷🔷🔷	Mediterranean Seafood	$23-$40	80
⑱ p. 75	Maine Lobster Shack	🔷🔷	Seafood	$12-$35	80
⑲ p. 75	Di'Millo's on the Water	🔷🔷	Seafood	$11-$51	79
⑳ p. 75	Sapporo Restaurant	🔷🔷	Japanese	$9-$23	80
㉑ p. 75	Emilitsa	🔷🔷🔷	Greek	$21-$31	79
㉒ p. 75	Nosh Kitchen Bar	🔷🔷	American	$11-$22	80
㉓ p. 75	Five Fifty-Five	🔷🔷🔷	American	$17-$38	80
㉔ p. 75	Yosaku	🔷🔷	Japanese	$8-$25	80
㉕ p. 75	Empire Chinese Kitchen	🔷🔷🔷	Asian	$14-$24	79
㉗ p. 75	Boda	🔷🔷🔷	Thai	$11-$19	79
㉘ p. 75	Local 188	🔷🔷	Spanish	$22-$39	80
㉙ p. 75	Becky's Diner	🔷🔷	American	$4-$14	79

WESTBROOK

Map Page	Hotel	Diamond Rated	Rate Range	Page
⑱ p. 75	Super 8	🔷🔷	$99-$130	87

SOUTH PORTLAND

Map Page	Hotels	Diamond Rated	Rate Range	Page
㉑ p. 75	Home2 Suites by Hilton Portland Airport	🔷🔷🔷	Rates not provided	84
㉒ p. 75	Comfort Inn Airport	🔷🔷	$85-$174	84
㉓ p. 75	**Holiday Inn Express & Suites**	🔷🔷🔷	$94-$359 SAVE	84
㉔ p. 75	**Portland Marriott at Sable Oaks**	🔷🔷🔷	$101-$342 SAVE	84
㉕ p. 75	**DoubleTree by Hilton**	🔷🔷🔷	$89-$399 SAVE	84
㉖ p. 75	Tru by Hilton Portland Airport Area	🔷🔷	Rates not provided	84
㉗ p. 75	Days Inn Airport/Maine Mall	🔷🔷	$53-$200	84
㉘ p. 75	Hampton by Hilton Portland Airport	🔷🔷🔷	Rates not provided	84
㉙ p. 75	Courtyard by Marriott Portland Airport	🔷🔷🔷	$82-$417	84

SOUTH PORTLAND (cont'd)

Map Page	Hotels (cont'd)	Diamond Rated	Rate Range	Page
30 p. 75	**Best Western Merry Manor Inn**	◈◈	$99-$329 [SAVE]	84

Map Page	Restaurants	Diamond Rated	Cuisine	Price Range	Page
32 p. 75	Saltwater Grille	◈◈◈	Regional Seafood	$12-$30	85
33 p. 75	Elsmere BBQ and Wood Grill	◈◈	Barbecue	$11-$36	85
34 p. 75	Q Street Diner	◈	American	$5-$12	85
35 p. 75	Pom's Thai Restaurant	◈◈	Thai	$8-$20	85
38 p. 75	B.GOOD	◈	Natural/Organic Sandwiches	$7-$15	85

AC HOTEL BY MARRIOTT PORTLAND DOWNTOWN WATERFRONT
(207)747-1640 **4**

◈◈◈
Hotel
$100-$527

AAA Benefit: Members save 5% or more!

Address: 158 Fore St 04101 **Location:** Between India and Hancock sts. **Facility:** 170 units. 6 stories, interior corridors. *Bath:* shower only. **Parking:** valet only. **Terms:** cancellation fee imposed. **Amenities:** safes. **Activities:** exercise room. **Guest Services:** valet laundry, area transportation.

[SAVE] [icons]
[BIZ icons]

CLARION HOTEL PORTLAND
(207)774-5611 **13**
◈◈◈ Hotel. **Address:** 1230 Congress St 04102

COURTYARD BY MARRIOTT PORTLAND DOWNTOWN/ WATERFRONT
(207)780-6000 **11**
◈◈◈ Hotel. **Address:** 321 Commercial St 04101

AAA Benefit: Members save 5% or more!

EMBASSY SUITES BY HILTON HOTEL
207/775-2200 **14**
◈◈◈ Hotel. **Address:** 1050 Westbrook St 04102

AAA Benefit: Members save 5% or more!

FIRESIDE INN & SUITES
207/774-5601 **2**
◈◈ Hotel. **Address:** 81 Riverside St 04103

HAMPTON INN PORTLAND DOWNTOWN-WATERFRONT
207/775-1454 **5**
◈◈ Hotel. **Address:** 209 Fore St 04101

AAA Benefit: Members save 5% or more!

From simple to spectacular:

AAA.com/travelguides/restaurants

HILTON GARDEN INN PORTLAND AIRPORT
(207)828-1117 **15**
◈◈◈ Hotel. **Address:** 145 Jetport Blvd 04102

AAA Benefit: Members save 5% or more!

HILTON GARDEN INN PORTLAND DOWNTOWN WATERFRONT
207/780-0780 **6**
◈◈◈ Hotel. **Address:** 65 Commercial St 04101

AAA Benefit: Members save 5% or more!

HOLIDAY INN BY THE BAY
207/775-2311 **12**

◈◈◈
Hotel
Rates not provided

Address: 88 Spring St 04101 **Location:** Center. **Facility:** 239 units. 11 stories, interior corridors. **Parking:** on-site (fee) and valet. **Terms:** check-in 4 pm. **Amenities:** safes. **Pool:** heated indoor. **Activities:** sauna, exercise room. **Guest Services:** valet and coin laundry, area transportation.

[SAVE icons]
[CALL icons]
[icons]

Waterfront view that extends to the Casco Bay Islands. In the heart of downtown Portland

HYATT PLACE PORTLAND OLD PORT
(207)775-1000 **8**

◈◈◈
Contemporary Hotel
$119-$999

HYATT PLACE· **AAA Benefit:** Members save 5% or more!

Address: 433 Fore St 04101 **Location:** At Union St; in Old Port. **Facility:** 130 units. 7 stories, interior corridors. **Parking:** on-site (fee) and valet. **Pool:** heated indoor. **Activities:** exercise room. **Guest Services:** valet and coin laundry, area transportation. **Featured Amenity:** breakfast buffet.

[SAVE icons]
[BIZ icons]

/ SOME UNITS [icons]

(See map & index p. 75.)

PORTLAND HARBOR HOTEL   (207)775-9090 **9**

Hotel
$169-$650

Address: 468 Fore St 04101 **Location:** In the Old Port; at Union St. **Facility:** This property has a 19th-century feel but with modern-day amenities and comforts. Enjoy the greenery on the lovely patio and the relaxing fire pit. 101 units. 5 stories, interior corridors. **Parking:** valet only. **Terms:** check-in 4 pm, 2-3 night minimum stay - seasonal and/or weekends, cancellation fee imposed. **Activities:** bicycles, exercise room. **Guest Services:** valet laundry, area transportation.

SAVE / SOME UNITS

PORTLAND REGENCY HOTEL & SPA

(207)774-4200 **7**

Historic Hotel
$129-$509

Address: 20 Milk St 04101 **Location:** In the Old Port; between Market and Silver sts; downtown. **Facility:** This converted 19th-century armory (circa 1895) is on the National Register of Historic Places. Guest rooms have a modern-classic design with a nostalgic feel. 95 units. 5 stories, interior corridors. **Parking:** valet only. **Terms:** cancellation fee imposed, resort fee. **Amenities:** safes. **Dining:** 2 restaurants. **Activities:** sauna, hot tub, steamroom, health club, spa. **Guest Services:** valet laundry, area transportation.

CALL BIZ / SOME UNITS

RAMADA PLAZA PORTLAND   (207)774-5861 **1**
Hotel. **Address:** 155 Riverside St 04103

RESIDENCE INN BY MARRIOTT PORTLAND DOWNTOWN/WATERFRONT   (207)761-1660 **3**

Extended Stay Contemporary Hotel
$94-$629

Residence INN **AAA Benefit:** Members save 5% or more!

Address: 145 Fore St 04101 **Location:** In the Old Port; near Casco Bay ferry terminal. **Facility:** 179 units, some two bedrooms, efficiencies and kitchens. 5 stories, interior corridors. **Parking:** on-site (fee). **Terms:** check-in 4 pm, cancellation fee imposed. **Pool:** heated indoor. **Activities:** hot tub, exercise room. **Guest Services:** valet and coin laundry, boarding pass kiosk, area transportation.

Featured Amenity: full hot breakfast.

SAVE / SOME UNITS

@ **For complete hotel,**

dining and attraction listings:

AAA.com/travelguides

THE WESTIN PORTLAND HARBORVIEW

(207)775-5411 **10**

Historic Hotel
$73-$286

WESTIN HOTELS & RESORTS   **AAA Benefit:** Members save 5% or more!

Address: 157 High St 04101 **Location:** At Congress St. **Facility:** This stately hotel features a contemporary interior with plush designs and up-to-date amenities. Westin "Heavenly Beds" are offered in all guest rooms. 289 units. 15 stories, interior corridors. **Parking:** on-site (fee) and valet. **Terms:** cancellation fee imposed. **Amenities:** safes. **Activities:** health club, spa. **Guest Services:** valet laundry, area transportation.

SAVE CALL BIZ / SOME UNITS

WHERE TO EAT

AMATO'S
Pizza Sandwiches. Quick Serve.
LOCATIONS:
Address: 71 India St 04101 **Phone:** 207/773-1682
Address: 312 St. John St 04102 **Phone:** 207/828-5978
Address: 1379 Washington Ave 04103 **Phone:** 207/797-5514

BACK BAY GRILL   207/772-8833 **15**

Regional American Fine Dining
$26-$38

AAA Inspector Notes: The owner-chef uses fresh, high-quality local and regional ingredients in the French-inspired seasonal menu. You might find lavender-marinated duck breast, cast-iron-seared scallops paired with a truffle vinaigrette, or mixed greens with candied walnuts. The wine list is diverse, offering an excellent variety of global selections. Colorful murals add a lively feel. The location, near the main post office, is a bit off the beaten path, but this restaurant is well worth the effort. **Features:** full bar. **Reservations:** suggested. **Address:** 65 Portland St 04101 **Location:** I-295 exit 6A, just e to Portland St, then just n. **Parking:** street only. D CALL

BECKY'S DINER   207/773-7070 **29**
American. Casual Dining. **Address:** 390 Commercial St 04101

BODA   207/347-7557 **27**
Thai. Casual Dining. **Address:** 671 Congress St 04101

DAVID'S RESTAURANT   207/773-4340 **13**

American Casual Dining
$13-$32

AAA Inspector Notes: This intimate restaurant treats you to innovative dishes, including the signature pepper-crusted rare tuna, and other creative items. The interesting setting has an open kitchen, small tables, mosaic tile floors, a lengthy bar and seasonal outdoor seating. Lunch is served on weekdays only. **Features:** full bar. **Reservations:** suggested. **Address:** 22 Monument Square 04101 **Location:** In Arts District. **Parking:** no self-parking. L D CALL

DI'MILLO'S ON THE WATER   207/772-2216 **19**
Seafood. Casual Dining. **Address:** 25 Long Wharf 04101

EMILITSA   207/221-0245 **21**
Greek. Casual Dining. **Address:** 547 Congress St 04101

EMPIRE CHINESE KITCHEN   207/747-5063 **25**
Asian. Casual Dining. **Address:** 575 Congress St 04101

(See map & index p. 75.)

EVENTIDE OYSTER CO.   207/774-8538 (4)
♥♥♥♥ Seafood. Casual Dining. **Address:** 86 Middle St 04101

FIVE FIFTY-FIVE   207/761-0555 (23)
♥♥♥ American. Fine Dining. **Address:** 555 Congress St 04101

FLATBREAD COMPANY   207/772-8777
♥♥ Pizza Natural/Organic. Casual Dining. **Address:** 72 Commercial St 04101

FORE STREET RESTAURANT   207/775-2717 (6)
♥♥♥♥ New American. Fine Dining. **Address:** 288 Fore St 04101

GRITTY MCDUFF'S   207/772-2739 (12)
♥♥ American. Brewpub. **Address:** 396 Fore St 04101

THE HOLY DONUT   207/775-7776 (10)
♥♥ Breads/Pastries Coffee/Tea. Quick Serve. **Address:** 7 Exchange St 04101

HUGO'S RESTAURANT   207/774-8538 (5)

♥♥♥♥♥
Regional American Fine Dining $24-$90

AAA Inspector Notes: The chef-inspired menu is a blend of local, regional and international ingredients that are always the highest quality. The daily-changing menu features à la carte dining, a five-course tasting menu and the chef's tasting menu. The dining rooms look onto an open kitchen, where the team of chefs create truly outstanding dishes. **Features:** full bar. **Reservations:** suggested. **Address:** 88 Middle St 04101 **Location:** Just ne of Franklin St; close to the Old Port.

(D)

LOCAL 188   207/761-7909 (28)
♥♥ Spanish. Casual Dining. **Address:** 685 Congress St 04101

MAINE LOBSTER SHACK   207/835-0700 (18)
♥♥ Seafood. Casual Dining. **Address:** 425 Fore St 04101

MEKONG ASIAN BISTRO   207/773-8424 (1)
♥♥ Thai. Casual Dining. **Address:** 865 Forest Ave 04103

NOSH KITCHEN BAR   207/553-2227 (22)
♥♥ American. Casual Dining. **Address:** 551 Congress St 04101

OLD PORT SEA GRILL AND RAW BAR   207/879-6100 (7)
♥♥♥ Seafood. Casual Dining. **Address:** 93 Commercial St 04101

THE OLD PORT TAVERN   207/774-0444 (11)
♥♥ American. Casual Dining. **Address:** 11 Moulton St 04101

PORTLAND LOBSTER CO   207/775-2112 (14)
♥ Seafood. Quick Serve. **Address:** 180 Commercial St 04101

RIBOLLITA   207/774-2972 (3)
♥♥♥ Regional Italian. Casual Dining. **Address:** 41 Middle St 04101

SAPPORO RESTAURANT   207/772-1233 (20)
♥♥ Japanese. Casual Dining. **Address:** 230 Commercial St 04101

SCALES   207/805-0444 (9)
♥♥♥ New Seafood. Casual Dining. **Address:** 68 Commercial St 04101

SEBAGO BREWING COMPANY   207/775-2337
♥♥ American. Brewpub. **Address:** 211 Fore St 04101

SILLY'S   207/772-0360 (2)
♥♥ American. Casual Dining. **Address:** 40 Washington Ave 04101

STREET & COMPANY   207/775-0887 (17)
♥♥♥♥ Mediterranean Seafood. Casual Dining. **Address:** 33 Wharf St 04101

TANDOOR   207/775-4259 (8)
♥♥♥ Indian. Casual Dining. **Address:** 88 Exchange St 04101

VIGNOLA CINQUE TERRE   207/772-1330 (16)
♥♥♥ Italian. Casual Dining. **Address:** 10 Dana St 04101

YOSAKU   207/780-0880 (24)
♥♥ Japanese. Casual Dining. **Address:** 1 Danforth St 04101

PRESQUE ISLE (C-6) pop. 9,692, elev. 445'

When Maxie Anderson, Ben Abruzzo and Larry Newman climbed into the gondola of the *Double Eagle II* on Aug. 11, 1978, they began an adventure momentous in the history of aviation. Six days later they landed in a field in France, having completed the first successful transatlantic hot air balloon flight. A replica of the balloon, at Double Eagle II Park on Spragueville Road just beyond Echo Lake, indicates the starting point of the flight.

The Maine Solar System Model, the world's largest complete 3-D scale model of the solar system, begins on the campus of the University of Maine and runs 40 miles along US 1 to Topsfield. The model includes the sun, nine planets, seven moons and three dwarf planets.

For the most part, however, Presque Isle's interests are more down to earth. The city is the chief industrial and commercial center of Aroostook County. Nearby, the University of Maine's 375-acre experiment station explores improved methods of growing and marketing potatoes as well as other crops. The university's Reed Fine Art Gallery, at 181 Main Street, serves as a cultural resource for the community and features works by local and regional artists; phone (207) 768-9442.

Recreation is available year-round at Aroostook State Park *(see Recreation Areas Chart)*, 4 miles south on US 1, then west and south via a park road. In the winter snowmobile enthusiasts enjoy over 1,600 miles of groomed trails in the area. Cross-country skiing, other recreational activities and winter camping also are available.

Central Aroostook Chamber of Commerce: 3 Houlton Rd., Presque Isle, ME 04769. **Phone:** (207) 764-6561.

Shopping: The Aroostook Centre Mall, 830 Main St., offers roughly 15 stores, including JCPenney.

HAMPTON INN BY HILTON PRESQUE ISLE   207/760-9292
♥♥♥ Hotel. **Address:** 768 Main St 04769

AAA Benefit: Members save 5% or more!

WHERE TO EAT

GOVERNOR'S RESTAURANT & BAKERY   207/769-2274
♥♥ American. Casual Dining. **Address:** 350 Main St 04769

ORIENTAL PEARL RESTAURANT   207/762-3268
🍷🍷 Chinese. Casual Dining. **Address:** 745 Main St 04769

RANGELEY

PLEASANT STREET INN BED & BREAKFAST   (207)864-5916
🍷🍷🍷 Bed & Breakfast. **Address:** 104 Pleasant St 04970

RANGELEY SADDLEBACK INN   207/864-3434
🍷🍷 Hotel. **Address:** 2303 Main St 04970

WHERE TO EAT

THE BLUE ORCHID   207/864-9035
🍷🍷 Traditional Thai Noodles. Casual Dining. **Address:** 2473
Main St 04970

FORKS IN THE AIR MOUNTAIN BISTRO   207/864-2883
🍷🍷🍷 Regional American. Casual Dining. **Address:** 2485
Main St 04970

ROCKLAND (J-5) pop. 7,297, elev. 35'

Rockland, one of Maine's largest fishing ports, is known as the Lobster Capital of the World and the Schooner Capital of Maine—ferries to several nearby islands are available along with schooners for daily and weeklong cruises. Shipbuilding, commercial fishing, granite quarrying and limekilns have contributed to area history and economy. The poet Edna St. Vincent Millay was born in Rockland.

A granite breakwater, extending seven-eighths of a mile across Penobscot Bay, leads to the Rockland Breakwater Lighthouse at Jameson Point in Rockland Harbor, built around 1888. Self-guiding tours are available on weekends from Memorial Day through Columbus Day. The town's historic Main Street district is now a shopping area. Owls Head Light, 5 miles southeast, offers outstanding views of Penobscot Bay.

In early August it's a true crustacean celebration at the 🔻 Maine Lobster Festival, which features boat rides, crafts, cooking contests and the coronation of the Maine Sea Goddess. Come hungry—there's nearly 10 tons of lobster to go around.

Penobscot Bay Regional Chamber of Commerce—Rockland: 1 Park Dr., Rockland, ME 04841. **Phone:** (207) 596-0376 or (800) 562-2529.

MAINE LIGHTHOUSE MUSEUM is at 1 Park Dr. The facility contains a large collection of lighthouse artifacts as well as exhibits of U.S. Coast Guard relics, including working lights, horns, bells and lifesaving devices. Lighthouse models, Fresnel lenses, flags, uniforms and fog bells are displayed. A video explains the inner workings of the Fresnel lens. **Hours:** Mon.-Fri. 10-5, Sat.-Sun. 10-4, June 1 to mid-Oct.; Mon.-Sat. 10-4, mid-Oct. to early Nov.; Thurs.-Sat. 10-4, rest of year. Closed major holidays. Phone ahead to confirm schedule. **Cost:** $8; $6 (ages 60+); free (ages 0-12). **Phone:** (207) 594-3301.

PROJECT PUFFIN VISITOR CENTER is at 311 Main St. Interactive displays and exhibits provide information about the National Audubon Society's seabird restoration program. A 20-minute orientation film gives an overview of puffin conservation efforts on the coastal islands of Maine. Visitors can watch a live video feed from puffin nesting sites May through August. An art gallery hosts changing exhibits. **Time:** Allow 30 minutes minimum. **Hours:** Daily 10-5 (also some Wed. 5-7, July-Aug.), June-Oct.; Wed.-Sun. 10-5, in May; Thurs.-Sun. 10-4, mid-Nov. through mid-Dec. Closed July 4 and Labor Day. **Cost:** Donations. **Phone:** (207) 596-5566.

BERRY MANOR INN   (207)596-7696

Historic Bed & Breakfast
$125-$325

Address: 81 Talbot Ave 04841 **Location:** Just w of Union St; center. Located in a residential area. **Facility:** A lovely front porch, pleasant parlors and tastefully decorated guest rooms distinguish this 1898 Victorian mansion. All guest rooms feature a gas or wood-burning fireplace, and some have jetted tubs. 12 units. 3 stories (no elevator), interior corridors. **Terms:** 2 night minimum stay - seasonal and/or weekends, 14 day cancellation notice-fee imposed. **Activities:** massage. **Featured Amenity: full hot breakfast.**

ROCKLAND HARBOR HOTEL   (207)594-2131

Hotel
$119-$379

Address: 520 Main St 04841 **Location:** On US 1; between Talbot and Summer sts. **Facility:** 82 units. 5 stories, interior/exterior corridors. **Terms:** check-in 4 pm, cancellation fee imposed. **Activities:** exercise room. **Guest Services:** coin laundry. **Featured Amenity: full hot breakfast.**

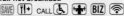

WHERE TO EAT

ATLANTIC BAKING COMPANY   207/596-0505
🍷 Breads/Pastries. Quick Serve. **Address:** 351 Main St 04841

CAFE MIRANDA   207/594-2034
🍷🍷🍷 International. Casual Dining. **Address:** 15 Oak St 04841

HOME KITCHEN CAFE   207/596-2449
🍷🍷 American. Casual Dining. **Address:** 650 Main St 04841

IN GOOD COMPANY   207/593-9110
🍷🍷 American. Casual Dining. **Address:** 415 Main St 04841

THE PEARL   207/593-8629
🍷🍷 Seafood. Casual Dining. **Address:** 275 Main St 04841

PRIMO   207/596-0770
🍷🍷🍷🍷 Mediterranean. Fine Dining. **Address:** 2 Main St (SR 73) 04841

ROCKLAND CAFE   207/596-7556

American Casual Dining
$8-$30

AAA Inspector Notes: Popular with local residents, this family café presents a menu with a nice selection of shrimp and haddock platters as well as sublime carrot cake, lemon meringue pie and giant muffins, which are prepared on the premises. All-you-can-eat seafood is a draw. **Features:** beer & wine. **Address:** 441 Main St 04841 **Location:** Just n of Limerick St; center. **Parking:** on-site and street. B L D

Fresh Maine lobster all-you-can-eat seafood open 7 days

RUSTICA CUCINA ITALIANA   207/594-0015
Italian. Casual Dining. **Address:** 315 Main St 04841

ROCKPORT elev. 59'

THE CLADDAGH MOTEL & SUITES   (207)594-8479
Motel. **Address:** 1044 Commercial St 04856

THE COUNTRY INN AT CAMDEN/ROCKPORT
(207)236-2725

Hotel
$119-$249

Address: 8 Country Inn Way 04856 **Location:** Jct SR 90, 0.9 mi n on US 1. **Facility:** 46 units, some cottages. 1-2 stories, interior/exterior corridors. **Terms:** 3 day cancellation notice-fee imposed. **Pool:** heated indoor. **Activities:** sauna, hot tub, miniature golf, playground, exercise room, massage. **Guest Services:** valet and coin laundry. **Featured Amenity:** continental breakfast.

GLEN COVE INN & SUITES   (207)594-4062

Motel
$79-$219

Address: 866 Commercial St 04856 **Location:** Jct SR 90, 3 mi s on US 1. **Facility:** 34 units. 1 story, exterior corridors. **Terms:** closed 11/1-4/30, 2 night minimum stay - seasonal and/or weekends, 3 day cancellation notice-fee imposed. **Pool:** heated outdoor. **Guest Services:** coin laundry. **Featured Amenity:** continental breakfast.

ISLAND VIEW INN   207/596-0040
Hotel. **Address:** 904 Commercial St 04856

SAMOSET RESORT ON THE OCEAN   (207)594-2511

Resort Hotel
$129-$499

Address: 220 Warrenton St 04856 **Location:** Oceanfront. Jct SR 90, 4.8 mi s on US 1, 0.5 mi e. **Facility:** All rooms overlook the ocean or golf course. The impressive outdoor pool area, with bar, offers guests splendid ocean views. In season there is an exceptional selection of recreational activities. 182 units, some cottages. 4 stories, interior/exterior corridors. **Parking:** on-site and valet. **Terms:** closed weekdays 11/10- 4/12, check-in 4 pm, 7 day cancellation notice-fee imposed, resort fee. **Amenities:** safes. **Dining:** 2 restaurants, also, La Bella Vita, see separate listing. **Pool:** heated outdoor, heated indoor. **Activities:** hot tub, steamroom, boat dock, regulation golf, tennis, recreation programs, kids club, playground, lawn sports, health club, spa. **Guest Services:** valet laundry, luggage security pick-up, area transportation.

SCHOONER BAY MOTOR INN   (207)236-2205
Motel. **Address:** 337 Commercial St 04856

STRAWBERRY HILL SEASIDE INN   207/594-5462
Hotel. **Address:** 886 Commercial St 04856

WHERE TO EAT

3 DOGS CAFE   207/230-0955
Traditional Desserts. Quick Serve. **Address:** 309 Commercial St 04856

47 WEST   207/706-7006
New Coffee/Tea Sandwiches. Quick Serve. **Address:** 47 West St 04856

LA BELLA VITA   207/594-2511
Italian. Fine Dining. **Address:** 220 Warrenton St 04856

THE MARKET BASKET   207/236-4371
Deli. Quick Serve. **Address:** 235 Commercial St 04856

OFFSHORE RESTAURANT   207/596-6804
American. Casual Dining. **Address:** 770 Commercial St 04856

SACO (K-2) pop. 18,482, elev. 75'
• Hotels & Restaurants map & index p. 58

Like its sister city Biddeford *(see place listing p. 47)*, Saco (SAH-co) was settled in 1631 at a site first noted by Capt. John Smith in 1614; in 1762 the town was incorporated as Pepperellborough. Pepperellborough became Saco in 1805.

A few years later the first major industry, an ironworks, was established. Due to an abundance of readily available waterpower, Saco remained predominantly industrial until recently. The economy now has a broader base, with commerce taking the leading role.

Besides powering the city's industries, the Saco River provides opportunities for fishing, boating and swimming on its 4-mile run to the sea. Ferry Beach State Park *(see Recreation Areas Chart)* occupies 117 acres on the east bank; a stand of tupelo trees, rare at this northern latitude, grows in the park. Also nearby is one of the region's favorite seaside resorts, Old Orchard Beach *(see place listing p. 69)*.

HAMPTON INN BY HILTON   (207)282-7222 22

Hotel
$103-$321

AAA Benefit: Members save 5% or more!

Address: 48 Industrial Park Rd 04072 **Location:** I-95 exit 36; I-195 exit 1, just ne. **Facility:** 100 units. 5 stories, interior corridors. **Terms:** 1-7 night minimum stay, cancellation fee imposed. **Pool:** heated outdoor. **Activities:** exercise room. **Guest Services:** valet and coin laundry, area transportation. **Featured Amenity:** continental breakfast.

For more details, rates and reservations:
AAA.com/travelguides/hotels

(See map & index p. 58.)

RAMADA SACO OLD ORCHARD BEACH AREA
(207)286-9600 **23**

Hotel
$75-$260

Address: 352 North St 04072 **Location:** I-95 exit 36, 0.6 mi sw to SR 112, then 0.4 mi nw. **Facility:** 88 units. 4 stories, interior corridors. **Terms:** 2 night minimum stay - seasonal and/or weekends, cancellation fee imposed. **Pool:** heated outdoor. **Guest Services:** valet and coin laundry. **Featured Amenity: breakfast buffet.**

SACO MOTEL   207/284-6952 **24**
Vintage Motel. **Address:** 473 Main St 04072

WAGON WHEEL MOTEL I & II   207/283-3258 **21**
Classic Motel. **Address:** 726 Portland Rd 04072

WHERE TO EAT

THE LOBSTER CLAW POUND & RESTAURANT
207/282-0040 **18**
Seafood. Casual Dining. **Address:** 41 Ocean Park Rd 04072

SCARBOROUGH pop. 4,403
• Hotels & Restaurants map & index p. 58, 75

CANDLEWOOD SUITES PORTLAND-SCARBOROUGH
(207)883-6800 **16**
Extended Stay Hotel. **Address:** 700 Roundwood Dr 04074

FAIRFIELD INN BY MARRIOTT PORTLAND MAINE MALL
(207)883-0300 **15**
Hotel. **Address:** 2 Cummings Rd 04074

AAA Benefit:
Members save 5% or more!

HOMEWOOD SUITES BY HILTON PORTLAND
207/775-2700 **14**
Extended Stay Hotel. **Address:** 200 Southborough Dr 04074

AAA Benefit:
Members save 5% or more!

RESIDENCE INN BY MARRIOTT PORTLAND/SCARBOROUGH
(207)883-0400 **17**
Extended Stay Hotel. **Address:** 800 Roundwood Dr 04074

AAA Benefit:
Members save 5% or more!

SEA-WARD ON THE OCEANFRONT GUEST HOUSE
(207)883-6666 **18**
Historic Motel. **Address:** 7 Bliss St 04074

WHERE TO EAT

AMATO'S   207/883-2402
Pizza Sandwiches. Quick Serve. **Address:** 234 US Rt 1 04074

THE BAIT SHED   207/883-4571 **15**
Seafood. Casual Dining. **Address:** 84 Jones Creek Dr 04074

BAYLEY'S SEAFOOD RESTAURANT   207/885-9754 **13**
Seafood. Quick Serve. **Address:** 165 Pine Point Rd 04074

KEN'S PLACE   207/883-6611 **14**
Seafood. Quick Serve. **Address:** 207 Pine Point Rd 04074

SEBAGO BREWING COMPANY   207/874-2337
American. Brewpub. **Address:** 201 Southborough Dr 04074

SPURWINK COUNTRY KITCHEN   207/799-1177 **12**
American. Casual Dining. **Address:** 150 Spurwink Rd 04074

SKOWHEGAN (H-4) pop. 6,297, elev. 175'

The Abenaki Indians called this island in the Kennebec River *skowhegan*—"a place to watch"—as they looked for salmon in the depths below the falls. One still watches: A 62-foot Native American sculpted in wood by Bernard Langlais rises above town in honor of those who first watched from this spot.

In 1771 the island's second settlers arrived, drawn by timber and the river's plenty. Their village was brushed by Revolutionary history in 1775, when Col. Benedict Arnold's expedition crossed the island en route to Québec; a granite boulder marks the site.

Although Skowhegan gradually evolved into a predominantly manufacturing city, the colorful history of log driving on the Kennebec did not end until 1976. A paper pulp mill with an 800-ton daily capacity, 7 miles south on US 201, is further evidence of the area's continued interest in lumbering.

Lakewood Theater, on Lake Wesserunsett 6 miles north of Skowhegan on US 201 to 76 Theatre Rd. in Madison, is Maine's state theater. Established in 1901, it is one of the oldest continuously operating summer stock theaters in the country. Matinee and evening performances run mid-May to mid-September; phone (207) 474-7176.

Skowhegan Area Chamber of Commerce: 23 Commercial St., Skowhegan, ME 04976. **Phone:** (207) 474-3621.

BELMONT MOTEL   207/474-8315
Motel. **Address:** 273 Madison Ave 04976

WHERE TO EAT

HERITAGE HOUSE   207/474-5100
American. Casual Dining. **Address:** 182 Madison Ave 04976

M THAI   207/474-5064
Traditional Thai. Casual Dining. **Address:** 105 N Water St 04976

SOUTHPORT elev. 50'

OCEAN GATE RESORT   (207)633-3321
Historic Hotel. **Address:** 70 Ocean Gate Rd 04576

WHERE TO EAT

ROBINSON'S WHARF   207/633-3830
Seafood. Casual Dining. **Address:** 20 Hendricks Hill Rd 04576

SOUTH PORTLAND (K-3) pop. 25,002, elev. 20'
• Hotels & Restaurants map & index p. 58, 75

CUSHING'S POINT MUSEUM AT BUG LIGHT PARK, off Madison Street in Bug Light Park, presents local and nautical history with exhibits about shipwrecks, lighthouses, sardine canneries and the South Portland shipyards where World War II Liberty ships were built. **Time:** Allow 45 minutes minimum. **Hours:** Daily 10-4, May-Oct.; Sat.-Sun. 10-4, Nov.-Dec. Phone ahead to confirm schedule. **Cost:** Donations. **Phone:** (207) 767-7299.

BEST WESTERN MERRY MANOR INN
(207)774-6151 **30**

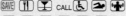

Hotel
$99-$329

Best Western. **AAA Benefit:** Members save up to 15% and earn bonus points!

Address: 700 Main St 04106 **Location:** I-95 exit 45, 1.3 mi e to US 1. **Facility:** 153 units. 4 stories, interior/exterior corridors. **Terms:** cancellation fee imposed. **Amenities:** safes. **Pool:** heated outdoor. **Activities:** hot tub, exercise room. **Guest Services:** valet and coin laundry.

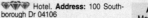

COMFORT INN AIRPORT
(207)775-0409 **22**
Hotel. **Address:** 90 Maine Mall Rd 04106

COURTYARD BY MARRIOTT PORTLAND AIRPORT
(207)253-5005 **29**
Hotel. **Address:** 100 Southborough Dr 04106

AAA Benefit: Members save 5% or more!

DAYS INN AIRPORT/MAINE MALL
(207)772-3450 **27**
Hotel. **Address:** 461 Maine Mall Rd 04106

DOUBLETREE BY HILTON
(207)775-6161 **25**

Hotel
$89-$399

DOUBLETREE BY HILTON **AAA Benefit:** Members save 5% or more!

Address: 363 Maine Mall Rd 04106 **Location:** I-95 exit 45, just n. Opposite Maine Mall. **Facility:** 220 units. 7-9 stories, interior corridors. **Terms:** 1-7 night minimum stay, cancellation fee imposed. **Amenities:** safes. **Pool:** heated indoor. **Activities:** exercise room, in-room exercise equipment. **Guest Services:** valet laundry, area transportation.

HAMPTON BY HILTON PORTLAND AIRPORT
207/773-4400 **28**
Hotel. **Address:** 171 Philbrook Ave 04106

AAA Benefit: Members save 5% or more!

HOLIDAY INN EXPRESS & SUITES
(207)775-3900 **23**

Hotel
$94-$359

Address: 303 Sable Oaks Dr 04106 **Location:** I-95 exit 45, just n on Maine Mall Rd, then just w on Running Hill Rd. **Facility:** 130 units. 6 stories, interior corridors. **Amenities:** safes. **Pool:** heated indoor. **Activities:** exercise room. **Guest Services:** valet and coin laundry, area transportation. **Featured Amenity: breakfast buffet.**

HOME2 SUITES BY HILTON PORTLAND AIRPORT
207/517-3636 **21**
Extended Stay Hotel. **Address:** 50 Maine Mall Rd 04106

AAA Benefit: Members save 5% or more!

PORTLAND MARRIOTT AT SABLE OAKS
(207)871-8000 **24**

Hotel
$101-$342

MARRIOTT **AAA Benefit:** Members save 5% or more!

Address: 200 Sable Oaks Dr 04106 **Location:** I-95 exit 45, just n on Maine Mall Rd, then just w on Running Hill Rd. **Facility:** 226 units. 6 stories, interior corridors. **Terms:** check-in 4 pm, cancellation fee imposed. **Amenities:** Some: safes. **Pool:** heated indoor. **Activities:** exercise room. **Guest Services:** valet and coin laundry, boarding pass kiosk, area transportation.

TRU BY HILTON PORTLAND AIRPORT AREA
207/221-3131 **26**
Hotel. **Address:** 369 Maine Mall Rd 04106

Members save 5% or more!

WHERE TO EAT

AMATO'S
207/767-5916
Pizza Sandwiches. Quick Serve. **Address:** 1108 Broadway 04106

(See maps & indexes p. 58, 75.)

B.GOOD 207/536-4406 (38)
◆ Natural/Organic Sandwiches. Quick Serve. **Address:** 200 Gorham Rd 04106

ELSMERE BBQ AND WOOD GRILL 207/619-1948 (33)
◆◆ Barbecue. Casual Dining. **Address:** 448 Cottage Rd 04106

POM'S THAI RESTAURANT 207/347-3000 (35)
◆◆ Thai. Casual Dining. **Address:** 209 Western Ave 04106

Q STREET DINER 207/767-0299 (34)
◆ American. Casual Dining. **Address:** 9 Q St 04106

SALTWATER GRILLE 207/799-5400 (32)
◆◆◆ Regional Seafood. Casual Dining. **Address:** 231 Front St 04106

SOUTHWEST HARBOR (I-6) pop. 720, elev. 468'
• **Hotels & Restaurants map & index p. 37**
• **Part of Acadia National Park area — see map p. 28**

Located on the southwest side of Somes Sound and bordered by a natural fjord, this fishing and boatbuilding center shares Mount Desert Island with Acadia National Park *(see place listing p. 28)*. With about 70 lobster fishermen operating from its wharves, Southwest Harbor is the archetype of the New England coastal village.

Bass Harbor Head Light, 3 miles south on SR 102A, is a favorite spot for photographers. Local conditions are ideal for boating, swimming and other water sports. Schooner cruises, deep-sea fishing excursions and canoe rentals are available.

Southwest Harbor & Tremont Chamber of Commerce: 329 Main St., Southwest Harbor, ME 04679. **Phone:** (207) 244-9264.

CLARK POINT INN 207/244-9828 (11)
◆◆◆ Bed & Breakfast. **Address:** 109 Clark Point Rd 04679

THE KINGSLEIGH INN (207)244-5302 (12)
◆◆◆ Historic Bed & Breakfast. **Address:** 373 Main St 04679

WHERE TO EAT

CAFE 2 & EAT-A-PITA 207/244-4344 (11)
◆◆ American. Casual Dining. **Address:** 326 Main St 04679

CAFE DRY DOCK 207/244-5842 (12)
◆◆ American. Casual Dining. **Address:** 357 Main St 04679

THOMASTON pop. 1,875, elev. 20'

HAMPTON INN & SUITES ROCKLAND/THOMASTON
207/594-6644
◆◆◆ Hotel. **Address:** 190 New County Rd 04861

AAA Benefit:
Members save 5% or more!

WHERE TO EAT

THE SLIPWAY 207/354-4155
◆◆ Seafood. Casual Dining. **Address:** 24 Public Landing Rd 04861

THOMASTON CAFE 207/354-8589
◆◆ Regional American. Gastropub. **Address:** 154 Main St 04861

TRENTON
• **Hotels & Restaurants map & index p. 37**
• **Part of Acadia National Park area — see map p. 28**

TRENTON BRIDGE LOBSTER POUND 207/667-2977 (5)
◆ Seafood. Quick Serve. **Address:** 1237 Bar Harbor Rd 04605

VINALHAVEN ISLAND (J-5) elev. 100'

Vinalhaven Island, 9 miles long and 6 miles wide, is the largest of Penobscot Bay's Fox Islands and the third largest along the Maine coast. This working island village is a popular day-trip destination with visitors and locals alike. The Maine State Ferry Service transports passengers, automobiles and trucks on a 1.25-hour cruise from Rockland to Carver's Harbor; phone (207) 596-5400.

Incorporated in 1789, Vinalhaven at one time had numerous granite quarries that attracted settlers and provided a booming industry. Many buildings in Washington, D.C., and New York were made of Vinalhaven granite. Two abandoned spring-fed quarries are now town parks and popular swimming holes. Another abandoned site, Armbrust Hill, also is a town park.

The island is home to one of the most productive lobster-fishing fleets in the world. Parks, rocky beaches, hiking trails and natural areas offer a variety of recreational opportunities. Lane's Island, south of Vinalhaven and accessible by bridge, is a nature preserve.

WATERVILLE (I-4) pop. 15,722, elev. 112'
• **Hotels p. 86** • **Restaurants p. 86**

Abenaki Indians once met for tribal councils and summer encampments at the Kennebec River's Ticonic Falls, near the site of Waterville. The area is now a center for commerce and education.

The city of Waterville was established in 1802. The arrival of the steamship *Ticonic* in 1832 introduced Waterville's era as a prosperous freight and passenger port. By mid-century, as river traffic declined due to railroad advances, energies turned to new possibilities. A dam was erected at Ticonic Falls in 1868; 5 years later the first of many large factories was established. The city is an important industrial center for paper, biotechnology, health care and professional services.

Waterville also benefits from the presence of two colleges and several cultural organizations. Especially popular are theater, dance, music and comedy performances at the Waterville Opera House; phone (207) 873-7000 for ticket information.

West of the city lies the Belgrade Lakes region, whose largest lake, Great Pond, inspired the play and movie "On Golden Pond." Miles of hiking trails lace the city, and fishing and boating on the Kennebec River are other popular outdoor pastimes.

The Maine International Film Festival draws a crowd in July to Railroad Square Cinema, 17 Railroad Square, for 10 days of independent and international films. The Taste of Waterville brings more than 7,000 foodies to downtown on the first Wednesday in August and includes food booths, live entertainment, a beer garden and children's activities.

Mid-Maine Chamber of Commerce: 50 Elm St., Waterville, ME 04901. **Phone:** (207) 873-3315.

BEST WESTERN PLUS WATERVILLE GRAND HOTEL
(207)873-0111

Hotel
$99-$299

 Best Western PLUS **AAA Benefit:** Members save up to 15% and earn bonus points!

Address: 375 Main St 04901 **Location:** I-95 exit 130 (Main St), on SR 104. **Facility:** 138 units. 3 stories, interior corridors. **Terms:** cancellation fee imposed. **Pool:** heated indoor. **Activities:** hot tub, exercise room. **Guest Services:** valet and coin laundry.

FIRESIDE INN & SUITES   207/873-3335
Hotel. **Address:** 376 Main St 04901

HAMPTON INN WATERVILLE   207/873-0400
Hotel. **Address:** 425 Kennedy Memorial Dr 04901

AAA Benefit: Members save 5% or more!

WHERE TO EAT

GOVERNOR'S RESTAURANT & BAKERY   207/872-0677
American. Casual Dining. **Address:** 376 Main St 04901

THE LAST UNICORN RESTAURANT   207/873-9363
American. Casual Dining. **Address:** 8 Silver St 04901

MAINELY BREWS RESTAURANT AND BREWHOUSE
207/873-2457
Traditional Burgers Pizza. Brewpub. **Address:** 1 Post Office Rd 04901

MING LEE CHINESE RESTAURANT   207/873-2828
Chinese. Casual Dining. **Address:** 365 Main St 04901

PAD THAI TOO   207/859-8900
Thai Noodles Vegetarian. Casual Dining. **Address:** 400 Kennedy Memorial Dr 04901

WELLS (L-2) elev. 203'
• Hotels & Restaurants map & index p. 58

Within a year of its settlement in 1640 Wells boasted a mill on the Webhannet River and showed signs of becoming a flourishing trading port. Although it ultimately fulfilled its potential, Native American hostility made the village's first century precarious. Wells was one of only four English communities to survive the second French and Indian War, which occurred 1688-97.

Stubborn courage may have been at the heart of Wells' survival. For 2 days in 1692, 15 soldiers ensconced in the Joseph Storer House repulsed the attacks of 500 Indians and French. The house, south on US 1, still stands as a private home and business.

Wells remained primarily a fishing and farming center until the "discovery" of Wells Beach, Laudholm Beach and Drakes Island Beach by vacationers in the early 20th century. Since then visitors have thronged to the 7-mile-long strand to sun, swim and just relax. The town also is a popular shopping center with a variety of stores, shops and factory outlets.

Wells Chamber of Commerce: 136 Post Rd., Wells, ME 04090. **Phone:** (207) 646-2451.

CARRIAGE HOUSE MOTEL, COTTAGES & SUITES
(207)646-2159 **54**
Motel. **Address:** 1404 Post Rd 04090

ELMWOOD RESORT HOTEL   207/646-1038 **55**
Condominium. **Address:** 1351 Post Rd 04090

THE GARRISON   207/646-3497 **56**
Motel. **Address:** 1099 Post Rd 04090

HAMPTON INN & SUITES BY HILTON
(207)646-0555 **57**

Hotel
$267-$380

  **Hampton** **AAA Benefit:** Members save 5% or more!

Address: 900 Post Rd 04090 **Location:** 0.7 mi n of jct SR 9B. **Facility:** 87 units. 3 stories, interior corridors. **Terms:** 1-7 night minimum stay, cancellation fee imposed. **Pool:** heated indoor. **Activities:** hot tub, exercise room. **Guest Services:** valet and coin laundry. **Featured Amenity: full hot breakfast.**

WELLS-MOODY MOTEL   207/646-5601 **58**
Motel. **Address:** 119 Post Rd 04054

WHERE TO EAT

BILLY'S CHOWDER HOUSE   207/646-7558 **35**
Seafood. Casual Dining. **Address:** 216 Mile Rd 04090

CONGDON'S FAMILY RESTAURANT & BAKERY
207/646-4219 **34**

American Casual Dining
$8-$19

AAA Inspector Notes: The family-run restaurant and bakery is known for its doughnuts. Home-style cooking is at the menu's heart. **Address:** 1090 Post Rd 04090 **Location:** I-95 exit 19, 1.6 mi e on SR 109, then 0.9 mi s on US 1.

FISHERMAN'S CATCH   207/646-8780 **31**
Seafood. Casual Dining. **Address:** 134 Harbor Rd 04090

(See map & index p. 58.)

MAINE DINER

American
Casual Dining
$6-$32

207/646-4441 30

AAA Inspector Notes: The Maine Diner is popular with locals and tourists alike. The varied menu features tasty local fish, including the signature lobster pie, burgers, salads and breakfast (served all day). The staff is friendly, prompt and attentive. **Features:** beer & wine. **Address:** 2265 Post Rd 04090 **Location:** 1.8 mi n.

B L D

MIKE'S CLAM SHACK

Regional
Seafood
Casual Dining
$9-$30

207/646-5999 33

AAA Inspector Notes: This eatery started out as a clam shack in 1948 but has grown into a popular full-service restaurant. Fresh local seafood is at the heart of the menu, but you'll also find prime rib, burgers, chicken, stir-fry and pasta. A takeout window is still available seasonally. **Features:** full bar, happy hour. **Address:** 1150 Post Rd (US 1) Rd 04090 **Location:** I-95 exit 19, 1.5 mi e on SR 109 to US 1, then 1 mi s.

L D

THE STEAKHOUSE

207/646-4200 32

Steak. Casual Dining. **Address:** 1205 Post Rd 04090

VARANO'S ITALIAN RESTAURANT

207/641-8550 36

Italian. Casual Dining. **Address:** 60 Mile Rd 04090

WELLS BEACH
• Hotels & Restaurants map & index p. 58

ATLANTIC OCEANFRONT MOTEL

(207)646-7061 61

Motel. **Address:** 37 Atlantic Ave 04090

WESTBROOK pop. 17,494
• Hotels & Restaurants map & index p. 75

SUPER 8

(207)854-1881 18

Hotel. **Address:** 208 Larrabee Rd 04092

WHERE TO EAT

AMATO'S

207/856-2120

Pizza Sandwiches. Quick Serve. **Address:** 120 Main St 04092

FROG & TURTLE

207/591-4185

American. Gastropub. **Address:** 3 Bridge St 04092

PORTLAND PIE CO.

207/591-6248

Pizza. Casual Dining. **Address:** 869 Main St 04092

WISCASSET pop. 1,097, elev. 11'

Wiscasset at one time was Maine's chief port. The Embargo Act of 1807 seriously crippled its prosperous sea trade, and the town never regained its stature as a seaport. However, the legacy of that era is evidenced by Wiscasset's mansions, built by ship owners and merchants in the 18th and early 19th centuries.

Lincoln County Museum and Old Jail, 133 Federal St., is a fortresslike granite building used as a jail 1811-1913. Original graffiti from the 19th century still exists on cell walls. A brick jailer's home attached to the jail houses antiques and decorative arts as well as changing exhibits; phone (207) 882-6817.

RED'S EATS

207/882-6128

Regional Seafood. Quick Serve. **Address:** 41 Water St 04578

SEA BASKET RESTAURANT

207/882-6581

Seafood. Quick Serve. **Address:** 303 Bath Rd 04578

YORK (L-2)
• Hotels & Restaurants map & index p. 58

First settled in 1624, York is one of Maine's oldest, most historic places. Reminders of York's past include residential areas dating from the 18th century, Colonial churches, farmhouses with large woodpiles of white birch, stone walls along tree-lined streets and an old burying ground where quaint epitaphs are favorites for stone rubbings.

Ancient traditions are strong, but there also are new industries and plentiful facilities for recreation. The York River provides a setting for boating, and Agamenticus Mountain has facilities for picnicking, biking and hiking. George Marshall Store Gallery, 140 Lindsay Rd., includes rotating exhibits by local artists; phone (207) 351-1083.

The Greater York Region Chamber of Commerce: 1 Stonewall Ln., York, ME 03909. **Phone:** (207) 363-4422.

BEST WESTERN YORK INN

(207)363-8903 91

Motel
$69-$450

AAA Benefit: Members save up to 15% and earn bonus points!

Address: 2 Brickyard Ln 03909 **Location:** I-95 exit 7, 1 mi s. **Facility:** 87 units. 2 stories, interior corridors. **Terms:** cancellation fee imposed. **Pool:** heated indoor. **Activities:** exercise room.

MICROTEL INN & SUITES BY WYNDHAM

(207)363-0800 90

Hotel. **Address:** 6 Market Place Dr 03909

WHERE TO EAT

CLAY HILL FARM

207/361-2272 55

American. Fine Dining. **Address:** 220 Clay Hill Rd 03902

RUBY'S GENUINE BRICK OVEN

207/363-7980 58

American. Casual Dining. **Address:** 433 US Rt 1 03909

WALKERS MAINE

207/351-1145 56

New American. Fine Dining. **Address:** 1273 US Rt 1 03902

WILD WILLY'S BURGERS

207/363-9924 57

Burgers. Quick Serve. **Address:** 765 US Rt 1 03909

YORK BEACH (L-2) elev. 23'
• Hotels p. 88 • Restaurants p. 88
• Hotels & Restaurants map & index p. 58

YORK'S WILD KINGDOM ZOO AND AMUSEMENT PARK, I-95 exit 7, then 2 mi. n. to 1 Animal Park Rd., is home to exotic animals from around the

(See map & index p. 58.)

world, including camels, lions and a white Bengal tiger. The Butterfly Kingdom exhibit, animal shows and a petting zoo also are offered. An amusement park features 20 rides.

Time: Allow 3 hours minimum. Hours: Zoo daily 10-6, late June-early Sept.; Mon.-Fri. 10-5, Sat.-Sun. 10-6, late May-late June and early to late Sept. Amusements daily noon-8, late June-early Sept.; Sat.-Sun. noon-6, late May-late June and early to late Sept. Last admission 1 hour before closing. Phone ahead to confirm schedule. Cost: Zoo $14.75; $9 (ages 4-12); $1 (ages 1-3). Combination zoo and rides $23.75; $18.50 (ages 4-12); $5.25 (ages 1-3). Hours and rates may vary; phone ahead. Phone: (207) 363-4911. ⊞

THE ANCHORAGE INN   207/363-5112 **87**
◈◈ Hotel. **Address:** 265 Long Beach Ave 03910
THE UNION BLUFF HOTEL   207/363-1333 **86**
◈◈◈ Classic Hotel. **Address:** 8 Beach St 03910

WHERE TO EAT

FOX'S LOBSTER HOUSE   207/363-2643 **51**
◈◈ Seafood. Casual Dining. **Address:** 8 Sohier Park Rd 03910
SUN & SURF   207/363-2961 **52**
◈◈ Regional Seafood. Casual Dining. **Address:** 264 Long Beach Ave 03910
UNION BLUFF PUB & GRILL   207/363-1333 **50**
◈◈ American. Casual Dining. **Address:** 8 Beach St 03910

YORK HARBOR (L-2) pop. 3,033, elev. 56'
• Hotels & Restaurants map & index p. 58

The fashionable resort member of the Yorks, York Harbor has enjoyed this role since the Civil War. Well-to-do residents of Boston, Philadelphia and other large cities built rambling three-story "cottages" and grand hotels in which to while away their summers, cooled by the New England sea breezes. York Harbor's summer colony once rivaled those of Bar Harbor *(see place listing p. 35)* and Newport, R.I.

The harbor itself, with the town wharves and marina, remains as busy now as in the 18th century, when it was the Yorks' marketplace and the scene of lively market fairs. It is a favored stopover among yachtsmen and an equally popular starting point for deep-sea fishing trips.

One block south of SR 1703 and US 1 a footpath leads to Wiggly Bridge, a restored suspension bridge spanning the York River. From York Harbor, Long Sands Beach extends northeastward past York Beach toward Cape Neddick Light, popularly known as the Nubble Light. One of the most photographed lighthouses in Maine, the Nubble extends a rocky thumb into the sea; from a tiny island just off its tip the Cape Neddick Light, built in 1879, once guided seamen.

The Sayward-Wheeler House at 9 Barrell Ln. Ext., open the second and fourth Saturday of each month from June to mid-October, contains antique furniture and items brought back as booty from the expedition against the French at Louisbourg in 1745; phone (207) 384-2454.

DOCKSIDE GUEST QUARTERS   207/363-2868   **96**
🔶🔶🔶 Country Inn. **Address:** 22 Harris Island Rd 03909

STAGE NECK INN   207/363-3850   **95**
🔶🔶🔶🔶   **Address:** 8 Stage Neck Rd 03911 **Location:** Oceanfront. Off US 1A via Harbor Beach Rd. **Facility:** Situated at the mouth of York Harbor's Rocky Neck, this hotel features breathtaking views and well-designed, amenity-rich, plush guest rooms. The Maine-centric gift shop is worth a visit. 58 units. 3 stories, interior corridors. **Amenities:** safes. **Pool:** heated outdoor, heated indoor. **Activities:** sauna, hot tub, tennis, exercise room, spa. **Guest Services:** valet and coin laundry. **Featured Amenity:** breakfast buffet. *(See ad this page.)*

Resort Hotel
Rates not provided

SAVE 🍴 🛎 🍸 CALL 🛗 🚴 🛄 BIZ 📶 ❌
📱 💳

YORK HARBOR INN   207/363-5119   **94**
🔶🔶🔶 Historic Country Inn. **Address:** 480 York St 03911

WHERE TO EAT

DOCKSIDE RESTAURANT ON YORK HARBOR   207/363-2722   **61**
🔶🔶🔶 Regional American. Casual Dining. **Address:** 22 Harris Island Rd 03909

▼ See AAA listing this page ▼

Mount Washington

New Hampshire

Live free or die.

To understand New Hampshire's blunt motto, it's necessary to peek into the state's feisty and pathfinding past.

Twenty years after English sea captain Martin Pring sailed up the lower Piscataqua River to explore the region, Europeans established the first white settlements at Odiorne's Point and Dover in 1623. Others followed in nearly a century of allegiance to the English crown.

When the colonists would have no more, New Hampshire declared independence from England, and in 1776 became the first colony to adopt a provisional constitution and government.

Durham was a hotbed of this Revolutionary activity. Led by native son Maj. Gen. John Sullivan, patriots took gunpowder from the British and stored it in a town meetinghouse; a tablet marks the site. Several historic houses along the Portsmouth Harbour Trail

Franconia Notch State Park

owe their significance to the strife. A then-renowned haven for dissenters, Exeter now is home to the American Independence Museum.

Out of this epic struggle for freedom, a simple motto was born.

In post-independence New Hampshire, the spirited maxim had even broader implications. It meant immunity from religious persecution to the Shakers, who built villages in Canterbury and Enfield.

The influence of the state's majestic backdrop of mountains, caves, lakes and wide open spaces encouraged creative figures to freely express themselves. Poet John Greenleaf Whittier wrote "Sunset on the Bearcamp" about the river of the same name. An ascent of Mount Monadnock inspired Ralph Waldo Emerson's poem "Monadnoc." Many writings of Robert Frost drew upon his life on a Derry farm.

Author Thomas Bailey Aldrich penned "The Story of a Bad Boy," which includes references to his Portsmouth boyhood home. Composer Edward MacDowell thrived in the woodland retreat of Peterborough, which he later introduced to scores of other artists.

From the White Mountains to Lake Winnipesaukee, the largely pristine Granite State epitomizes much of what is amazing—and liberating—about nature.

Mountain roads like Kancamagus Highway

(SR 112) wind through White Mountain National Forest, skirting breathtaking vistas of the peaks. In autumn the vivid hues of changing leaves are unmatched in their glory and beauty.

Railways and tramways climb to the top of Cannon Mountain, Loon Mountain and Mount Washington, the Northeast's tallest peak at 6,288 feet. Well-trodden hiking paths through the entire mountainous region often lead to tumbling waterfalls.

At the Bottom, Looking Up

The low-level vantage points of mountain gaps give a different perspective. Impressive characteristics of Franconia Notch, which splits the Kinsman and Franconia ranges, are The Flume Gorge, a long chasm flanking Mount Liberty; the Lost River, which often disappears as it snakes through boulder caves and potholes in Kinsman Notch; and Dixville Notch, which boasts striking sights like the Cathedral Spires and Table Rock.

Walk amid granite boulders and mineral formations in Plymouth's Polar Caves, seven caves formed by glacial activity more than 20,000 years ago.

Climb aboard a steamship or boat in Portsmouth and cruise through Portsmouth Harbor to the Isles of Shoals. Marvel at Lake Winnipesaukee's natural spectacles—coves and islands set against an outline of mountain peaks; cruises depart from Weirs Beach and Wolfeboro.

Kick back, shake off your encumbrances and live life to its fullest in New Hampshire. It's certainly the better of the motto's two options!

Recreation

If New Hampshire needs a recreation slogan, here's an idea: "Have skis, will travel."

The state sport is unrivaled in popularity.

Like it fast? You'll find more than 150 downhill skiing and snowboarding trails among the White Mountain region's three largest resorts: Attitash Bear Peak in Bartlett, Loon Mountain in Lincoln, and Waterville Valley.

Tubing parks are among the additional facilities at Cranmore Mountain Resort in North Conway, Gunstock Mountain Resort in Gilford, King Pine Ski Area in East Madison, Pats Peak in Henniker and Whaleback in Lebanon.

If you prefer skiing on more level ground, there are 24 cross-country facilities that fit the bill. Lengthy trails and scenic vistas characterize Jackson X-C in Jackson and The Franconia Inn in Franconia.

In the state's northernmost quarter snowmobiling is sure to get your motor running. A 7,000-mile interconnecting trail system weaves through breathtaking scenery.

When the snow melts away, you'll warm to New Hampshire's more temperate pursuits.

Bicyclists are in for a treat when they pedal through the Granite State: endless vistas of dark green mountainsides and clear blue skies. The trail system is extensive, particularly along the Connecticut River, around Lake Winnipesaukee and in the Merrimack Valley region, from Concord to Nashua.

The easy 1-mile hike up Blue Job Mountain, near Strafford, culminates in great views of Boston and Mount Washington. If you have half a day, take on White Dot Trail on Mount Monadnock, one of the most climbed mountains in the world.

Got nerves of steel? Cathedral Ledge, in Echo Lake State Park near Bartlett, and Franconia Notch State Park, near Franconia and Lincoln, are hot spots for rock climbing.

The Swift River beckons to white-water rafting enthusiasts. Kayaking is good on the Androscoggin River, which can be slightly rough upstream from Berlin.

Strong winds over the surface of Lake Winnipesaukee make for excellent sailing. For boating and swimming, check out Newfound, Squam and Sunapee lakes.

Cathedral Ledge in Echo Lake State Park

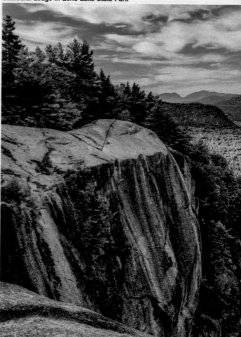

Historic Timeline

1603	English sea captain Martin Pring becomes the first European to visit New Hampshire.
1622	Captain John Mason is given a land grant to the area and names it after the English county of Hampshire.
1776	New Hampshire becomes the first colony to declare independence from England.
1788	New Hampshire is the ninth and deciding state to ratify the U.S. Constitution.
1808	Concord becomes the state capital.
1852	New Hampshire native Franklin Pierce is elected president of the United States.
1920	The state begins holding the first-in-the-nation presidential primary.
1944	At the Bretton Woods Conference, delegates from 44 nations agree on solutions to international monetary problems.
1964	The state adopts the first legal lottery in the 20th-century United States.
1986	Concord teacher Christa McAuliffe, the first educator to fly in space, is killed when the space shuttle *Challenger* explodes.
1999	New Hampshire is the first state to have a female governor, Senate president and House speaker all at the same time.

What To Pack

Temperature Averages Maximum/Minimum	JANUARY	FEBRUARY	MARCH	APRIL	MAY	JUNE	JULY	AUGUST	SEPTEMBER	OCTOBER	NOVEMBER	DECEMBER
Concord	32/11	34/12	42/22	56/32	69/42	78/51	83/56	81/54	72/46	62/36	48/27	35/15
Dixville Notch	21/-3	24/-2	34/9	46/24	60/36	69/47	74/52	72/50	63/42	51/32	38/22	26/7
Franconia	25/5	28/7	36/16	47/28	61/39	70/48	74/53	73/51	65/43	54/33	42/24	31/12
Hanover	29/9	34/12	43/22	57/33	70/44	79/54	83/59	81/57	71/49	59/37	46/28	34/16
Manchester	32/5	36/8	44/18	56/29	68/40	77/50	82/55	80/53	72/44	61/32	50/24	37/12
Portsmouth	34/15	37/18	46/26	56/34	68/44	77/53	83/59	81/57	72/50	61/39	50/32	39/21

From the records of The Weather Channel Interactive, Inc.

Good Facts To Know

ABOUT THE STATE

POPULATION: 1,316,470.

AREA: 9,349 square miles; ranks 46th.

CAPITAL: Concord.

HIGHEST POINT: 6,288 ft., Mount Washington.

LOWEST POINT: Sea level, Atlantic Ocean.

TIME ZONE(S): Eastern. DST.

GAMBLING

MINIMUM AGE FOR GAMBLING: 21.

REGULATIONS

TEEN DRIVING LAWS: For the first 6 months, no more than one unrelated passenger under age 25. Driving is not permitted 1 a.m.-4 a.m. The minimum age for an unrestricted driver's license is 18 years. For more information about New Hampshire driver's license regulations, phone (603) 227-4000.

SEAT BELT/CHILD RESTRAINT LAWS: Children ages 7-17 and at least 57 inches tall are required to be in a seat belt; child restraints are required for children under age 7 and under 57 inches tall. AAA recommends the use of seat belts and appropriate child restraints for the driver and all passengers.

CELLPHONE RESTRICTIONS: Texting and handheld cellphone use while driving is prohibited for all drivers. Drivers under age 18 may not use a cellphone—even if it is equipped with hands-free technology—while driving. Through its law against negligent driving, New Hampshire holds drivers accountable for all distractions causing a crash.

HELMETS FOR MOTORCYCLISTS: Not required.

RADAR DETECTORS: Permitted. Prohibited for use by commercial vehicles.

MOVE OVER LAW: Driver is required to slow down and vacate a lane nearest police, fire, rescue, utility and road maintenance vehicles stopped on the side of the road using audible or flashing signals. Law includes tow trucks.

FIREARMS LAWS: Vary by state and/or county. Contact the New Hampshire State Police, Permits and Licensing Unit, 33 Hazen Dr., Room 106 Concord, NH 03305; phone (603) 223-3873.

HOLIDAYS

HOLIDAYS: Jan. 1 ▪ Martin Luther King Jr. Day, Jan. (3rd Mon.) ▪ Washington's Birthday/Presidents Day, Feb. (3rd Mon.) ▪ Memorial Day, May (last Mon.) ▪ July 4 ▪ Labor Day, Sept. (1st Mon.) ▪ Columbus Day, Oct. (2nd Mon.) ▪ Veterans Day, Nov. 11 ▪ Thanksgiving, Nov. (4th Thurs.) ▪ day after Thanksgiving ▪ Christmas, Dec. 25.

MONEY

TAXES: New Hampshire does not have a statewide sales tax. There is a 9 percent Meals & Rentals Tax.

VISITOR INFORMATION

INFORMATION CENTERS: State welcome centers provide details about attractions, accommodations, historic sites, parks and events. They are maintained year-round at Canterbury, I-93N between exits 18 and 19 ▪ Hooksett, I-93N and I-93S between exits 10 and 11 ▪ Lebanon, I-89S between exits 17 and 18 ▪ Littleton, I-93S before exit 44 ▪ Nashua, US 3 exit 6 ▪ North Conway, US 16 and US 302 ▪ Salem, I-93N before exit 1 ▪ Sanbornton, I-93S between exits 20 and 22 ▪ Seabrook, I-95N before exit 1 ▪ Springfield, I-89N between exits 12A and 13 ▪ and Sutton, I-89S between exits 9 and 10. Information centers are maintained Memorial Day to mid-October at Antrim ▪ Colebrook ▪ Epsom ▪ Rumney ▪ and Shelburne.

FURTHER INFORMATION FOR VISITORS:
Division of Travel and Tourism Development
1 Eagle Sq.
Suite 100
Concord, NH 03301
(603) 271-2665
(800) 386-4664

NATIONAL FOREST INFORMATION:
White Mountain National Forest
71 White Mountain Dr.
Campton, NH 03223
(603) 536-6100
TTY (603) 536-3665

FISHING AND HUNTING REGULATIONS:
Fish and Game Department
11 Hazen Dr.
Concord, NH 03301
(603) 271-3421

Maine Annual Events

Please call ahead to confirm event details.

 Visit **AAA.com/travelguides/events** to find AAA-listed events for every day of the year

WINTER

Dec. - Christmas at Canterbury / Canterbury 603-783-9511
- Candlelight Stroll / Portsmouth 603-433-1100

Jan. - New Hampshire Snow Sculpture Competition / Jackson 603-383-9356
- White Mountain Classic 30K Jackson / 603-383-9355
- Independence Weekend Celebration Lincoln / 603-745-8111

Feb. - Winter Wine Festival / New Castle / 603-373-6566
- Mountain Dew Vertical Challenge Newbury / 603-763-3500

SPRING

Mar. - The Hampton Half Marathon & 5K Hampton / 603-659-2824
- Hannes Schneider Meister Cup Race North Conway / 603-823-7177
- Attitash Grandstand Mogul Jam Bartlett / 603-374-2600

Apr. - Intergalactic Cardboard Sled Race Newbury / 603-763-3500
- Machine Quilters Exposition Quilt Festival / Manchester / 866-675-4355
- Last Run Luau Pond Skimming Waterville Valley / 603-236-8311, ext. 3456

May - Chowder and Brews Fest / Waterville Valley / 603-236-8175
- Wildquack Duck River Festival Jackson / 603-383-9356

SUMMER

June - Master Sand Sculpting Classic Hampton Beach / 603-548-6002
- WOKQ Chowder Festival Portsmouth / 603-436-2848
- Celebration of Lupines / Franconia 603-823-5661

July - Hillsborough Balloon Festival and Fair / Hillsborough / 603-464-0377
- American Independence Festival Exeter / 603-772-2622

Aug. - North Country Moose Festival Colebrook / 603-237-8939
- League of New Hampshire Craftsmen's Fair / Newbury 603-224-3375

FALL

Sept. - Hampton Beach Seafood Festival Hampton Beach / 603-926-8718
- New Hampshire Highland Games Lincoln / 603-229-1975

Oct. - Return of the Pumpkin People Jackson / 603-383-9356
- Attitash Oktoberfest / Bartlett 800-223-7669
- Apple Harvest Day and 5K Road Race / Dover / 603-742-2218

Nov. - Winter Holiday Stroll / Nashua 603-883-5700
- Concord Tree Lighting Celebration Concord / 603-496-2917
- Christmas Celebration and Parade Littleton / 603-444-6561

Love the great outdoors? Find places to camp at AAA.com/campgrounds

Carousel at Canobie Lake Park, Salem

Strawbery Banke, Portsmouth

Saint-Gaudens National Historic Site, Cornish

Autumn in the White Mountains

Hillsborough Balloon Festival and Fair

Index: Great Experience for Members

AAA editor's picks of exceptional note

Saint-Gaudens
National Historic Site

Canterbury Shaker
Village

Mount Washington
Cog Railway

Cannon Mountain
Aerial Tramway

See Orientation map on p. 100 for corresponding grid coordinates, if applicable.
*Indicates the GEM is temporarily closed.

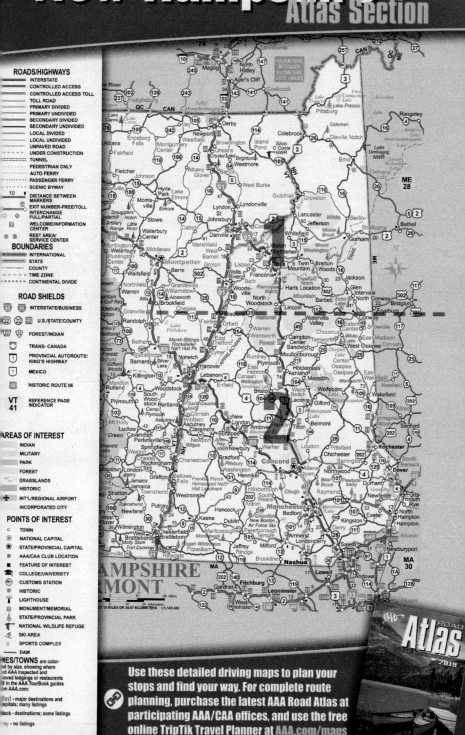

ROADS/HIGHWAYS

- INTERSTATE
- CONTROLLED ACCESS
- CONTROLLED ACCESS TOLL
- TOLL ROAD
- PRIMARY DIVIDED
- PRIMARY UNDIVIDED
- SECONDARY DIVIDED
- SECONDARY UNDIVIDED
- LOCAL DIVIDED
- LOCAL UNDIVIDED
- UNPAVED ROAD
- UNDER CONSTRUCTION
- TUNNEL
- PEDESTRIAN ONLY
- AUTO FERRY
- PASSENGER FERRY
- SCENIC BYWAY
- DISTANCE BETWEEN MARKERS
- EXIT NUMBER-FREE/TOLL
- INTERCHANGE FULL/PARTIAL
- WELCOME/INFORMATION CENTER
- REST AREA/ SERVICE CENTER

BOUNDARIES

- INTERNATIONAL
- STATE
- COUNTY
- TIME ZONE
- CONTINENTAL DIVIDE

ROAD SHIELDS

- INTERSTATE/BUSINESS
- U.S./STATE/COUNTY
- FOREST/INDIAN
- TRANS- CANADA
- PROVINCIAL AUTOROUTE/ KING'S HIGHWAY
- MEXICO
- HISTORIC ROUTE 66
- REFERENCE PAGE INDICATOR

AREAS OF INTEREST

- INDIAN
- MILITARY
- PARK
- FOREST
- GRASSLANDS
- HISTORIC
- INT'L/REGIONAL AIRPORT
- INCORPORATED CITY

POINTS OF INTEREST

- TOWN
- NATIONAL CAPITAL
- STATE/PROVINCIAL CAPITAL
- AAA/CAA CLUB LOCATION
- FEATURE OF INTEREST
- COLLEGE/UNIVERSITY
- CUSTOMS STATION
- HISTORIC
- LIGHTHOUSE
- MONUMENT/MEMORIAL
- STATE/PROVINCIAL PARK
- NATIONAL WILDLIFE REFUGE
- SKI AREA
- SPORTS COMPLEX
- DAM

CITIES/TOWNS are colored by size, showing where and AAA inspected and approved lodgings or restaurants found in the AAA TourBook guides on AAA.com:

- Red - major destinations and capitals; many listings
- Black - destinations; some listings
- Grey - no listings

Atlas ROAD 2019

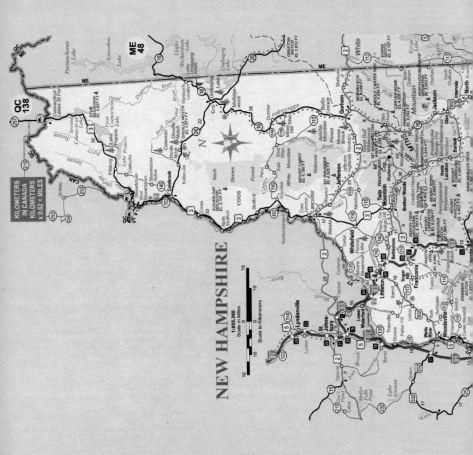

NEW HAMPSHIRE

1:855,360
Scale in Miles
0   10
Scale in Kilometers
0   10

KILOMETERS
IN CANADA
KILOMETERS
x 0.62 = MILES

QC
138

ME
48

ME

ME

CAN

COOS

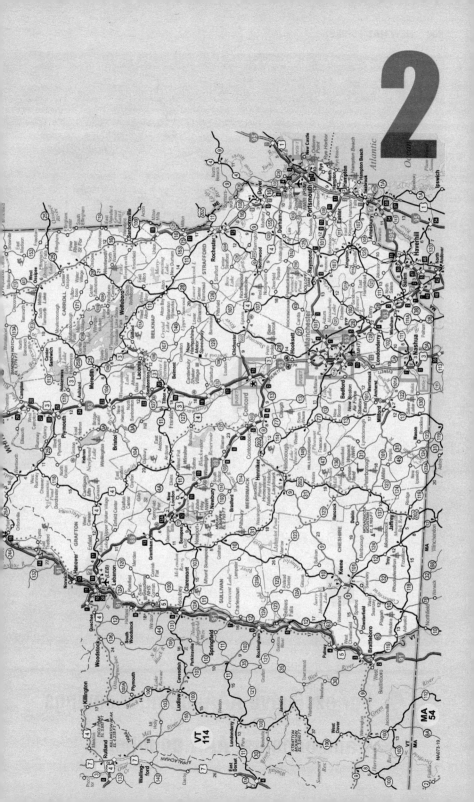

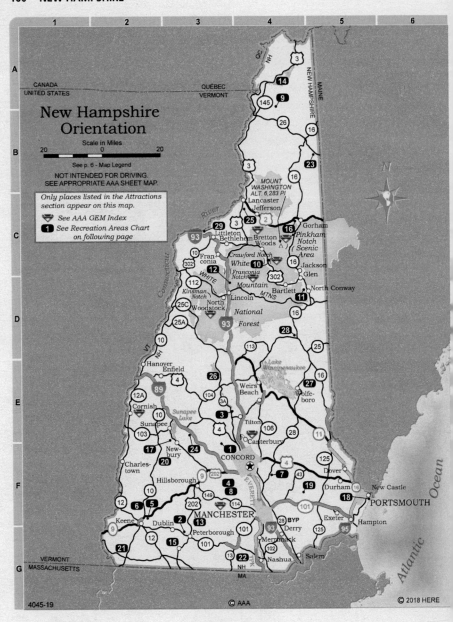

New Hampshire
Orientation

Scale in Miles

See p. 6 - Map Legend

NOT INTENDED FOR DRIVING.
SEE APPROPRIATE AAA SHEET MAP.

Only places listed in the Attractions
section appear on this map.

⬧ See AAA GEM Index

1 See Recreation Areas Chart
on following page

Recreation Areas Chart

The map location numerals in column 2 show an area's location on the preceding map.

 Find thousands of places to camp at AAA.com/campgrounds

	MAP LOCATION	CAMPING	PICNICKING	HIKING TRAILS	BOATING	BOAT RAMP	BOAT RENTAL	FISHING	SWIMMING	PET FRIENDLY	BICYCLE TRAILS	WINTER SPORTS	VISITOR CENTER	LODGE/CABINS	FOOD SERVICE
NATIONAL FORESTS *(See place listings.)*															
White Mountain (C-4) 770,000 acres. Northern New Hampshire. Scenic. Cross-country and downhill skiing, hunting, rock climbing, sledding, snowmobiling, snowshoeing.			•	•	•	•			•	•	•	•	•	•	•
ARMY CORPS OF ENGINEERS															
Blackwater Dam (F-3) 18 mi. n. of Concord off SR 127. Canoeing, hunting, kayaking; horse trails.	1		•		•	•		•		•	•				
Edward MacDowell Lake (F-3) 1,198 acres 4 mi. w. of Peterborough off SR 101. Cross-country skiing, hunting, snowshoeing.	2		•	•	•	•		•				•			
Franklin Falls Dam (E-3) 2,800 acres 15 mi. along Pemigewassett River, 2 mi. n. of Franklin off SR 127. Canoeing, cross-country skiing, hunting, kayaking, snowmobiling, snowshoeing.	3		•	•				•		•	•	•			
Hopkinton-Everett Lake (F-3) 7,992 acres off I-89 exit 6, then 3 mi. w. on SR 127. Canoeing, hunting, snowmobiling; horseshoes, model airplane field.	4		•	•	•	•		•		•	•	•			
Otter Brook Lake (F-2) 458 acres 2 mi. e. of Keene off SR 101 on Branch Rd. Canoeing, cross-country skiing, hunting, ice fishing, sailing, snowmobiling, snowshoeing. Electric boat motors only.	5		•	•	•	•		•	•	•	•	•			
Surry Mountain Lake (F-2) 1,865 acres 6 mi. n. of Keene off SR 12A. Canoeing, cross-country skiing, hunting, ice fishing, kayaking, snowmobiling, snowshoeing; beach, horseshoes, nature trails, volleyball.	6	•	•	•	•	•	•		•	•	•	•	•		
STATE															
Bear Brook (F-4) 10,000 acres 2 mi. e. of Allenstown off SR 28. Cross-country skiing, horseback riding, snowmobiling, snowshoeing; archery range, museums.	7	•	•	•	•		•		•	•	•	•	•	•		•
Clough (F-3) 140 acres 5 mi. e. of Weare between SRs 114 and 13. Mountain biking; beach.	8		•	•	•	•		•	•	•	•				•
Coleman (A-4) 1,605 acres 12 mi. e. of Colebrook off SR 26. Cross-country skiing, hunting, snowmobiling; all-terrain vehicle trails.	9	•	•	•	•	•	•	•		•		•		•		
Crawford Notch (C-4) 5,775 acres 12 mi. w. of Bartlett on US 302. Snowshoeing.	10	•	•	•				•		•		•	•		
Echo Lake (D-4) 396 acres 1.5 mi. w. of US 302 on Westside Rd. in North Conway. Scenic. Canoeing, kayaking, rock climbing.	11		•	•	•		•		•	•					
Franconia Notch (C-3) 6,440 acres 5 mi. n. of North Woodstock off US 3. Canoeing, cross-country skiing, downhill skiing, kayaking, snowmobiling, snowshoeing; bike rental.	12	•	•	•	•	•	•	•	•	•	•	•	•		•
Greenfield (F-3) 401 acres 1 mi. w. of Greenfield off SR 136. Snowshoeing; canoe and kayak rentals, playground.	13	•	•	•	•		•		•	•	•	•			•
Lake Francis (A-4) 1,684 acres 7 mi. n. of Pittsburg off US 3. Canoeing, cross-country skiing, hunting, kayaking, snowmobiling, snowshoeing; all-terrain vehicle trails, canoe rentals, playground.	14	•	•		•	•	•	•		•		•			
Monadnock (G-3) 699 acres 4 mi. n.w. of Jaffrey off SR 124. Cross-country skiing, snowshoeing.	15	•	•	•						•		•	•		•
Moose Brook (C-4) 755 acres 2 mi. w. of Gorham off US 2. Cross-country skiing; mountain biking trails. Pets restricted to designated areas.	16	•	•	•				•	•	•	•	•			•
Mount Sunapee (F-2) 2,893 acres w. of Newbury at jct. SRs 103 and 103B. Scenic. Downhill skiing; beach, playground.	17		•	•	•		•		•	•		•	•		•
Odiorne Point (F-5) 370 acres on SR 1A in Rye. Cross-country skiing; science center.	18		•	•	•			•		•	•	•	•		
Pawtuckaway (F-4) 5,500 acres 4 mi. n.e. of Raymond off SR 156. Cross-country skiing, rock climbing, snowmobiling; beach, canoe and kayak rentals, playground, tower.	19	•	•	•	•	•	•	•	•	•	•	•	•	•	•
Pillsbury (F-2) 3,702 acres 3.5 mi. n. of Washington on SR 31. Cross-country skiing, mountain biking, snowmobiling; canoe and kayak rentals, playground.	20	•	•	•	•	•	•	•	•		•	•	•		

Recreation Areas Chart

The map location numerals in column 2 show an area's location on the preceding map.

Find thousands of places to camp at AAA.com/campgrounds

	MAP LOCATION	CAMPING	PICNICKING	HIKING TRAILS	BOATING	BOAT RAMP	BOAT RENTAL	FISHING	SWIMMING	PET FRIENDLY	BICYCLE TRAILS	WINTER SPORTS	VISITOR CENTER	LODGE/CABINS	FOOD SERVICE
Pisgah (G-2) 13,500 acres off SR 63 in Chesterfield. Horseback riding, hunting, mountain biking, snowmobiling, snowshoeing; all-terrain vehicle trails.	21		•	•				•		•	•	•			
Silver Lake (G-4) 80 acres 14 mi. n.e. of Mason on SR 122. Canoeing, kayaking; beach.	22		•	•	•	•	•	•	•						•
Umbagog Lake (B-5) 19 mi. s.e. of Dixville Notch on SR 26; some portions accessible only by boat. Canoeing, kayaking; beach.	23	•	•		•	•	•	•	•					•	
Wadleigh (F-3) 8 mi. n.e. of Newbury off Chaulk Pond Rd. Canoeing, kayaking; playground.	24		•	•	•			•	•	•					
Weeks (C-4) 420 acres 2 mi. s. of Lancaster off SR 3. Historic. Scenic. Downhill and cross-country skiing, snowmobiling, snowshoeing; tower.	25		•	•								•	•		
Wellington (E-3) 183 acres 4 mi. n. of Bristol off SR 3A. Beach, horseshoes, kayak rentals, volleyball.	26		•	•	•	•		•	•	•					•
Wentworth (E-5) 50 acres 7 mi e. of Wolfeboro on SR 109. Canoeing, kayaking.	27		•		•			•	•						
White Lake (D-4) 603 acres 1 mi. n. of West Ossipee on SR 16. Canoeing, cross-country skiing, kayaking, snowshoeing; playground.	28	•	•		•			•	•				•		•
OTHER															
Moore Reservoir (C-3) 3,500 acres 8 mi. w. of Littleton off I-93 via SRs 18 and 135.	29		•	•	•	•	•		•	•	•	•		•	

Exciting Itineraries | Engaging Experiences | Exclusive Values

AAA Vacations   CAA Vacations

DESIGNED FOR AAA/CAA MEMBERS

AAA/CAA Vacations® offers vacation options and experiences all over the world. In addition to our 24/7 Member Care and Best Price Guarantee*, we deliver value with every itinerary.

These exclusive values may include:

- Savings or spending credits
- Complimentary excursions
- Pre-night hotel stay
- Complimentary specialty dining
- Priority check-in
- Pre-paid gratuities
- *And more!*

**Call your AAA/CAA Travel Agent
or visit
AAA.com/AAAVacations
CAA.ca/CAAVacations**

* If you book a qualifying *AAA/CAA Vacations®* cruise or tour package and find a valid better rate for the exact itinerary within 24 hours of your booking, AAA/CAA will match the lower rate and send you a $50 *AAA/CAA Vacations®* future travel credit certificate. Certain restrictions apply. Visit AAA.com/AAAVacations or CAA.ca/CAAVacations for full details.

BARTLETT (D-4) pop. 373, elev. 2,630'
• Hotels & Restaurants map & index p. 121

With Bear Mountain to the south, Mount Parker to the north and symmetrical Mount Carrigan rising at the western end of the valley, Bartlett is a year-round recreation center. The land along the Saco River east of its emergence from Crawford Notch was granted to William Stark and several others for their service in the French and Indian War; the village was incorporated in 1790.

From Bartlett a scenic road runs south through Bear Notch to the Kancamagus Highway (see attraction listing p. 135).

THE BARTLETT INN   603-374-2353   33
 Bed & Breakfast. Address: 1477 US 302 03812

NORTH COLONY MOTEL   (603)374-6679   32
 Motel. Address: 1025 US 302 03812

BEDFORD

BEDFORD VILLAGE INN AND THE GRAND AT BEDFORD VILLAGE INN   (603)472-2001

Country Inn
$219-$499

Address: 2 to 12 Olde Bedford Way 03110 **Location:** On SR 101, 0.3 mi w of jct SR 114. Located in a quiet area. **Facility:** These two exceptional inns, the original inn and now The Grand, are located on expansive grounds. Guests check in at the property where they are staying. 64 units. 3 stories, interior/exterior corridors. **Terms:** 10 day cancellation notice-fee imposed, resort fee. **Amenities:** safes. **Dining:** 3 restaurants, also, Bedford Village Inn Restaurant, see separate listing. **Pool:** heated outdoor. **Activities:** hot tub, exercise room, spa. **Guest Services:** valet laundry. **Featured Amenity: continental breakfast.**

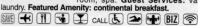

HAMPTON INN & SUITES BY HILTON MANCHESTER BEDFORD   (603)623-2040

Hotel
$117-$520

AAA Benefit: Members save 5% or more!

Address: 8 Hawthorne Dr 03110 **Location:** Just e of US 3; 1 mi s of jct SR 101. **Facility:** 92 units. 4 stories, interior corridors. **Terms:** 1-7 night minimum stay, cancellation fee imposed. **Pool:** heated indoor. **Activities:** exercise room. **Guest Services:** valet and coin laundry. **Featured Amenity: continental breakfast.**

WHERE TO EAT

BEDFORD VILLAGE INN RESTAURANT   603/472-2001

American
Fine Dining
$15-$59

AAA Inspector Notes: Historic. This 1810 farmhouse has been transformed into an elegant setting with several intimate dining rooms and a classic design. The creative menu offers a variety of memorable dishes made with a perfect blend of local and global ingredients. Save room for "The Chocolate Bag," which is the signature dessert. This delectable delight is in fact an edible chocolate bag filled with both dark and white chocolate mousse atop a sponge cake with berries. **Features:** full bar, patio dining, Sunday brunch. **Reservations:** suggested. **Address:** 2 Olde Bedford Way 03110 **Location:** On SR 101, 0.3 mi w of jct SR 114; in Bedford Village Inn and The Grand at Bedford Village Inn.

CHEN YANG LI RESTAURANT   603/641-6922
 Asian. Casual Dining. **Address:** 124 S River Rd 03110

PIZZA BELLA   603/472-8560
Pizza. Quick Serve. **Address:** 178 SR 101 03110

T-BONES GREAT AMERICAN EATERY   603/641-6100
American. Casual Dining. **Address:** 25 S River Rd 03110

BETHLEHEM (C-3) pop. 972, elev. 1,437'

THE ROCKS off I-93 exit 40, then .5 mi. e. on US 302 to Glessner Rd., then e. to 4 Christmas Ln. The 1882 estate of Chicago businessman John Jacob Glessner, a founder of International Harvester, sits on the grounds. Scenic trails with wildlife viewing and hiking and skiing opportunities wind throughout the 1,400 acres.

Glessner's grandchildren donated the land to the Society for Protection of New Hampshire Forests in 1978. A sustainable Christmas tree farm with more than 43,000 trees is open to the public, as is an interactive maple sugar house and museum. **Time:** Allow 2 hours minimum. **Hours:** Estate daily dawn-dusk. Maple sugar museum daily 10-4, July 1 to mid-Oct. **Cost:** Trails free. **Phone:** (603) 444-6228 or (800) 639-5373.

ADAIR COUNTRY INN & RESTAURANT   603/444-2600
Historic Country Inn. **Address:** 80 Guider Ln 03574

WHERE TO EAT

THE MAIA PAPAYA   603/869-9900
Vegetarian Coffee/Tea. Quick Serve. **Address:** 2161 Main St 03574

ROSA FLAMINGO'S   603/869-3111
Italian. Casual Dining. **Address:** 2312 Main St (US 302) 03574

BOW

HAMPTON INN BY HILTON CONCORD/BOW
(603)224-5322

fyi
Hotel
$143-$299

AAA Benefit: Members save 5% or more!

Under major renovation, call for details. **Last Rated:** **Address:** 515 South St 03304 **Location:** I-89 exit 1, just nw. **Facility:** 145 units. 3-4 stories, interior corridors. **Terms:** 1-7 night minimum stay, cancellation fee imposed. **Pool:** heated indoor. **Activities:** limited exercise equipment. **Guest Services:** valet and coin laundry. **Featured Amenity:** breakfast buffet.

WHERE TO EAT

CHEN YANG LI RESTAURANT & PUB   603/228-8508
Chinese. Casual Dining. **Address:** 520 South St 03304

BRETTON WOODS (C-4) elev. 1,631'

With the opening of the Mount Washington Hotel in July 1902, Bretton Woods became a well-known resort. Wealthy families spent pre-Depression summers at this lavish European-style spa. Some 50 trains arrived daily, and private railroad cars sat on a siding by the golf course, waiting to take passengers home.

A second surge of fame came in July 1944 when the International Monetary Conference convened at the hotel, refurbished for the occasion by the federal government. This meeting set the gold standard at $35 an ounce, thereby stabilizing post-World War II currency and establishing the American dollar as the cornerstone of international financial exchange. The conference room is now a small museum.

MOUNT WASHINGTON COG RAILWAY is 6 mi. n.w. on SR 302, then 6 mi. n.e. to 3168 Base Station Rd. Opened in 1869, the historic railway bills itself as the first mountain-climbing cog railway in the world. Coal-fired steam and biodiesel-powered trains take passengers on a scenic 3-hour round-trip to the top of Mount Washington—the highest peak in the Northeast. The base station features a museum that has media and interactive presentations.

Time: Allow 3 hours minimum. **Hours:** Train departs two to 10 times daily on the half-hour beginning at 8, 9 or 10:30, May-Nov. Phone ahead to confirm schedule. **Cost:** Train fares include admission to Cog Railway Museum in Marshfield Base Station. Steam train $78. Biodiesel train $72; $68 (ages 65+); $41(ages 4-12); free (ages 0-3 on adult lap). Advance ticket purchase is recommended; all sales are final and no refunds or exchanges are issued. **Phone:** (603) 278-5404 or (800) 922-8825. *(See ad p. 118.)*

THE LODGE AT BRETTON WOODS   603/278-4000
Motel. **Address:** 2653 US 302 E 03575

OMNI BRETTON ARMS INN   603/278-3000
Historic Country Inn. **Address:** 173 Mount Washington Hotel Rd 03575

OMNI MOUNT WASHINGTON RESORT   603/278-1000
Classic Historic Hotel. **Address:** 310 Mount Washington Rd 03575

THE TOWNHOMES AT BRETTON WOODS   603/278-2000
Vacation Rental House.

WHERE TO EAT

THE DINING ROOM AT OMNI BRETTON ARMS INN
603/278-1000

American Fine Dining $28-$56

AAA Inspector Notes: A luxurious setting and classical music set the tone for an intimate dining experience. The chef frequently creates new menus to take advantage of fresh, seasonal ingredients. Menu selections include lamb chops with braised lentils, zucchini, squash, green apple and a currant demi-glacé, as well as a breast of duck with sweet potatoes, cipollini, pickled asparagus, baby carrots and sugar beets in a lavender-orange sauce. **Features:** full bar. **Reservations:** suggested. Semiformal attire. **Address:** 173 Mount Washington Rd 03575 **Location:** Center; in Omni Bretton Arms Inn.

FABYAN'S STATION RESTAURANT & LOUNGE   603/278-2222
American. Casual Dining. **Address:** US 302 03575

THE MAIN DINING ROOM AT THE OMNI MOUNT WASHINGTON RESORT   603/278-1000

◆◆◆◆
Continental
Fine Dining
$28-$46

AAA Inspector Notes: This casually refined dining room has breathtaking, panoramic views of the mountains and stunning grounds. Nightly orchestra accompaniment enhances the dining experience. Menu items may include stuffed oysters, smoked brook trout, pan-seared bass, linguine with Cape Cod clams, chilled Maine lobster, and prime rib with creamy horseradish. The waitstaff provides splendid, skillful service. **Features:** full bar. **Reservations:** suggested. Semiformal attire. **Address:** 310 Mount Washington Hotel Rd 03575 **Location:** Center; in Omni Mount Washington Resort. **Parking:** on-site and valet. [B] [D] CALL [&]

CANTERBURY (E-4) elev. 375'

CANTERBURY SHAKER VILLAGE is off I-93 exit 18, following signs to 288 Shaker Rd. During the village's heyday in the 1850s, more than 300 Shakers—members of a religious sect known for the ecstatic dancing that took place during church services—lived, worked and worshiped in the village. Today it's a museum and historic site with 25 restored original buildings and four reconstructions set among nearly 700 acres of pretty New England countryside.

The oldest buildings go back all the way to 1792, when the village was established, about 2 decades after the Shakers first arrived from England. Canterbury Village was one of the most important of the 19 virtually self-sufficient communities the Shakers established from Maine to Kentucky in the 18th and 19th centuries.

Living a nearly monastic lifestyle that stressed pacifism, communal ownership, celibacy, gender equality, industriousness and simple living, the Shakers built large dormitories, barns and workshops with minimal ornamentation, a feature you'll notice immediately as you stroll among the unadorned utilitarian clapboard buildings. You'll also notice the separate entrances and sleeping areas for men and women; another hallmark of the Shaker lifestyle.

"Hands to work and hearts to God" was one Shaker motto, and Shaker communities prospered as they became known for the beautifully crafted objects they made. The village museum houses a large collection of these items, including Shaker furniture, noted for its elegant simplicity. And at various locations in the village, you can watch artisans recreate the traditional Shaker crafts of broom making, letterpress printing, oval box making, spinning and weaving, among others.

Guided tours introduce visitors to the 200-year history, culture and innovations of the Canterbury Shakers. If you want to see the village at your own pace, you can opt for the self-guiding tour; a printed guide describing the network of nature trails on-site is available at the Visitor Education Center.

Time: Allow 3 hours minimum. **Hours:** Wed.-Sun. 10-4, early May to day before Labor Day; daily 10-5, Labor Day to mid-Oct.; Sat.-Sun. 10-4, mid-Oct. through Nov. 30. **Cost:** Admission $19; $9 (ages

6-17); $45 (family). **Phone:** (603) 783-9511. GT [†]

CHARLESTOWN (F-2) pop. 1,152, elev. 369'

The 12 families who lived in this northwestern outpost in 1744 found their position increasingly precarious as King George's War accelerated. In 1746 Abenaki Indian raids confined them to the fortified village, and that winter they abandoned the settlement. Capt. Phineas Stevens led less than 50 provincial soldiers returned in April. Their withstanding a 3-day siege by 700 French and Native Americans was celebrated in Boston.

Charlestown revived as settlers returned to the fertile Connecticut River Valley. During the Revolutionary War the town's wide main streets supposedly served as a training ground for the soldiers of Gen. John Stark, hero of the Battle of Bennington *(see Bennington, Vt., p. 150)*. Main Street has many buildings that date from the late 18th and early 19th century.

COLEBROOK pop. 1,394

NORTHERN COMFORT MOTEL   603/237-4440

◆◆
Motel
Rates not provided

Address: 1 Trooper Scott Phillips (US 3) Hwy 03576 **Location:** 1.5 mi s on US 3. **Facility:** 19 units, some kitchens. 1 story, exterior corridors. *Bath:* shower only. **Pool:** heated outdoor. **Activities:** snowmobiling, playground.

[SAVE] [⚓] [📶] [✕] [▤] [▣]
/SOME UNITS [🦌]

CONCORD (F-4) pop. 42,695, elev. 264'
• Hotels p. 106 • Restaurants p. 106

The political and financial center of the state—and capital since 1808—Concord also is a major industrial, transportation and distribution point. At the root of its prosperity is easy accessibility. Historically, settlement and commerce followed the Merrimack River and later, a canal to Boston. Now a convergence of highways forms the city's busy lifelines.

A trading post operating as early as 1660, the locale gained notoriety in 1697 as the place where Hannah Dustin, abducted by Penacook Indians in a raid on Haverhill, Mass., scalped her sleeping captors and escaped.

Settlement came somewhat more slowly. Not until 1725 was the land granted to settlers, who named it the Plantation of Penacook, from the name Native Americans gave to a nearby bend in the river. In 1765 the area was renamed Concord.

Because generally peaceful relations with the Penacook people had allowed Concord to grow, by the Revolutionary War it was a sturdy community able to send companies to fight at Lexington and

Concord, Mass., Bunker Hill and other battle sites. A tablet at Walker and Bouton streets marks the site where New Hampshire ratified the Constitution on June 21, 1788.

Industry began to develop during the early 1800s. Wheelwright Lewis Downing and coach builder J. Stephens Abbot created a product that was instrumental in opening the frontier—the bouncing, high-wheeled Concord coach used by Wells Fargo and other stage lines throughout the West.

A few reminders of Concord's past stand along some of the town's wide, shaded streets. The Rev. Timothy Walker House, 276 N. Main St., dates from 1734, making it the oldest house in Concord; it is closed to the public. The structure at 132 N. Main St. once was the Eagle Hotel, a popular tavern 1825-56; it is now the site of a restaurant. Tuck Library, established in the early 1900s and operated by the New Hampshire Historical Society, is at 30 Park St.

A community-wide effort resulted in the restoration of the Capitol Theatre, built in the neo-Egyptian style in 1927 to house vaudeville shows. The Capitol Center for the Arts, with the Chubb Theatre as its centerpiece, presents touring Broadway shows, concerts, entertainers and dance troupes. The 1,300-seat theater is at 44 S. Main St.; phone (603) 225-1111.

The city balances its governmental and business orientation with ample opportunities for recreation. Among several city parks offering both summer and winter sports are 20-acre White Park at Centre and Washington streets and 16-acre Merrill Park at Eastman and Carpenter streets.

Greater Concord Chamber of Commerce: 49 S. Main St., Suite 104, Concord, NH 03301. **Phone:** (603) 224-2508.

Self-guiding tours: Concord on Foot, a tour of downtown, includes historical and architecturally interesting buildings. Brochures are available at the chamber of commerce and at the New Hampshire Historical Society for $2.

CANTERBURY SHAKER VILLAGE—see Canterbury p. 105.

SUSAN N. MCLANE AUDUBON CENTER is at 84 Silk Farm Rd. Visitors can view wildlife and observe raptors up close. Miles of well-marked hiking trails and a large picnic area are available. In addition to serving as the headquarters of the New Hampshire Audubon, the center offers educational programs year-round. **Hours:** Grounds daily dawn-dusk. Center and sanctuary Mon.-Fri. 10-5, Sat. 10-4. **Cost:** Donations. **Phone:** (603) 224-9909.

BEST WESTERN CONCORD INN & SUITES
(603) 228-4300

 Hotel $99-$199

 Best Western. **AAA Benefit:** Members save up to 15% and earn bonus points!

Address: 97 Hall St 03301 **Location:** I-93 exit 13, just n on Main St, then 0.5 mi w. **Facility:** 65 units. 3 stories, interior corridors. **Terms:** cancellation fee imposed. **Pool:** heated indoor. **Activities:** hot tub, exercise room. **Guest Services:** coin laundry.

THE CENTENNIAL HOTEL   603/227-9000
Historic Hotel. **Address:** 96 Pleasant St 03301

CONCORD COMFORT INN   (603) 226-4100
Hotel. **Address:** 71 Hall St 03301

COURTYARD BY MARRIOTT-CONCORD   (603) 225-0303
Hotel. **Address:** 70 Constitution Ave 03301
AAA Benefit: Members save 5% or more!

FAIRFIELD INN BY MARRIOTT CONCORD   (603) 224-4011
Hotel. **Address:** 4 Gulf St 03301
AAA Benefit: Members save 5% or more!

HOLIDAY INN   603/224-9534
Hotel. **Address:** 172 N Main St 03301

RESIDENCE INN BY MARRIOTT CONCORD   (603) 226-0012
Extended Stay Hotel. **Address:** 91 Hall St 03301
AAA Benefit: Members save 5% or more!

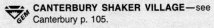

WHERE TO EAT

ANGELINA'S RISTORANTE ITALIANO   603/228-3313
Regional Italian. Casual Dining. **Address:** 11 Depot St 03301

THE BARLEY HOUSE RESTAURANT & TAVERN 603/228-6363
American. Casual Dining. **Address:** 132 N Main St 03301

THE COMMON MAN   603/228-3463
Regional American. Casual Dining. **Address:** 25 Water St 03301

GRANITE RESTAURANT & BAR   603/227-9000
American. Fine Dining. **Address:** 96 Pleasant St 03301

HERMANOS COCINA MEXICANA   603/224-5669

◈◈◈

**Mexican
Casual Dining
$8-$20**

AAA Inspector Notes: This eatery has a vibrant color scheme and Aztec decorations. The vast menu features traditional Mexican favorites, including some with a twist like "Bruce's Slow-Cooked Chili" made with sirloin beef, pinto beans, tomatoes and more. Do not miss the strawberry burrito for dessert. Live jazz is played five nights a week in the lounge. **Features:** full bar. **Address:** 11 Hills Ave 03301 **Location:** Just off Storrs St; downtown. **Parking:** street only. L D CALL ⒧

MAKRIS LOBSTER & STEAK HOUSE   603/225-7665

◈◈◈

**Seafood
Casual Dining
$10-$25**

AAA Inspector Notes: This friendly, family-run restaurant serves up fresh New England seafood in a casual, no-frills atmosphere. **Features:** full bar, patio dining. **Address:** 354 Sheep Davis Rd 03301 **Location:** I-393 exit 3, 0.5 mi on SR 106. L D

MARGARITAS MEXICAN RESTAURANT   603/224-2821
◈◈ Mexican. Casual Dining. **Address:** 1 Bicentennial Square 03301

THE RED BLAZER   603/224-4101
◈◈ American. Casual Dining. **Address:** 72 Manchester St 03301

SIAM ORCHID   603/228-3633
◈◈ Thai. Casual Dining. **Address:** 12 N Main St 03301

CONWAY pop. 1,823
• Hotels & Restaurants map & index p. 121

CAFE NOCHE MEXICAN   603/447-5050 ㉞
◈◈ Mexican. Casual Dining. **Address:** 147 Main St 03818

JONATHON'S SEAFOOD RESTAURANT & FISH MARKET
603/447-3838 ㉝
◈◈ Seafood. Casual Dining. **Address:** 280 East Side Rd 03818

CORNISH (E-2) elev. 620'

In the first decade of the 20th century this township on the Connecticut River gained fame as a major New England art colony. The central force behind the reputation was sculptor Augustus Saint-Gaudens, but Maxfield Parrish and other notables in arts and letters also found a haven in the village.

About 2 miles south of Saint-Gaudens National Historic Site *(see attraction listing)* off SR 12A is the Cornish-Windsor Covered Bridge, one of the longest covered bridges in the United States. Built in 1866 and 450 feet long, the bridge spans the Connecticut River and links New Hampshire to Windsor, Vt.

◣GEM **SAINT-GAUDENS NATIONAL HISTORIC SITE** is off SR 12A at 139 Saint-Gaudens Rd. The 1885-1907 home and studio of sculptor Augustus Saint-Gaudens originally was a country tavern built in 1817. Complemented by formal gardens, the house retains Saint-Gaudens' furnishings.

Other buildings include the Little Studio, which contains bas-reliefs, portraits and monuments; the New Gallery, with casts of some of the sculptor's largest works, cameos and coin models; the Picture Gallery, where contemporary art exhibitions are displayed; and the stable, which features a collection of horse-drawn vehicles. Hiking trails wind through the

190-acre site. Concerts are held on Sundays from early July to mid-August.

Leashed dogs are allowed on the grounds. **Time:** Allow 2 hours minimum. **Hours:** Grounds open daily dawn-dusk. Buildings open daily 9-4:30, late May-Oct. 31. **Cost:** (Valid for 7 days) $10; free (ages 0-16). **Phone:** (603) 675-2175. 🐾

CRAWFORD NOTCH (C-4) elev. 1,214'

Created when the Pleistocene ice sheet pushed through a narrow preglacial pass, majestic Crawford Notch stretches from Bartlett on the south to Saco Lake on the north. The Saco River and US 302 wind along its floor between steep, wooded Webster and Willey mountains. Behind Mount Webster rises Mount Jackson, the southernmost peak of the Presidential Range.

The scars of many landslides mark the mountainsides. In 1826 a landslide thundered down Willey Mountain, killing the fleeing family whose name the peak bears, but sparing the family's home. The event is recounted in "The Ambitious Guest," one of Nathaniel Hawthorne's "Twice-Told Tales." Near the site of the Willey House is the headquarters for Crawford Notch State Park *(see Recreation Areas Chart)*, which embraces much of the notch; phone (603) 374-2272.

The Willey Slide also disrupted the Tenth New Hampshire Turnpike, one of a series of roads that laced the notch following Timothy Nash's discovery of the gap during a 1771 hunting expedition. Spurred by the governor's promise of a land grant if Nash could bring a horse through the notch, the hunter and a companion hauled the animal up and down the rocks by ropes.

As improvements made the route passable for freight traffic, the turnpike became instrumental in the opening of New Hampshire's North Country. Promptly repaired after the 1826 landslide, the road served as a channel for commerce until the railroad crossed the notch in 1875.

DOVER (F-5) pop. 29,987, elev. 77'
• Hotels p. 108 • Restaurants p. 108

Considered the oldest permanent settlement in the state, Dover was founded in 1623 by fishermen and traders who plied the tidewaters of the Great Bay area and landed at Pomeroy Cove, now called Dover Point. By the late 1600s population growth necessitated moving the settlement from Dover Point, on SR 4 at the Piscataqua River, to its present location.

The harnessing of the Cochecho Falls' water power caused the shift from a fishing and farming economy to one based on industry. Sawmills and gristmills gave way to cotton mills when the embargoes imposed during the War of 1812 curtailed mercantile interests.

Apple Harvest Day, held the first Saturday in October, attracts more than 350 vendors and 50,000 attendees to the downtown area. The Cochecho Arts Festival, a summer-long concert series, provides a showcase for local and regional musicians.

Greater Dover Chamber of Commerce and Visitor Center: 550 Central Ave., Dover, NH 03820. **Phone:** (603) 742-2218.

CHILDREN'S MUSEUM OF NEW HAMPSHIRE, 6 Washington St., has an assortment of hands-on exhibits. Youngsters can command a yellow submarine, build and test flying machines, learn about life in the mills and experience a music matrix where they can visualize sound waves. **Time:** Allow 1 hour minimum. **Hours:** Tues.-Sat. 10-5 (also Mon. 10-5 during summer, holidays and school vacations), Sun. noon-5. **Cost:** $10; $9 (ages 65+); free (under 1). **Phone:** (603) 742-2002.

COMFORT INN & SUITES   (603)750-7507
♦♦♦ Hotel. **Address:** 10 Hotel Dr 03820

HAMPTON INN   (603)516-5600

♦♦♦♦
Hotel
$159-$269

AAA Benefit: Members save 5% or more!

Address: 9 Hotel Dr 03820 **Location:** SR 16 exit 9, 0.4 mi ne. **Facility:** 93 units. 3 stories, interior corridors. **Terms:** 1-7 night minimum stay, cancellation fee imposed. **Pool:** heated indoor. **Activities:** exercise room. **Guest Services:** valet and coin laundry, area transportation.

SAVE 🛏 CALL 🖫 🛳 🗖 BIZ
HS 📶 ✕ 🖬 🖼 🖵

HOMEWOOD SUITES BY HILTON DOVER   603/516-0929
♦♦♦ Extended Stay Hotel. **Address:** 21 Members Way 03820

AAA Benefit: Members save 5% or more!

WEATHERVANE SEAFOOD RESTAURANT   603/749-2341
♦♦ Seafood. Casual Dining. **Address:** 2 Dover Point Rd 03820

DURHAM (F-5) pop. 10,345, elev. 81'

Settled in 1635 and separated from Dover in 1732, historic Durham was the home of Maj. Gen. John Sullivan, a Revolutionary War hero and three-time governor of New Hampshire.

A tablet marks the site of the old meetinghouse where, in 1774, Sullivan and his band of Durham patriots supposedly stored the gunpowder they had taken from the British at Fort William and Mary in New Castle *(see place listing p. 119).* Although the British attempted to retrieve the gunpowder, the shallow river halted their frigate at Portsmouth.

The ensuing century of rural and maritime activity ended in 1893. A bequest to the state removed the College of Agriculture and Mechanical Arts (which

later became the University of New Hampshire) from Hanover, where it had been founded in association with Dartmouth College in 1866, to Durham. University and community quickly blended, and Durham assumed its role as a college town. The university's Paul Creative Arts Center is a focus for cultural activities; phone (603) 862-7222 for the ticket office.

HOLIDAY INN EXPRESS DURHAM-UNH   603/868-1234
♦♦♦ Hotel. **Address:** 2 Main 03824.

THREE CHIMNEYS INN   603/868-7800
♦♦♦ Historic Country Inn. **Address:** 17 Newmarket Rd 03824

ENFIELD (E-2) pop. 1,540, elev. 760'

In 1782 two Shaker brothers from Mount Lebanon, N.Y., came to a village in the rolling woodlands near the eastern shore of Lake Mascoma. With others they formed the society that led to the establishment of Enfield, one of 19 Shaker communities to flourish in the United States. In 1793 they moved to the west side of the lake, where a permanent settlement was built.

The Enfield Shakers numbered 330 in the 1850s, but entries into the celibate order declined steadily after the Civil War. The last 10 members moved to the Canterbury society *(see Canterbury Shaker Village attraction listing p. 105)* in 1923.

ENFIELD SHAKER MUSEUM, 447 SR 4A, is a restored 19th-century village dedicated to preserving the legacy of the Enfield Shakers. A self-guiding walking tour includes the herb, production and community gardens; the 1854 Cow Barn; the stone mill, feast grounds and cemetery; the Great Stone Dwelling; the Ministry East/West Brethren Shops; the Mary Keane Chapel; and the laundry and dairy complex. A tour guide is available in the Great Stone Dwelling. Museum displays include Shaker artifacts and furniture. **Time:** Allow 1 hour minimum. **Hours:** Mon.-Sat. 10-5, Sun. noon-5, May 1-late Dec. Last admission 1 hour before closing. Closed major holidays. Phone ahead to confirm schedule. **Cost:** $12; $8 (ages 11-17); $3 (ages 6-10). Prices may vary; phone ahead. **Phone:** (603) 632-4346.

EXETER (F-5) pop. 9,242, elev. 58'

Behind the peaceful charm of Exeter at the falls of the Squamscott River lies a history of outspoken dissent. The settlement was begun in 1638 by the Rev. John Wheelwright, whose radical views and religious nonconformity led to his expulsion from Boston. Wheelwright's individualism seemed to set the tone for the community, for revolutionary attitudes and politics were characteristic from the outset.

Exeter citizenry defied Royal commands, flouted talk of liberty and burned in effigy British lords Bute and North. When the war began, it was natural that the capital was moved from Tory-controlled Portsmouth to this Patriot stronghold.

Exeter is a mixture of industry and academia; Phillips Exeter Academy, a distinguished secondary school, was founded in 1781 and has conducted classes since 1783. Another link to the town's past is its architectural heritage, which is preserved with pride.

Every October, more than 50 brewers and 20 restaurants satisfy taste buds at the Powder Keg Beer and Chili Festival; phone (603) 772-2411.

Exeter Area Chamber of Commerce: 24 Front St., Unit 101, Exeter, NH 03833. **Phone:** (603) 772-2411.

THE EXETER INN   603/772-5901
▼▼▼▼ Historic Boutique Country Inn. **Address:** 90 Front St 03833

FAIRFIELD INN & SUITES BY MARRIOTT   (603)772-7411

Hotel
$78-$315

Fairfield **AAA Benefit:** Members save 5% or more!

Address: 138 Portsmouth Ave 03833 **Location:** SR 101 exit 11, just s. **Facility:** 71 units. 3 stories, interior corridors. **Terms:** cancellation fee imposed. **Pool:** heated indoor. **Activities:** exercise room. **Guest Services:** valet and coin laundry.

SAVE ECO ▮+▮ CALL ⬧ ⬧ ⬧
BIZ HS 🛜 ✕ ⬧ ⬧ ⬧

HAMPTON INN & SUITES BY HILTON   603/658-5555
▼▼▼ Hotel. **Address:** 59 Portsmouth Ave 03833

AAA Benefit: Members save 5% or more!

INN BY THE BANDSTAND   (603)772-6352
▼▼▼▼ ▼▼▼▼
Historic Country Inn
$199-$429

Address: 6 Front St 03833 **Location:** Center; across from Bandstand. **Facility:** Built in 1809, this stately Federal-style property blends luxury comforts with historic designs. A few parking spaces are located behind the inn, accessed via the Water St. Municipal parking lot. 8 units. 3 stories (no elevator), interior corridors. **Terms:** 15 day cancellation notice-fee imposed. **Featured Amenity:** full hot breakfast.

SAVE ⬧ ⬧ 🛜 ✕ ☎ ⬧
/SOME UNITS ⬧ ⬧ ⬧

WHERE TO EAT

EPOCH RESTAURANT & BAR   603/778-3762
▼▼▼ Regional American. Casual Dining. **Address:** 90 Front St 03833

THE GREEN BEAN   603/778-7585
▼ Sandwiches Soup. Quick Serve. **Address:** 33 Water St 03833

FRANCONIA (C-3) elev. 990'

In June Franconia hosts the ▼▼ Celebration of Lupines, featuring afternoon teas, sporting events, arts and crafts, horse-drawn wagon rides and tours of historic homes and gardens.

BEST WESTERN WHITE MOUNTAIN INN   (603)823-7422

Hotel
$100-$225

Best Western. **AAA Benefit:** Members save up to 15% and earn bonus points!

Address: 87 Wallace Hill Rd 03580 **Location:** I-93 exit 38, just e. **Facility:** 60 units. 2 stories (no elevator), interior corridors. **Terms:** 3 day cancellation notice-fee imposed. **Pool:** heated indoor. **Activities:** hot tub, exercise room. **Guest Services:** coin laundry.

SAVE ⬧ ⬧ BIZ 🛜 ✕ ⬧
⬧ ⬧ /SOME UNITS ⬧

LOVETTS INN BY LAFAYETTE BROOK   603/823-7761
▼▼▼ Historic Country Inn. **Address:** 1474 Profile Rd 03580

WHERE TO EAT

FRANCONIA INN   603/823-5542
▼▼▼ Regional American. Casual Dining. **Address:** 1172 Easton Rd (Rt 116) 03580

FRANCONIA NOTCH (C-4) elev. 1,821'

Franconia Notch is perhaps the most celebrated mountain gap in the East. A gap between the towering Kinsman and Franconia ranges, it has more scenic spots than any other White Mountain notch. It is crossed by I-93 from Echo Lake, southwest of Twin Mountain, to Lincoln.

The grandeur of the notch most likely was first seen by white settlers in the late 18th century. Its fame spread quickly, and by the mid-1800s it was a favorite tourist destination, with huge hotels to accommodate a plethora of visitors. Although the hotels no longer exist, throngs of visitors continue to enjoy the area's scenic and recreational aspects, many of which are within Franconia Notch State Park *(see Recreation Areas Chart)*.

Echo Lake is bounded by mountains on three sides. Named for the acoustical phenomenon resulting from its setting, the lake is the largest body of water in the notch and offers boating, fishing and swimming. The beach is open daily 9-6, mid-June through Labor Day; Fri.-Sun. and Memorial Day 9-6, late May to mid-June; Fri.-Sun 9-5, day after Labor Day-Columbus Day.

Franconia Notch Regional Chamber of Commerce: 421 Main St., P.O. Box 755, Franconia, NH 03580. **Phone:** (603) 823-5661.

▼GEM **CANNON MOUNTAIN AERIAL TRAMWAY,** off I-93 exit 34B, extends from Valley Station to the top of Cannon Mountain. During the summer, when this popular ski mountain isn't buried in snow and swarming with skiers and snowboarders, you can hop aboard an 80-passenger aerial tram car that will whisk you to the summit where you can enjoy spectacular views of the surrounding mountains and valleys of Franconia Notch State Park and the White Mountain National Forest. Foot trails lead from the observation platform to overlooks from which, on a clear day, you can see four states and the province of Québec.

The current tramway, inaugurated in 1980, is the second to operate on this breathtaking spot. Its predecessor is said to have been the first aerial tram in North America, having made its first trip up to the 4,080-foot-high summit back in 1938.

RV campsites are available. **Time:** Allow 1 hour minimum. **Hours:** Daily 8:30-5:30, mid-May to mid-Oct. (weather permitting). **Cost:** Round-trip $19; $16 (ages 6-12). One-way trip $15. **Phone:** (603) 823-8800. 🔺 🍴

THE FLUME GORGE, 852 Daniel Webster Hwy. (SR 3), at the s. end of Franconia Notch State Park, is a chasm extending nearly 800 feet along the flank of Mount Liberty. A mountain stream tumbles in a series of waterfalls and pools between its 60- to 90-foot-high granite walls. An optional shuttle bus takes visitors the first half-mile; it is then a 1.5-mile walk through the flume back to the visitor center. A well-constructed boardwalk leads through the gorge; there are, however, some steep grades. Within the flume are two covered bridges, waterfalls and cascades.

Time: Allow 1 hour minimum. **Hours:** Daily 8:30-5, early May-late Oct. Phone ahead to confirm schedule. **Cost:** $16; $13 (ages 6-12). Prices may vary; phone ahead. **Phone:** (603) 745-8391.

GILFORD   elev. 738'

FIRESIDE INN & SUITES	603/293-7526
♦♦ Hotel. **Address:** 17 Harris Shore Rd 03249	
THE INN AT SMITH COVE	(603)293-1111
♦♦♦ Country Inn. **Address:** 19 Roberts Rd 03249	

WHERE TO EAT

LYONS' DEN RESTAURANT & TAVERN	603/293-8833
♦♦ American. Casual Dining. **Address:** 25 Dock Rd 03249	
PATRICK'S PUB & EATERY	603/293-0841
♦♦ Irish. Casual Dining. **Address:** 18 Weirs Rd 03249	

GLEN   (D-4) elev. 544'
• Hotels & Restaurants map & index p. 121

An access point to both Franconia Notch *(see place listing p. 109)* and Pinkham Notch *(see place listing p. 126),* Glen is an important link in the chain of communities in the Mount Washington Valley. Nearby ski areas include a large cross-country skiing center.

COVERED BRIDGE HOUSE	(603)383-9109	29
♦♦♦ Historic Bed & Breakfast. **Address:** 404 US 302 03838		
GOLDEN APPLE INN	603/383-9680	28
♦♦♦ Motel. **Address:** 322 US 302 03838		

WHERE TO EAT

WHITE MOUNTAIN CIDER CO.	603/383-9061	30
♦♦♦ American. Fine Dining. **Address:** 207 US 302 03838		

GORHAM   pop. 1,600, elev. 801'

A gateway to the Great North Woods, Gorham is home to several miles of scenic and challenging trails, including a section of the Appalachian Trail.

MOOSE BROOK MOTEL	(603)466-5400
♦ Motel. **Address:** 65 Lancaster Rd 03581	
ROYALTY INN	(603)466-3312
♦ Hotel. **Address:** 130 Main St 03581	
TOP NOTCH INN	603/466-5496
♦♦ Motel. **Address:** 265 Main St 03581	
TOWN & COUNTRY INN & RESORT	603/466-3315
♦♦ Classic Hotel. **Address:** 20 US 2 03581	

WHERE TO EAT

J'S CORNER RESTAURANT & LOUNGE	603/466-5132
♦♦ American. Casual Dining. **Address:** 277 Main St 03581	

MARY'S PIZZA	603/752-6150

♦♦ Italian Casual Dining $8-$18	**AAA Inspector Notes:** *Classic.* Established in 1947, this third-generation family diner specializes in award-winning pizzas and homemade pasta dishes. Fettuccine Alfredo, spaghetti with white clam sauce, linguine and manicotti are available in both small and large por-

tions. **Features:** beer & wine, senior menu. **Address:** 9 Cascade Flats 03581 **Location:** 3.5 mi n on SR 16 from jct US 2; 2 mi s on SR 16 from jct SR 110. L D

MR. PIZZA FAMILY RESTAURANT & CRACKER JACK LOUNGE	603/466-5573
♦♦ American. Casual Dining. **Address:** 160 Main St 03581	
TOWN & COUNTRY INN & RESORT DINING ROOM	603/466-3315
♦♦ American. Casual Dining. **Address:** 20 SR 2 03581	
YOKOHAMA RESTAURANT	603/466-2501
♦♦ Japanese. Casual Dining. **Address:** 288 Main St 03581	

HAMPTON   (F-5) pop. 9,656, elev. 52'

One of New Hampshire's earliest towns, Hampton was settled in 1638. The town first was called the Plantation of Winnacunnet. *Winnacunnet* is an Abenaki Indian word meaning "pleasant pines." The first tax-supported public school was established in Winnacunnet in 1649 for the education of both boys and girls. The Tuck Museum on Meeting House Green, 40 Park Ave., depicts facets of Hampton's history; phone (603) 929-0781. Across from the Green, Founders Park contains 42 stones representing the town's earliest families.

Nearby Hampton Beach buzzes with activity during the summer, reeling in tourists with its countless water activities, weekly fireworks shows, free evening concerts and fun annual events. The biggest event is the 🦞 Hampton Beach Seafood Festival, an extravaganza of food and crafts held on the beach the weekend after Labor Day. In June, talented sand artists participate in the Master Sand Sculpting Competition.

Hampton Area Chamber of Commerce: 1 Lafayette Rd., Hampton, NH 03842. **Phone:** (603) 926-8718, or (603) 926-8717 for the visitor center at Hampton Beach.

LAMIE'S INN   603/926-0330
♥♥♥ Historic Country Inn. **Address:** 490 Lafayette Rd 03842

SPRINGHILL SUITES BY MARRIOTT HAMPTON
PORTSMOUTH   603/910-5600
♥♥♥ Hotel. **Address:** 299 Exeter
Rd 03842

AAA Benefit:
Members save 5%
or more!

THE VICTORIA INN   603/929-1437
♥♥♥ Classic Bed & Breakfast. **Address:** 430 High St 03842

WHERE TO EAT

THE GALLEY HATCH RESTAURANT & KAY'S KAFE
                                                603/926-6152
♥♥ American. Casual Dining. **Address:** 325 Lafayette Rd 03842

OLD SALT EATING & DRINKING PLACE   603/926-8322
♥♥ American. Casual Dining. **Address:** 490 Lafayette Rd 03842

RON'S LANDING AT ROCKY BEND   603/929-2122
♥♥ Seafood. Casual Dining. **Address:** 379 Ocean Blvd 03842

HAMPTON BEACH pop. 2,275

ASHWORTH BY THE SEA HOTEL   603/926-6762
♥♥ Classic Hotel. **Address:** 295 Ocean Blvd 03842

HANOVER (E-2) pop. 8,636, elev. 603'

When Rev. Eleazar Wheelock arrived in Hanover to establish the school that was to be an experiment in spreading Christian education to the Abenaki Indians and other youth, he found a staid agricultural village of about 20 families. The purpose of the school failed so Wheelock enlarged it to include a college for the education of whites in the classics, philosophy and literature. In 1769 and despite objections from Lord Dartmouth, the head of the British Board of Trustees, Wheelock named the school Dartmouth College. The community and the college quickly established a symbiotic relationship that continues to the present, each growing and prospering with the other.

Hanover Area Chamber of Commerce: 53 S. Main St., Suite 208, P.O. Box 5105, Hanover, NH 03755. **Phone:** (603) 643-3115.

THE HANOVER INN DARTMOUTH   (603)643-4300

♥♥♥ ♥♥♥
Historic Boutique Hotel
$199-$729

Address: 2 E Wheelock St 03755 **Location:** Center. **Facility:** This renowned, 18th-century hotel's historic pedigree stands in stark contrast to its modern appointments. It successfully blends the old with the new throughout. Rooms offer solid wood furniture. 108 units. 5 stories, interior corridors. **Parking:** valet only. **Amenities:** safes. **Activities:** exercise room. **Guest Services:** valet laundry.

SIX SOUTH ST HOTEL HANOVER   603/643-0600
♥♥♥ Hotel. **Address:** 6 South St 03755

WHERE TO EAT

JESSE'S   603/643-4111
♥♥ Steak Seafood. Casual Dining. **Address:** 224 Lebanon St 03755

LOU'S RESTAURANT & BAKERY   603/643-3321
♥♥ Breakfast Breads/Pastries. Casual Dining. **Address:** 30 Main St 03755

MOLLY'S RESTAURANT & BAR   603/643-2570
♥♥ American. Casual Dining. **Address:** 43 S Main St 03755

TUK TUK THAI CUISINE   603/277-9192
♥♥ Thai. Casual Dining. **Address:** 5 S Main St 03755

HILLSBOROUGH (F-3) pop. 1,976, elev. 580'

Hillsborough comprises several villages that feature Early American architecture, some of which is pre-Revolutionary. Stone arch bridges, built 1830-60 by Scottish stonemasons, are made from locally excavated granite. The town also was the home of the 14th president of the United States, Franklin Pierce.

Fox State Forest, on Center Road 2 miles north, covers 1,445 wooded acres. Its 20 miles of hiking paths become cross-country ski trails in winter; snowshoeing and snowmobiling also are available. Information about local plants and wildlife is available at headquarters; phone (603) 464-3453.

Greater Hillsborough Area Chamber of Commerce: 3 School St., P.O. Box 541, Hillsborough, NH 03244. **Phone:** (603) 464-5858.

Self-guiding tours: Maps for a walking tour of homes in the historic district are available at the chamber of commerce.

HOLDERNESS

THE MANOR ON GOLDEN POND   (603)968-3348

**Historic
Country Inn
$235-$510**

Address: 31 Manor Dr 03245 **Location:** I-93 exit 24, 4.5 mi e on US 3. **Facility:** Located on a knoll overlooking Squam Lake, this English-style mansion is graced with lovely grounds and some private cottages. Some suites have a fireplace or a hot tub. Tea is served at 4 p.m. daily. 24 units. 1-3 stories (no elevator), interior/exterior corridors. **Terms:** 2 night minimum stay - seasonal and/or weekends, 30 day cancellation notice-fee imposed. **Dining:** The Manor on Golden Pond-Van Horn Dining Room, see separate listing. **Pool:** heated outdoor. **Activities:** tennis, spa. **Guest Services:** valet laundry. **Featured Amenity: full hot breakfast.**

WHERE TO EAT

THE MANOR ON GOLDEN POND-VAN HORN DINING ROOM
603/968-3348

**New
American
Fine Dining
$24-$40**

AAA Inspector Notes: *Historic.* The Manor's delectable cuisine offers a variety of fresh, savory entrées that are artistically presented and wonderfully flavorful, with a hint of French influence. The décor is elegant and relaxed; service is superb. **Features:** full bar, patio dining. **Reservations:** required. **Address:** 31 Manor Dr 03245 **Location:** I-93 exit 24, 4.5 mi e on US 3; in The Manor on Golden Pond. [D]

WALTER'S BASIN   603/968-4412
American. Casual Dining. **Address:** 859 US Rt 3 03245

HOOKSETT pop. 4,147

FAIRFIELD INN & SUITES BY MARRIOTT HOOKSETT
(603)606-5485
Hotel. **Address:** 8 Bell Ave 03106

AAA Benefit:
Members save 5% or more!

JACKSON (C-4) elev. 764'
• Hotels & Restaurants map & index p. 121

The village of Jackson, nestled between several mountain peaks in the White Mountain National Forest, offers visitors numerous year-round recreational opportunities in a picturesque setting.

Jackson Area Chamber of Commerce: 18 Main St., P.O. Box 304, Jackson, NH 03846. **Phone:** (603) 383-9356.

INN AT ELLIS RIVER   (603)383-9339   21
Bed & Breakfast. **Address:** 17 Harriman Rd 03846

THE INN AT THORN HILL AND SPA   (603)383-4242   24

**Country Inn
$99-$450**

Address: 40 Thorn Hill Rd 03846 **Location:** Off SR 16A. **Facility:** The main inn has 16 luxurious guest rooms that feature gas fireplaces. Also offered are three pleasant cottages. 19 units, some cottages. 3 stories, interior corridors. **Terms:** 2 night minimum stay - weekends, 14 day cancellation notice-fee imposed. **Dining:** The Inn at Thorn Hill, see separate listing. **Activities:** sauna, cross country skiing, snowmobiling, trails, spa. **Guest Services:** valet laundry. **Featured Amenity: full hot breakfast.**

THE LODGE AT JACKSON VILLAGE   603/383-0999   22
Hotel. **Address:** 153 SR 16 03846

NORDIC VILLAGE RESORT & SUITES   603/383-9101   25
Resort Condominium. **Address:** SR 16 03846

THE SNOWFLAKE INN   603/383-8259   20
Bed & Breakfast. **Address:** 95 Main St (SR 16A) 03846

WHERE TO EAT

HIGHFIELDS RESTAURANT   603/383-9111   22
American. Casual Dining. **Address:** 179 Carter Notch Rd 03846

THE INN AT THORN HILL   603/383-4242   26
Regional American. Fine Dining. **Address:** 40 Thorn Hill Rd 03846

RED FOX BAR & GRILLE   603/383-4949   27
American. Casual Dining. **Address:** 49 New Hampshire (SR 16) 03846

THE WENTWORTH DINING ROOM   603/383-9700   23
Regional American. Fine Dining. **Address:** 1 Carter Notch Rd 03846

THE WILDCAT INN & TAVERN   603/383-4245   25
New American. Casual Dining. **Address:** 94 Main St 03846

YESTERDAYS OF JACKSON VILLAGE   603/383-4457   24
American. Casual Dining. **Address:** 100 SR 16A (Main St) 03846

JEFFERSON (C-4) elev. 1,400'

Known locally as Jefferson Hill, Jefferson is primarily a summer resort community. From high on the flank of Mount Starr King, it commands a wide view of the Israel River Valley and the White Mountains southwest to the Franconias.

A marker just west on US 2 commemorates inventor and pioneer aeronaut Thaddeus S.C. Lowe, born nearby in 1823. During the Civil War Lowe organized and directed a Union balloon force; later he invented several important devices for use in atmospheric observation and metallurgical processing.

THE LANTERN RESORT   603/586-7151
Motel. **Address:** 571 Presidential Hwy 03583

KEENE (F-2) pop. 23,409, elev. 496'

The 1762 Wyman Tavern, 339 Main St., is one of Keene's important early buildings. In 1770 the well-known inn was the scene of the first meeting of the trustees of Dartmouth College; 5 years later Capt. Isaac Wyman led 29 Minutemen from the tavern to Lexington at the onset of the Revolutionary War. The Historical Society of Cheshire County offers seasonal tours of the tavern; phone (603) 352-1895.

Keene's industrial future was cast during the 19th century when the city became known for the production of glass and pottery. Henry Schoolcraft's flint glass bottles have become collectors' items, as has the white pottery made 1871-1926 by the Hampshire Pottery.

The Keene State College Redfern Arts Center on Brickyard Pond is the locale of plays, concerts and recitals during the academic year; phone (603) 358-2168. The restored Colonial Theatre at 95 Main St. features plays, concerts and opera as well as movies; phone (603) 357-1233.

Six covered bridges can be found on side roads off SR 10 between Keene and Winchester. Three of these bridges span the Ashuelot River: south of SR 119 at Ashuelot; east of SR 10 at West Swanzey; and a mile north of SR 32 at Swanzey Village. Still another covered bridge crosses the South Branch of the Ashuelot River east of SR 32, a half-mile south of Swanzey Village.

Greater Keene Chamber of Commerce: 48 Central Sq., Keene, NH 03431. **Phone:** (603) 352-1303.

Shopping: The Colony Mill Marketplace, 222 West St., is a restored woolen mill that contains a group of shops. On Main Street, visitors can find boutiques, art shops and locally owned restaurants.

BEST WESTERN PLUS KEENE HOTEL   (603)357-3038

♦♦
Hotel
$109-$300

Best Western PLUS

AAA Benefit: Members save up to 15% and earn bonus points!

Address: 401 Winchester St 03431 **Location:** SR 10, just s of jct SR 12 and 101. **Facility:** 122 units. 2 stories, interior corridors. **Terms:** cancellation fee imposed. **Pool:** heated indoor. **Activities:** exercise room. **Guest Services:** coin laundry. **Featured Amenity:** breakfast buffet.

 HS

COURTYARD BY MARRIOTT KEENE DOWNTOWN
(603)354-7900

♦♦♦ Hotel. **Address:** 75 Railroad St 03431

AAA Benefit: Members save 5% or more!

FAIRFIELD INN & SUITES BY MARRIOTT KEENE DOWNTOWN
(603)357-7070

♦♦♦ Historic Hotel. **Address:** 30 Main St 03431

AAA Benefit: Members save 5% or more!

HOLIDAY INN EXPRESS   603/352-7616

♦♦♦
Hotel
Rates not provided

Address: 175 Key Rd 03431 **Location:** SR 101, just n, via Winchester St, then 0.3 mi w. Located in a business park. **Facility:** 80 units. 2 stories, interior corridors. **Pool:** heated indoor. **Activities:** exercise room. **Guest Services:** coin laundry. **Featured Amenity:** continental breakfast.

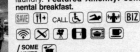

WHERE TO EAT

ELM CITY BREWING COMPANY   603/355-3335
♦♦ American. Gastropub. **Address:** 222 West St 03431

KINSMAN NOTCH (D-3) elev. 1,863'

Rather than turn back when he found that he had taken the wrong road en route to a land grant at Landaff, pioneer Asa Kinsman, his wife and two Woodstock townsmen hacked their way through the rugged intervening miles to their destination. Thus was traversed—and named—Kinsman Notch, a pass between Mount Moosilauke and the Kinsman Range.

Kinsman, like the other White Mountain notches, was deepened and widened by the Pleistocene ice sheet. As the glaciers melted and frost weakened the fractures in the north face of the notch, huge blocks of granite plunged into Lost River Gorge to form the narrow passages among which the river gets lost.

LACONIA (E-4) pop. 15,951, elev. 507'
• Restaurants p. 114

A log cabin, the first structure on the site of Laconia, was probably erected in 1766. Before then the presence of Sachem Indians had prevented settlement, although the area had been granted as early as 1727. Growth was slow until the railroad reached the community—then called Meredith Bridge—in 1848. Thereafter mills and factories proliferated, and Laconia became a trading and manufacturing center.

Paugus Bay and lakes Winnisquam and Opechee extend into Laconia's city limits, bringing opportunities for water sports. About 5 miles north is Lake Winnipesaukee, the largest lake in the state and a major resort center (see Weirs Beach p. 133).

Cultural activities are presented at the Belknap Mill, a noted center for arts and humanities. Outdoor concerts are presented in spring and summer at the grandstand next to Belknap Mill.

Lakes Region Chamber of Commerce: 383 S. Main St., Laconia, NH 03246. **Phone:** (603) 524-5531.

BAY TOP MOTEL   (603)366-2225
♦ Motel. **Address:** 1025 Weirs Blvd 03246

BIRCH KNOLL MOTEL   (603)366-4958
♦ Motel. **Address:** 867 Weirs Blvd 03247

WHERE TO EAT

FRATELLO'S ITALIAN GRILLE   603/528-2022
 Italian. Casual Dining. **Address:** 799 Union Ave 03246

WATER STREET CAFE   603/524-4144
 American. Casual Dining. **Address:** 141 Water St 03246

LANCASTER (C-4) pop. 1,725, elev. 887'

Charming old houses create an atmosphere of the past in this busy trading center, settled in 1764 as the first town in northern New Hampshire. Its setting at the confluence of the Israel and Connecticut rivers is enhanced by the serrated Pilot Range to the northeast and the Presidential Range to the southeast. Abundant recreational activities are available, including hiking, biking, camping, fishing, hunting, skiing and snowmobiling.

Lancaster is a waypoint along the Connecticut River Byway, a scenic, 500-mile route that traverses through more than 50 communities on both sides of the Connecticut River in New Hampshire and Vermont. Brochures and information are available at the Great North Woods Welcome Center (closed in winter), 25 Park St; phone (603) 788-3212.

Northern Gateway Chamber of Commerce: 25 Park St., P.O. Box 537, Lancaster, NH 03584. **Phone:** (603) 788-2530 or (877) 788-2530.

LEBANON pop. 13,151

COURTYARD BY MARRIOTT HANOVER LEBANON
(603)643-5600

ᗺᗺᗺ
Hotel
$89-$421

COURTYARD® **AAA Benefit:** Members save 5% or more!

Address: 10 Morgan Dr 03766 **Location:** I-89 exit 18, 2 mi n on SR 120 exit Centerra Pkwy, then s. **Facility:** 124 units. 4 stories, interior corridors. **Terms:** cancellation fee imposed. **Pool:** heated indoor. **Activities:** hot tub, exercise room. **Guest Services:** valet and coin laundry, boarding pass kiosk, area transportation.

 ⊞ ⊠ CALL ♿ ⇄

⇄ BIZ HS 📶 ✕ 🔒 ⊟ ▭

ELEMENT BY WESTIN HANOVER-LEBANON
(603)448-5000

ᗺᗺᗺ
Extended Stay
Contemporary
Hotel
$100-$362

AAA Benefit: Members save 5% or more!

Address: 25 Foothill St 03766 **Location:** I-89 exit 18, 1.8 mi n on SR 120, e on Altaria Park, then just n. **Facility:** 120 efficiencies. 5 stories, interior corridors. *Bath:* shower only. **Terms:** cancellation fee imposed. **Amenities:** safes. **Pool:** heated indoor. **Activities:** bicycles, exercise room. **Guest Services:** valet and coin laundry, area transportation. **Featured Amenity: continental breakfast.**

⊞ ⊠ ⊞ CALL ♿ ⇄ ⇄ BIZ HS 📶 ✕

🔒 ⊟ ▭ / SOME UNITS 🐾

HILTON GARDEN INN HANOVER LEBANON
603/448-3300

ᗺᗺᗺ Hotel. **Address:** 35 Lombard Rd 03766

AAA Benefit: Members save 5% or more!

RESIDENCE INN BY MARRIOTT HANOVER LEBANON
(603)643-4511

ᗺᗺᗺᗺ
Extended Stay
Hotel
$109-$454

Residence INN. **AAA Benefit:** Members save 5% or more!

Address: 32 Centerra Pkwy 03766 **Location:** I-89 exit 18, 2.5 mi n on SR 120. **Facility:** 114 units, some two bedrooms, efficiencies and kitchens. 3 stories, interior corridors. **Parking:** winter plug-ins. **Terms:** cancellation fee imposed. **Activities:** exercise room. **Guest Services:** valet and coin laundry, area transportation. **Featured Amenity: breakfast buffet.**

⊞ ⊞ ⊞ CALL ♿ 🖐 BIZ 📶 ✕ 🔒 ⊟

▭ / SOME UNITS 🐾

LINCOLN (D-3) pop. 993, elev. 808'

Lincoln is the western terminus of one of the state's most popular scenic drives, the Kancamagus Highway *(see attraction listing p. 135)*. With North Woodstock, its sister community across the Pemigewasset River, Lincoln serves those who visit the nearby recreational developments. The North Country Center for the Arts offers year-round productions at Jean's Playhouse; phone (603) 745-6032 for information or (603) 745-2141 for tickets.

In September the ᗺ New Hampshire Highland Games, featuring Scottish music, dancing and athletic competitions, is held at Loon Mountain Resort.

BLUEGREEN VACATIONS SOUTH MOUNTAIN, AN ASCEND RESORT COLLECTION MEMBER
(603)745-9300

ᗺᗺᗺ Hotel. **Address:** 23 Innseason Dr 03251

ECONO LODGE INN & SUITES
(603)745-3661

ᗺᗺ
Motel
$89-$389

Address: 381 US Rt 3 03251 **Location:** I-93 exit 33 (US 3), 0.3 mi ne. **Facility:** 51 units, some two bedrooms. 1-2 stories (no elevator), interior/exterior corridors. **Terms:** check-in 4 pm, resort fee. **Pool:** outdoor, heated indoor. **Activities:** sauna, hot tub, exercise room. **Guest Services:** coin laundry. **Featured Amenity: continental breakfast.**

⊞ ⊞ ⊠ 🖐 📶 ✕ 🔒

▭ / SOME UNITS

THE MOUNTAIN CLUB ON LOON   603/745-2244
ᗺᗺᗺ Resort Hotel. **Address:** 90 Loon Mountain Rd 03251

MOUNT COOLIDGE MOTEL   603/745-8052
ᗺ Motel. **Address:** 386 US 3 03251

NORDIC INN CONDOMINIUM RESORT   (603)745-2230
ᗺᗺ Condominium. **Address:** 227 Main St 03251

RIVERGREEN RESORT HOTEL & CONDIMINIUMS AT LOON MOUNTAIN   603/745-2450
ᗺᗺ Hotel. **Address:** 48 Cooper Memorial Dr 03251

RODEWAY INN   (603)745-2267

Motel
$65-$254

Address: 417 US Rt 3 03251 **Location:** I-93 exit 33 (US 3), 0.5 mi ne. **Facility:** 30 units. 2 stories (no elevator), exterior corridors. **Terms:** check-in 4 pm. **Pool:** heated outdoor. **Guest Services:** coin laundry. **Featured Amenity:** continental breakfast.

• Hotels p. 116 • Restaurants p. 117

WHERE TO EAT

BLACK MTN. BURGER CO.   603/745-3444
Burgers. Casual Dining. **Address:** 264 Main St 03251

CHIENG GARDENS   603/745-8612
Chinese. Casual Dining. **Address:** 165 Main St 03251

THE COMMON MAN   603/745-3463
Regional American. Casual Dining. **Address:** 10 Pollard Rd 03251

GORDI'S FISH & STEAK HOUSE   603/745-6635
Steak. Casual Dining. **Address:** 260 Main St 03251

GYPSY CAFÉ   603/745-4395
International. Casual Dining. **Address:** 117 Main St 03251

LITTLETON (C-3) pop. 4,412, elev. 875'

Prior to the Civil War Littleton was a station on the branch of the Underground Railroad that led northward to Vermont and Canada. It is now better known as a resort center and stopover for travelers bound for the White Mountains.

The Ammonoosuc River's 235-foot descent through Littleton was the catalyst for the city's transformation into a manufacturing and commercial center. The job of energy production now falls to Moore Station, a hydroelectric plant on the Connecticut River, 8 miles west on SR 18. One of New England's largest such projects, it impounds Moore Reservoir (see Recreation Areas Chart).

Littleton Area Chamber of Commerce: 107 Main St., Littleton, NH 03561. **Phone:** (603) 444-6561.

Self-guiding tours: A free brochure describing a walking tour of 22 historic sites along Main Street is available from the chamber of commerce.

COUNTRY SQUIRE MOTEL   (603)444-5610
Motel. **Address:** 172 W Main St 03561

EXIT 41 TRAVEL INN   603/259-3085
Motel. **Address:** 337 Cottage St 03561

HAMPTON INN BY HILTON LITTLETON   603/444-0025
Hotel. **Address:** 580 Meadow St 03561

AAA Benefit: Members save 5% or more!

LITTLETON MOTEL   (603)444-5780
Motel. **Address:** 166 Main St 03561

WHERE TO EAT

ASIAN GARDEN RESTAURANT   603/444-9888
Asian. Casual Dining. **Address:** 551 Meadow St 03561

CHANG THAI CAFE   603/444-8810
Traditional Thai Sushi Vegetarian. Casual Dining. **Address:** 77 Main St 03561

THE LITTLE GRILLE   603/444-0395
American. Casual Dining. **Address:** 62 Cottage St 03561

LITTLETON DINER   603/444-3994
Traditional Breakfast Comfort Food. Casual Dining. **Address:** 145 Main St 03561

MANCHESTER (F-4) pop. 109,565, elev. 210'
• Hotels p. 116 • Restaurants p. 117

Logging helped to sustain early settlers in Manchester, and by 1810 the first cotton and woolen mills were in operation. The village was on its way to becoming the American counterpart of its British namesake, then the largest textile producing city in the world. In 1831 a group of Boston financiers bailed out a struggling cotton mill called the Amoskeag Cotton and Woolen Factory and reincorporated it as the Amoskeag Manufacturing Co.

Nearly 5 million yards of cloth were shipped each week from the brick mills, which employed thousands of workers and covered more than 8 million square feet. The mills thrived until the 1920s when a combination of stresses on the industry such as obsolete machinery, labor unrest and strong competition from the South, sapped its strength. In 1935 Amoskeag filed for bankruptcy and the mills fell silent.

But Manchester was not doomed to obscurity. A group of local businessmen pooled $5 million, purchased the mile-long ranks of mills and reactivated them with a diversified array of industries. Manchester is the state's industrial giant as well as its largest city and the home of nearly 10 percent of its population.

Just as the mills and the company houses have new tenants, so does the fully restored 1915 Palace Theatre at 80 Hanover St. Known for its excellent acoustics and large stage, the theater hosts performances by the New Hampshire Philharmonic, the Opera League of New Hampshire and the theater's own professional company; phone (603) 668-5588.

Manchester also is noted for its association with Gen. John Stark, who was born in Londonderry in 1728 and moved with his family to Derryfield—now Manchester—when he was 8. Stark fought the Abenaki Indians with Maj. William Rogers and his Rogers' Rangers, a backwoods fighting team that is considered the forerunner of today's Army Rangers. Stark died in 1822, having outlived every Patriot general except Marquis de Lafayette. His childhood home stands at 2000 Elm St.; his grave is in Stark Park, off N. River Road overlooking the river.

Greater Manchester Chamber of Commerce: 54 Hanover St., Manchester, NH 03101. **Phone:** (603) 666-6600.

Shopping: The Mall of New Hampshire, 1500 S. Willow St., features JCPenney, Macy's and Sears. Elm Street and Hanover Street in downtown boast dozens of locally owned shops.

THE CURRIER MUSEUM OF ART, 150 Ash St., is in a 1929 Beaux Arts building reminiscent of an Italian Renaissance palace. A complementary modern addition was built in 2008.

The museum showcases an internationally respected collection of European and American paintings, sculpture and decorative arts from the 13th century to the present. The collection features more than 11,000 objects including works by Frank Stella, Edward Hopper, Winslow Homer, Henri Matisse, Claude Monet, Georgia O'Keeffe, Pablo Picasso and Andrew Wyeth. American furniture and works by New Hampshire artists and craftsmen also are on view. Changing exhibitions, lectures and concerts are offered.

Time: Allow 1 hour, 30 minutes minimum. **Hours:** Sun.-Mon. and Wed.-Fri. 11-5, Sat. 10-5. Closed Jan. 1, Easter, Memorial Day, July 4, Thanksgiving and Christmas. **Cost:** $15; $13 (ages 65+); $10 (students ages 18+ with ID); $5 (ages 13-17); free (ages 0-12 and to New Hampshire residents 2nd Sat. of the month 10-noon). Combination ticket with Zimmerman House $25; $24 (ages 65+); $16 (students with ID); $8 (ages 7-17). Ages 0-6 are not permitted on Zimmerman House tour. **Phone:** (603) 669-6144. ⊓

Zimmerman House is reached by van from The Currier Museum of Art, 150 Ash St. Frank Lloyd Wright designed the house, the interiors, all the furniture, the gardens and even the mailbox. Built for Isadore J. and Lucille Zimmerman in 1950, the structure is one of Wright's Usonian houses and is the only Wright home open to the public in New England.

Time: Allow 1 hour, 30 minutes minimum. **Hours:** Tours depart Thurs.-Mon. at 11:30 and 2, Apr.-Oct.; Mon. and Thurs.-Fri. at 2, Sat.-Sun. at 11:30 and 2, Nov. 1-early Jan. Closed Jan. 1, Easter, Memorial Day, July 4, Thanksgiving and Christmas. Phone ahead to confirm schedule. **Cost:** (Includes The Currier Museum of Art) $25; $24 (ages 65+); $16 (students with ID); $8 (ages 7-17). Ages 0-6 are not permitted on the tour. Reservations are required. **Phone:** (603) 669-6144. GT

SEE SCIENCE CENTER, 200 Bedford St., has interactive exhibits that focus on a variety of topics including electricity, momentum, light and gravity. The LEGO Millyard exhibit features more than 3 million LEGO bricks. **Time:** Allow 1 hour minimum. **Hours:** Mon.-Fri. 10-4, Sat.-Sun. 10-5. Closed major holidays. **Cost:** $9; free (ages 0-2). **Phone:** (603) 669-0400.

BEST WESTERN PLUS EXECUTIVE COURT INN & CONFERENCE CENTER (603)627-2525

Hotel
$110-$170

Best Western PLUS

AAA Benefit: Members save up to 15% and earn bonus points!

Address: 13500 S Willow St 03103 **Location:** I-293 exit 1, 0.5 mi s on SR 28, then 1 mi e. **Facility:** 134 units. 3 stories, interior corridors. **Terms:** cancellation fee imposed. **Amenities:** Some: safes. **Pool:** heated indoor. **Activities:** hot tub, game room, exercise room. **Guest Services:** valet and coin laundry, area transportation.

COMFORT INN (603)668-2600
🔶🔶 Hotel. **Address:** 298 Queen City Ave 03102

COURTYARD BY MARRIOTT MANCHESTER BOSTON REGIONAL AIRPORT (603)641-4900
🔶🔶🔶 Hotel. **Address:** 700 Huse Rd 03103
AAA Benefit: Members save 5% or more!

DOUBLETREE BY HILTON MANCHESTER DOWNTOWN 603/625-1000
🔶🔶🔶 Hotel. **Address:** 700 Elm St 03101
AAA Benefit: Members save 5% or more!

FAIRFIELD INN BY MARRIOTT MANCHESTER-BOSTON REGIONAL AIRPORT (603)625-2020
🔶🔶 Hotel. **Address:** 860 S Porter Ext 03103
AAA Benefit: Members save 5% or more!

HILTON GARDEN INN MANCHESTER DOWNTOWN 603/669-2222
🔶🔶🔶 Hotel. **Address:** 101 S Commercial St 03101
AAA Benefit: Members save 5% or more!

HOLIDAY INN EXPRESS HOTEL & SUITES-MANCHESTER AIRPORT 603/669-6800
🔶🔶🔶 Hotel. **Address:** 1298 S Porter St 03103

HOLIDAY INN MANCHESTER AIRPORT 603/641-6466
🔶🔶🔶 Hotel. **Address:** 2280 Brown Ave 03103

HOMEWOOD SUITES BY HILTON 603/668-2200
🔶🔶🔶 Extended Stay Hotel. **Address:** 1000 Perimeter Rd 03103
AAA Benefit: Members save 5% or more!

LA QUINTA INN & SUITES MANCHESTER (603)669-5400
🔶🔶🔶 Hotel. **Address:** 21 Front St 03102

SPRINGHILL SUITES BY MARRIOTT MANCHESTER-BOSTON REGIONAL AIRPORT (603)668-9400
🔶🔶🔶 Hotel. **Address:** 975 Perimeter Rd 03103
AAA Benefit: Members save 5% or more!

TOWNEPLACE SUITES BY MARRIOTT
MANCHESTER-BOSTON REGIONAL AIRPORT   (603)641-2288
◈◈ Extended Stay Hotel. **Address:**
686 Huse Rd 03103

> **AAA Benefit:**
> Members save 5%
> or more!

WHERE TO EAT

AIRPORT DINER   603/623-5040
◈◈ American. Casual Dining. **Address:** 2280 Brown Ave
03103

CACTUS JACK'S GREAT WEST GRILL   603/627-8600
◈◈ American. Casual Dining. **Address:** 782 S Willow St
03103

CHEN'S GARDEN   603/836-5608
◈ Chinese. Casual Dining. **Address:** 956 Second St 03102

COTTON   603/622-5488
◈◈◈ New American. Casual Dining. **Address:** 75 Arms St
03101

GAUCHOS CHURRASCARIA BRAZILIAN STEAKHOUSE
                                                            603/669-9460
◈ Brazilian. Casual Dining. **Address:** 62 Lowell St 03101

GOLDEN TAO   603/518-7076
◈ Chinese. Casual Dining. **Address:** 270 Amory St 03102

HANOVER STREET CHOPHOUSE   603/644-2467
◈◈ Steak. Fine Dining. **Address:** 149 Hanover St 03101

LA CARRETA   603/628-6899
◈◈ Mexican. Casual Dining. **Address:** 545 Daniel Webster
Hwy 03104

NINETY NINE RESTAURANT   603/641-5999
◈◈ American. Casual Dining. **Address:** 1685 S Willow St
03103

PICCOLA RISTORANTE   603/606-5100
◈◈ Italian. Casual Dining. **Address:** 815 Elm St 03101

PURITAN BACKROOM   603/669-6890
◈◈ American. Casual Dining. **Address:** 245 Hooksett Rd
03104

THE SHASKEEN IRISH PUB & RESTAURANT   603/625-0246
◈◈ Irish. Casual Dining. **Address:** 909 Elm St 03101

SHORTY'S MEXICAN ROADHOUSE   603/625-1730
◈◈ Mexican. Casual Dining. **Address:** 1050 Bicentennial Dr
03105

XO ON ELM   603/560-7998
◈◈◈ Northern American. Casual Dining. **Address:** 827 Elm
St 03101

MEREDITH pop. 1,718

BAY POINT AT MILL FALLS   (603)279-7006
◈◈◈ Hotel. **Address:** 1 SR 25 03253

🔗 **Use the free travel planning
tools at AAA.com/maps**

CHASE HOUSE AT MILL FALLS   (603)279-7006
◈◈◈ Hotel. **Address:** 300 Daniel Webster Hwy 03253

CHURCH LANDING AT MILL FALLS   (603)279-7006

**Hotel
$279-$650**

Address: 281 Daniel Webster Hwy
03253 **Location:** Waterfront. Jct US 3
and SR 104, 0.6 mi n. **Facility:** 73 units,
some cottages. 4 stories, interior/exterior
corridors. **Terms:** 2-3 night minimum
stay - seasonal and/or weekends, 7 day
cancellation notice-fee imposed, resort
fee. **Amenities:** Some: safes. **Pool:**
heated outdoor, heated indoor. **Activities:** hot tub, limited beach access, boat
dock, fishing, ice skating, game room,
exercise room, spa. **Guest Services:**
valet laundry.

MEREDITH INN B & B   (603)279-0000
◈◈◈ Bed & Breakfast. **Address:** 2 Waukewan St 03253

WHERE TO EAT

CAMP   603/279-3003
◈◈ American. Casual Dining. **Address:** 300 Daniel Webster
Hwy 03253

GIUSEPPE'S SHOW TIME PIZZERIA   603/279-3313
◈ Italian. Casual Dining. **Address:** 312 Daniel Webster Hwy
03253

HART'S TURKEY FARM RESTAURANT   603/279-6212

◈◈ **American
Casual Dining
$13-$32**

AAA Inspector Notes: Operated by the
Hart family since 1954, this popular
family restaurant specializes in home-
style cooking, particularly turkey preparations. Also on the menu are beef,
pasta and seafood dishes. Almost every-
thing is made on the premises. Contrib-
uting to the décor is an extensive collection of turkey plates.
Features: full bar, senior menu. **Address:** 233 Daniel Webster
Hwy 03253 **Location:** Jct US 3 and SR 104. 🄻 🄳

SUNSHINE & PA'S RESTAURANT   603/279-5280
◈◈ American. Casual Dining. **Address:** 11 Main St 03253

TOWN DOCKS   603/279-3445
◈ Seafood. Casual Dining. **Address:** 289 Daniel Webster Hwy
03253

MERRIMACK (G-4) elev. 122'

ANHEUSER-BUSCH LLC is e. off Everett Tpke. exit
10 at 221 Daniel Webster Hwy. Tours include a visit
to the brew hall, cold cellars, sampling room, packaging facilities and Clydesdale stables. Behind-the-
scenes Beermaster Tours include a visit to the
brewhouse, hop room, primary fermentation cellar,
lager cellar, packaging facility, quality assurance
room and finishing cellar. Beermaster Tours and Day
Fresh Tours include a beer sample directly from a
finishing tank.

Note: Pants and closed-toe shoes are required
for the Beermaster Tour. **Time:** Allow 1 hour, 30 minutes minimum. **Hours:** Daily 10-5, June-Aug.; daily
10-4, Sept.-Dec.; Thurs.-Mon. 10-4, rest of year.
Beermaster Tour schedule varies; phone ahead.
Closed Jan. 1, Easter, Thanksgiving, Christmas
Eve, Christmas and Dec. 31. **Cost:** General tours
free. Beermaster Tours $25 (ages 21+); $10 (ages

13-20). Day Fresh Tour $10; free (ages 0-20). Children must be with an adult; children ages 0-12 are not permitted on Beermaster Tour. Reservations are required for Beermaster and Day Fresh tours. **Phone:** (603) 595-1202. GT

HOLIDAY INN EXPRESS & SUITES   603/429-3600
ⓌⓌⓌ Hotel. **Address:** 4 Amherst Rd 03054

WHERE TO EAT

BUCKLEY'S GREAT STEAKS AT RIDDLE'S TAVERN
                                            603/424-0995
ⓌⓌⓌⓌ Steak. Fine Dining. **Address:** 438 Daniel Webster Hwy 03054

THE COMMON MAN   603/429-3463
ⓌⓌ Regional American. Casual Dining. **Address:** 304 Daniel Webster Hwy 03054

MOUNT WASHINGTON elev. 6,288'

At 6,288 feet, Mount Washington, in the Presidential Range of the White Mountains, is the Northeast's highest peak. The weather at its summit rivals that of Antarctica: the average annual temperature is below freezing. Fifteen feet of snow is the winter norm, and summer temperatures rarely exceed 72 F. The highest wind velocity ever recorded—231 mph—occurred in April 1934.

Conditions can change in minutes from balmy to subfreezing. Nevertheless, in clear weather, the summit rewards visitors with a panorama that includes the Atlantic Ocean, Maine, New Hampshire, Québec and Vermont.

 MOUNT WASHINGTON COG RAILWAY— see Bretton Woods p. 104.

NASHUA (G-4) pop. 86,494, elev. 161'

New Hampshire's second most populous city, located at the confluence of the Merrimack and Nashua rivers, has a history dating to the 1650s. Way back then it was known as Dunstable, founded as a fur-trading settlement. Like other New England riverfront towns, Nashua's 19th-century development was fueled by textile mills running on water power—an industry that today is only a historical footnote.

Mine Falls Park, a green retreat in the heart of downtown, has forest and wetland habitats where visitors hike, bike and fish during the summer and go cross-country skiing in winter. The Nashua Canal Trail follows a 3-mile-long canal, dug by hand in the 1880s, through a lush wooded setting along the Nashua River. The park has several access points; take US 3 (Everett Turnpike) to exit 5W (SR 111/W. Hollis Street); proceed west to Riverside Street and follow signs to the parking areas.

COURTYARD BY MARRIOTT NASHUA   (603)880-9100
ⓌⓌⓌ Hotel. **Address:** 2200 Southwood Dr 03063
> **AAA Benefit:** Members save 5% or more!

DOUBLETREE BY HILTON NASHUA   603/886-1200
ⓌⓌⓌ Hotel. **Address:** 2 Somerset Pkwy 03063
> **AAA Benefit:** Members save 5% or more!

HAMPTON INN BY HILTON NASHUA   603/883-5333
ⓌⓌⓌ Hotel. **Address:** 407 Amherst St 03063
> **AAA Benefit:** Members save 5% or more!

HOLIDAY INN & SUITES NASHUA   603/888-1551
ⓌⓌⓌ
Hotel
Rates not provided

Address: 9 Northeastern Blvd 03062 **Location:** US 3 exit 4, just w, then 0.3 mi n. **Facility:** 198 units, some efficiencies. 4 stories, interior corridors. **Terms:** check-in 4 pm. **Pool:** outdoor. **Activities:** exercise room. **Guest Services:** valet and coin laundry.

[SAVE] [🍴] [👤] [💺] [CALL] [♿] [�']
[🚼] [BIZ] [📶] [✕] [▭]
/SOME UNITS [🐾] [🛄] [🖼]

HOMEWOOD SUITES BY HILTON GATEWAY HILLS NASHUA
                                            603/546-7470
ⓌⓌⓌ Extended Stay Hotel. **Address:** 15 Tara Blvd 03062
> **AAA Benefit:** Members save 5% or more!

▼ See AAA listing p. 104 ▼

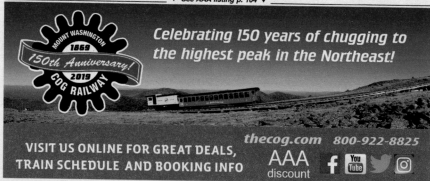

RADISSON HOTEL NASHUA   603/888-9970
◈◈◈ Hotel. **Address:** 11 Tara Blvd 03062

RESIDENCE INN BY MARRIOTT NASHUA   (603)882-8300
◈◈◈ Extended Stay Hotel. **Ad-**   **AAA Benefit:**
dress: 25 Trafalgar Sq 03063   Members save 5%
                                            or more!

WHERE TO EAT

110 GRILL   603/943-7443
◈◈ American. Casual Dining. **Address:** 27 Trafalgar Sq
03063

LA CARRETA RESTAURANTE MEXICANO   603/891-0055
◈◈ Mexican. Casual Dining. **Address:** 139 Daniel Webster
Hwy 03060

LILAC BLOSSOM   603/886-8420
◈◈ Chinese. Casual Dining. **Address:** 650 Amherst St 03063

MARTHA'S EXCHANGE RESTAURANT & BREWING CO
                                           603/883-8781
◈◈ American. Casual Dining. **Address:** 185 Main St 03060

MT'S LOCAL KITCHEN & WINE BAR   603/595-9334
◈◈◈ Regional American. Casual Dining. **Address:** 212 Main
St 03060

NOT YOUR AVERAGE JOE'S   603/318-7777
◈◈ American. Casual Dining. **Address:** 221 Daniel Webster
Hwy 03060

PIG TALE   603/864-8740
◈◈◈ New American. Casual Dining. **Address:** 449 Amherst
St 03063

SURF   603/595-9293
◈◈◈ Seafood. Fine Dining. **Address:** 207 Main St 03060

NEWBURY (E-3) elev. 1,112'

Beginning the first Saturday in August, Newbury's 9-day ◈ League of New Hampshire Craftsmen's Fair is said to be the oldest craft fair in the country; phone (603) 224-3375.

SUNAPEE LAKE LODGE   603/763-2010
◈◈ Hotel. **Address:** 1403 SR 103 03255

NEW CASTLE (F-5) elev. 20'
• Hotels & Restaurants map & index p. 128

Narrow streets with old houses flush to the curbs lend a Colonial air to New Castle, founded as a fishing village on Great Island in the late 1600s. To the east of the square is a historic site containing the remnants of Fort Constitution, the site of the first overt acts of rebellion against the British Crown.

Originally Fort Constitution was the British stronghold Fort William and Mary. On Dec. 14, 1774, following a little-known warning ride by Paul Revere, Portsmouth's Sons of Liberty, accompanied by Durham and New Castle patriots, captured the fort and seized the British powder and arms. Stored in Durham *(see place listing p. 108)*, the munitions were used against the British 4 months later at the battle of Bunker Hill.

President Theodore Roosevelt won a Nobel Peace Prize for work done in New Castle. In 1905 he negotiated the Treaty of Portsmouth, which ended the Russo-Japanese War.

WENTWORTH BY THE SEA, A MARRIOTT HOTEL & SPA   (603)422-7322   🔟⑥

◈◈◈◈
Historic Hotel
$176-$712

AAA Benefit: Members save 5% or more!

Address: 588 Wentworth Rd 03854 **Location:** Waterfront. On SR 1B, 2 mi e of SR 1A. **Facility:** Steeped in history and once host to dignitaries and Hollywood icons, this stately 19th-century hotel has been beautifully restored. Guest rooms afford varying views; all have plush comforts. 161 units, some efficiencies. 5 stories, interior/exterior corridors. **Parking:** on-site and valet. **Terms:** check-in 4 pm, 3 day cancellation notice-fee imposed. **Amenities:** safes. **Pool:** heated outdoor, heated indoor. **Activities:** sauna, hot tub, marina, regulation golf, tennis, exercise room, spa. **Guest Services:** valet laundry, boarding pass kiosk, area transportation.

[SAVE] 🍴 ♿ 🍷 CALL ♿ 🏊 🛏 BIZ 📶 ✕
📠 🖥 /SOME UNITS 🐾

NEW LONDON pop. 1,415

FLYING GOOSE BREW PUB & GRILLE   603/526-6899
◈◈ American. Brewpub. **Address:** 40 Andover Rd 03257

MILLSTONE 74 MAIN   603/526-4201
◈◈ American. Fine Dining. **Address:** 74 Newport Rd 03257

NORTH CONWAY (D-5) pop. 2,349, elev. 546'
• Hotels p. 124 • Restaurants p. 125
• Hotels & Restaurants map & index p. 121

So taken was he with the view of Mount Washington from North Conway's main street that artist Benjamin Champney set up his easel in the middle of the road in August 1850 and painted the scene. Subsequently he and other artists depicted Thompson's Falls and many other nearby spots. Champney supposedly sold several of his New Hampshire landscapes to a chromolithograph company that circulated reproductions.

As the commercial center of the Mount Washington Valley recreation area, the community thrives on a year-round throng of visitors who come not only for outdoor sports and sightseeing, but also for dining, shopping and nightlife.

Mount Washington Valley Chamber of Commerce: 2617 Main St., P.O. Box 2300, North Conway, NH 03860. **Phone:** (603) 356-5701, or (800) 367-3364 out of N.H.

Shopping: Bargain hunters enjoy Main Street, where the L.L. Bean Shopping Center, Red Barn Factory Stores, Settler's Green and White Mountain Outlets feature such stores as Brooks Brothers, Eddie Bauer, Nautica and Ralph Lauren.

(See map & index p. 121.)

MOUNT WASHINGTON OBSERVATORY WEATHER DISCOVERY CENTER is at 2779 White Mountain Hwy. Interactive exhibits explore the science of climate and weather. Visitors can speak with meteorologists at the Mount Washington summit, forecast the weather in a mock television studio, and learn how tornadoes form. Mount Washington is said to have some of the world's most extreme weather, and the observatory plays an important role in recording and researching atmospheric conditions.

Time: Allow 1 hour minimum. **Hours:** Daily 10-5, early May-early Oct.; 10-3, rest of year. Closed Jan. 1, Easter, Thanksgiving and Christmas. Phone ahead to confirm schedule. **Cost:** $2; $1 (ages 7-17). **Phone:** (603) 356-2137.

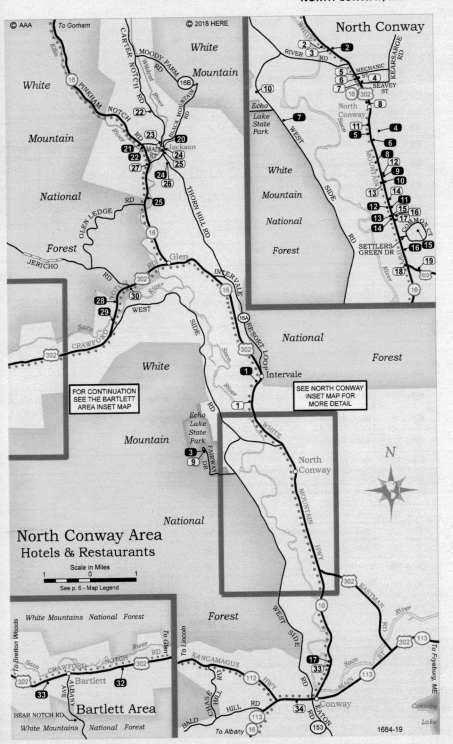

© AAA   To Gorham   © 2018 HERE

North Conway

White Mountain

White Mountain National Forest

PINKHAM NOTCH

Ellis River

16

CARTER NOTCH RD   MOODY FARM RD   Walcott River   BLACK MOUNTAIN RD

16B

22

23   20   Jackson   Main St

21   22   24

27   24   25

26

25   THORN HILL RD

16

Glen

GLEN LEDGE RD   NOTCH RD

JERICHO

302   WEST   Saco River   CRAWFORD

28

29   30   WEST

302   White Mountain

INTERVALE   16   SIDE   Saco River   RESORT LOOP   302   16A

1   Intervale

1

FOR CONTINUATION SEE THE BARTLETT AREA INSET MAP

Echo Lake State Park   FAIRWAY DR

3
9

National

Forest

North Conway Area
Hotels & Restaurants

Scale in Miles
1   0   1
See p. 6 - Map Legend

White Mountains National Forest

Bartlett Area

To Bretton Woods   Saco River   CRAWFORD NOTCH   302

33   Bartlett   ALBANY AVE   32

BEAR NOTCH RD
White Mountains National Forest

To Lincoln   KANCAMAGUS   CHASE HILL RD   112   HWY   BALD HILL RD   HILL RD

To Albany   16   113   To Albany

North Conway inset:
White River   2   RD
2   3   KEARSARGE RD   MECHANIC ST
6   5   4
7   SEAVEY ST
10   16   302   8
Echo Lake State Park   North Conway   Saco River
7   11   4
WEST   5   6
8   12
9
10
SIDE   13   14
12   11
RD   13   15   16
14   17   COMMON CT
SETTLERS GREEN DR   16   15
18   19
16   302

Intervale   National   Forest

SEE NORTH CONWAY INSET MAP FOR MORE DETAIL

North Conway   MOUNTAIN HWY   WHITE

302   EASTMAN RD   River   To Fryeburg, ME
16   113

WEST SIDE RD   Saco   MAIN ST   302   113
17   33   34   Conway   153   Eaton
Conway Lake

N

1684-19

North Conway Area

This index helps you "spot" where approved hotels and restaurants are located on the corresponding detailed maps. Hotel daily rate range is for comparison only. Restaurant price range is a combination of lunch and/or dinner. Turn to the listing page for more information and consult display ads for special promotions.

 For more details, rates and reservations: AAA.com/travelguides/hotels

NORTH CONWAY

Map Page	Hotels	Diamond Rated	Rate Range	Page
1 p. 121	The 1785 Inn	♦♦	$99-$199	124
2 p. 121	**Eastern Inn & Suites**	♦♦	$89-$185 SAVE	124
3 p. 121	**White Mountain Hotel & Resort**	♦♦♦	Rates not provided SAVE	125
4 p. 121	Red Elephant Inn	♦♦♦	Rates not provided	124
5 p. 121	**Briarcliff Motel**	♦♦	Rates not provided SAVE	124
6 p. 121	Red Jacket Mountain View Resort and Indoor Water Park	♦♦♦	Rates not provided	124
7 p. 121	The Farm by the River Bed & Breakfast with Stables	♦♦	Rates not provided	124
8 p. 121	**North Conway Mountain Inn**	♦♦	Rates not provided SAVE	124
9 p. 121	**Comfort Inn & Suites**	♦♦♦	$145-$229 SAVE	124
10 p. 121	Fox Ridge Resort	♦♦	Rates not provided	124
11 p. 121	Residence Inn by Marriott, North Conway	♦♦♦	$96-$417	125
12 p. 121	**Golden Gables Inn**	♦♦	Rates not provided SAVE	124
13 p. 121	Hampton Inn & Suites by Hilton North Conway	♦♦♦	Rates not provided	124
14 p. 121	**Holiday Inn Express Hotel & Suites**	♦♦♦	Rates not provided SAVE	124
15 p. 121	**North Conway Grand Hotel**	♦♦♦	Rates not provided SAVE	124
16 p. 121	**Green Granite Inn**	♦♦	Rates not provided SAVE	124
17 p. 121	Merrill Farm Resort	♦♦	$69-$169	124

Map Page	Restaurants	Diamond Rated	Cuisine	Price Range	Page
① p. 121	Moat Mountain Smoke House & Brewing Co.	♦♦	Barbecue	$11-$28	125
② p. 121	May Kelly's Cottage	♦♦	Irish	$12-$26	125
③ p. 121	Delaney's Hole in the Wall	♦♦	American	$10-$24	125
④ p. 121	Hooligan's	♦♦	American	$8-$21	125
⑤ p. 121	Horsefeathers	♦♦	American	$9-$27	125
⑥ p. 121	The Metropolitan Coffee House	♦	Sandwiches Breads/Pastries	$3-$10	125
⑦ p. 121	The Stairway Café	♦♦	Breakfast	$5-$12	125
⑧ p. 121	Peach's Restaurant	♦♦	American	$7-$14	125
⑨ p. 121	Ledges Dining Room	♦♦♦	American	$6-$39	125
⑩ p. 121	Lobster Trap	♦♦	Seafood	$5-$30	125
⑪ p. 121	Muddy Moose Restaurant & Pub	♦♦	American	$10-$25	125
⑫ p. 121	China Chef	♦♦	Chinese	$6-$17	125
⑬ p. 121	Sea Dog Brewing Co.	♦♦	American	$10-$26	125
⑭ p. 121	A Taste of Thai Restaurant	♦♦	Thai	$8-$26	125

Map Page	Restaurants (cont'd)	Diamond Rated	Cuisine	Price Range	Page
⑮ p. 121	The Blueberry Muffin	◆	American	$3-$10	125
⑯ p. 121	Wicked Fresh Craft Burgers	◆	Burgers	$8-$15	125
⑰ p. 121	Merlino's Family Steakhouse	◆◆◆	Steak	$9-$34	125
⑱ p. 121	Black Cap Grille	◆◆	American	$10-$28	125
⑲ p. 121	The Peking Sunrise Restaurant Lounge	◆◆	Chinese	$10-$31	125

JACKSON

Map Page	Hotels	Diamond Rated	Rate Range	Page
⑳ p. 121	The Snowflake Inn	◆◆◆	Rates not provided	112
㉑ p. 121	Inn at Ellis River	◆◆◆	$149-$339	112
㉒ p. 121	The Lodge at Jackson Village	◆◆	Rates not provided	112
㉔ p. 121	**The Inn at Thorn Hill and Spa**	◆◆◆◆	$99-$450 [SAVE]	112
㉕ p. 121	Nordic Village Resort & Suites	◆◆	Rates not provided	112

Map Page	Restaurants	Diamond Rated	Cuisine	Price Range	Page
㉒ p. 121	Highfields Restaurant	◆◆◆	American	$15-$32	112
㉓ p. 121	The Wentworth Dining Room	◆◆◆	Regional American	$26-$42	112
㉔ p. 121	Yesterdays of Jackson Village	◆	American	$5-$12	112
㉕ p. 121	The Wildcat Inn & Tavern	◆◆◆	New American	$11-$28	112
㉖ p. 121	The Inn at Thorn Hill	◆◆◆	Regional American	$26-$33	112
㉗ p. 121	Red Fox Bar & Grille	◆◆	American	$13-$39	112

GLEN

Map Page	Hotels	Diamond Rated	Rate Range	Page
㉘ p. 121	Golden Apple Inn	◆◆◆	Rates not provided	110
㉙ p. 121	Covered Bridge House	◆◆◆	$99-$139	110

Map Page	Restaurant	Diamond Rated	Cuisine	Price Range	Page
㉚ p. 121	White Mountain Cider Co.	◆◆◆	American	$12-$30	110

BARTLETT

Map Page	Hotels	Diamond Rated	Rate Range	Page
㉜ p. 121	North Colony Motel	◆◆	$59-$179	103
㉝ p. 121	The Bartlett Inn	◆◆	Rates not provided	103

CONWAY

Map Page	Restaurants	Diamond Rated	Cuisine	Price Range	Page
㉝ p. 121	Jonathon's Seafood Restaurant & Fish Market	◆◆	Seafood	$9-$24	107
㉞ p. 121	Cafe Noche Mexican	◆◆	Mexican	$6-$17	107

Turn dreams into plans using

AAA travel planning tools: AAA.com/maps

(See map & index p. 121.)

THE 1785 INN (603)356-9025 **1**
 Historic Country Inn. **Address:** 3582 White Mountain Hwy 03860

BRIARCLIFF MOTEL 603/356-5584 **5**

Motel
Rates not provided

Address: 2304 White Mountain Hwy 03860 **Location:** 0.5 mi s on US 302/SR 16. **Facility:** 31 units. 1 story, exterior corridors. **Pool:** heated outdoor. **Guest Services:** coin laundry.

[SAVE] 🛬 🛜 ⊗ 🛢 🖥

COMFORT INN & SUITES (603)356-8811 **9**

Hotel
$145-$229

Address: 2001 White Mountain Hwy 03860 **Location:** 1.4 mi s on US 302/SR 16. **Facility:** 59 units. 3 stories, interior corridors. **Terms:** check-in 4 pm. **Amenities:** safes. **Pool:** heated indoor. **Activities:** miniature golf, exercise room. **Guest Services:** coin laundry. **Featured Amenity:** full hot breakfast.

[SAVE] [Y↑] CALL [&] 🛬 🛜
🛜 ⊗ 🛢 🖥 🖥

EASTERN INN & SUITES (603)356-5447 **2**

Hotel
$89-$185

Address: 2955 White Mountain Hwy 03860 **Location:** 0.5 mi n on US 302/SR 16. **Facility:** 56 units. 2 stories (no elevator), interior corridors. **Terms:** check-in 4 pm, 3 day cancellation notice-fee imposed. **Pool:** heated indoor. **Activities:** hot tub, cross country skiing, playground, game room, picnic facilities, trails, exercise room. **Guest Services:** coin laundry. **Featured Amenity:** continental breakfast.

[SAVE] 🛬 🚶 🛜 ⊗ 🛢
/ SOME UNITS 🖥

THE FARM BY THE RIVER BED & BREAKFAST WITH STABLES 603/356-2694 **7**
 Historic Bed & Breakfast. **Address:** 2555 West Side Rd 03860

FOX RIDGE RESORT 603/356-3151 **10**
 Hotel. **Address:** 1979 White Mountain Hwy 03860

GOLDEN GABLES INN 603/356-2878 **12**

Motel
Rates not provided

Address: 1814 White Mountain Hwy 03860 **Location:** Jct US 302/SR 16, 1 mi n. **Facility:** 66 units, some two bedrooms and kitchens. 1-2 stories (no elevator), interior/exterior corridors. **Pool:** heated outdoor. **Activities:** hot tub, snowmobiling, bicycles, playground, picnic facilities. **Guest Services:** coin laundry.

[SAVE] [Y↑] 🛬 🛜 ⊗ 🛢
/ SOME UNITS 🖥

GREEN GRANITE INN 603/356-6901 **16**

Hotel
Rates not provided

Address: 1515 White Mountain Hwy 03860 **Location:** 2.3 mi s on US 302/SR 16. **Facility:** 91 units, some condominiums. 2 stories (no elevator), interior/exterior corridors. **Terms:** check-in 4 pm. **Amenities:** safes. **Pool:** outdoor, heated indoor. **Activities:** hot tub, playground, game room, picnic facilities, exercise room. **Guest Services:** coin laundry. **Featured Amenity:** breakfast buffet.

[SAVE] [Y↑] 🛬 🚶 [BIZ] 🛜 ⊗
🛢 🖥 / SOME UNITS 🐾 🖥

HAMPTON INN & SUITES BY HILTON NORTH CONWAY 603/356-7736 **13**
 Hotel. **Address:** 1788 White Mountain Hwy 03860

> **AAA Benefit:** Members save 5% or more!

HOLIDAY INN EXPRESS HOTEL & SUITES 603/356-2551 **14**

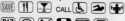
Hotel
Rates not provided

Address: 1732 White Mountain Hwy 03860 **Location:** 2 mi s on US 302/SR 16. **Facility:** 78 units. 3 stories, interior corridors. **Pool:** heated indoor. **Activities:** hot tub, snowmobiling. **Guest Services:** coin laundry. **Featured Amenity:** breakfast buffet.

[SAVE] [Y↑] CALL [&] 🛬 [BIZ] 🛜
⊗ 🛢 🖥 / SOME UNITS 🖥

MERRILL FARM RESORT (603)447-3866 **17**
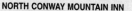 Motel. **Address:** 428 White Mountain Hwy 03860

NORTH CONWAY GRAND HOTEL 603/356-9300 **15**

Hotel
Rates not provided

Address: 72 Common Ct 03860 **Location:** 0.5 mi n of southern jct US 302/SR 16, 0.3 mi e at sign; behind Settlers Green Outlet Village. **Facility:** 200 units. 4 stories, interior corridors. **Terms:** check-in 4 pm. **Amenities:** safes. **Pool:** heated outdoor, heated indoor. **Activities:** sauna, hot tub, ice skating, recreation programs in summer, playground, game room, exercise room. **Guest Services:** coin laundry.

[SAVE] [Y↑] 🍽 CALL [&] 🛬 🚶
[BIZ] 🛜 ⊗ 🛢 🖥 🖥

NORTH CONWAY MOUNTAIN INN 603/356-2803 **8**

Motel
Rates not provided

Address: 2114 White Mountain Hwy 03860 **Location:** 1 mi s on US 302/SR 16. **Facility:** 34 units, some two bedrooms. 2 stories (no elevator), exterior corridors.

[SAVE] [Y↑] 🛜 ⊗ 🛢 🖥
/ SOME UNITS 🐾

RED ELEPHANT INN 603/356-3548 **4**
 Historic Bed & Breakfast. **Address:** 28 Locust Ln 03860

RED JACKET MOUNTAIN VIEW RESORT AND INDOOR WATER PARK 603/356-5411 **6**
 Resort Hotel. **Address:** 2251 White Mountain Hwy 03860

(See map & index p. 121.)

RESIDENCE INN BY MARRIOTT, NORTH CONWAY
(603)356-3024 **11**

◆◆◆ Extended Stay Hotel. **Address:** 1801 White Mountain Hwy 03860

AAA Benefit: Members save 5% or more!

WHITE MOUNTAIN HOTEL & RESORT
603/356-7100 **3**

◆◆◆
Resort Hotel
Rates not provided

Address: 2560 West Side Rd 03860 **Location:** Jct SR 16/113/153 at Conway traffic light, turn onto Washington St to West Side Rd (do not cross covered bridge), then 5 mi on left. **Facility:** Located in the quiet and peaceful development of Hale's, this property affords grand views of Mt. Kearsarge and Mt. Cranmore. Rooms are equipped with DVD players and iPod stations. 79 units. 3 stories, interior corridors. **Dining:** Ledges Dining Room, see separate listing. **Pool:** heated outdoor. **Activities:** sauna, hot tub, regulation golf, tennis, cross country skiing, sledding, game room, trails, exercise room, massage. **Guest Services:** coin laundry. **Featured Amenity: full hot breakfast.**

SAVE ECO ◯ ◯ ◯ CALL ◯ ◯ ◯ BIZ ◯
◯ ◯ ◯ / SOME UNITS ◯

WHERE TO EAT

A TASTE OF THAI RESTAURANT   603/356-7624 **14**
◆◆ Thai. Casual Dining. **Address:** 1857 White Mountain Hwy 03860

BLACK CAP GRILLE   603/356-2225 **18**
◆◆ American. Casual Dining. **Address:** 1498 White Mountain Hwy 03860

THE BLUEBERRY MUFFIN   603/356-5736 **15**
◆ American. Casual Dining. **Address:** 1769 White Mountain Hwy 03860

CHINA CHEF   603/356-3788 **12**
◆ Chinese. Casual Dining. **Address:** 2025 White Mountain Hwy 03860

DELANEY'S HOLE IN THE WALL   603/356-7776 **3**
◆◆ American. Casual Dining. **Address:** 2966 White Mountain Hwy 03860

FLATBREAD COMPANY   603/356-4470
◆ Pizza Natural/Organic. Casual Dining. **Address:** 2760 White Mountain Hwy 03860

HOOLIGAN'S   603/356-6110 **4**
◆◆ American. Casual Dining. **Address:** 21 Kearsarge Rd 03860

HORSEFEATHERS   603/356-6862 **5**
◆◆ American. Casual Dining. **Address:** 2679 White Mountain Hwy 03860

LEDGES DINING ROOM   603/356-7100 **9**
◆◆◆ American. Fine Dining. **Address:** 2560 West Side Rd 03860

LOBSTER TRAP   603/356-5578 **10**
◆◆ Seafood. Casual Dining. **Address:** 2840 West Side Rd 03860

MAY KELLY'S COTTAGE   603/356-7005 **2**
◆◆ Irish. Casual Dining. **Address:** 3002 White Mountain Hwy 03860

MERLINO'S FAMILY STEAKHOUSE   603/356-6006 **17**
◆◆ Steak. Casual Dining. **Address:** 1717 White Mountain Hwy 03860

THE METROPOLITAN COFFEE HOUSE   603/356-2332 **6**
◆ Sandwiches Breads/Pastries. Quick Serve. **Address:** 2680 White Mountain Hwy 03860

MOAT MOUNTAIN SMOKE HOUSE & BREWING CO.
603/356-6381 **1**
◆◆ Barbecue. Casual Dining. **Address:** 3378 White Mountain Hwy 03860

MUDDY MOOSE RESTAURANT & PUB   603/356-7696 **11**
◆◆ American. Casual Dining. **Address:** 2344 White Mountain Hwy 03860

NINETY NINE RESTAURANT   603/356-9909
◆◆ American. Casual Dining. **Address:** 1920 White Mountain Hwy 03860

PEACH'S RESTAURANT   603/356-5860 **8**
◆◆ American. Casual Dining. **Address:** 2506 White Mountain Hwy 03860

THE PEKING SUNRISE RESTAURANT LOUNGE
603/356-6976 **19**
◆◆ Chinese. Casual Dining. **Address:** 1179 Eastman Rd (US 302) 03860

SEA DOG BREWING CO.   603/356-0590 **13**
◆◆ American. Brewpub. **Address:** 1976 White Mountain Hwy 03860

THE STAIRWAY CAFÉ   603/356-5200 **7**
◆◆ Breakfast. Casual Dining. **Address:** 2649 White Mountain Hwy 03860

WICKED FRESH CRAFT BURGERS   603/730-5907 **16**
◆ Burgers. Quick Serve. **Address:** 19 Barnes Rd 03860

NORTH WOODSTOCK (D-3) pop. 528, elev. 738'

• Hotels p. 126 • Restaurants p. 126

Western White Mountains Chamber of Commerce: 126 Main St., North Woodstock, NH 03262. **Phone:** (603) 745-6621.

LOST RIVER GORGE & BOULDER CAVES is at 1712 Lost River Rd. (SR 112). Thousands of years ago, the water from melting glaciers scoured out this 300-feet-deep gorge. As centuries passed, water seeped into cracks within the walls, expanded as it froze and split away massive blocks of granite that tumbled into the gorge, stacking up and hiding the river in places—hence the name "Lost."

But you won't get lost as you explore this heavily wooded setting thanks to a wide loop trail of gravel paths, wooden boardwalks and more stairs than you'd want to count. You'll have postcard-worthy views of the river as it cascades over, around and under the huge, moss-covered boulders. If you're up to it, and don't mind confined spaces and a little dirt, you can clamber down ladders into lantern-lit caves among the rocks with colorful names like Judgment Hall of Pluto, Devil's Kitchen, Cave of Odin, the Dungeon and, if you dare, the Lemon Squeezer.

Informative signs along the way describe various features of the gorge, and platforms and benches offer spots beneath the maple and birch trees where you can pause to catch your breath. A forest boardwalk trail leads visitors across a covered bridge to a tree house and a suspension bridge over the upper gorge.

The self-guided boardwalk trail through the gorge covers 1 mile, includes over 1,000 stairs, and takes roughly 60 to 90 minutes to complete; sturdy walking shoes are advised. The boulder caves can be individually bypassed. **Note:** Baby strollers, wheelchairs and dogs are not allowed in the gorge. **Time:** Allow 1 hour minimum. **Hours:** Daily 9-6, July-Aug.; 9-5, May-June and Sept.-Oct. Last admission 1 hour before closing. Evening Lantern Tour departs select days at dusk, late May to mid-Oct. **Cost:** $21; $17 (ages 4-12). Evening Lantern Tour $35; not recommended for ages 0-4. Reservations are required for Evening Lantern Tour. **Phone:** (603) 745-8031. GT 🍴 🏕

WILDERNESS INN BED & BREAKFAST   (603)745-3890
🔻🔻 Bed & Breakfast. **Address:** 57 S Main St 03262

WHERE TO EAT

CAFE LAFAYETTE DINNER TRAIN   603/745-3500
🔻🔻🔻 Continental. Fine Dining. **Address:** 3 Crossing at River Place (Rt 112) 03262

WOODSTOCK STATION   603/745-3951

🔻🔻
American Casual Dining $9-$27

AAA Inspector Notes: This restaurant is set in an old railroad station. Menu offerings include chimichangas, homemade root beer and salads. A favorite is the chili in a bread bowl that's made with spent grain from the brewing process. Servers are prompt, friendly and attentive. **Features:** full bar. **Address:** 135 Main St 03262 **Location:** I-93 exit 32, 0.5 mi w on SR 112, then just n on US 3; in Woodstock Inn, Station & Brewery. 📶 B L D

PETERBOROUGH (G-3) pop. 3,103, elev. 723'

Peterborough and the arts have been virtually synonymous since the late 19th century. In 1907 composer Edward MacDowell decided to share with other artists the peace and inspiration he had found at his nearby woodland retreat. Although he died the next year, the MacDowell Colony flourished. Pulitzer Prizes, Guggenheim Fellowships and many other international awards have been bestowed upon painters, sculptors, printmakers, filmmakers, writers and composers who have worked in Peterborough.

Because the colony closely guards the privacy of its resident artists, only Colony Hall and MacDowell's gravesite are accessible to the public; phone (603) 924-3886.

Nearly as venerable is the Peterborough Players, a professional summer theater company that performs in a theater within a converted 18th-century barn at Stearns Farm, just 3 miles from downtown at 55 Hadley Rd.; phone (603) 924-7585.

Greater Peterborough Chamber of Commerce: 10 Wilton Rd. (SR 101), P.O. Box 401, Peterborough, NH 03458. **Phone:** (603) 924-7234.

🔻 PINKHAM NOTCH SCENIC AREA (C-4)

Walled by the Presidential Range on the west and by Mount Moriah, North Carter Mountain, Carter Dome and other mountains on the east, Pinkham Notch is one of the easternmost of the New Hampshire White Mountain notches.

In 1790 Joseph Pinkham, whose name was bestowed on the notch, allegedly brought his possessions to his new home via pig-drawn sled. The rough trace that Pinkham and his companions followed has since evolved into scenic SR 16, which threads through the pass between Jackson and Gorham. On the south slope the road parallels the Ellis River and offers access to such spots as Glen Ellis Falls and Crystal Cascade along the Tuckerman Ravine Trail.

The ravine's sheer west wall challenges expert downhill skiers. The notch and its attractions are within the White Mountain National Forest.

A visitor center on SR 16 between North Conway and Gorham is sponsored by the Appalachian Mountain Club. The center offers hikers and other travelers trail and weather information, food, educational displays about outdoor recreation in the White Mountains, free guided walks and evening lectures; phone (603) 466-2721.

PLYMOUTH pop. 4,456, elev. 514'

FAIRFIELD INN & SUITES BY MARRIOTT PLYMOUTH
                                       (603)536-0100
🔻🔻🔻 Hotel. **Address:** 12 Ridgeview Ln 03264

AAA Benefit: Members save 5% or more!

WHERE TO EAT

ITALIAN FARMHOUSE   603/536-4536
🔻🔻 Italian. Casual Dining. **Address:** 337 Daniel Webster Hwy 03264

PORTSMOUTH (F-5) pop. 20,779, elev. 14'
• Hotels p. 130 • Restaurants p. 131
• Hotels & Restaurants map & index p. 128

To their delight, when the sea-weary travelers on the *Pied Cow* disembarked on the west bank of the Piscataqua River in 1630, they found the ground covered with wild strawberries. Thus was founded and named Strawbery Banke, the little settlement that took root around a tidal inlet and grew into the seaport of Portsmouth.

The passengers on the *Pied Cow* were not the first to settle in the area. In 1623 members of the Laconia Co. had come to the Piscataqua to establish a plantation and fishery. Part of the group continued upriver to Dover. The remainder settled at Odiorne Point, 2 miles east of Portsmouth, where they built the first house in New Hampshire. Odiorne Point is a state park that preserves an area little changed in the last 3 centuries *(see Recreation Areas Chart)*.

Strawbery Banke, however, changed greatly. Fishing and farming sustained residents at first, but the ready supply of good timber and an excellent harbor soon engaged them in shipbuilding. Portsmouth—the name was changed in 1653—

(See map & index p. 128.)

began attracting the merchant class in large numbers.

The community also served as the seat of the provincial government. As a center of political activity and a vital trade circuit that linked it with Great Britain and the West Indies, Portsmouth naturally was the focus of many Patriot vs. Tory confrontations prior to the Revolutionary War. British ammunition and stores taken from Fort William and Mary by Portsmouth patriots on Dec. 14, 1774, were used in the first battles of the revolution.

Private shipbuilding reached its apex in the early 19th century, producing many of the swift clipper ships that graced the sea. Two of America's first warships, the *Ranger* and the *America*, were built in Portsmouth Harbor under the direction of John Paul Jones. Thereafter, shipping and shipbuilding declined as steamships and the competing Massachusetts ports gained popularity.

In 1800 the historic U.S. Navy Yard on Seavey's Island *(see Kittery, Maine, p. 64)* became the impetus behind Portsmouth's economy, since augmented by diversified industry and a healthy summer resort trade.

Portsmouth's history is documented in many restored buildings and neighborhoods. Colonial structures as well as the finely detailed houses built by wealthy 19th-century sea captains line the narrow, winding streets of these sections.

The Old Harbor area at Bow and Ceres streets once was the focus of a thriving mercantile seaport; craft shops, restaurants and boutiques now occupy its chandleries and warehouses. Seacoast Repertory Theatre, an all-year equity theater, is in a renovated brewery at 125 Bow St.; phone (603) 433-4472 for tickets.

Similarly the 14 Federal and Georgian buildings of The Hill, at Deer and High streets, have been refurbished and now are used as offices. Seven of the structures were erected during or before the Revolutionary War. Across Mechanic Street from Prescott Park is the city's oldest cemetery, Point of Graves, which contains gravestones dating from 1682.

The Music Hall, 28 Chestnut St., is a beautifully restored Victorian-era theater with a striking Beaux Arts lobby and an ornate auditorium. Just around the corner at 131 Congress St. is the theater's sister venue, The Music Hall Loft, a trendy, intimate space offering the same menu of plays, movies, concerts and literary events. Phone (603) 436-2400 for the box office.

The Chamber Collaborative of Greater Portsmouth: 500 Market St., P.O. Box 239, Portsmouth, NH 03802. **Phone:** (603) 610-5510.

STRAWBERY BANKE MUSEUM is bounded by Marcy, Court, Washington and Hancock sts. The 10-acre historic waterfront neighborhood offers eight gardens and more than 30 buildings from the period 1695-1955, with costumed role-players and traditional craft demonstrations.

The 1777 William Pitt Tavern, 1780 Wheelwright House, 1795 Drisco House, 1815 Chase House, 1830 Rider-Wood House, 1872 Goodwin Mansion and 1919 Shapiro House have been restored and furnished in different periods to show the changes in lifestyle and architectural fashion over 350 years. The boyhood home of editor and author Thomas Bailey Aldrich, known as the Nutter House to readers of his book "The Story of a Bad Boy," is another highlight.

Information about self-guiding tours, guided walking tours and holiday events is available at the Tyco Visitor Center at 14 Hancock St. An outdoor skating rink is open daily 9-9 December 1 through February. Special events and programs are offered year-round.

Time: Allow 1 hour, 30 minutes minimum. **Hours:** Daily 10-5, May-Oct. Guided garden tours depart daily at 1. Guided 90-minute museum tours are given Sat.-Sun. on the hour 10-2, in Nov. Candlelight Stroll holiday event Sat. 5-9, Sun. 4-8, first three weekends in Dec. Skating daily 9-9, Dec.-Mar. Closed Christmas Eve, Christmas and Dec. 31. Phone ahead to confirm schedule. **Cost:** (Valid for 2 consecutive days) $19.50; $9 (ages 5-17); $49 (family, two adults and two children ages 5-17); free (active military with ID and their families). Garden tour free. Museum or holiday house tour $15; $10 (ages 5-17); $40 (family). **Phone:** (603) 433-1100, or (603) 433-1107 for the visitor center. GT 🍴 🚻

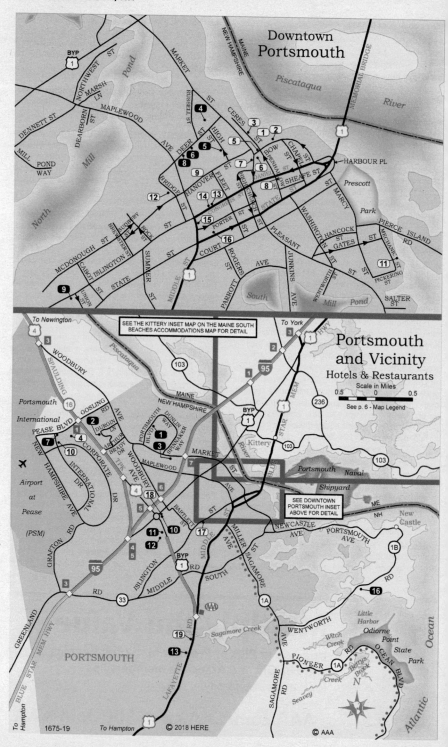

Downtown Portsmouth

Portsmouth and Vicinity
Hotels & Restaurants
Scale in Miles
See p. 6 - Map Legend

SEE THE KITTERY INSET MAP ON THE MAINE SOUTH BEACHES ACCOMMODATIONS MAP FOR DETAIL

SEE DOWNTOWN PORTSMOUTH INSET ABOVE FOR DETAIL

© 2018 HERE

© AAA

1675-19

Portsmouth and Vicinity

This index helps you "spot" where approved hotels and restaurants are located on the corresponding detailed maps. Hotel daily rate range is for comparison only. Restaurant price range is a combination of lunch and/or dinner. Turn to the listing page for more information and consult display ads for special promotions.

 For more details, rates and reservations: AAA.com/travelguides/hotels

PORTSMOUTH

Map Page	Hotels	Diamond Rated	Rate Range	Page
1 p. 128	Homewood Suites by Hilton	◇◇◇	Rates not provided	130
2 p. 128	Hampton Inn by Hilton Portsmouth Central	◇◇◇	Rates not provided	130
3 p. 128	**Courtyard by Marriott**	◇◇◇	$79-$358 SAVE	130
4 p. 128	**Sheraton Portsmouth Harborside Hotel**	◇◇◇	$215-$472 SAVE	131
5 p. 128	Hilton Garden Inn Portsmouth Downtown	◇◇◇	Rates not provided	130
6 p. 128	**Residence Inn by Marriott Downtown/Waterfront**	◇◇◇	$110-$458 SAVE	131
7 p. 128	**Residence Inn by Marriott**	◇◇◇	$55-$430 SAVE	131
8 p. 128	**Hampton Inn & Suites Portsmouth Downtown**	◇◇◇	$159-$483 SAVE	130
9 p. 128	Martin Hill Inn	◇◇◇	$145-$260	130
10 p. 128	**Best Western Plus Portsmouth Hotel & Suites**	◇◇	$99-$249 SAVE	130
11 p. 128	Port Inn Portsmouth, An Ascend Collection Member	◇◇◇	$109-$130	130
12 p. 128	**Fairfield by Marriott-Portsmouth Seacoast**	◇◇◇	$75-$262 SAVE	130
13 p. 128	Quality Inn Portsmouth	◇◇	$100-$173	130

Map Page	Restaurants	Diamond Rated	Cuisine	Price Range	Page
① p. 128	Old Ferry Landing	◇	Seafood	$8-$28	131
② p. 128	The Wellington Room	◇◇◇	American	$20-$35	132
③ p. 128	The Oar House Restaurant	◇◇	American	$12-$54	131
④ p. 128	Redhook Brewery	◇	American	$12-$21	132
⑤ p. 128	The Dolphin Striker	◇◇	Seafood	$14-$34	131
⑥ p. 128	Fat Belly's	◇	American	$9-$20	131
⑦ p. 128	The Portsmouth Brewery	◇◇	American	$13-$28	132
⑧ p. 128	Ristorante Massimo	◇◇◇	Italian	$26-$39	132
⑨ p. 128	Row 34	◇◇◇	Seafood	$16-$32	132
⑩ p. 128	Paddy's An American Grille	◇◇	American	$9-$27	131
⑪ p. 128	Geno's Chowder and Sandwich Shop	◇	American	$4-$15	131
⑫ p. 128	Thai Paradise	◇◇	Thai	$10-$22	132
⑬ p. 128	the Friendly Toast	◇◇	Breakfast	$8-$14	131
⑭ p. 128	Café Mediterraneo	◇◇	Italian	$8-$25	131
⑮ p. 128	Jumpin' Jay's Fish Café	◇◇◇	Seafood	$17-$32	131
⑯ p. 128	The Library Restaurant	◇◇◇	American Steak	$10-$40	131
⑰ p. 128	The Portsmouth Bread Box	◇	Pizza	$7-$13	131
⑱ p. 128	Roundabout Diner & Lounge	◇◇	American	$10-$22	132

Map Page	Restaurants (cont'd)	Diamond Rated	Cuisine	Price Range	Page
19 p. 128	**Dinnerhorn Restaurant & Bratskellar Pub**	◈◈	Seafood	$9-$26	131

NEW CASTLE

Map Page	Hotel	Diamond Rated	Rate Range	Page
16 p. 128	**Wentworth By The Sea, A Marriott Hotel & Spa**	◈◈◈◈	$176-$712 SAVE	119

BEST WESTERN PLUS PORTSMOUTH HOTEL & SUITES
(603)436-7600 **10**

Hotel $99-$249

Best Western PLUS. **AAA Benefit:** Members save up to 15% and earn bonus points!

Address: 580 US Hwy 1 Bypass 03801 **Location:** I-95 exit 5, jct US 1 Bypass and Portsmouth Traffic Circle. **Facility:** 168 units, some two bedrooms and efficiencies. 2-6 stories, interior/exterior corridors. **Terms:** check-in 4 pm, cancellation fee imposed. **Dining:** Roundabout Diner & Lounge, see separate listing. **Pool:** outdoor, heated indoor. **Activities:** hot tub, exercise room. **Guest Services:** valet and coin laundry.

SAVE ❘❘ ❘ CALL ⟨⟩ ⟰ 🛂 BIZ 🛜 ❘ 🖥 🖥 / SOME UNITS HS

COURTYARD BY MARRIOTT
(603)436-2121 **3**

Hotel $79-$358

COURTYARD **AAA Benefit:** Members save 5% or more!

Address: 1000 Market St 03801 **Location:** I-95 exit 7, just w. **Facility:** 133 units. 4 stories, interior corridors. **Terms:** cancellation fee imposed. **Amenities:** safes. **Pool:** heated indoor. **Activities:** exercise room. **Guest Services:** valet and coin laundry, area transportation.

SAVE ECO ❘❘ ❘ CALL ⟨⟩ ⟰ 🛂 BIZ 🛜 ❘ 🖥 🖥 / SOME UNITS HS

FAIRFIELD BY MARRIOTT-PORTSMOUTH SEACOAST
(603)436-6363 **12**

Hotel $75-$262

Fairfield **AAA Benefit:** Members save 5% or more!

Address: 650 Borthwick Ave 03801 **Location:** I-95 exit 5, jct US 1 Bypass and Portsmouth Traffic Circle. **Facility:** 102 units. 4 stories, interior corridors. **Terms:** cancellation fee imposed. **Pool:** outdoor. **Activities:** exercise room. **Guest Services:** valet and coin laundry, boarding pass kiosk, area transportation. **Featured Amenity:** breakfast buffet.

SAVE CALL ⟨⟩ ⟰ 🛂 BIZ 🛜

🛂 ❘ 🖥 🖥

HAMPTON INN & SUITES PORTSMOUTH DOWNTOWN
(603)430-3033 **8**

Hotel $159-$483

AAA Benefit: Members save 5% or more!

Address: 23 Portwalk Pl 03801 **Location:** At Hanover St and Portwalk Pl; downtown. **Facility:** 120 units. 5 stories, interior corridors. **Parking:** valet only. **Terms:** 1-7 night minimum stay, cancellation fee imposed. **Pool:** heated indoor. **Activities:** exercise room. **Guest Services:** valet and coin laundry. **Featured Amenity:** continental breakfast.

SAVE ❘ ❘❘ ❘ CALL ⟨⟩ ⟰

🛂 BIZ HS 🛜 ✕ ❘ 🖥 🖥

HAMPTON INN BY HILTON PORTSMOUTH CENTRAL
603/431-6111 **2**

◈◈◈ Hotel. **Address:** 99 Durgin Ln 03801

AAA Benefit: Members save 5% or more!

HILTON GARDEN INN PORTSMOUTH DOWNTOWN
603/431-1499 **5**

◈◈◈ Hotel. **Address:** 100 High St 03801

AAA Benefit: Members save 5% or more!

HOMEWOOD SUITES BY HILTON
603/427-5400 **1**

◈◈◈ Extended Stay Hotel. **Address:** 100 Portsmouth Blvd 03801

AAA Benefit: Members save 5% or more!

MARTIN HILL INN
(603)436-2287 **9**

◈◈◈ Historic Bed & Breakfast. **Address:** 404 Islington St 03801

PORT INN PORTSMOUTH, AN ASCEND COLLECTION MEMBER
(603)436-4378 **11**

◈◈◈ Motel. **Address:** 505 US Hwy 1 Bypass 03801

QUALITY INN PORTSMOUTH
(603)433-3338 **13**

◈◈ Hotel. **Address:** 1190 Lafayette Rd 03801

(See map & index p. 128.)

RESIDENCE INN BY MARRIOTT   (603)436-8880 7

Residence INN

Extended Stay Hotel
$55-$430

AAA Benefit: Members save 5% or more!

Address: 1 International Dr 03801 **Location:** Spaulding Tpke (US 4) exit 1, just 0.5 mi w. **Facility:** 90 units, some two bedrooms, efficiencies and kitchens. 3 stories, interior corridors. **Terms:** cancellation fee imposed. **Pool:** heated indoor. **Activities:** exercise room. **Guest Services:** valet and coin laundry, area transportation.

RESIDENCE INN BY MARRIOTT DOWNTOWN/WATERFRONT   (603)422-9200 6

Residence INN

Extended Stay Contemporary Hotel
$110-$458

AAA Benefit: Members save 5% or more!

Address: 100 Deer St 03801 **Location:** Downtown; at Portwalk Place. **Facility:** 128 efficiencies. 5 stories, interior corridors. **Parking:** valet only. **Terms:** check-in 4 pm, cancellation fee imposed. **Pool:** heated indoor. **Activities:** exercise room. **Guest Services:** valet and coin laundry. **Featured Amenity:** breakfast buffet.

SHERATON PORTSMOUTH HARBORSIDE HOTEL   (603)431-2300 4

Sheraton

Hotel
$215-$472

AAA Benefit: Members save 5% or more!

Address: 250 Market St 03801 **Location:** At Russell St; downtown. **Facility:** 193 units, some two bedrooms and kitchens. 5 stories, interior corridors. **Parking:** on-site (fee) and valet. **Terms:** cancellation fee imposed. **Amenities:** safes. **Pool:** heated indoor. **Activities:** exercise room. **Guest Services:** valet laundry.

WHERE TO EAT

THE BEACH PLUM   603/964-7451
Seafood. Quick Serve. **Address:** 2800 Lafayette Rd 03801

CAFÉ MEDITERRANEO   603/427-5563 14
Italian. Casual Dining. **Address:** 119 Congress St 03801

DINNERHORN RESTAURANT & BRATSKELLAR PUB
603/436-0717 19

Seafood Casual Dining
$9-$26

AAA Inspector Notes: Convenient to businesses south of downtown, the casual restaurant displays pleasant contemporary decor. The menu focuses primarily on seafood, including raw bar items, but also includes steak, chicken, pizza and pasta entrees. Smaller portions are available at lunch. **Features:** full bar. **Address:** 980 Lafayette Rd 03801 **Location:** I-95 exit 5, 1.3 mi s on US 1.

THE DOLPHIN STRIKER   603/431-5222 5
Seafood. Fine Dining. **Address:** 15 Bow St 03801

FAT BELLY'S   603/610-4227 6
American. Casual Dining. **Address:** 2 Bow St 03801

THE FRIENDLY TOAST   603/430-2154 13
Breakfast. Casual Dining. **Address:** 113 Congress St 03801

GENO'S CHOWDER AND SANDWICH SHOP
603/427-2070 11
American. Casual Dining. **Address:** 177 Mechanic St 03801

JUMPIN' JAY'S FISH CAFÉ   603/766-3474 15
Seafood. Casual Dining. **Address:** 150 Congress St 03801

THE LIBRARY RESTAURANT   603/431-5202 16
American Steak. Fine Dining. **Address:** 401 State St 03801

MARGARITAS MEXICAN RESTAURANT   603/431-5828
Mexican. Casual Dining. **Address:** 775 Lafayette Rd 03801

THE OAR HOUSE RESTAURANT   603/436-4025 3
American. Casual Dining. **Address:** 55 Ceres St 03801

OLD FERRY LANDING   603/431-5510 1
Seafood. Casual Dining. **Address:** 10 Ceres St 03801

PADDY'S AN AMERICAN GRILLE   603/430-9450 10
American. Casual Dining. **Address:** 27 International Dr 03801

THE PORTSMOUTH BREAD BOX   603/436-1631 17
Pizza. Quick Serve. **Address:** 460 Islington St 03801

🔗 What's for dinner?

AAA.com/travelguides/restaurants

(See map & index p. 128.)

THE PORTSMOUTH BREWERY   603/431-1115 (7)
🍷🍷 American. Brewpub. **Address:** 56 Market St 03801

REDHOOK BREWERY   603/430-8600 (4)
🍷 American. Casual Dining. **Address:** 1 Redhook Way 03801

RISTORANTE MASSIMO   603/436-4000 (8)
🍷🍷🍷 Italian. Fine Dining. **Address:** 59 Penhallow St 03801

ROUNDABOUT DINER & LOUNGE   603/431-1440 (18)
🍷🍷 American. Casual Dining. **Address:** 580 US Hwy 1 Bypass 03801

ROW 34   603/319-5011 (9)
🍷🍷🍷 Seafood. Casual Dining. **Address:** 5 Portwalk Pl 03801

THAI PARADISE   603/431-9193 (12)
🍷🍷 Thai. Casual Dining. **Address:** 96 Bridge St 03801

THE WELLINGTON ROOM   603/431-2989 (2)
🍷🍷🍷 American. Fine Dining. **Address:** 67 Bow St, 2nd Floor 03801

ROCHESTER pop. 29,752

HOLIDAY INN EXPRESS HOTEL & SUITES ROCHESTER
    (603)994-1175
🍷🍷🍷 Hotel. **Address:** 77 Farmington Rd 03867.

RYE

THE CARRIAGE HOUSE   603/964-8251
🍷🍷🍷 American. Casual Dining. **Address:** 2263 Ocean Blvd 03870

PETEY'S SUMMERTIME SEAFOOD & BAR   603/433-1937
🍷 Seafood. Casual Dining. **Address:** 1323 Ocean Blvd 03870

SALEM (G-4) elev. 147'

AMERICA'S STONEHENGE, 5 mi. e. of I-93 exit 3 on SR 111, then 1 mi. s. to 105 Haverhill Rd., encompasses prehistoric stone structures proven by carbon dating to form the oldest known megalithic site on this continent. Continuing research indicates the site may be 4,000 years old; inscriptions deciphered offer possible evidence that Celt-Iberians used this site from about 800 to 300 B.C. Inscriptions are displayed and reading material is available as well a mobile app with an audio tour. Five alpacas are on the premises.

Time: Allow 1 hour minimum. **Hours:** Daily 9-5. Last admission 1 hour before closing. Closed Thanksgiving and Christmas. **Cost:** $12.50; $10.50 (ages 65+); $7.50 (ages 6-12). **Phone:** (603) 893-8300.

CANOBIE LAKE PARK is .2 mi. e., then 1 mi. n. of I-93 exit 2 to 85 N. Policy St. The amusement park offers more than 85 rides, games and activities and features live entertainment. Highlights include three roller coasters, a giant sky wheel, an 1890s carousel with hand-carved horses, a lake cruise, a log flume water ride, a water coaster and an interactive waterplay complex. During the park's annual SCREEEM-FEST in October, visitors can brave haunted houses, play Halloween-themed games and sample seasonal foods in addition to enjoying the park's regular ride offerings.

Time: Allow 4 hours minimum. **Hours:** Daily a.m.-10 p.m., Memorial Day-Labor Day; hours va Sat.-Sun., late Apr.-day before Memorial Day ar day after Labor Day-late Sept. SCREEEMFEST Fri Sun. in Oct. Phone ahead to confirm schedule **Cost:** (Includes rides and shows) $42; $26 (age 60+ and children under 48 inches tall); free (age 0-3). After 5 p.m. $25. Phone for SCREEEMFES prices. Prices may vary; phone ahead. **Phone** (603) 893-3506. 🍴 ⊠

HOLIDAY INN-SALEM NEW HAMPSHIRE   603/893-551
🍷🍷🍷 Hotel. **Address:** 1 Keewaydin Dr 03079

LA QUINTA INN & SUITES SALEM   (603)893-472
🍷🍷🍷 Hotel. **Address:** 8 Keewaydin Dr 03079

WHERE TO EAT

THE COLOSSEUM RESTAURANT   603/898-119
🍷🍷 Italian. Casual Dining. **Address:** 264 N Broadway 03079

T-BONES GREAT AMERICAN EATERY   603/893-344
🍷🍷 American. Casual Dining. **Address:** 311 S Broadwa 03079

TUSCAN KITCHEN   603/952-487
🍷🍷🍷 Italian. Casual Dining. **Address:** 67 Main St 03079

WEATHERVANE SEAFOOD RESTAURANT   603/893-626
🍷🍷 Seafood. Casual Dining. **Address:** 41 S Broadway 03079

SUNAPEE (E-3) elev. 914'

Sunapee is one of several resort communitie that line many-lobed, 10-square-mile Lake Sunapee A vacation spot since the mid-19th century, the area affords a variety of year-round outdoor recreation Located in west-central New Hampshire, the locale should not be confused with the "Lakes Region," lo cated in the eastern part of the state. The lake' name is derived from a Penacook Indian word be lieved to mean "goose lake." Boat cruises may be taken on the lake.

During the 1860s Sunapee seemed to attrac residents with a flair for invention. In 1868 Joh Smith devised a machine that permitted the loca clothespin factory—a major industry at the time—t produce 125 finished clothespins per minute.

The following year, after a decade of study, Enos Clough drove a horseless carriage throughout the area, but its tendency to terrify horses resulted in it being banned. Clough sold the contraption to a La conia man who ran it into a fence; the engine was fi nally installed in a boat.

Lake Sunapee Region Chamber of Commerce 328 Main St., P.O. Box 532, New London, NH 03257. **Phone:** (603) 526-6575 or (877) 526-6575.

URKEHAVEN MOTEL AND LODGE   (603)763-2788

Motel
$99-$189

Address: 179 Burkehaven Hill Rd 03782 **Location:** I-89 exit 12, 5 mi w on SR 11, 0.4 mi e on Main St (Lake Ave), then 0.8 mi se, follow signs to harbor. **Facility:** 10 units. 1 story, exterior corridors. *Bath:* shower only. **Terms:** 2 night minimum stay - seasonal, 7 day cancellation notice-fee imposed. **Pool:** heated outdoor. **Featured Amenity: breakfast buffet.**

[icons] SAVE [icons] / SOME UNITS [icon]

TILTON (E-4) elev. 456'

hopping: SAVE Tanger Outlets, just n. on US 3 from 93 exit 20 at 120 Laconia Rd., features stores such s American Eagle Outfitters, Nike Factory Store, ommy Hilfiger and Under Armour.

AMPTON INN & SUITES BY HILTON TILTON   603/286-3400
d 03276 Hotel. **Address:** 195 Laconia

AAA Benefit:
Members save 5% or more!

OLIDAY INN EXPRESS & SUITES   (603)286-4550
 Hotel. **Address:** 75 Tilton Rd 03276

UPER 8 OF TILTON   (603)286-8882
 Motel. **Address:** 7 Tilton Rd 03276

WHERE TO EAT

NINETY NINE RESTAURANT   603/286-4994
 American. Casual Dining. **Address:** 154 Laconia Rd 03276

TILT'N DINER   603/286-2204
 American. Casual Dining. **Address:** 61 Laconia Rd 03276

WATERVILLE VALLEY

SILVER FOX INN   (603)236-3699
 Hotel. **Address:** 70 Packards Rd 03215

WHERE TO EAT

COYOTE GRILL   603/236-4919
 American. Casual Dining. **Address:** 98 Valley Rd 03215

WEIRS BEACH (E-4) elev. 535'

A boardwalk, waterslide, weekly fireworks displays, yachting, fishing, swimming and other water sports are among the diversions at Weirs Beach, New Hampshire's inland version of a seaside resort.

Weirs Beach lies on the shore of Lake Winnipesaukee. Its name is thought to mean "Smile of the Great Spirit." The title is apt, for island-studded Winnipesaukee is considered one of the most picturesque lakes in the state. It also is the largest; the many bays and deep coves create a 283-mile shoreline.

Endicott Rock, a large boulder, was marked by emissaries of Gov. John Endicott of Massachusetts Colony. Proceeding 3 miles north, they established the northern boundary of Massachusetts, a line that held until the separation of New Hampshire and Massachusetts in 1740.

WHITEFIELD pop. 1,142

MOUNTAIN VIEW GRAND RESORT & SPA (603)837-2100

Classic Historic Hotel

$149-$809

Address: 101 Mountain View Rd 03598 **Location:** 2.5 mi n on US 3, just e. **Facility:** This sprawling 1865 hotel supports sustainability initiatives; 12% of its electricity is provided by an on-site wind farm. Guests love the luxurious amenities and the beautiful mountain views. 141 units. 4 stories, interior corridors. **Parking:** on-site and valet. **Terms:** 2 night minimum stay - seasonal, 10 day cancellation notice-fee imposed, resort fee. **Amenities:** safes. **Dining:** 2 restaurants. **Pool:** heated outdoor, heated indoor. **Activities:** sauna, hot tub, regulation golf, tennis, cross country skiing, snowmobiling, sledding, ice skating, recreation programs, kids club, bicycles, playground, game room, lawn sports, trails, health club, spa. **Guest Services:** valet laundry. *(See ad this page.)*

WHITE MOUNTAINS AND WHITE MOUNTAIN NATIONAL FOREST (C-4)

Elevations in the forest range from 440 ft. south of Deer Hill near Colton Brook to 6,288 ft. on Mount Washington. Refer to AAA maps for additional elevation information.

North of New Hampshire's central plateau, the White Mountains rise in dramatic relief, cloaked with forests and laced with streams. Among the range and ridges are the highest mountains in the Northeast, the Presidential Range, which culminate in the bare granite summit of 6,288-foot Mount Washington *(see place listing p. 118)*. Mounts Adams, Jefferson, Monroe and Madison also exceed 5,000 feet in elevation.

Passes known as notches pierce the uplift; Crawford, Franconia, Kinsman and Pinkham notches provide some of the best scenic features in the state. More than 800,000 acres of the region lie within the White Mountain National Forest, which extends into Maine.

The names of several mountains in the southern section of the forest commemorate some of the state's best-known Native Americans. Mount Passaconaway honors the chieftain who united 17 tribes into the Penacook Confederacy in the mid-17th century. Mount Kancamagus remembers Passaconaway's grandson Kancamagus, the last sagamore of the confederacy, who strove for peace with white settlers until he was provoked to attack Dover in 1689.

Because the White Mountains are as noted for outdoor recreation—particularly skiing and hiking—as for their beauty, they are one of the nation's most heavily used forest areas. Some of the ski resorts are world renowned. In summer anglers ply the rivers for several species of trout, and campers take advantage of the numerous campgrounds.

From spring through late fall the extensive network of trails, including the Appalachian Trail along the mountains' spine, lures hikers and backpackers. Many places, such as the Great Gulf Wilderness, are accessible only on foot. Only experienced back-country travelers thoroughly familiar with the terrain

and weather should attempt the higher elevations—in any season.

There are visitor information centers at the Pemigewasset Ranger Station, 71 White Mountain Dr. in Campton, phone (603) 536-6100; at the Saco Ranger Station, 33 Kancamagus Highway (SR 112) near Conway, phone (603) 447-5448; and at the Androscoggin Ranger Station, 300 Glen Rd. in Gorham, phone (603) 466-2713. White Mountains Visitor Center, 200 Kancamagus Hwy. (SR 112) in North Woodstock, is open daily 9-3:30, late May-late Oct. and Fri.-Sun. 9-3:30, rest of year; phone (603) 745-3816.

For further information phone (603) 536-6100 or TTY (603) 536-3665. *See Recreation Areas Chart.*

KANCAMAGUS HIGHWAY (SR 112), traverses the forest between Conway and Lincoln. It follows the Swift River Valley, passing Rocky Gorge Scenic Area, old Passaconaway and Sabbaday Falls. After crossing 2,860-foot Kancamagus Pass, the highway drops into the Pemigewasset Valley. Overlooks, picnic sites and campgrounds are scattered along the 34.5-mile route.

Self-guiding trails are near Covered Bridge Campground and at the Russell Colbath Historic Site, 12 miles from Conway near the junction with Bear Notch Road, which leads to Bartlett *(see place listing p. 103).* About 1.5 miles west of Lincoln *(see place listing p. 114)* is the White Mountains Visitor Center, which dispenses recreation information year-round. Seasonal interpretive programs and brochures detailing the history of the area are available. **Phone:** (603) 447-5448 for the Saco Visitor Center, or (603) 745-3816 for the White Mountains Visitor Center.

WOLFEBORO (E-4) pop. 2,838, elev. 508'

Known as one of the oldest summer resorts in America, Wolfeboro attained this status in 1768 when Gov. John Wentworth of Massachusetts built the country's first summer home. A marker at the site, 5 miles east on SR 109, commemorates the estate. By the time the governor's manor house burned in 1820, it was no longer unique. Summer homes and resorts now line Lake Wentworth and the southeastern shore of Lake Winnipesaukee. Although it has an air of sedate venerability, modern Wolfeboro is a major lake port.

Wolfeboro Area Chamber of Commerce: 32 Central Ave., P.O. Box 547, Wolfeboro, NH 03894. **Phone:** (603) 569-2200 or (800) 516-5324.

THE WRIGHT MUSEUM OF WORLD WAR II, n.w. of jct. SRs 109 and 28 at 77 Center St., displays memorabilia of the U.S. home front 1939-45. Exhibits illustrate details of American life as well as major events of World War II as they unfolded in Europe and the Pacific. An extensive collection of vehicles, equipment, clothing and other relics is on permanent display and enhanced by music and news broadcasts of the period, film clips and vintage periodicals.

Time: Allow 1 hour minimum. **Hours:** Mon.-Sat. 10-4, Sun. noon-4, May-Oct. **Cost:** $10; $8 (ages 60+ and military with ID); $6 (ages 5-17). **Phone:** (603) 569-1212.

PIPING ROCK RESORT   603/569-1915

Motel
Rates not provided

Address: 680 N Main St 03894 **Location:** Waterfront. 3.1 mi n on SR 109 N. **Facility:** 18 units, some two bedrooms, three bedrooms, efficiencies, kitchens and cottages. 2 stories (no elevator), exterior corridors. **Activities:** boat dock, fishing, snowmobiling, playground, lawn sports, trails.

WOLFEBORO INN   603/569-3016
Hotel. **Address:** 90 N Main St 03894

WHERE TO EAT

WOLFE'S TAVERN   603/569-3016
American. Casual Dining. **Address:** 90 N Main St 03894

WOODSVILLE pop. 1,126

ALL SEASONS MOTEL   (603)747-2157

Motel
$70-$130

Address: 36 Smith St 03785 **Location:** I-91 exit 17, 4.1 mi e on US 302, then just s. **Facility:** 14 units, some efficiencies. 1 story, exterior corridors. **Terms:** cancellation fee imposed. **Pool:** outdoor. **Activities:** playground, picnic facilities.

NOOTKA LODGE   (603)747-2418

Motel
$75-$230

Address: 4982 Dartmouth College Hwy 03785 **Location:** I-91 exit 17, 4.5 mi e on US 302. **Facility:** 33 units, some two bedrooms, efficiencies, kitchens and houses. 2 stories (no elevator), interior/exterior corridors. **Terms:** 7 day cancellation notice-fee imposed, resort fee. **Pool:** outdoor. **Activities:** hot tub, snowmobiling, game room, picnic facilities, trails, exercise room.

WHERE TO EAT

SHILOH'S RESTAURANT   603/747-2525
American. Casual Dining. **Address:** 202 Central St 03785

Fall foliage in Stowe

Vermont

Samuel de Champlain, the French explorer who in 1609 visited what is now Vermont, called it *les verts mont*—"green mountains"—after the lush ridges that form the spine of the state. Visit Vermont and you'll discover its namesake hue just about everywhere.

Take the Green Mountains and Green Mountain National Forest in central Vermont: From a distance, peaks appear swathed in deep blue-green, the palette of balsam, hemlock and white pine trees.

Maple trees adorned with emerald, five-fingered leaves contribute to the state's maple syrup production. Light green apples hang on orchard trees throughout the state in late summer, awaiting harvest. Fields of kelly green crops display the state's green thumb.

Rainbow-colored hot air balloons float over dark green valleys and aqua lakes. And various shades of green can be found stitched

Red covered bridge in Arlington

or woven into quilts, baskets and other Vermont handicrafts.

The Green Mountain State

In an attic, an elderly woman discovers a book containing portraits of the "Green Mountain State." Images fill her head as she recalls her childhood in Vermont. Deciding to revisit a pleasant past, she dusts off the cover and cracks the binding.

Page one: A stark white steeple pierces the deep blue sky. Lofty, green-leafed trees surround the church.

It's summer in Stowe, and Mount Mansfield, the state's tallest peak, keeps watch over the town. The outline of the mountain resembles a face, so much so that it's easy to make out the formations locals call the Forehead, Nose and Chin.

The woman sips her tea and flips to page 11: A light blue truck is parked under a red covered bridge. Bands of soft light filter through the wooden lattice on one side wall, and the outlines of two lip-locked lovers can be seen in the glow of the setting sun.

Page 14: Light from a full moon cloaked in clouds casts a violet glow over a field quilted in white.

She clutches the afghan around her shoulders and turns to page 16. Buckets are crookedly attached to the trunks of sugar maple trees, tapped to catch oozing sap in spring. Page 17 shows beige, gallon-sized jugs filled with the sugary stuff lining a shelf.

Flames of fall color dominate pages 20 and 21. She can easily distinguish the softwoods from the hardwoods in a photograph of

Green Mountain National Forest. Softwoods remain a deep green, while the leaves on oak, maple, beech, ash and cherry trees showcase the same hues as school buses, blackberries, pumpkins and rosy lips.

Next, a father searches for the perfect pick off an apple tree while his son slyly tastetests those already in the bucket. The flush of the boy's cheeks matches the red of the apples, and the scene calls to mind a Norman Rockwell painting—the artist lived in Arlington 1939-53 and used many townsfolk as models.

She flips to page 26: The granite spire of the Bennington Battle Monument reaches 306 feet into the cloudless sky. The monument honors the 1777 defeat of the British forces at this site by the Green Mountain Boys, a Vermont militia group.

Turning to the last page, she is greeted by the gap-toothed grins of two young girls. Their fingers are covered with dripping ice cream, their faces a sticky delight. The sugar cone wrappers display "Ben & Jerry's" in trademark bubble letters, and one of the girls' shirts reads "I loVERMONT."

As she slowly closes the book, she can't think of a reason not to love Vermont.

Recreation

Mogul maniacs hit the slopes at Killington/Pico (the "Beast of the East"); Mount Snow; Stratton, known as the birthplace of snowboarding; Bromley in Manchester Center; Okemo in Ludlow; Sugarbush in Warren; Mad River Glen in Waitsfield; Stowe; Smugglers' Notch Resort in Jeffersonville; Burke Mountain in East Burke; and Bolton Valley.

Snowmobiling on more than 1,800 miles of well-marked "corridor" throughout the state heats up winter chills. Cross-country skiing trails are at Hildene, The Lincoln Family Home in Manchester Village; Prospect Mountain; and Viking and Wild Wings, both near Arlington.

But Vermont is versatile. Hiking and biking trails also accommodate cross-country skiers and snowmobilers; fishing and boating become ice fishing and ice boating in winter; and ski slopes run alpine slides in summer.

Biking is best in central Vermont's Green Mountains. In fall, blueberries grow on wild bushes that crowd the Hogback Mountain Trail on the south side of Hogback Mountain.

For another good Green Mountains ride, head to Ripton and catch the Natural Turnpike, a 23-mile paved path that circles to South Lincoln and offers a great view of Mount Abraham. Linking to the Natural Turnpike is Steammill Road, where you may glimpse moose relaxing near a former steam mill.

Hikers love Camel's Hump Trail. Crossing brooks and passing stands of birch trees, it runs between Burlington and Montpelier. Aptly named, the 270-mile Long Trail ascends to the Camel's Hump summit.

In Mount Mansfield State Forest, numerous paths lead trekkers to the Chin of Mount Mansfield for a spectacular 360-degree panorama. The famed Appalachian Trail meanders along the Green Mountains' crown; continue south at Shelburne Pass to intersect with the lower portion of the Long Trail.

Put the wind in your sails on expansive Lake Champlain. More than 400 other freshwater lakes—especially Lake Seymour, Lake Willoughby, and Caspian and Crystal lakes in the north—are also good places to row a boat.

Rafters and canoeists put in and paddle the waters of the Connecticut, Batten Kill and White rivers. Otter Creek, the longest river in the state, provides a good view of the Green Mountains. The Winooski River starts at Montpelier and runs 58 miles through deep Winooski Gorge, around dams and eventually to Lake Champlain.

Snowmobiling in the winter

Historic Timeline

1609	French explorer Samuel de Champlain discovers the Green Mountains and the lake that now bears his name.
1775	Ethan Allen, the Green Mountain Boys and Benedict Arnold capture Fort Ticonderoga from the British.
1785	The nation's first marble quarry is begun in East Dorset by Isaac Underhill.
1864	Confederate soldiers raid St. Albans in the northernmost land battle of the Civil War.
1881	Native son Chester A. Arthur becomes the 21st president of the United States following James A. Garfield's assassination.
1923	Calvin Coolidge of Plymouth Notch becomes the 30th president.
1940	Ida M. Fuller of Ludlow becomes the first recipient of a monthly Social Security check, for $22.54.
1968	Vermont becomes the first state to ban roadside billboards.
1984	Madeleine M. Kunin becomes the first woman governor of Vermont.
1987	The Growth Management Law sets statewide goals to protect natural resources and to promote land preservation.
2008	South Burlington-based ice cream icon Ben & Jerry's celebrates its 30th anniversary.

What To Pack

Temperature Averages Maximum/Minimum	JANUARY	FEBRUARY	MARCH	APRIL	MAY	JUNE	JULY	AUGUST	SEPTEMBER	OCTOBER	NOVEMBER	DECEMBER
Bennington	29/9	32/10	41/20	53/31	66/42	74/50	79/55	77/53	69/45	58/35	45/28	34/16
Burlington	27/9	29/10	38/20	53/33	67/44	77/54	82/59	80/57	71/49	57/39	44/29	31/15
Derby Line	26/6	31/8	41/19	54/31	69/43	77/52	81/57	79/55	70/47	57/37	43/27	31/13
Montpelier	25/7	28/10	38/20	51/32	65/43	73/52	78/57	76/55	67/46	55/36	42/28	31/14
Norwich	29/9	34/12	43/22	57/33	70/44	79/54	83/59	81/57	71/49	59/37	46/28	34/16
Shoreham	27/9	30/10	41/22	55/34	68/46	76/55	81/59	78/57	69/48	57/37	45/28	33/16

From the records of The Weather Channel Interactive, Inc.

Good Facts To Know

POPULATION: 625,741.

AREA: 9,616 square miles; ranks 45th.

CAPITAL: Montpelier.

HIGHEST POINT: 4,393 ft., Mount Mansfield.

LOWEST POINT: 95 ft., Lake Champlain.

TIME ZONE(S): Eastern. DST.

GAMBLING

MINIMUM AGE FOR GAMBLING: 21.

REGULATIONS

TEEN DRIVING LAWS: No passengers are allowed for the first 3 months without a licensed parent, guardian or other licensed adult at least 25 years old. No passengers, except for immediate family (of any age), are allowed for the following 3 months. The minimum age for an unrestricted driver's license is 16 years, 6 months. Phone (802) 828-2000 for more information about Vermont driver's license regulations.

SEAT BELT/CHILD RESTRAINT LAWS: Seat belts are required for driver and all passengers ages 18 and over. Children ages 8-17 are required to use a seat belt or child restraint. Child restraints are required for children under age 8; children under age 1 or less than a lbs. are required to be in a rear-facing child restraint. AAA recommends the use of seat belts and appropriate child restraints for the driver and all passengers.

CELLPHONE RESTRICTIONS: All drivers are prohibited from text messaging and using handheld cellphones. Drivers under 18 are prohibited from any cellphone use.

HELMETS FOR MOTORCYCLISTS: Required for all riders.

RADAR DETECTORS: Permitted for personal vehicles but prohibited for use by commercial vehicles.

MOVE OVER LAW: Driver must slow down and vacate the lane nearest stopped police, fire, rescue and tow truck vehicles using audible or flashing signals.

FIREARMS LAWS: Vary by state and/or county. Contact the Vermont State Police Headquarters, 45 State Dr., Waterbury, VT 05671; phone (802) 244-7345.

HOLIDAYS

HOLIDAYS: Jan. 1 ▪ Martin Luther King Jr. Day, Jan. (3rd Mon.) ▪ Washington's Birthday/Presidents Day, Feb. (3rd Mon.) ▪ Town Meeting Day, Mar. (1st Tues.) ▪ Memorial Day, May (4th Mon.) ▪ July 4 ▪ Bennington Battle Day, Aug. 16 ▪ Labor Day, Sept. (1st Mon.) ▪ Veterans Day, Nov. 11 ▪ Thanksgiving, Nov. (4th Thurs.) ▪ Christmas, Dec. 25.

MONEY

TAXES: Vermont's statewide sales tax is 6 percent; the towns of Burlington, Colchester, Dover, Killington, Manchester, Middlebury, Rutland, South Burlington, St. Albans, Stratton, Williston, Winhall and Wilmington impose an additional 1 percent sales tax. The state's Meals and Rooms Tax assesses a tax of 9 percent on lodgings and food and 10 percent on alcoholic beverages; 15 Vermont communities impose an extra 1 percent tax on lodgings, food and alcoholic beverages.

VISITOR INFORMATION

INFORMATION CENTERS: Year-round welcome centers are open in Montpelier (daily 8-8) ▪ on I-91 near the Canadian border at Derby Line ▪ on SR 4A at Fair Haven ▪ on I-91 at Guilford ▪ on I-93 at Lower Waterford ▪ and on I-91 at Lyndonville.

State and visitor information booths, open during the summer, are in Alburg ▪ Barre ▪ Bellows Falls ▪ Bennington ▪ Brandon ▪ Brattleboro ▪ Bristol ▪ Burlington ▪ Castleton ▪ Chester ▪ Hardwick ▪ Island Pond ▪ Jeffersonville ▪ Killington ▪ Ludlow ▪ Manchester ▪ Middlebury ▪ Montpelier ▪ Quechee ▪ Randolph ▪ Rutland ▪ St. Albans ▪ St. Johnsbury ▪ Swanton ▪ Vergennes ▪ Waitsfield ▪ Wells River ▪ White River Junction ▪ Wilmington ▪ and Woodstock.

FURTHER INFORMATION FOR VISITORS:
Vermont Department of Tourism and Marketing
National Life Building
1 National Life Dr., 6th floor
Montpelier, VT 05620-0501
(802) 828-3237
(800) 837-6668

NATIONAL FOREST INFORMATION:
Green Mountain and Finger Lakes National Forest
231 N. Main St.
Rutland, VT 05701
(802) 747-6700
(802) 747-6766

FISHING AND HUNTING REGULATIONS:
Vermont Department of Fish and Wildlife
1 National Life Dr., Davis 2
Montpelier, VT 05620
(802) 828-1190 (licenses)
(802) 828-1000

RECREATION INFORMATION:
State of Vermont Parks and Reservations
1 National Life Dr., Davis 2
Montpelier, VT 05620
(802) 828-1534 (Commissioner)
(802) 522-0730 (Business Office)
(888) 409-7579 (Reservations)

Vermont Annual Events

Please call ahead to confirm event details.

 Visit AAA.com/travelguides/events to find
AAA-listed events for every day of the year

WINTER

Dec. - Coolidge Holiday Open House
Plymouth / 802-672-3773
- Vermont International Festival
Essex Junction / 802-863-6713
- Christmas at the Farm / Woodstock
802-457-2355

Jan. - Vermont Farm Show / Essex
Junction / 802-828-1319
- Stowe Winter Carnival / Stowe
802-253-7321

Feb. - Winter Carnival / Brattleboro
802-254-5808
- Middlebury College Winter Carnival
Middlebury / 802-443-3103

SPRING

Mar. - Burlington Home Show / Burlington
800-237-6024
- Bud Light Reggaefest / Mount
Snow / 802-464-4191

Apr. - Sugar Slalom / Stowe / 802-253-770
- Pond Skimming / Killington
802-422-6200
- Vermont Maple Festival / St.
Albans / 802-524-5800

May - Spring Open Studio Weekend
Montpelier / 802-223-3380
- Kids' Day / Burlington / 802-864-012
- Sheep Shearing and Herding with
Border Collies / Woodstock
802-457-2355

SUMMER

June - Vermont Quilt Festival / Essex
Junction / 802-872-0034
- Quechee Hot Air Balloon Craft and
Music Festival / Quechee
802-295-7900
- Discover Jazz Festival / Burlington
802-863-7992

July - Stoweflake Hot Air Balloon Festival
Stowe / 802-253-7355
- Old Vermont 4th / Woodstock
802-457-2355
- Warren 4th of July / Warren
802-485-7092

Aug. - Bennington Battle Day Festivities and
Parade / Bennington / 802-447-0550
- Central Vermont Chamber Music
Festival / Randolph / 802-728-6464
- Vermont State Fair / Rutland
802-775-5200

FALL

Sept. - Garlic and Herb Festival / Benningtor
802-368-7147
- Colors of the Kingdom / St.
Johnsbury / 802-748-3678
- Glory Days Festival / White
River Junction / 802-295-5036

Oct. - Oktoberfest / Stowe / 802-253-3928
- Harborween Celebration / Vergennes
802-475-2311
- Essex Fall Craft and Fine Art Show
Essex Junction / 802-878-4786

Nov. - Fine Craft & Art Show / South
Burlington / 802-872-8600
- Manchester Merriment / Manchester
802-362-6313
- Santa Claus Parade and Holiday
Lighting Ceremony / Burlington
802-863-1648

 For complete hotel, dining and

attraction listings: AAA.com/travelguides

Manchester Merriment

Autumn by a creek in the Green Mountains

Gondolas to Mt. Mansfield in Stowe

President Calvin Coolidge State Historic Site, Plymouth

Park-McCullough Historic Estate, North Bennington

Index: Great Experience for Members

AAA editor's picks of exceptional note

Bennington Battle Monument

Marsh-Billings-Rockefeller Mansion

Shelburne Museum

Hildene, The Lincoln Family Home

See Orientation map on p. 147 for corresponding grid coordinates, if applicable.
* Indicates the GEM is temporarily closed.

Bennington (G-1)
Bennington Battle Monument *(See p. 151.)*
Bennington Museum *(See p. 151.)*

Manchester (F-2)
Hildene, The Lincoln Family Home
(See p. 157.)

Marsh-Billings-Rockefeller National Historical Park (D-3)
Marsh-Billings-Rockefeller Mansion
(See p. 159.)

North Bennington (G-1)
Park-McCullough Historic Estate *(See p. 162.)*

Norwich (D-3)
Montshire Museum of Science *(See p. 163.)*

Plymouth (E-3)
President Calvin Coolidge State Historic Site
(See p. 163.)

Proctor (E-2)
Wilson Castle *(See p. 163.)*

Shelburne (C-1)
Shelburne Museum *(See p. 166.)*

Woodstock (E-3)
Billings Farm & Museum *(See p. 174.)*

Vermont Atlas Section

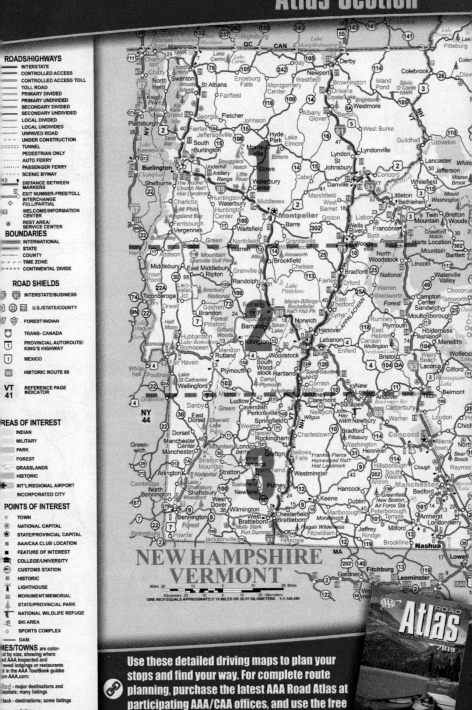

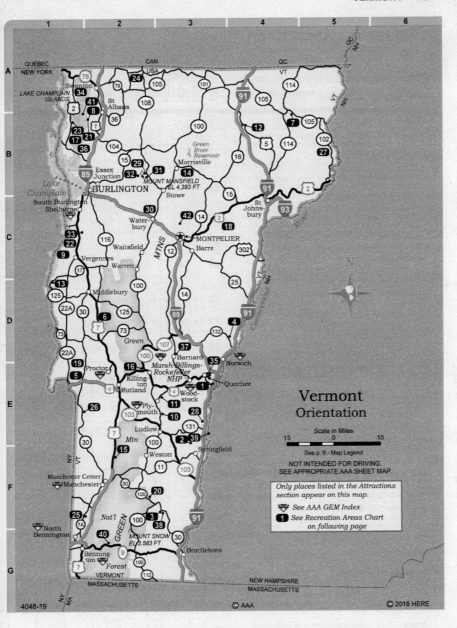

1 2 3 4 5 6

QUÉBEC
NEW YORK

CAN
USA

QC
VT

LAKE CHAMPLAIN
ISLANDS

Swanton

St Albans

Lake
Champlain

Essex
Junction

BURLINGTON

South Burlington
Shelburne

Green
River
Reservoir

Morrisville

MOUNT MANSFIELD
EL 4,393 FT

Stowe

St
Johns-
bury

Water-
bury

MONTPELIER

Barre

Waitsfield

Vergennes

Warren

Middlebury

Proctor

Green

Killing-
ton

Rutland

Ply-
mouth

Ludlow

Weston

Mtn

Barnard

Marsh-Billings-
Rockefeller
NHP

Norwich

Woodstock

Quechee

Springfield

Vermont
Orientation

Scale in Miles

15   0   15

See p. 6 - Map Legend

NOT INTENDED FOR DRIVING.
SEE APPROPRIATE AAA SHEET MAP.

*Only places listed in the Attractions
section appear on this map.*

See AAA GEM Index

1 See Recreation Areas Chart
on following page

Manchester Center
Manchester

North
Bennington

Nat'l

GREEN

MOUNT SNOW
EL 3,583 FT

Bennington

Forest

Brattleboro

VERMONT
MASSACHUSETTS

NEW HAMPSHIRE
MASSACHUSETTS

NY
MA

4048-19

© AAA

© 2018 HERE

N

Connecticut River

MTNS

Recreation Areas Chart

The map location numerals in column 2 show an area's location on the preceding map.

 Find thousands of places to camp at AAA.com/campgrounds

	MAP LOCATION	CAMPING	PICNICKING	HIKING TRAILS	BOATING	BOAT RAMP	BOAT RENTAL	FISHING	SWIMMING	PET FRIENDLY	BICYCLE TRAILS	WINTER SPORTS	VISITOR CENTER	LODGE/CABINS	FOOD SERVICE
NATIONAL FORESTS *(See place listings.)*															
Green Mountain (E-2) 420,000 acres. South-central Vermont. Cross-country and downhill skiing, horseback riding, hunting, snowboarding, snowmobiling, snowshoeing.			•	•	•	•	•		•	•	•	•	•		
ARMY CORPS OF ENGINEERS															
North Hartland Lake (E-3) 1 mi. n. of North Hartland off US 5. Canoeing, cross-country skiing, snowmobiling, snowshoeing; playground. Non-motorized boats only.	1	•	•	•	•	•	•	•	•	•		•	•		
North Springfield Lake (E-3) 1,361 acres .5 mi. n.e. of North Springfield off SR 106. Cross-country skiing, hunting, snowmobiling, snowshoeing. Canoes and flat-bottomed boats only.	2		•		•	•		•	•			•			
Townshend Lake (F-2) 6 mi. n. of Townshend on SR 30. Cross-country skiing, hunting, snowmobiling, snowshoeing.	3	•	•	•	•	•		•	•	•		•			
Union Village Dam (D-4) 5 mi. s. of Thetford Center on SR 132. Cross-country skiing, hunting, snowmobiling.	4		•	•				•	•						
STATE															
Bomoseen (E-1) 3,576 acres (two areas) .5 mi. n. of West Castleton. Historic. Beach, nature center, nature trails.	5	•	•	•	•	•	•	•	•	•		•			•
Branbury (D-2) 64 acres 3 mi. e. of Salisbury off US 7 on SR 53. Beach, nature center, nature trails, playground, waterfalls.	6	•	•	•	•	•	•	•	•	•		•		•	•
Brighton (B-4) 610 acres 2 mi. e. of Island Pond off SR 105. Amphitheater, beach, nature center, nature trails, theater. Pets allowed in campground only.	7	•	•	•	•	•	•	•	•	•		•		•	
Burton Island (A-2) 253 acres in Lake Champlain; access by boat only from Kamp Kill Kare State Park. Marina, nature center, nature trails.	8	•	•	•	•	•	•	•	•	•		•			•
Button Bay (C-1) 253 acres .5 mi. w. of Vergennes on SR 22A, then 6.5 mi. n. w. via Panton and Basin Harbor rds. Kayak rentals, nature center, nature trails, swimming pool.	9	•	•	•	•	•	•	•	•	•		•			
Camp Plymouth (E-3) 295 acres off SR 100 n. of Ludlow. Beach.	10	•	•	•		•		•	•	•				•	•
Coolidge (E-3) 21,416 acres 2 mi. n. of Plymouth via SR 100A. Snowmobiling; nature center, playground.	11	•	•	•				•		•		•			
Crystal Lake (B-4) 16 acres in Barton on SR 16. Beach, playground.	12		•	•				•	•	•				•	•
D.A.R. (D-1) 95 acres 1 mi. n. of Chimney Point on SR 17. Bird-watching, sailing.	13	•	•		•			•		•		•			
Elmore (B-3) 700 acres at Elmore on SR 12. Beach, playground.	14	•	•	•		•		•	•	•					•
Emerald Lake (F-2) 430 acres at North Dorset on US 7. Historic. Beach, cemetery, nature center, nature trails, playground. Non-motorized boats only.	15	•	•	•		•	•	•	•	•		•			•
Gifford Woods (E-2) 285 acres 2 mi. n. of Killington on SR 100.	16	•	•	•				•		•			•		
Grand Isle (B-1) 226 acres 5 mi. n. of South Hero off US 2. Nature center, playground.	17	•	•	•	•	•	•	•	•	•	•	•		•	
Groton State Forest (C-4) 26,175 acres (seven areas) midway between Montpelier and St. Johnsbury. Snowmobiling.	18	•	•	•	•	•	•	•	•	•		•		•	•
Half Moon Pond (E-1) 50 acres 10 mi. n.w. of Castleton off SR 30. Beach, nature programs, nature trails, playground. Non-motorized boats only.	19	•		•	•			•	•	•		•		•	
Jamaica (F-3) 772 acres 1 mi. e. of Jamaica on SR 30. Nature center.	20	•	•	•				•	•	•		•			
Kamp Kill Kare (B-2) 17.75 acres 4 mi. w. of St. Albans on SR 36, then 3.5 mi. s.w. on Point Rd. Kayak rentals, playground.	21		•		•	•	•	•	•			•			
Kingsland Bay (C-1) 264 acres 3 mi. n.w. of Ferrisburgh off Hawkins Rd. Historic. Sailing.	22		•	•	•		•	•	•	•		•			
Knight Point (B-1) 54 acres 3 mi. s. of North Hero off US 2. Art center, beach, playground.	23		•	•	•			•	•	•		•			
Lake Carmi (A-2) 482 acres 3 mi. s. of East Franklin on SR 236. Beach, nature trails, playground.	24	•	•	•	•	•	•	•	•	•		•		•	•

Recreation Areas Chart

The map location numerals in column 2 show an area's location on the preceding map.

Find thousands of places to camp at AAA.com/campgrounds

	MAP LOCATION	CAMPING	PICNICKING	HIKING TRAILS	BOATING	BOAT RAMP	BOAT RENTAL	FISHING	SWIMMING	PET FRIENDLY	BICYCLE TRAILS	WINTER SPORTS	VISITOR CENTER	LODGE/CABINS	FOOD SERVICE
Lake St. Catherine (F-1) 117 acres 3 mi. s. of Poultney on SR 30. Canoeing, kayaking; nature center, nature trails, playground.	25	•	•	•	•	•	•	•	•	•		•			•
Lake Shaftsbury (E-2) 84 acres 10 mi. n. of Bennington via US 7A. Beach, nature trail, playground.	26		•	•				•	•	•				•	•
Maidstone (B-5) 469 acres 5 mi. s. of Bloomfield on SR 102, then 5 mi. s.w. on State Forest Hwy. Beach, nature trails, playground.	27	•	•	•	•	•		•	•	•			•		
Mt. Ascutney (E-3) 2,506 acres 3 mi. s.w. of Windsor on SR 44 off US 5. Scenic. Hang gliding, snowmobiling.	28	•	•	•						•		•			
Mount Mansfield State Forest (B-2) 39,765 acres. Cross-country skiing, downhill skiing, snowmobiling.	29	•	•	•								•			
Little River (C-2) 60 acres 1.5 mi. w. of Waterbury on US 2, then 3.5 mi. n. on Little River Rd. Water skiing; beach, playground.	30	•	•	•	•	•	•	•	•	•		•	•		
Smugglers Notch (B-3) 32 acres 8 mi. w. of Stowe on SR 108. Historic. Nature programs.	31	•	•	•						•		•	•		
Underhill (B-2) 1 mi. n.e. of Underhill Center on Pleasant Valley Rd., then 2.6 mi. e. on Mountain Rd.	32	•	•	•						•		•			
Mount Philo (C-1) 168 acres 14 mi. s. of Burlington off US 7. Scenic. Bird-watching; playground.	33	•	•	•						•			•		
North Hero (A-1) 400 acres 8 mi. n. of North Hero off US 2. Nature trails, playground.	34		•		•	•		•	•	•					
Quechee (D-3) 688 acres 7 mi. w. of White River Junction off US 4.	35		•	•				•		•			•		
Sand Bar (B-1) 15 acres n.w. of Burlington using I-89, exit 17 (Champlain Islands) then 4 mi n on US 2. Beach, playground.	36		•		•	•	•	•	•	•					•
Silver Lake (D-3) 34 acres .5 mi. e. of Barnard off SR 12. Beach, playground.	37	•	•		•		•	•	•	•					•
Townshend (F-3) 1,095 acres 4.8 mi. w. of Townshend at 2755 State Forest Rd.	38	•	•	•	•			•	•	•					
Wilgus (E-3) 89 acres 1 mi. s. of Ascutney on US 5. Canoeing, kayaking; nature trails.	39	•	•	•	•			•		•				•	
Woodford (G-2) 398 acres 10 mi. e. of Bennington on SR 9. Nature trails, playground.	40	•	•	•	•		•	•	•	•					
Woods Island (A-2) 125 acres 4 mi. n. of Burton Island State Park in Lake Champlain; accessible by private boat only. Permit camping only.	41	•	•	•	•			•	•	•					
OTHER															
Wrightsville Beach (C-3) 4 mi. n. of Montpelier off SR 12. Disc golf (18 holes); canoe and kayak rentals. Dogs are permitted before Memorial Day and after Labor Day for a fee.	42		•	•	•			•	•	•	•				•

BARNARD (D-3) elev. 1,309'

A town of summer cottages and winter hideaways, Barnard has been home to some of the state's most elite citizens. Journalist Dorothy Thompson and her husband, novelist Sinclair Lewis, lived at their picturesque white frame house, Twin Farms, during the 1930s. Thompson was one of the few female correspondents during World War II. She is buried in Village Cemetery on North Road.

THE MAPLE LEAF INN   (802)234-5342

♦♦♦♦♦
Bed & Breakfast
$165-$280

Address: 5890 VT 12 05031 **Location:** Just s on SR 12; center. **Facility:** This Victorian-style farmhouse sits on 16 bucolic acres in a serene setting near picturesque Silver Lake. Guest rooms are individually decorated with plush bedding; many have a jetted bathtub. 7 units. 3 stories (no elevator), interior corridors. **Terms:** 2 night minimum stay - seasonal and/or weekends, 14 day cancellation notice-fee imposed. **Activities:** cross country skiing, snowmobiling, bicycles. **Featured Amenity: full hot breakfast.** SAVE BIZ 🛜 ✕

WHERE TO EAT

BARNARD INN RESTAURANT & MAX'S TAVERN
802/234-9961
♦♦♦ New American. Fine Dining. **Address:** 5518 SR 12 05031

BARRE pop. 9,052, elev. 515'

Although Barre (BARE-ie) started out not much different from other fledgling late 18th-century New England towns, a quirk of geology established its fate.

Originally chartered as Wildersburgh in 1780, the area's first settlers arrived in 1788, followed soon thereafter by emigrants from New Hampshire and Massachusetts. A name change resulted in Barre replacing Wildersburgh, though exactly how the change occurred has been lost to history. Two stories prevail—one version involves a bout of fisticuffs, the other has to do with offering naming rights to the person who contributed the most money toward the construction of a meeting house (the winning bid, by the way, was £62).

The huge quantity of granite found nearby is the geological phenomenon that altered the course of Barre's history. Shortly after the conclusion of the War of 1812, many highly skilled stonecutters from Italy, Scotland and other nations came to ply their trade. The arrival of the railroad simplified transportation, and the city adopted the moniker Granite Center of the World. Barre has been the largest granite-producing district in the country since 1900.

Barre granite, known for its almost flawless texture, comes in two shades: white and blue-gray. Fine works created from the local stone can be found throughout the region, including the state house in nearby Montpelier (see place listing p. 160).

You don't have to go far, though, to find some prime examples of granite craftsmanship. Pay a visit to Barre Opera House at 6 N. Main St.; phone (802) 476-8188. Hope Cemetery, established in 1895, has many artistic, often whimsical memorials, all crafted out of Barre gray granite. And the Robert Burns Monument, at 60 Washington St., was cut by local artisans in 1899 and is considered one of the finest pieces of granite sculpture in the world. In addition to a statue of Burns, the sculpture includes four panels that depict scenes from his poems and from his cottage in Ayr, Scotland.

Many large plants still produce granite sculpture for use in monuments and tombstones, and factory and quarry tours are available in nearby Graniteville at Rock of Ages Visitors Center.

Central Vermont Chamber of Commerce: 33 Stewart Rd., P.O. Box 336, Barre, VT 05641 **Phone:** (802) 229-5711 or (802) 229-4619.

Self-guiding tours: A downtown walking tour covers the town's common, memorials, a number of 19th-century churches, the Opera House, Masonic Temple, library, post office and fire station. You can pick up a walking tour brochure at the chamber of commerce, the library and local merchants.

LADDER 1 GRILL   802/883-2000
♦♦ American. Casual Dining. **Address:** 8 S Main St 05641

MR. Z'S   802/479-3259
♦♦ Italian. Casual Dining. **Address:** 379 N Main St 05641

THE STEAK HOUSE RESTAURANT   802/479-9181
♦♦ Steak. Casual Dining. **Address:** 1239 US 302 05641

BENNINGTON (G-1) pop. 9,074, elev. 728'
• Hotels p. 152 • Restaurants p. 153

Bennington is set in a valley between Mount Anthony, part of the Taconic Range, and the foothills of the Green Mountains (see place listing p. 155). In the Battle of Bennington on Aug. 16, 1777, the Americans under Gen. John Stark defeated a British expedition sent by Gen. John Burgoyne. The conflict is commemorated each year in mid-August during the Bennington Battle Day Celebration.

Bennington's three covered bridges are reminders of times gone by. The Silk Road Bridge, Paper Mill Village Bridge and Henry Bridge all are easily accessible from off SR 67A on Murphy Road. US 7A north to Manchester and SR 9 east to Brattleboro provide scenic drives.

Hemmings Car Lover's Store and Sunoco Station displays vintage automobile memorabilia in an old-fashioned, full-service gas station at 216 Main St.; phone (802) 447-9652.

Three miles north at 121 Historic SR 7A in Shaftsbury is the Robert Frost Stone House Museum, in which the Pulitzer Prize-winning poet lived and composed poetry from 1920-29. Educational and literary displays cover Frost's life and art; phone (802) 447-6200.

Outdoor activities available in the area include cross-country skiing, snowshoeing, snowmobiling, canoeing, kayaking, hiking and fishing. Popular recreational areas are Lake Paran, Woodford State Park *(see Recreation Areas Chart)* and Lake Shaftsbury State Park *(see Recreation Areas Chart)*.

Held Labor Day weekend, the Southern Vermont Garlic and Herb Festival draws more than 13,000 allium lovers with food, music and crafts.

Bennington Area Chamber of Commerce: 100 Veterans Memorial Dr., Bennington, VT 05201. **Phone:** (802) 447-3311.

Self-guiding tours: Maps of two walking tours of historic buildings, houses and streets are available from the chamber of commerce. The chamber also has bike tour maps and driving tour maps that feature covered bridges.

Shopping: Bennington Potters Yard, 324 County St., offers free self-guiding tours of the pottery works which produce fine and decorative art pottery for the home; phone (800) 205-8033. Works in other media are offered in galleries throughout town.

BENNINGTON BATTLE MONUMENT, 1 mi. w. on SR 9 (Main St.), then .3 mi. n. on Monument Ave. to 15 Monument Cir., commemorates the Revolutionary War battle of Aug. 16, 1777, between British General John Burgoyne's forces and a group of Vermont, New Hampshire and Massachusetts volunteers led by General John Stark.

The British, running low on supplies, were attempting to reach the depot in Bennington where U.S. military provisions and food were stocked. The Americans met the redcoats before they could reach the storage site, however, and the Battle of Bennington, which ensued, was actually fought about 5 miles west at Walloomsac, N.Y. The loss to the Americans (both in manpower and the failure to restock their supplies) proved to be a factor in Burgoyne's surrender following the Battle of Saratoga in October, said to be a major turning point in the war.

The stone obelisk, when completed in 1889, was the tallest battle monument in the world; at 306 feet, it is still the tallest structure in Vermont. The monument was not dedicated, though, until 1891, with President Benjamin Harrison in attendance.

From the upper lookout chamber, reached by elevator or on occasion by walking the 412 steps, three states (Vermont, New York and Massachusetts) can be seen. A diorama and exhibits illustrate the battle, and an iron kettle belonging to General Burgoyne is displayed. A granite monument to Seth Warner who, with the Green Mountain Boys, helped win the battle, a statue of Stark and other monuments surround the attraction. Events are scheduled throughout the season.

Time: Allow 30 minutes minimum. **Hours:** Daily 9-5, mid-Apr. through Oct. 31. **Cost:** $5; $1 (ages 6-14). **Phone:** (802) 447-0550.

BENNINGTON CENTER FOR THE ARTS, 44 Gypsy Ln., is home to seven visual arts galleries and a covered bridge museum. The center's 700-piece collection is displayed on a rotating basis; a Native American exhibit, Floyd Scholz bird carvings and Eric Sloane paintings are displayed year-round. Concerts, lectures and workshops are offered throughout the year.

Time: Allow 30 minutes minimum. **Hours:** Wed.-Mon. 10-5. Closed Jan. 1, Thanksgiving and Christmas. **Cost:** (Includes entire complex) $9; $8 (ages 62+ and students ages 13-22 with ID); free (ages 0-12); $20 (family). **Phone:** (802) 442-7158.

Vermont Covered Bridge Museum, inside the Bennington Center for the Arts at 44 Gypsy Ln., describes the history of the state's and nation's covered bridges, many of which were destroyed in a late 1920s flood. Visitors view miniature replicas of covered bridges and learn about the bridges' builders, architectural styles and locations. A resource center contains information about covered bridges across the country. **Time:** Allow 30 minutes minimum. **Hours:** Wed.-Mon. 10-5. **Cost:** (Includes entire Bennington Center for the Arts complex) $9; $8 (ages 62+ and students ages 13-22 with ID); free (ages 0-12); $20 (family). **Phone:** (802) 442-7158.

BENNINGTON MUSEUM is at 75 Main St., 1 mi. w. of jct. SRs 7 and 9 in The Shires of Vermont. The museum houses a collection reflective of the region's art, history and innovation. Home to what is said to be the largest public collection of paintings by Anna Mary Robertson "Grandma" Moses, the museum's Grandma Moses Gallery displays her paintings and belongings as well as photographs and family memorabilia. The gallery is adjacent to the Grandma Moses Schoolhouse, a family and children's activity center where visitors can barter in a country store and learn what it was like to attend school in the 19th century.

Permanent exhibits include the Bennington Flag, one of the oldest Stars and Stripes flags in existence; firearms; and American paintings and sculpture from the 18th and 19th centuries. The story of the Battle of Bennington is told in the museum's Military Gallery, and the Bennington Pottery Gallery showcases a renowned collection of 19th-century ceramics produced by local companies.

The Early Vermont Gallery presents life in Vermont from the time when the earliest European settlers arrived in 1761 with only the bare necessities to the early 1800s when Vermont craftsmen achieved a level of sophistication rivaling Boston and New York. (1760s to early-1800s). Explored through stories and vignettes, this gallery showcases over 85 major pieces and smaller items from the Museum's extensive historical collection of over 30,000 objects.

The Bennington Modernism Gallery includes works by avant-garde artists working in Bennington from the early 1950s to the mid-1970s. As the gallery changes, it may feature works by such artists as

Pat Adams, Paul Freeley, Helen Frankenthaler, Kenneth Noland and David Smith. The Gilded Age Vermont Gallery highlights industrial and cultural innovations in the region through objects either made or owned in Bennington or created by artists with connections to the area. Exhibits include paintings by William Morris Hunt and Frederick MacMonnies; glass and metal works by Louis Comfort Tiffany; and the Martin Wasp, a 1920s luxury automobile made in Bennington by Karl Martin. The Works on Paper Gallery features drawings, prints, paintings and photographs by contemporary and historic artists.

Changing exhibits are available year-round. A genealogy research library and the Hadwen Woods and George Aiken Wildflower Trail also are on the grounds.

Cellphone audio tours are available. **Time:** Allow 1 hour minimum. **Hours:** Daily 10-5, June-Oct.; Thurs.-Tues. 10-5, Feb.-May and Nov.-Dec. Closed Easter, July 4, Thanksgiving and Christmas (closes at 1 on Dec. 24 and 31). **Cost:** $10; $9 (ages 62+); free (ages 0-17). **Phone:** (802) 447-1571.

BEST WESTERN BENNINGTON (802)442-6311

Motel
$99-$209

Best Western.

AAA Benefit: Members save up to 15% and earn bonus points!

Address: 220 Northside Dr 05201 **Location:** Jct SR 9, 1.2 mi n on US 7, then 0.7 mi n on Historic SR 7A. **Facility:** 58 units. 1-2 stories (no elevator), interior/exterior corridors. **Terms:** cancellation fee imposed. **Amenities:** safes. **Pool:** outdoor. **Activities:** exercise room. **Guest Services:** valet and coin laundry. *(See ad this page.)*

FOUR CHIMNEY'S INN 802/447-3500
◆◆◆ Historic Bed & Breakfast. **Address:** 21 West Rd 05201

HAMPTON INN BY HILTON (802)440-9862

Hotel
$119-$298

Hampton

AAA Benefit: Members save 5% or more!

Address: 51 Hannaford Square 05201 **Location:** SR 279 exit 1, just s. **Facility:** 80 units. 3 stories, interior corridors. **Terms:** 1-7 night minimum stay, cancellation fee imposed. **Pool:** heated indoor. **Activities:** sauna, exercise room. **Guest Services:** valet and coin laundry. **Featured Amenity:** full hot breakfast.

/SOME UNITS

THE HARWOOD HILL 802/442-6278
◆ Motel. **Address:** 864 Harwood Hill Rd 05201

KNOTTY PINE MOTEL (802)442-5487
◆ Vintage Motel. **Address:** 130 Northside Dr 05201

▼ See AAA listing this page ▼

WHERE TO EAT

ALLEGRO RISTORANTE   802/442-0990
▼▼▼▼ Italian. Fine Dining. **Address:** 520 Main St 05201

LIL' BRITAIN FISH & CHIP SHOP   802/442-2447
▼ British. Casual Dining. **Address:** 116 North St 05201

MADISON BREWING CO. PUB & RESTAURANT 802/442-7397
▼▼ American. Brewpub. **Address:** 428 Main St 05201

THE PUBLYK HOUSE   802/442-7500
▼▼▼ American. Casual Dining. **Address:** 782 Harwood Hill
05201

BRATTLEBORO (G-3) pop. 7,414, elev. 226'

It was here that the state's first permanent English settlement, Fort Dummer, was established in 1724.

Rudyard Kipling, in collaboration with New York architect Henry Rutgers Marshall, built a house for his American bride north of Brattleboro in Dummerston and named it Naulakha, which means "precious jewel." Kipling wrote "Captains Courageous" and the two "Jungle Book" stories during his residence there. The Landmark Trust USA, a non-profit foundation dedicated to preserving historically significant homes, restored the house, which is available for rent by reservation and accommodates up to eight guests at a time; phone (802) 254-6868.

Also of interest is Brooks Memorial Library, which has changing art and photography exhibits, an extensive genealogy room and a children's room; phone (802) 254-5290. Running west to Bennington is SR 9, which offers scenic views in the vicinity of Hogback Mountain.

Brattleboro Area Chamber of Commerce: 180 Main St., Brattleboro, VT 05301. **Phone:** (802) 254-4565 or (877) 254-4565.

HAMPTON INN BY HILTON BRATTLEBORO
(802)254-5700

▼▼▼ **Hotel**
$109-$215

AAA Benefit: Members save 5% or more!

Address: 1378 Putney Rd 05301 **Location:** I-91 exit 3, 0.6 mi n on US 5. **Facility:** 73 units. 4 stories, interior corridors. **Terms:** 1-7 night minimum stay, cancellation fee imposed. **Pool:** heated indoor. **Activities:** hot tub, exercise room. **Guest Services:** coin laundry.

[SAVE] CALL [⬆] [🚗] [♿] [BIZ] [HS]
[📶] [✕] [🎥] [🛏] [🍽] [🖥]

HOLIDAY INN EXPRESS HOTEL & SUITES   (802)257-2400
▼▼▼ Hotel. **Address:** 100 Chickering Dr 05301

WHERE TO EAT

DUO RESTAURANT   802/254-4141
▼▼ American. Casual Dining. **Address:** 136 Main St 05301

BURLINGTON (B-1) pop. 42,417, elev. 112'
• Hotels p. 154 • Restaurants p. 154

Built on the terraced slopes of Lake Champlain, Burlington is the largest city in Vermont and is an important industrial, retail and educational center. It is the headquarters of navigation on the lake and a principal port of air entry on the United States-Canada border.

The area first was settled in 1775, but most of its inhabitants left with the onset of the American Revolution, and settlement did not resume until after the war. Revolutionist Ethan Allen tended a farm north of the city and is buried in Greenmount Cemetery on Colchester Avenue. The Ethan Allen Monument, a 35-foot-tall Doric column topped with an 8-foot-tall statue of the patriot, marks the site of his grave.

The city's oldest section is along Battery Street near the lakefront. Explore other historic areas including Pearl, South Willard and Church streets, the University Green and City Hall Park. Church Street Marketplace, a five-block pedestrian mall, is in the historic district.

On the upper level of town is the University of Vermont, founded in 1791. Champlain College, established in 1878 as the Burlington Collegiate Institute but renamed in 1958, spreads out along S. Willard Street in the city's Hill Section, within walking distance of downtown. Some dormitories occupy handsomely renovated Victorian-era mansions. Free campus tours of Champlain College are available; phone (802) 860-2727 for reservation information.

The Burlington Bikepath, a 7.5-mile scenic route from Oakledge Park to the path's terminus at the Winooski River, traverses Burlington's historic waterfront, skirts Lake Champlain's shoreline, passes through woodland areas and ultimately connects to the Colchester Bike Path.

Burlington is at the end of the scenic portion of two highways: I-89, which runs 95 miles southeast to White River Junction, and SR 7, which runs south to Middlebury.

You'll be tapping your toes at the ▼ Discover Jazz Festival, a 10-day event that kicks off summer in Burlington. In early June, more than 100 performances by local talent and international jazz legends take place at intimate venues, parks, restaurants and the Church Street Marketplace. Plus, classes, films, meet-the-artist sessions and workshops offer festivalgoers greater insight into this enduring American art form.

Lake Champlain Regional Chamber of Commerce: 60 Main St., Suite 100, Burlington, VT 05401. **Phone:** (802) 863-3489 or (877) 686-5253.

Shopping: Burlington Town Center, I-89 exit 14W, features some 50 stores, including Ann Taylor LOFT, Chico's, J. Crew, L.L. Bean, Macy's and Williams-Sonoma.

Downtown, Church Street Marketplace provides shops, services and restaurants in a festive atmosphere that includes street musicians and sidewalk cafés. University Mall on Dorset Street offers more than 70 stores including anchors The Bon-Ton, JC-Penney, Kohl's and Sears.

ECHO, LEAHY CENTER FOR LAKE CHAMPLAIN is downtown on the waterfront, just w. of jct. College and Battery sts., at 1 College St. In this nature and science center, numerous tanks hold 70 live species you can find in the area. Enhance learning with more than 100 interactive experiences for all ages. Northfield Savings Bank 3D Theater screens nature and science films daily.

Some permanent exhibits include Action Lab, a 3-D augmented reality watershed sand table; Into the Lake, a shipwreck for kids to explore and discover live sturgeon and learn about invasive species; and Indigenous Expressions, a look at the Native Americans who lived in the Lake Champlain basin. In Champ Lane, a 2,500-square-foot interactive learning space, families can climb in a tree house, captain a ship, shop in a market, explore water play and care for animals in the Kids Lab. Rotating exhibits change seasonally.

Time: Allow 1 hour, 30 minutes minimum. **Hours:** Daily 10-5. Café closes 1 hour before closing. Closed Thanksgiving, Christmas Eve and Christmas. **Cost:** $14.50; $12.50 (ages 60+ and college students with ID); $11.50 (ages 3-17). Theater additional $5. **Parking:** Parking is available for a fee. **Phone:** (802) 864-1848 or (877) 324-6386. [T]

LAKE CHAMPLAIN FERRIES—see Lake Champlain p. 156.

ROBERT HULL FLEMING MUSEUM, 61 Colchester Ave. on the University of Vermont campus, opened in 1931. Displays of European, American, African, ancient Egyptian, and Middle Eastern art and anthropology as well as paintings by 20th-century American artists are featured. Rotating exhibits are shown periodically.

Hours: Tues.-Fri. 10-4 (also Wed. 4-7), Sat.-Sun. noon-4, Labor Day-late May. Closed major holiday weekends and school breaks. **Cost:** $5; $3 (ages 7-17 and 60+); $10 (family, two adults and all minor children). **Phone:** (802) 656-0750, or (802) 656-2090 for recorded information.

SHELBURNE MUSEUM—see Shelburne p. 166.

COURTYARD BY MARRIOTT BURLINGTON HARBOR HOTEL
(802)864-4700
WWWW Hotel. **Address:** 25 Cherry St 05401

| AAA Benefit: Members save 5% or more! |

HILTON BURLINGTON   (802)658-6500

Contemporary Hotel
$129-$999

AAA Benefit: Members save 5% or more!

Address: 60 Battery St 05401 **Location:** Waterfront. At Battery and College sts; just n of ferry terminal; center. **Facility:** 258 units. 8 stories, interior corridors. **Parking:** on-site (fee). **Terms:** 1-7 night minimum stay, cancellation fee imposed. **Amenities:** safes. **Pool:** heated indoor. **Activities:** hot tub, bicycles, exercise room. **Guest Services:** valet laundry, area transportation.

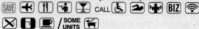

HILTON GARDEN INN BURLINGTON DOWNTOWN
802/951-0099
WWW Contemporary Hotel. **Address:** 101 Main St 05401

| AAA Benefit: Members save 5% or more! |

HOTEL VERMONT   802/651-0080
WWW Boutique Hotel. **Address:** 41 Cherry St 05401

WHERE TO EAT

AMERICAN FLATBREAD   802/861-2999
WW Pizza. Casual Dining. **Address:** 115 St. Paul St 05401

ASIANA NOODLE SHOP   802/862-8828
WW Asian Noodles Sushi. Casual Dining. **Address:** 88 Church St 05401

AUGUST FIRST BAKERY & CAFE   802/540-0060
W Breads/Pastries Breakfast. Casual Dining. **Address:** 149 S Champlain St 05401

BUENO Y SANO   802/864-9900
W Mexican. Quick Serve. **Address:** 213 College St 05401

EL CORTIJO TAQUERIA & CANTINA   802/497-1668
WW Mexican. Casual Dining. **Address:** 189 Bank St 05401

THE FARMHOUSE TAP & GRILL   802/859-0888
WW Regional American. Gastropub. **Address:** 160 Bank St 05401

HALVORSON'S UPSTREET CAFE   802/658-0278
WW American. Casual Dining. **Address:** 16 Church St 05401

HEN OF THE WOOD RESTAURANT BURLINGTON
802/540-0534
WWW New American. Fine Dining. **Address:** 55 Cherry St 05401

LEUNIG'S BISTRO & CAFE   802/863-3759
WWW New American. Fine Dining. **Address:** 115 Church St 05401

MONARCH & THE MILKWEED   802/310-7828
WWW New Comfort Food Desserts. Casual Dining. **Address:** 111 St Paul St 05401

PASCOLO RISTORANTE   802/497-1613
WWW Italian. Casual Dining. **Address:** 83 Church St 05401

PENNY CLUSE CAFE   802/651-8834
WW Breakfast Sandwiches. Casual Dining. **Address:** 169 Cherry St 05401

PHO HONG 802/865-8031
♦♦ Vietnamese. Casual Dining. **Address:** 325 N Winooski Ave 05401

RI-RA IRISH PUB 802/860-9401
♦♦ Irish. Casual Dining. **Address:** 123 Church St 05401

THE SCUFFER TAP & TABLE 802/864-9451
♦♦ American. Casual Dining. **Address:** 148 Church St 05401

THE SKINNY PANCAKE 802/540-0188
♦♦ American. Casual Dining. **Address:** 60 Lake St 05401

SWEETWATERS 802/864-9800
♦♦ American. Casual Dining. **Address:** 120 Church St 05401

TRATTORIA DELIA 802/864-5253
♦♦♦ Italian. Casual Dining. **Address:** 152 St. Paul St 05401

THE VERMONT PUB & BREWERY 802/865-0500
♦♦ American. Casual Dining. **Address:** 144 College St 05401

COLCHESTER

DAYS INN COLCHESTER (802)655-0900
♦♦ Hotel. **Address:** 124 College Pkwy 05446

HAMPTON INN BY HILTON & VERMONT EVENT CENTER
(802)655-6177
♦♦♦ Hotel. **Address:** 42 Lower Mountain View Dr 05446

AAA Benefit: Members save 5% or more!

MOTEL 6 #1407 (802)654-6860
♦ Hotel. **Address:** 74 S Park Dr 05446

RESIDENCE INN BY MARRIOTT, BURLINGTON-COLCHESTER
(802)655-3100
♦♦♦ Extended Stay Contemporary Hotel. **Address:** 71 Rathe Rd 05446

AAA Benefit: Members save 5% or more!

WHERE TO EAT

GUILTY PLATE DINER 802/399-2011
♦♦ American. Casual Dining. **Address:** 164 Porters Point Rd 05446

THE LIGHTHOUSE RESTAURANT AND LOUNGE
802/448-3361
♦♦ American. Casual Dining. **Address:** 38 Lower Mountain View Dr 05446

MCGILICUDDY'S ON THE GREEN 802/871-5480
♦♦ Irish. Sports Bar. **Address:** 18 Severance Rd 05446

ESSEX JUNCTION (B-2) pop. 9,271, elev. 344'

The ⚑ Vermont Quilt Festival, held in late June at the Champlain Valley Exposition, features hundreds of new and antique quilts. The Champagne and Chocolate Preview kicks off what is called New England's oldest and largest quilt show. You'll find quilt appraisals, classes, demonstrations, gallery talks, guest speakers and a merchants' mall with more than 80 vendors.

Shopping: Essex Outlets, off I-89 at 21 Essex Way, is home to such national retailers as Brooks Brothers and OshKosh B'gosh. A digital movie theater with stadium seating also is on-site.

BAYMONT INN & SUITES BURLINGTON/ESSEX JUNCTION
(802)872-5200
♦♦ Extended Stay Hotel. **Address:** 27 Susie Wilson Rd 05452

THE ESSEX, VERMONT'S CULINARY RESORT & SPA
(802)878-1100
♦♦♦ Resort Hotel. **Address:** 70 Essex Way 05452

WHERE TO EAT

JUNCTION 802/878-1100

♦♦♦♦ American Fine Dining $20-$40

AAA Inspector Notes: Whimsically decorated with table settings attached to the ceiling and culinary-themed artwork on the walls, this restaurant features a theater kitchen where guests are seated at a white marble table. Meals begin by individually speaking with the chef who explains the origins and preparations of each course. Expertly trained staff members accommodate special requests and offer personalized options. **Features:** full bar. **Reservations:** suggested. **Address:** 70 Essex Way 05452 **Location:** SR 289 exit 10, 0.3 mi s; in The Essex, Vermont's Culinary Resort & Spa. **Parking:** on-site and valet. [D]

FAIRFAX

THE INN AT BUCK HOLLOW FARM (802)849-2400

♦♦♦ Historic Bed & Breakfast $89-$145

Address: 2150 Buck Hollow Rd 05454 **Location:** 6 mi n of jct SR 104 via Buck Hollow Rd. Located in a rural area. **Facility:** This 1790 carriage house is on 400 acres and features individually decorated rooms. Sit for a spell in front of the fireplace in the sun room. Cross-country ski for miles directly from the property. 4 units. 2 stories (no elevator), interior corridors. **Terms:** 14 day cancellation notice-fee imposed. **Pool:** heated outdoor. **Activities:** hot tub, cross country skiing. **Featured Amenity:** full hot breakfast.

SAVE 🛏 📶 ✕ ☎ / SOME UNITS 🐕

GREEN MOUNTAINS AND GREEN MOUNTAIN NATIONAL FOREST (E-2)

Elevations in the forest range from 878 ft. near Rochester to 4,083 ft. Mount Ellen in Warren. Refer to AAA maps for additional elevation information.

Extending the length of Vermont, the Green Mountains comprise several distinct ranges. The highest peaks lie in the north; several—including Mount Mansfield (see place listing p. 162), the tallest mountain in Vermont—exceed 4,000 feet.

The 420,000-acre Green Mountain National Forest was established in 1932 after uncontrolled logging, fire and flooding had ravaged Vermont. It stretches across nearly two-thirds of the state's length, following the main range of the Green Mountains. The forest is divided into two sections. The southern half extends from the Vermont-Massachusetts border to SR 140 near Wallingford; the northern half extends from US 4 northeast of Rutland to SR 17 near Bristol.

The forest encompasses eight wilderness areas as well as the White Rocks National Recreation Area, south of Wallingford, and the Moosalamoo National Recreation Area, east of Lake Dunmore. Ranger stations are located at 2538 Depot St. in Manchester Center, phone (802) 362-2307; 1007 SR 7S in Middlebury, phone (802) 388-4362; and 99 Ranger Rd. in Rochester, phone (802) 767-4261.

Natural resources in this area play an important role in the economy of Vermont and the Northeast. In addition, the region's scenic beauty and a broad range of recreational opportunities attract thousands of visitors annually. Along with 60,000 acres of designated wilderness, there are 900 miles of hiking trails—including the Appalachian/Long Trail and the Robert Frost Interpretive Trail—approximately 400 miles of snowmobile trails, seven cross-country ski areas and three downhill ski areas.

Developed campgrounds (no RV hook-ups) and picnic sites are available as well. For more information, phone (802) 747-6700. *See Recreation Areas Chart.*

KILLINGTON (E-2) elev. 1,286'

With its long snow season and challenging peaks, today's Killington is home to one of the largest ski resorts in the East. Other popular winter recreational activities include snowmobiling, snowshoeing, cross-country skiing and dog sledding. When green returns to the mountains, the area provides abundant opportunities for hiking, mountain biking, tennis and golf.

Killington Pico Area Association: 2319 US 4, P.O. Box 114, Killington, VT 05751. **Phone:** (802) 773-4181 or (800) 337-1928.

BIRCH RIDGE INN   802/422-4293
🍷🍷🍷 Hotel. **Address:** 37 Butler Rd 05751

KILLINGTON GRAND RESORT HOTEL & CONFERENCE
CENTER   802/422-5001
🍷🍷🍷 Resort Hotel. **Address:** 228 E Mountain Rd 05751

KILLINGTON MOTEL   802/773-9535
🍷🍷 Motel. **Address:** 1946 US 4 05751

KILLINGTON MOUNTAIN LODGE, BW SIGNATURE
COLLECTION   802/422-4302
🍷🍷🍷 Hotel. **Address:** 2617 Killington Rd 05751

> **AAA Benefit:**
> Members save up to 15% and earn bonus points!

MOUNTAIN SPORTS INN   802/422-3315
🍷 Hotel. **Address:** 813 Killington Rd 05751

SNOWED INN   802/422-3407
🍷🍷🍷 Bed & Breakfast. **Address:** 104 Miller Brook Rd 05751

WHERE TO EAT

BIRCH RIDGE INN RESTAURANT   802/422-4293
🍷🍷🍷 American. Fine Dining. **Address:** 37 Butler Rd 05751

FOUNDRY AT SUMMIT POND   802/422-5335
🍷🍷🍷 Steak. Casual Dining. **Address:** 63 Summit Path 05751

IPIE PIZZERIA   802/422-4111
🍷🍷 Pizza Sandwiches. Quick Serve. **Address:** 1307 Killington Rd 05751

LIQUID ART COFFEEHOUSE   802/422-2787
🍷🍷 Coffee/Tea Sandwiches. Casual Dining. **Address:** 37 Miller Brook Rd 05751

PEPPINO'S   802/422-3293
🍷🍷 Italian. Casual Dining. **Address:** 747 Killington Rd 05751

LAKE CHAMPLAIN (B-1)

Extending from Canada southward for 120 miles, Lake Champlain varies from a quarter of a mile to 12 miles wide. Two-thirds of its area lies in Vermont; the rest, except for a small Canadian portion, is in New York. Lake Champlain—with its Hudson River connector, the Champlain Canal—accommodates large vessels to make navigation possible from New York City to Montréal and the Great Lakes. It briefly became the sixth Great Lake in 1998 after president Bill Clinton signed a Senate bill reauthorizing the Sea Grant Program, but 2 months later the designation was rescinded.

Legends of Lake Champlain's own version of the Loch Ness Monster have persisted since French explorer Samuel de Champlain, the lake's discoverer, allegedly sighted what he described as a serpentine creature 20 feet long, as thick as a barrel and with a head like a horse. Occasional sightings of the elusive creature, affectionately named "Champ," still occur, but whether a distant cousin of the legendary Scottish sea serpent really resides in the lake remains a matter of speculation.

LAKE CHAMPLAIN FERRIES depart from Burlington, Charlotte and Grand Isle. Offered are scenic links between Vermont and New York via three crossings: Burlington to Port Kent, N.Y. (crossing time 1 hour); Charlotte to Essex, N.Y. (crossing time 25 minutes); and Grand Isle to Plattsburgh, N.Y. (crossing time 12 minutes).

Hours: Grand Isle ferry operates daily 24 hours year-round. Charlotte ferry operates year-round (ice conditions permitting); hours vary. Burlington ferry runs mid-June to late Sept.; hours vary. Phone ahead to confirm schedule. **Cost:** Grand Isle or Charlotte one-way passenger fare $4.50; $4 (ages 65+); $2.25 (ages 6-12). Grand Isle or Charlotte one-way fare for driver and vehicle 19 feet or less $10.75. Burlington one-way passenger fare $8.10; $6.80 (ages 65+); $3.10 (ages 6-12). Burlington one-way fare for driver and vehicle 19 feet or less $30. A fuel surcharge may apply. Cash only. **Phone:** (802) 864-9804.

LAKE CHAMPLAIN ISLANDS (A-1)

The Lake Champlain Islands are a picturesque summer resort area, affording a broad expanse of inland sea with the Adirondack Mountains on the west and the Green Mountains on the east. US 2 off I-89 connects the islands with the Vermont mainland, New York and Canada.

St. Anne's Shrine on Isle La Motte is on the site of Fort Ste. Anne, the first European settlement in Vermont. The shrine contains a statue of Samuel de Champlain that was sculpted at Expo '67 in Montréal; phone (802) 928-3362.

LOWER WATERFORD

RABBIT HILL INN   (802)748-5168
♥♥♥ Historic Country Inn. **Address:** 48 Lower Waterford Rd 05848

WHERE TO EAT

RABBIT HILL INN DINING ROOM   802/748-5168
♥♥♥♥
Regional American Fine Dining
$26-$39

AAA Inspector Notes: The candlelight experience provided by this charming inn dates back to the early 1800s. Seasonal farm-to-table menus offer artistically prepared food combinations, such as salt and pepper octopus, slow poached monkfish, braised lamb ragout and Parisienne gnocchi. Extravagant desserts and the rabbit-shaped butter served with a warm bread loaf are almost too pretty to eat. **Features:** full bar. **Reservations:** required. **Address:** 48 Lower Waterford Rd 05848 **Location:** I-93 exit 44 northbound, 2.6 mi n on SR 18; exit 1 southbound, 6 mi s on SR 18; in Rabbit Hill Inn. D

LUDLOW (E-3) pop. 811, elev. 1,064'

Situated on SRs 100/103 along the Black River, Ludlow offers views of mountain ranges, lakes and fertile farmland. Vermonters in this area pioneered the manufacture of reworked wool to combat cloth shortages after the Civil War.

Ludlow is home to the 600-acre campus of the Fletcher Farm School for the Arts and Crafts, 611 SR 103S, where artisans and craftspeople have been teaching the general public traditional techniques and exploring new media and methods since 1947. Classes last from 2 days to 1 week. In the summer a shop features items made by members of the Society of Vermont Artists and Craftsmen; phone (802) 228-8770 for class information and shop schedule.

Okemo Valley Regional Chamber of Commerce: 57 Pond St., P.O. Box 333, Ludlow, VT 05149. **Phone:** (802) 228-5830.

PETTIGREW INN   802/228-4846
♥♥♥ Historic Bed & Breakfast. **Address:** 13 Pleasant St 05149

WHERE TO EAT

SAM'S STEAKHOUSE   802/228-2087
♥♥ Steak. Casual Dining. **Address:** 91 Rt 103 S 05149

MANCHESTER (F-2) pop. 749, elev. 695'
• Hotels p. 158

Manchester, a year-round resort area guarded by Mount Equinox to the west, encompasses the communities of Manchester, Manchester Depot and Manchester Center. Elm-lined streets and marble sidewalks characterize Manchester, which is primarily residential; Manchester Center is more of a retail area.

Shopping: Battenkill & Highridge Outlet Centers, Manchester Designer Outlets and Marble Mill on Depot Street (SR 11/30) all house factory outlets.

AMERICAN MUSEUM OF FLY FISHING, 4070 Main St. (SR 7A), chronicles the history of fly fishing dating back to A.D. 200. The museum has a library, angling-related art and an impressive collection of rods, reels and flies. **Hours:** Tues.-Sat. 10-4 (also Sun. 10-4, June-Oct.). Closed major holidays. **Cost:** $5; $3 (ages 5-14); $10 (family). **Phone:** (802) 362-3300.

 SAVE **HILDENE, THE LINCOLN FAMILY HOME,** 1.5 mi. s. on SR 7A to 1005 Hildene Rd., is a 24-room Georgian Revival mansion built in 1905 as a summer home for Robert Todd Lincoln, Abraham Lincoln's only child to live to maturity.

Robert Lincoln, who became president and chairman of the Pullman Co., was so impressed by the beauty of the Manchester area when he visited with his mother and brother Tad in 1864 that he returned years later to build this 412-acre estate. Lincoln descendants lived in the house until 1975.

Visitors can watch a brief video orientation in the welcome center, take a guided or self-guiding tour of the home, hear an original Aeolian 1,000-pipe organ and stroll through the formal gardens. Displays include personal Lincoln artifacts and a restored 1903 wooden Pullman Palace car. Cheese-making can be viewed at Hildene Farm. Interpretative walking trails wind through woods and meadows, and cross-country skiing and snowshoeing are available in winter.

Time: Allow 1 hour, 30 minutes minimum. **Hours:** Daily 9:30-4:30. Cross-country skiing and snowshoeing are available mid-Dec. to early Mar. (weather permitting). Closed Easter, Thanksgiving, Christmas Eve, Christmas and day after Christmas. **Cost:** $23; $6 (ages 6-16). Phone ahead for skiing and snowshoeing fees; equipment rental is available. **Phone:** (802) 362-1788. GT 🎋

Mount Equinox Skyline Drive begins on SR 7A between Manchester and Arlington (toll house). The 5.2-mile winding route takes you to the 3,848-foot summit of Mount Equinox. Parking areas offer panoramic views of the Green, White, Adirondack, Taconic and Berkshire mountains as well as rivers, lakes and valley communities along the way.

Note: Buses; RVs; trailers; truck campers; vans that can accommodate more than eight passengers; and vehicles carrying bikes, canoes or kayaks are not permitted on the toll road. Have your brakes checked and be sure your vehicle is in good condition before attempting the drive. **Time:** Allow 1 hour minimum. **Hours:** Daily 9-4, Memorial Day-Oct. 31 (weather permitting). Last vehicle allowed up at 4.

Cost: $20 (per private vehicle driver); $12 (per motorcycle driver); $5 (per passenger in private vehicle); free (ages 0-10 and motorcycle passenger). **Phone:** (802) 362-1114. 🐾 🎨

SOUTHERN VERMONT ARTS CENTER is off SR 7A to West Rd., following signs to 930 Southern Vermont Arts Center Dr. Situated on a 407-acre campus on the slope of Mount Equinox, the center includes the Elizabeth de C. Wilson Museum of paintings and sculptures; the 400-seat Louise Arkell Pavilion; the Yester House art galleries; a sculpture garden; and a botany hiking trail.

    Time: Allow 2 hours minimum. **Hours:** Complex open Tues.-Sat. 10-5, Sun. noon-5. Phone ahead to confirm schedule. **Cost:** Free. **Phone:** (802) 362-1405.

BRITTANY MOTEL   802/362-1033
🛡️ Motel. **Address:** 1056 Main St 05254

HAMPTON INN & SUITES BY HILTON MANCHESTER
                             802/362-4000
🛡️🛡️🛡️ Hotel. **Address:** 4519 Main St 05255

AAA Benefit: Members save 5% or more!

NORTH SHIRE LODGE   (802)362-2336
🛡️🛡️ Motel. **Address:** 97 Main St 05254

MANCHESTER CENTER (F-2) pop. 2,120, elev. 748'

    Manchester Center is a census-designated place in the northeastern part of the town of Manchester *(see place listing p. 157)*. Located in a scenic valley in the Green Mountain National Forest, Manchester is a resort destination offering outdoor recreational opportunities, art and cultural events, shopping and dining.

THE ASPEN AT MANCHESTER   802/362-2450
🛡️🛡️ Motel. **Address:** 5669 Main St 05255

CASABLANCA MOTEL   (802)362-2145
🛡️🛡️ Cabin. **Address:** 5927 Main St 05255

THE INN AT ORMSBY HILL   802/362-1163
🛡️🛡️🛡️🛡️ Historic Bed & Breakfast. **Address:** 1842 Main St 05255

MANCHESTER VIEW FINE LODGING   802/362-2739
🛡️🛡️🛡️ Motel. **Address:** 77 High Meadows Way 05255

TOLL ROAD INN   (802)362-1711
🛡️🛡️ Vintage Motel. **Address:** 2220 Depot St 05255

WHERE TO EAT

BISTRO HENRY   802/362-4982
🔶🔶
American Casual Dining $20-$44
AAA Inspector Notes: This chef-owned casual bistro serves a varied selection of seafood, steaks, and more. Favorites include stuffed shrimp, "Fat Henry's 1/2 Chicken" (barbecue), Parmesan-crusted sole, steaks with tasty sides, and a nice selection of wine. The decor is open, airy and relaxed. **Features:** full bar, patio dining. **Address:** 1942 Depot St 05255 **Location:** On SR 11/30, 0.3 mi e of jct US 7.
Ⓓ 🐾

CHRISTOS' PIZZA & PASTA   802/362-2408
🛡️ Greek Pizza. Quick Serve. **Address:** 4931 Historic SR 7A 05255

THE GOURMET DELI & CAFE   802/362-1254
🔶🔶
Breakfast Sandwiches Quick Serve $10-$13
AAA Inspector Notes: This restaurant offers patrons fresh sandwiches and soups in a quaint café atmosphere. For those who like beans, do not miss the 15-bean soup. This is also a great spot to start the day. A menu of hearty breakfast options may include buttermilk pancakes, breakfast sandwiches and two eggs any style. **Features:** beer & wine, patio dining. **Address:** 4961 Main St 05255 **Location:** In Green Mountain Village Shoppes. Ⓑ Ⓛ 🐾

MANCHESTER PIZZA HOUSE   802/362-3338
🛡️ Pizza. Casual Dining. **Address:** 351 Depot St 05255

MISTRAL'S AT TOLL GATE   802/362-1779
🛡️🛡️🛡️ French. Fine Dining. **Address:** 10 Toll Gate Rd 05255

RAVEN'S DEN STEAKHOUSE & TAPROOM 802/768-8779
🛡️🛡️ Steak. Casual Dining. **Address:** 1844 Depot St 05255

UP FOR BREAKFAST   802/362-4204
🛡️🛡️ Breakfast. Casual Dining. **Address:** 4935 Main St 05255

YE OLDE TAVERN   802/362-0611
🛡️🛡️🛡️ Regional American. Casual Dining. **Address:** 5183 Main St 05255

MANCHESTER VILLAGE

THE EQUINOX, A LUXURY COLLECTION GOLF RESORT & SPA   (802)362-4700
🔶🔶🔶 🔶🔶🔶
Historic Resort Hotel $200-$769

THE LUXURY COLLECTION

AAA Benefit: Members save 5% or more!

Address: 3567 Main St 05254 **Location:** 1.3 mi s on Historic SR 7A, from jct SR 11/30. **Facility:** Anchored in the village center, this stately 1790 resort features luxury appointments in a blend of modern and classic styles. The Spa at Equinox is a perfect spot to unwind and decompress. 150 units. 4 stories, interior corridors. **Parking:** on-site and valet. **Terms:** check-in 4 pm, 14 day cancellation notice-fee imposed, resort fee. **Amenities:** safes. **Pool:** heated indoor. **Activities:** sauna, hot tub, steamroom, fishing, regulation golf, tennis, recreation programs in summer, bicycles, playground, lawn sports, trails, health club, spa. **Guest Services:** valet laundry, area transportation.
[SAVE] [ECO] 🍴 📶 🛎️ CALL ♿ 👤 🏊 💪 [BIZ] 📶
✖️ 🎬 / SOME UNITS 🐾 [HS]

THE INNS AT EQUINOX   802/362-4700
🔶🔶🔶
Hotel Rates not provided

Address: 3567 Main St 05254 **Location:** Jct SR 11/30, 1.3 mi s on Historic SR 7A; at The Equinox, A Luxury Collection Golf Resort & Spa. **Facility:** 49 units, some kitchens. 2-3 stories (no elevator), interior/exterior corridors. **Terms:** check-in 4 pm. **Dining:** 3 restaurants, also, The Marsh Tavern at The Equinox, see separate listing. **Pool:** heated indoor. **Activities:** sauna, hot tub, steamroom, fishing, regulation golf, tennis, bicycles, playground, trails, spa. **Guest Services:** valet laundry, area transportation.
[SAVE] 🍴 📶 🍸 🏊 💪 [BIZ]
📶 ✖️ 🎬 / SOME UNITS 🐾 🚪 📺 💻

TACONIC, A KIMPTON HOTEL (802)362-0147

♦♦♦ ♦♦♦
Boutique Hotel
$269-$699

Address: 3835 Main St 05254 **Location:** On Historic SR 7A, 1 mi s of jct SR 11/30. **Facility:** The eye-catching design at this Southern Vermont hotel is a blend of modernity and tradition. The Frette linens, plush furnishings and Atelier Bloem bath amenities will ensure a luxurious experience. 86 units, some cottages. 3 stories, interior/exterior corridors. *Bath:* shower only. **Terms:** 2-4 night minimum stay - seasonal and/or weekends, 3 day cancellation notice-fee imposed, resort fee. **Amenities:** safes. **Pool:** heated outdoor. **Activities:** bicycles, lawn sports, trails, exercise room, massage. **Guest Services:** valet laundry.

[SAVE] [🛎] [🍽] CALL [♿] [🚐] [🛏] [BIZ] [📶] [✕] [🎥]
[❽] / SOME UNITS [🐾]

WHERE TO EAT

THE MARSH TAVERN AT THE EQUINOX   802/362-4700
♦♦♦ American. Casual Dining. **Address:** 3567 Main St 05254

MARSH-BILLINGS-ROCKEFELLER NATIONAL HISTORICAL PARK (D-3)

The nation's only national park focusing on conservation history and the evolution of land stewardship in the United States, Marsh-Billings-Rockefeller National Historical Park is located off SR 12 in Woodstock. The park's woodlands, covering 550 acres, comprise an area known for its scenic beauty and are managed not only to preserve natural resources but also to maintain sustainable forestry.

The park was an outgrowth of the first environmental crisis faced by Vermonters: the large-scale deforestation of the Green Mountains in the mid-19th century as a result of settlement that began after the end of the American Revolution. It was named for George Perkins Marsh, an early conservationist who also served as a diplomat and member of Congress, and Frederick Billings, a railroad president and philanthropist who was a successful attorney in San Francisco before returning to his native state.

Billings purchased the Marsh family farm, not only establishing a progressive dairy operation but also developing one of the country's first blueprints for scientific forest management. His work was carried on by three generations of women—his wife Julia, their three daughters and Billings' granddaughter, Mary French. French subsequently married Laurance S. Rockefeller, bringing together two families with a strong commitment to conservation. The Rockefellers gifted their estate's residential and forestlands to the people of the United States, making possible the creation in 1992 of Vermont's first national park.

A fine way to experience the parkland is by walking some of the 20 miles of carriage roads and trails that crisscross Mount Tom. **Note:** Due to ongoing forestry and trail work, portions of the carriage roads and trails may be closed. Hike to the top of Mount Tom for beautiful views of Woodstock and the surrounding hills. Also within the national park is the

Marsh-Billings-Rockefeller Mansion *(see attraction listing).*

The Carriage Barn, the park's visitor center, has an exhibit about land stewardship. The visitor center is open daily 10-5, Memorial Day weekend-Oct. 31. The carriage roads and trails are open year-round. Park admission is free. For park information phone (802) 457-3368, ext. 222.

MARSH-BILLINGS-ROCKEFELLER MANSION, just inside the entrance to Marsh-Billings-Rockefeller National Historical Park at 54 Elm St., is the childhood home of pioneering environmentalist George Perkins Marsh. Conservationist Frederick Billings purchased the property in 1869 and built the Queen Anne-style residence that his granddaughter, Mary French Rockefeller, modernized in the 1950s. The house features Tiffany glass windows and beautifully detailed woodwork as well as the dining room complete with table settings.

Ranger-guided tours of the mansion and gardens explore the history of conservation, the stewardship ethic of the Marsh, Billings and Rockefeller families, and community-based conservation in a more modern context. In addition to original furnishings and personal items, the mansion displays works of art that include some of America's finest landscape paintings, highlighting the influence painting and photography had on the conservation movement.

Hours: Guided 30-minute Mansion Experience tours and 1-hour Legacy of Stewardship tours are given daily 10-4, Memorial Day weekend-Oct. 31. Phone ahead to confirm schedule. **Cost:** $8; $4 (ages 62+); free (ages 0-15). Reservations are recommended. **Phone:** (802) 457-3368, ext. 222. [GT]

MIDDLEBURY (D-2) pop. 6,588, elev. 366'
• Hotels p. 160 • Restaurants p. 160

Midway between Salisbury and New Haven, Middlebury was founded in 1761. A ranger district office at 1007 SR 7S provides maps and guides for hiking in nearby Green Mountain National Forest *(see place listing p. 155)*; phone (802) 388-4362.

Middlebury College was chartered in 1800; the present enrollment exceeds 2,500. The campus includes Painter Hall, Vermont's oldest college building, built in 1816. Emma Hart Willard, a pioneer in American women's education, began her work in 1807 when she became the principal of Middlebury Female Academy. The school plays host to the Bread Loaf Writers' Conference in summer.

Addison County Chamber of Commerce: 93 Court St., Middlebury, VT 05753. **Phone:** (802) 388-7951.

Self-guiding tours: Walking-tour maps are available from the chamber of commerce.

@ **Rest assured:**
AAA.com/travelguides/hotels

COURTYARD BY MARRIOTT MIDDLEBURY
(802)388-7600

Hotel
$123-$300

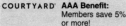 **AAA Benefit:** Members save 5% or more!

Address: 309 Court St 05753 **Location:** 1 mi s on US 7. **Facility:** 88 units. 3 stories, interior corridors. **Parking:** winter plug-ins. **Terms:** cancellation fee imposed. **Amenities:** *Some:* safes. **Pool:** heated indoor. **Activities:** hot tub, exercise room. **Guest Services:** valet and coin laundry.

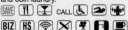

MIDDLEBURY INN
(802)388-4961

Historic Boutique Country Inn. **Address:** 14 Court Square 05753

SWIFT HOUSE INN
802/388-9925

Historic Country Inn. **Address:** 25 Stewart Ln 05753

 WHERE TO EAT

AMERICAN FLATBREAD
802/388-3300

Pizza Small Plates. Casual Dining. **Address:** 137 Maple St 05753

FIRE & ICE RESTAURANT
802/388-7166

American Casual Dining
$15-$35

AAA Inspector Notes: *Classic.* A city landmark for more than a quarter of a century, this restaurant features hand-cut steaks, prime rib, fresh seafood, homemade mashed potatoes and an impressive 55-item salad bar. The restaurant is divided into a number of informal dining rooms filled with an eclectic collection of memorabilia. **Features:** full bar. **Reservations:** suggested. **Address:** 26 Seymour St 05753 **Location:** Jct SR 125 and US 7, just w.

D

GREEN PEPPERS RESTAURANT
802-388-3164

Pizza. Casual Dining. **Address:** 10 Washington St 05753

MORGAN'S TAVERN AT MIDDLEBURY INN
802/388-4961

New American. Casual Dining. **Address:** 14 Court Square 05753

NOONIES DELI
802/388-0014

Deli. Quick Serve. **Address:** 137 Maple St 05753

ROSIE'S
802/388-7052

American. Casual Dining. **Address:** 886 Rt 7 S 05753

MONTPELIER (C-3) pop. 7,855, elev. 484'

Capital of the state, Montpelier is a center for the insurance and granite-quarrying industries. The city was the birthplace of Adm. George Dewey, hero of Manila Bay during the Spanish-American War. Hubbard Park, covering 185 acres on a hill behind the Capitol, offers a good view of the Worcester Mountains and the Winooski River Valley.

Also of architectural interest is the Supreme Court Building, 111 State St., which was constructed from Barre granite. The State Office Building, directly across from the Capitol, is a fine example of modern architecture. It is built of reinforced concrete, with Vermont marble facing on the exterior and polished, matched marble in the lobby.

Founded in Bristol in 1977, Lost Nation Theater stages dramas focusing on the power of human interaction. The theater is located on the second floor of Montpelier City Hall at 39 Main St.; phone (802) 229-0492 for the box office.

MORSE FARM MAPLE SUGARWORKS, 2.7 mi. n. on Main St. to 1168 County Rd., following signs, shows a video about the sugaring process. A sample of maple syrup is included. Tours show processing techniques as well as the history of syrup

making. Also on the premises is the Outdoor Museum of Folk Art.

Time: Allow 30 minutes minimum. **Hours:** Daily 9-8, June 1-Labor Day; 9-6, day after Labor Day-Oct. 31; 9-5, rest of year. Closed Jan. 1, Thanksgiving and Christmas. **Cost:** Free. **Phone:** (802) 223-2740. [GT]

CAPITOL PLAZA HOTEL & CONFERENCE CENTER
802/223-5252

Hotel
Rates not provided

Address: 100 State St 05602 **Location:** Center; 1 blk from state capitol building. **Facility:** 64 units. 4 stories, interior corridors. **Amenities:** safes. **Dining:** J. Morgan's Steakhouse, see separate listing. **Activities:** exercise room. **Guest Services:** valet laundry. *(See ad this page.)*

[SAVE] [ECO] [☰] [🛏] [Y]

CALL [🦽] [♿] [BIZ] [🛜] [✕]

[🍵] / SOME UNITS [🛄]

COMFORT INN & SUITES AT MAPLEWOOD
(802)229-2222

Hotel
$130-$249

Address: 213 Paine Tpke N 05602 **Location:** I-89 exit 7 (SR 62), 0.3 mi e. **Facility:** 90 units. 3 stories (no elevator), interior corridors. **Parking:** winter plug-ins. **Amenities:** safes. **Activities:** exercise room. **Guest Services:** coin laundry. **Featured Amenity:** full hot breakfast.

[SAVE] [☰] CALL [🦽] [♿] [BIZ] [HS]

[🛜] [✕] [🛄] [🍵] [🗔]

THE INN AT MONTPELIER
802/223-2727

Bed & Breakfast
Rates not provided

Address: 147 Main St 05602 **Location:** Just e of State St; center. **Facility:** This inn consists of two adjacent 19th-century homes and features multiple parlors and a wraparound veranda. Antique and reproduction furnishings complement the classic New England architecture. 19 units. 2 stories (no elevator), interior corridors. **Featured Amenity:** continental breakfast. [SAVE] [Y] [🛜] [✕]

🔗 **Use the free travel planning tools at AAA.com/maps**

▼ See AAA listing this page ▼

WHERE TO EAT

CAPITOL GROUNDS
802/223-7800
◈ American. Quick Serve. **Address:** 27 State St 05602

J. MORGAN'S STEAKHOUSE   802/223-5252
❤❤❤ Steak Seafood. Casual Dining. **Address:** 100 State St 05602 *(See ad p. 161.)*

LA BRIOCHE BAKERY & CAFE   802/229-0443
❤ Breads/Pastries Sandwiches. Quick Serve. **Address:** 89 Main St 05602

NECI ON MAIN   802/223-3188
❤❤ American. Casual Dining. **Address:** 118 Main St 05602

SARDUCCI'S RESTAURANT AND BAR   802/223-0229
❤❤ Italian. Casual Dining. **Address:** 3 Main St 05602

THE SKINNY PANCAKE   802/262-2253
❤❤ Natural/Organic. Casual Dining. **Address:** 89 Main St 05602

WAYSIDE RESTAURANT & BAKERY   802/223-6611
❤❤ American. Quick Serve. **Address:** 1873 US Rt 302 05602

MORRISVILLE (B-3) pop. 1,958, elev. 646'

Morrisville, like Vermont's other mountain-bound towns, grew rapidly when railroad service reached the area. Visible reminders of that event remain on Portland Street, where structures more closely resemble those of a Western boomtown than a New England village.

Lamoille Region Chamber of Commerce: 92 Lower Main St., Morrisville, VT 05661. **Phone:** (802) 888-7607.

NOYES HOUSE MUSEUM, 122 Lower Main St., is a two-story Federal-style brick building that contains local and regional history exhibits, photographs, furnishings, toys, household and farm tools, quilts, costumes and military artifacts. On guided tours, visitors learn about the residents, most notably the women, who were instrumental in shaping the town. **Time:** Allow 1 hour, 30 minutes minimum. **Hours:** Thurs. noon-4, Fri.-Sat. 10-4, June-Aug.; Fri. noon-4, Sat. 10-4, Sept.-Oct. **Cost:** $5; free (children). **Phone:** (802) 888-7617. GT

SUNSET MOTOR INN   (802)888-4956
❤❤ ❤❤
Motel
$105-$145

Address: 160 Vt Rt 15 W 05661 **Location:** Jct SR 100, just w. **Facility:** 55 units, some kitchens. 2 stories (no elevator), interior/exterior corridors. **Parking:** winter plug-ins. **Terms:** 7 day cancellation notice-fee imposed. **Pool:** outdoor. **Activities:** playground. **Guest Services:** coin laundry.

WHERE TO EAT

CHARLMONT RESTAURANT & PUB   802/888-4242
❤❤ American. Casual Dining. **Address:** 116 SR 15 W 05661

MOUNT MANSFIELD elev. 4,393'

The loftiest peak in both the Green Mountains and in Vermont, Mount Mansfield is 4,393 feet high and 5 miles long. Covering 34,000 acres of the mountain is Mount Mansfield State Forest *(see Recreation Areas Chart).* The forest can be reached by roads from Stowe through Smugglers' Notch or from Underhill Center.

The profile of Mount Mansfield is said to resemble a human face. The Long Trail and other trails lead to scenic spots and picnic areas. Campgrounds are available. The east side is a game refuge; hunting is permitted on the west side.

MOUNT SNOW (F-2) elev. 3,583'

In southern Vermont's Green Mountains, Mount Snow is a year-round resort. Recreational activities include alpine skiing from early November to early May and golf, tennis, swimming, boating, fishing and mountain biking the rest of the year.

NORTH BENNINGTON (G-1) pop. 1,643, elev. 287'

PARK-McCULLOUGH HISTORIC ESTATE is 1 blk. w. off SR 67A at 1 Park St. Built in 1865, this 35-room Victorian "summer home" contains original furnishings, decorative art pieces and period clothing belonging to the Park and McCullough families. The home remains essentially as it was more than 140 years ago.

Also on the premises are gardens, a carriage house with a collection of carriages, the 1904 Grapery Greenhouse and the 1865 Playhouse. Hiking trails are available and special programs are offered throughout the year.

Time: Allow 1 hour minimum. **Hours:** Grounds daily dawn-dusk. House Fri.-Sat. 10-2, Sun. noon-4 (also select Mon. holidays 10-2), late May to mid-Oct. **Cost:** Grounds free. Tour $15; $12 (senior citizens); $8 (ages 8-17). Cash or check only. **Phone:** (802) 442-5441. GT

PANGAEA RESTAURANT   802/442-7171
❤❤❤ American. Fine Dining. **Address:** 1 Prospect St 05257

NORWICH (D-3) pop. 878, elev. 398'

The King Arthur Flour Baking Education Center, Bakery and The Baker's Store at 135 SR 5S draws visitors from all over the United States and Canada. The store is staffed with experienced bakers who delight in answering technical baking questions and are quick to provide demonstrations and samples. The education center offers registrants the chance to work alongside some of the nation's finest master bakers. Classes from half a day to a full week cover subjects from chocolate to artisan breads to pasta; phone (802) 649-3361, or (800) 827-6836 to order a catalog.

MONTSHIRE MUSEUM OF SCIENCE, I-91 exit 13 to 1 Montshire Rd. off SR 10A, features more than 140 hands-on exhibits about science, natural history and technology. Permanent exhibits include freshwater aquariums; live animals; and Bubbles: Science in Soap, exploring surface tension and how it affects bubbles of all sizes. Daily activities are offered in the Science Discovery Lab. Visiting exhibitions also are offered throughout the year.

The museum is on 110 acres along the Connecticut River. Nature trails, outdoor exhibits and an outdoor science park with water features are on-site. Food is available in summer. **Time:** Allow 4 hours minimum. **Hours:** Daily 10-5. Closed Thanksgiving and Christmas. **Cost:** June 19-Labor Day $18; $15 (ages 2-17). Rest of year $16; $13 (ages 2-17). **Phone:** (802) 649-2200. 🅰️

KING ARTHUR FLOUR CAFE   802/649-3361
🍴 Breads/Pastries Sandwiches. Quick Serve. **Address:** 135 US Rt 5 S 05055

THE NORWICH INN   802/649-1143
🍴🍴 International. Fine Dining. **Address:** 325 Main St 05055

PLYMOUTH (E-3) elev. 1,407'

The small Green Mountain town of Plymouth is the birthplace of Calvin Coolidge. Vice President Coolidge was at home Aug. 3, 1923, when he heard the news of President Warren G. Harding's death. His father, a notary public, administered the oath of office to him in the parlor by the light of a kerosene lamp.

PRESIDENT CALVIN COOLIDGE STATE HISTORIC SITE, 3780 SR 100A, includes the birthplace, boyhood home and grave of Calvin Coolidge, the 30th president of the United States. The birthplace and homestead have original furnishings.

Other buildings include the President Calvin Coolidge Museum & Education Center, with an exhibit about Coolidge's career and changing displays of gifts presented to the president while in office; Wilder House, the childhood home of Coolidge's mother, which is now a restaurant; Wilder Barn, displaying a collection of 19th-century farm implements; the Plymouth Cheese Factory, built in 1890 by Coolidge's father and still making cheese using the original 1890 recipe; the 1850s General Store; the office of the 1924 summer White House; and Union Christian Church, an 1840 meetinghouse. The Aldrich House contains exhibits pertaining to the village and to Coolidge.

Time: Allow 2 hours minimum. **Hours:** Complex open daily 10-5, late May to mid-Oct. **Cost:** $10; $2 (ages 6-14); $25 (family, up to eight people). **Phone:** (802) 672-3773.

INN AT WATER'S EDGE   (802)228-8143
🍴🍴🍴 Historic Country Inn. **Address:** 45 Kingdom Rd 05149

PROCTOR (E-2) elev. 477'

In the narrow Otter Creek Valley, Proctor was named for Redfield Proctor, governor of the state 1878-80 and founder of the Vermont Marble Co., an international corporation. Appropriately, sidewalks and public buildings are constructed from the local marble.

VERMONT MARBLE MUSEUM is at 52 Main St. Said to contain one of the largest displays of its kind in the world, the museum illustrates the origin, quarrying and finishing of marble. More than 100 exhibits feature custom marble work, historic photographs, varied artifacts and the Earth Alive geology display room. The Hall of Presidents contains white marble relief statues of past U.S. presidents. The Tomb of the Unknown Soldier exhibit chronicles the history of the shrine, from the quarrying of the marble to the burial vault's arrival at Arlington National Cemetery.

Visitors also can observe the museum's sculptor in residence create marble carvings. **Hours:** Daily 10-5, mid-May to late Oct. **Cost:** $9; $7 (senior citizens); $4 (ages 6-17). **Phone:** (802) 459-2750 or (800) 427-1396.

WILSON CASTLE, 2708 West St., was built in 1867 on a 115-acre estate. Nineteen open proscenium arches overlooked by a towering turret, parapet and balcony dominate the elaborate facade of English brick and marble. The castle's 32 rooms feature 84 stained glass windows and 13 fireplaces finished with domestic tiles and bronze; not all rooms are included in the tour.

Furnishings include European and Far Eastern antiques and museum pieces, along with statuary, Chinese scrolls and Oriental rugs. Paintings, sculpture and photographs are displayed in an art gallery. Cattle barns, stables and a carriage house are on the grounds.

Hours: Guided tours of two of the three floors depart continuously daily 10-5, Memorial Day weekend to mid-Oct. **Cost:** $12; $11 (ages 62+); $6 (ages 6-12). **Phone:** (802) 773-3284. GT

QUECHEE (E-3) pop. 656, elev. 558'
• Hotels p. 164 • Restaurants p. 164

A scenic portion of Quechee Gorge, Vermont's Little Grand Canyon, lies west of Quechee (pronounced KWEE-chee). The bridge on US 4 that spans the gorge 165 feet above the Ottauquechee River provides a good view of this natural spectacle. A covered bridge leads into this small village, known in the 19th century for its busy woolen mills.

White River Junction Welcome Center: 100 Railroad Row, White River Junction, VT 05001. **Phone:** (802) 281-5050.

🔵 **For complete hotel, dining and attraction listings: AAA.com/travelguides**

Shopping: The Mill, 1760 Quechee Main St., is a complex of shops including Simon Pearce Glass, where visitors can observe the glass-blowing process. The Fat Hat Clothing Company, 1 Quechee Main St., sells clothing. Quechee Gorge Village, on Woodstock Road at Quechee Gorge, offers antiques, arts and crafts, seasonal miniature steam train rides, an antique carousel and a Cabot Creamery tasting center, one of only two in the state.

VERMONT INSTITUTE OF NATURAL SCIENCE is on SR 4, 3.5 mi. w. of I-89 exit 1 at 149 Natures Way. Located adjacent to scenic Quechee Gorge, this environmental learning center encompasses 47 acres inhabited by migratory songbirds, amphibians and other Vermont wildlife. Such raptors as owls, bald eagles, red-tailed hawks and peregrine falcons can be viewed in 17 outdoor enclosures.

Educational programs allow visitors to get an up-close look at live raptors, and nature trails encourage exploration. There is an outdoor adventure playscape and a Forest Canopy walk as well as the stroller- and wheelchair-friendly McKnight Trail which winds through the lush woodlands for .25 miles. **Hours:** Daily 10-5, May-Oct. Schedule varies rest of year; phone ahead. Closed Thanksgiving and Christmas. **Cost:** $16.50; $15.50 (ages 65+); $14.50 (ages 4-17). **Phone:** (802) 359-5000.

THE QUECHEE INN AT MARSHLAND FARM
(802)295-3133

Historic Country Inn
$109-$255

Address: 1119 Quechee Main St 05059 **Location:** 0.8 mi n of US 4. Located in a quiet area. **Facility:** Dating from the 18th century, this Colonial-style farmhouse provides a lovely retreat in a tranquil countryside setting. Rooms range from cozy to spacious and offer elegant country décor. 25 units. 2 stories (no elevator), interior corridors. **Terms:** 2 night minimum stay - seasonal, 14 day cancellation notice-fee imposed. **Dining:** The Quechee Inn at Marshland Farm Restaurant, see separate listing. **Activities:** self-propelled boats, fishing, cross country skiing, bicycles, trails. **Featured Amenity:** full hot breakfast.

WHERE TO EAT

PARKER HOUSE INN & BISTRO   802/295-6077
Mediterranean. Fine Dining. **Address:** 1792 Quechee Main St 05059

THE QUECHEE INN AT MARSHLAND FARM RESTAURANT   802/295-3133

American Fine Dining
$23-$36

AAA Inspector Notes: *Historic.* This restaurant occupies the beautiful, historic 1793 former home and farm of Colonel John Marsh, Vermont's first lieutenant governor, and is recorded on the National Register of Historic Places. Innovative chefs prepare a variety of complex recipes with excellent knowledge of their seasonal menu and dish preparations. **Features:** full bar. **Reservations:** suggested. **Address:** 1119 Quechee Main St 05059 **Location:** 1 mi n of US 4; in The Quechee Inn at Marshland Farm. D

SIMON PEARCE RESTAURANT   802/295-1470
Regional American. Casual Dining. **Address:** 1760 Quechee Main St 05059

RANDOLPH pop. 1,974

RANDOLPH VILLAGE PIZZA   802/728-9677
Pizza. Quick Serve. **Address:** 1 S Main St 05060

RUTLAND (E-2) pop. 16,495, elev. 562'

The immense quarrying and finishing industries in Rutland are responsible for the community's reputation as the "Marble City." An industrial center in the Otter Creek Valley, Rutland is protected by the Taconic Mountains to the west and three striking Green Mountain peaks—Killington, Pico and Shrewsbury—to the east. It is the closest city to Killington *(see place listing p. 156)* and functions as a base for visits to the Green Mountain National Forest *(see place listing p. 155).*

The state's oldest continuously published newspaper, the *Rutland Herald,* was founded in 1794. Rutland also was the birthplace of John Deere, a journeyman blacksmith who developed the first commercially successful, self-scouring steel plow and began a plow-building business that became today's well-known manufacturer of agricultural machinery and equipment.

The Chaffee Art Center, 16 S. Main St., occupies an elegant Victorian-era mansion and offers eight galleries displaying works by Vermont artists; phone (802) 775-0356.

If you like exhibits, fair food and carnival midways, the Vermont State Fair won't disappoint. Highlights of one of the oldest state fairs in the country include top-name entertainers, demolition derbies, harness racing, racing pigs, death-defying stunt performances and truck pulls. Held in mid-August, the fair closes with the Governor's Day Benefit Event.

Rutland Region Chamber of Commerce: 50 Merchants Row, Rutland, VT 05701. **Phone:** (802) 773-2747 or (800) 756-8880.

BEST WESTERN INN & SUITES RUTLAND/KILLINGTON
(802)773-3200

Motel
$129-$239

AAA Benefit: Members save up to 15% and earn bonus points!

Address: 5 Best Western Pl 05701 **Location:** Jct US 7, 2.6 mi e on US 4. **Facility:** 112 units, some two bedrooms and kitchens. 2 stories (no elevator), exterior corridors. **Parking:** winter plug-ins. **Terms:** check-in 4 pm, cancellation fee imposed. **Pool:** heated outdoor. **Activities:** tennis, playground, exercise room. **Guest Services:** valet and coin laundry.

COMFORT INN AT TROLLEY SQUARE   (802)775-2200
Hotel. **Address:** 19 Allen St 05701

HAMPTON INN BY HILTON RUTLAND/KILLINGTON
802/773-9066

♦♦♦ Hotel. **Address:** 47 Farrell Rd
05701

AAA Benefit:
Members save 5%
or more!

HOLIDAY INN RUTLAND/KILLINGTON   802/775-1911

♦♦ Hotel. **Address:** 476 Holiday Dr 05701

WHERE TO EAT

COUNTRYMAN'S PLEASURE RESTAURANT   802/773-7141

♦♦♦ Continental. Fine Dining. **Address:** 63 Town Line Rd 05701

KELVANS   802/775-1550

♦♦ American. Casual Dining. **Address:** 128 Merchants Row 05701

LITTLE HARRY'S   802/747-4848

♦♦ International. Casual Dining. **Address:** 121 West St 05701

NINETY NINE RESTAURANT   802/775-9288

♦♦ American. Casual Dining. **Address:** 288 US Route 7 S 05701

ROOTS THE RESTAURANT   802/747-7414

♦♦ American. Casual Dining. **Address:** 55 Washington St 05701

TABLE 24 RESTAURANT   802/775-2424

♦♦ Southwestern. Casual Dining. **Address:** 24 Wales St 05701

TOKYO HOUSE   802/786-8080

♦♦ Japanese. Casual Dining. **Address:** 106 West St 05701

THE YELLOW DELI   802/775-9800

♦♦ Deli. Casual Dining. **Address:** 23 Center St 05701

ST. ALBANS (B-2) pop. 6,918, elev. 383'

Nestled between Lake Champlain and the Green Mountains, the town once described by Henry Ward Beecher as "a place in the midst of a greater variety of scenic beauty than any other I can remember in America" had anything but a placid history to match its serene setting. St. Albans was a notorious center for smuggling operations on Lake Champlain in the early 1800s and was an important link on the Underground Railroad.

Its rowdy days left behind, St. Albans is headquarters for the New England Central Railway, a production and distribution center for dairy products and a manufacturing center of such products as maple sugar, sugar-making equipment, medical technology equipment and ice cream.

Franklin County Regional Chamber of Commerce: 2 N. Main St., Suite 101, St. Albans, VT 05478. **Phone:** (802) 524-2444.

ECONO LODGE   (802)524-5956

♦♦ Motel. **Address:** 287 S Main St (US 7) 05478

HAMPTON INN BY HILTON, ST. ALBANS   802/528-5020

♦♦♦ Hotel. **Address:** 43 Lake St
05478

AAA Benefit:
Members save 5%
or more!

LA QUINTA INN & SUITES ST. ALBANS   (802)524-3300

♦♦ Hotel. **Address:** 813 Fairfax Rd 05478

WHERE TO EAT

JEFF'S MAINE SEAFOOD   802/524-6135

♦♦ Seafood. Casual Dining. **Address:** 65 N Main St (US 7) 05478

MAPLE CITY DINER   802/528-8400

♦♦ Comfort Food Desserts. Casual Dining. **Address:** 17 Swanton Rd 05478

THAI HOUSE RESTAURANT   802/524-0999

♦♦ Thai. Casual Dining. **Address:** 333 Swanton Rd 05478

ST. JOHNSBURY (C-4) pop. 6,193, elev. 556'
• Hotels p. 166 • Restaurants p. 166

The converging valleys of the Moose, Passumpsic and Sleeper's rivers create a striking range of elevations upon which St. Johnsbury grew. The town was named after the French consul in New York, Saint Jean de Crèvecoeur, a friend of Ethan Allen and author of "Letters of an American Farmer." Crèvecoeur suggested the addition of "bury" to the town's name to distinguish it from the many towns named St. John.

Much of St. Johnsbury's history and growth centered on Thaddeus Fairbanks' invention of the platform scale in 1830 and George Cary's idea of flavoring plug tobacco with maple sugar. The town prospered with the success of the Fairbanks Scale and maple-sugar industries, still major contributors to the local economy. It is the industrial, retail and cultural center of the part of Vermont known as the Northeast Kingdom.

Northeast Kingdom Chamber of Commerce: 2000 Memorial Dr., Suite 11, St. Johnsbury, VT 05819. **Phone:** (802) 748-3678 or (800) 639-6379.

FAIRBANKS MUSEUM AND PLANETARIUM, 1302 Main St., houses a large collection that includes art and antiques, village and crafts tools and more than 75,000 natural-science specimens like shells, rocks and mounted animals. The museum also is home to the Eye in the Sky Weather Center (a working studio that is not open to visitors) and Vermont's only public planetarium. It also hosts a traveling exhibit that runs from one summer to the next. The 1891 building was designed by noted architect Lambert Packard to house the "cabinet of curiosities" of Franklin Fairbanks, nephew of Thaddeus Fairbanks, the inventor of the platform scale.

Time: Allow 1 hour, 30 minutes minimum. **Hours:** Daily 9-5. Planetarium show daily at 3:30 (additional shows are offered Sat.-Sun.; phone for schedule). Closed Jan. 1, Easter, July 4, Thanksgiving and Christmas. Phone ahead to confirm schedule in early Jan. **Cost:** Museum $9; $7 (ages 5-17, ages

62+ and students ages 18-25 with ID); $25 (family living in one household). One-hour planetarium show $6. Thirty-minute planetarium show $4. **Phone:** (802) 748-2372.

ST. JOHNSBURY ATHENAEUM, 1171 Main St., is a public library and art gallery containing 19th-century landscape paintings from the Hudson River School. The collection includes Albert Bierstadt's monumental "The Domes of the Yosemite." Donated to the town by Horace Fairbanks in 1871, the historic landmark has Victorian reading rooms showcasing elaborate woodwork and spiral staircases. Regularly scheduled public programs include poetry readings and educational lectures.

Note: "The Domes of the Yosemite" will be on display again after completion of conservation work in July, 2018. **Time:** Allow 30 minutes minimum. **Hours:** Mon., Wed. and Fri. 10-5:30, Tues. and Thurs. 2-7, Sat. 10-3. Closed major holidays. Phone ahead to confirm schedule. **Cost:** Donations. **Phone:** (802) 748-8291.

COMFORT INN & SUITES NEAR BURKE MOUNTAIN
(802)748-1500
♦♦♦ Hotel. **Address:** 703 US Rt 5 S 05819

FAIRBANKS INN   (802)748-5666
♦♦ Motel. **Address:** 401 Western Ave 05819

ANTHONY'S DINER   802-748-3613
♦ American. Casual Dining. **Address:** 321 Railroad St 05819

KHAM'S THAI CUISINE   802-751-8424
♦♦ Thai. Casual Dining. **Address:** 1112 Memorial Dr 05819

SHELBURNE (C-1) pop. 592, elev. 159'

Shelburne, with the Adirondack Mountains to the west and the Green Mountains to the east, was settled in 1763 by two German lumbermen and later named for an English earl. Many downtown shops occupy renovated farm buildings dating from the 1800s.

SHELBURNE MUSEUM, 6000 Shelburne Rd. (US 7), consists of several galleries and 25 historic structures. Spread over 45 acres, the buildings house diverse collections of fine and folk art and artifacts depicting early New England life. Among the structures are a horseshoe barn, jail, country store, schoolhouse, blacksmith shop, meetinghouse, stagecoach inn, lighthouse, hunting lodge, apothecary and furnished houses representing 4 centuries.

Attractions include a railroad depot, a private rail car and locomotive, a two-lane covered bridge, a round barn, a handcrafted model circus parade more than 500 feet long and the side-wheel steamboat *Ticonderoga.*

Displays of Americana feature a sizable group of wooden cigar-store figures; fine, folk and decorative art; tools; and coaches, carriages and wagons. The Electra Havemeyer Webb Memorial building houses European furnishings, sculpture and paintings by Jean Baptiste Corot, Gustave Courbet, Edgar Degas, Edouard Manet and Claude Monet, as well as works by American artist Mary Cassatt.

The Webb Gallery of American Art contains works by Albert Bierstadt, John Copley, Winslow Homer, Fitz Henry Lane, Grandma Moses, William Prior, Andrew Wyeth and other 18th-, 19th- and 20th-century artists. Formal gardens, ornamental trees and shrubs, and seasonal roses and lilacs adorn the grounds.

Open year-round, the Pizzagalli Center for Art and Education contains two floors of gallery space, as well as classrooms and an auditorium. **Time:** Allow 4 hours minimum. **Hours:** Daily 10-5, May-Dec.; Wed.-Sun. 10-5, rest of year. Closed Jan. 1, Thanksgiving, Christmas Eve (closes at 2), Christmas and Dec. 31. Phone ahead to confirm schedule for buildings, exhibitions and programs. **Cost:** May through Oct. $25; $23 (senior citizens); $14 (ages 13-17); $12 (ages 5-12); $65 (family, two adults and minor children). Rest of year $10; $5 (ages 5-18). **Phone:** (802) 985-3346. [▯] [▯]

DAYS INN SHELBURNE   (802)985-3334
♦♦ Hotel. **Address:** 3229 Shelburne Rd 05482

CHEF LEU'S HOUSE   802-985-5258
♦♦ Chinese. Casual Dining. **Address:** 3761 Shelburne Rd 05482

THE INN AT SHELBURNE FARMS   802-985-8498
♦♦♦ American. Fine Dining. **Address:** 1611 Harbor Rd 05482

SOUTH BURLINGTON (B-2) pop. 17,904, elev. 315'

Part of the Burlington metropolitan area, South Burlington is home to multiple residential neighborhoods, a commercial center and Burlington International Airport. The city's Red Rocks Park offers trails and a summer beach on Lake Champlain. South Burlington is just west of Vermont's Green Mountains, offering year-round recreational opportunities such as skiing, snowboarding, hiking, golfing and swimming.

BEST WESTERN PLUS WINDJAMMER INN &
CONFERENCE CENTER   (802)863-1125

Best Western PLUS **AAA Benefit:** Members save up to 15% and earn bonus points!

Hotel
$129-$359

Address: 1076 Williston Rd 05403 **Location:** I-89 exit 14E, 0.3 mi e on US 2. **Facility:** 158 units, some two bedrooms. 2 stories, interior corridors. **Parking:** winter plug-ins. **Terms:** 2 night minimum stay - seasonal. **Dining:** Windjammer, see separate listing. **Pool:** outdoor, heated indoor. **Activities:** exercise room. **Guest Services:** valet and coin laundry, area transportation. **Featured Amenity:** breakfast buffet.

[SAVE] [ECO] [▭] [▯] [▯] CALL [&] [▭] [▭] [BIZ] [▭]
[▭] [▯] [▭] [▭] / SOME UNITS [▭] [HS]

DOUBLETREE BY HILTON BURLINGTON VERMONT
(802)865-6600

Hotel
$164-$1029

DOUBLETREE
BY HILTON

AAA Benefit:
Members save 5% or more!

Address: 870 Williston Rd 05403 **Location:** I-89 exit 14W, just w on US 2. **Facility:** 309 units. 2-4 stories, interior corridors. **Parking:** winter plug-ins. **Terms:** check-in 4 pm, 1-7 night minimum stay, cancellation fee imposed. **Amenities:** safes. **Pool:** heated indoor. **Activities:** exercise room. **Guest Services:** valet laundry, area transportation.

GREEN MOUNTAIN SUITES HOTEL   (802)860-1212
Extended Stay Hotel. **Address:** 401 Dorset St 05403

HOLIDAY INN BURLINGTON   802/863-6363
Hotel. **Address:** 1068 Williston Rd 05403

HOLIDAY INN EXPRESS   802/860-6000
Hotel. **Address:** 1720 Shelburne Rd 05403

HOMEWOOD SUITES BY HILTON SOUTH BURLINGTON
802/652-4400
Extended Stay Hotel. **Address:** 5 Dorset St 05403

AAA Benefit:
Members save 5% or more!

LA QUINTA INN & SUITES SOUTH BURLINGTON
(802)865-3400
Hotel. **Address:** 1285 Williston Rd 05403

TRADER DUKE'S HOTEL   (802)658-0250

Hotel
$71-$177

MARRIOTT

AAA Benefit:
Members save 5% or more!

Address: 1117 Williston Rd 05403 **Location:** I-89 exit 14E, just e on US 2. **Facility:** 161 units. 2 stories, interior corridors. **Parking:** winter plug-ins. **Terms:** cancellation fee imposed. **Dining:** Duke's Public House, see separate listing. **Pool:** heated indoor. **Activities:** hot tub, exercise room. **Guest Services:** valet laundry, area transportation. Affiliated with Marriott Hotels, Resorts and Suites.

WHERE TO EAT

AL'S FRENCH FRYS   802/862-9203
American. Casual Dining. **Address:** 1251 Williston Rd 05403

DUKE'S PUBLIC HOUSE   802/658-0250
American. Casual Dining. **Address:** 1117 Williston Rd 05403

GUILD TAVERN   802/497-1207
Steak. Fine Dining. **Address:** 1633 Williston Rd 05403

LAKE VIEW HOUSE RESTAURANT   802/865-3900
American. Casual Dining. **Address:** 1710 Shelburne Rd 05403

PAULINE'S CAFÉ   802/862-1081
New American. Casual Dining. **Address:** 1834 Shelburne Rd 05403

PULCINELLA'S   802/863-1000
Southern Italian. Casual Dining. **Address:** 100 Dorset St 05403

THE ROTISSERIE   802/658-1838
American. Casual Dining. **Address:** 1838 Williston Rd 05403

WINDJAMMER   802/862-6585
Seafood Steak. Casual Dining. **Address:** 1076 Williston Rd 05403

SPRINGFIELD (F-3) pop. 3,979, elev. 400'

The Black River powered a variety of Springfield mills in the 18th and early 19th centuries. Though some mills still exist along the river, none uses waterpower.

Two state historic sites are nearby. The restored Eureka Schoolhouse is east of Springfield on SR 11. Begun in 1785 and completed 5 years later, this one-room schoolhouse is said to be the state's oldest and is one of Vermont's few remaining 18th-century public buildings. Today it houses an information center. Next to it stands the 37-foot-long Baltimore Covered Bridge, built in 1870. The bridge originally spanned Great Brook in North Springfield; it was moved to its present location in 1970.

The Great Hall, 100 River St., is a renovated factory building that accommodates large works of art; phone (802) 885-3061.

Springfield declared itself "Home of the Simpsons" after being chosen as the fictional hometown of Homer, Marge, Bart, Lisa and Maggie from the animated television series "The Simpsons."

Springfield Regional Chamber of Commerce: 56 Main St., Suite 2, Springfield, VT 05156. **Phone:** (802) 885-2779.

HOLIDAY INN EXPRESS   802/885-4516
Hotel. **Address:** 818 Charlestown Rd 05156

STOWE (B-3) pop. 495, elev. 722'
• Hotels p. 170 • Restaurants p. 171
• Hotels & Restaurants map & index p. 169

In the heart of the Green Mountains, Stowe is a year-round vacation destination offering fall foliage viewing and other outdoor pursuits. This historic, picture-perfect New England village, complete with a white-steepled church, is nestled beside 4,393-foot Mount Mansfield, Vermont's highest peak. The Von Trapps of "The Sound of Music" fame settled in Stowe in the 1940s; today family descendants operate an alpine lodge offering classical concerts and sing-alongs.

The area includes some of New England's best downhill ski runs. Cross-country skiing, snowshoeing, sleighing and ice-skating also are popular cold-weather endeavors. Once it warms up, visitors can indulge in hiking, rock climbing, golf, horseback

(See map & index p. 169.)

riding, kayaking, mountain biking and ziplining. Hikers, cyclists and skaters head to the Stowe Recreation Path, starting in the town center behind the village church (parking areas provide access along the route). Area outfitters rent bikes and family biking accessories. For more challenging terrain, hikers venture to nearby Smugglers Notch State Park *(see Recreation Areas Chart)*.

Recreational activities aside, Stowe also presents a thriving cultural and arts scene. Visitors can enjoy musical, theatrical and dance performances as well as outdoor concerts by the Vermont Symphony Orchestra. Artists and craftspeople display their wares in the village's assorted shops and galleries—works include glass, pottery, jewelry, woodcarvings, painting, hand-dyed yarns, sculpture and photography.

During the summer months, Stowe Mountain Resort's gondola takes passengers on a 7,000-foot ride to a point just below Mount Mansfield's summit, where they can view sweeping panoramas of lush mountain valleys; phone (802) 253-3000 or (800) 253-4754.

On Sundays from mid-May to mid-October, the Stowe Farmers' Market is the place to shop for fresh produce, garden supplies, locally made products and other Vermont specialties; the market is next to the Red Barn shops on SR 108.

In addition to the area's brilliant foliage, a highlight of Stowe's fall season is the traditional harvest festival ▼ Oktoberfest, held in early October. Don your lederhosen and dirndls and celebrate the 3-day event in a re-created Bavarian village at the Stowe Events Fields. This lively event includes oompah bands, German food and beers, a parade, pumpkin and face painting, dancing and crafts.

Stowe Area Association: 51 Main St., P.O. Box 1320, Stowe, VT 05672. **Phone:** (802) 253-7321 or (800) 467-8693.

THE HELEN DAY ART CENTER, 90 Pond St., is in an 1860 Greek Revival building. It presents changing exhibitions of the works of well-known local, national and international visual artists.

Time: Allow 30 minutes minimum. **Hours:** Tues.-Sat. 10-5. Closed major holidays. Phone ahead to confirm schedule. **Cost:** Donations. **Phone:** (802) 253-8358.

VERMONT SKI & SNOWBOARD MUSEUM is at 1 S. Main St. The museum utilizes permanent and changing exhibits to relate Vermont's skiing and snowboarding history—from handcrafted 8-foot-long skis to lost ski areas to the story of the 10th Mountain Division to Vermont Olympians. **Time:** Allow 1 hour minimum. **Hours:** Generally open Wed.-Sun. noon-5. Closed Thanksgiving and Christmas. Phone ahead to confirm schedule. **Cost:** $5; $10 (family). **Phone:** (802) 253-9911.

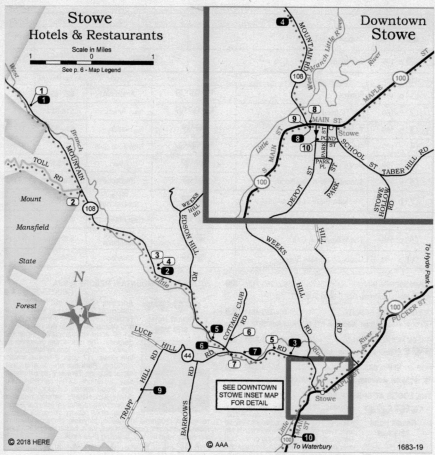

Stowe
Hotels & Restaurants

Scale in Miles
1   0   1

See p. 6 - Map Legend

Downtown Stowe

© 2018 HERE

© AAA

1683-19

Stowe

This index helps you "spot" where approved hotels and restaurants are located on the corresponding detailed maps. Hotel daily rate range is for comparison only. Restaurant price range is a combination of lunch and/or dinner. Turn to the listing page for more information and consult display ads for special promotions.

 For more details, rates and reservations: AAA.com/travelguides/hotels

STOWE

Map Page	Hotels	Diamond Rated	Rate Range	Page
1 this page	**The Lodge at Spruce Peak**	◆◆◆◆	$219-$899 SAVE	170
2 this page	**Topnotch Resort**	◆◆◆◆	Rates not provided SAVE	170
3 this page	Town & Country Resort Motor Inn	◆◆	Rates not provided	170
4 this page	Golden Eagle Resort	◆◆◆	Rates not provided	170
5 this page	Hob Knob Inn Bar & Lounge	◆◆	Rates not provided	170
6 this page	Stowe Motel & Snowdrift	◆◆	Rates not provided	170
7 this page	**Stoweflake Mountain Resort & Spa**	◆◆◆◆	$188-$926 SAVE	170
8 this page	Green Mountain Inn	◆◆◆	Rates not provided	170

STOWE (cont'd)

Map Page	Hotels (cont'd)	Diamond Rated	Rate Range	Page
9 p. 169	Trapp Family Lodge	◆◆◆	Rates not provided	171
10 p. 169	Commodores Inn	◆◆	Rates not provided	170

Map Page	Restaurants	Diamond Rated	Cuisine	Price Range	Page
1 p. 169	Solstice	◆◆◆	American	$27-$54	171
2 p. 169	Cliff House Restaurant	◆◆◆	New American	$16-$27	171
3 p. 169	Trattoria La Festa	◆◆	Italian	$16-$35	171
4 p. 169	Flannel	◆◆◆	New American	$7-$45	171
5 p. 169	Sushi Yoshi	◆◆	Asian	$9-$39	171
6 p. 169	Sunset Grille & Tap Room	◆◆	Barbecue	$8-$28	171
7 p. 169	Piecasso Pizzeria & Lounge	◆◆	Pizza Sandwiches	$9-$22	171
8 p. 169	Harrison's Restaurant & Bar	◆◆	New American	$13-$34	171
9 p. 169	The Whip Bar & Grill	◆◆	Regional American	$10-$36	171
10 p. 169	Depot Street Malt Shop	◆◆	American	$5-$9	171

COMMODORES INN   802/253-7131   **10**
◆◆ Hotel. **Address:** 823 S Main St 05672

GOLDEN EAGLE RESORT   802/253-4811   **4**
◆◆◆ Resort Motel. **Address:** 511 Mountain Rd 05672

GREEN MOUNTAIN INN   802/253-7301   **8**
◆◆◆ Historic Country Inn. **Address:** 18 Main St 05672

HOB KNOB INN BAR & LOUNGE   802/253-8549   **5**
◆◆ Motel. **Address:** 2364 Mountain Rd 05672

THE LODGE AT SPRUCE PEAK   (802)760-4700   **1**

◆◆◆◆
Resort Hotel
$219-$899

Address: 7412 Mountain Rd 05672 **Location:** Jct SR 100, 7.3 mi w on SR 108. **Facility:** This lodge is adjacent to a ski area, near ski lifts and the gondola to Mt. Mansfield. Relax year-round in the outdoor pool or rejuvenate in the luxurious spa and enjoy the views. 312 condominiums, some kitchens. 5 stories, interior corridors. **Parking:** on-site and valet. **Terms:** check-in 4 pm, 14 day cancellation notice-fee imposed, resort fee. **Amenities:** safes. Some: video games. **Dining:** 2 restaurants, also, Solstice, see separate listing. **Pool:** heated outdoor. **Activities:** sauna, hot tub, steamroom, regulation golf, tennis, downhill & cross country skiing, snowboarding, recreation programs in season, playground, game room, trails, health club, spa. **Guest Services:** valet and coin laundry.

STOWEFLAKE MOUNTAIN RESORT & SPA
(802)253-7355   **7**

◆◆◆
Resort Hotel
$188-$926

Address: 1746 Mountain Rd 05672 **Location:** Jct SR 100, 1.4 mi w on SR 108. **Facility:** Located near the village center and nearby ski areas, this resort is set on 60 acres of manicured lawns and gardens. The rooms are designed for comfort and many feature lovely mountain views. 117 units. 2 stories, interior corridors. **Parking:** on-site and valet, winter plug-ins. **Terms:** 2 night minimum stay - weekends, 15 day cancellation notice. **Pool:** heated outdoor, heated indoor. **Activities:** sauna, hot tub, steamroom, regulation golf, par 3 golf, tennis, cross country skiing, ice skating, recreation programs in season, bicycles, playground, game room, lawn sports, picnic facilities, trails, health club, spa. **Guest Services:** valet laundry, boarding pass kiosk.

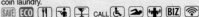

STOWE MOTEL & SNOWDRIFT   802/253-7629   **6**
◆◆ Motel. **Address:** 2135 Mountain Rd 05672

TOPNOTCH RESORT   802/253-8585   **2**

◆◆◆
Resort Hotel
Rates not provided

Address: 4000 Mountain Rd 05672 **Location:** Jct SR 100, 4.2 mi w on SR 108. **Facility:** This trendy hotel is close to the ski slopes. Set away from the road, it offers a quiet and upscale retreat. A selection of rooms with modern decor is offered; some have magnificent mountain views. 89 units, some kitchens and condominiums. 3 stories, interior/exterior corridors. **Parking:** on-site and valet. **Terms:** check-in 4 pm. **Amenities:** safes. **Dining:** Flannel, see separate listing. **Pool:** heated outdoor, heated indoor. **Activities:** sauna, hot tub, steamroom, tennis, recreation programs, game room, lawn sports, trails, health club, spa. **Guest Services:** valet laundry, area transportation. Affiliated with Preferred Hotels & Resorts.

TOWN & COUNTRY RESORT MOTOR INN
802/253-7595   **3**
◆◆ Motel. **Address:** 876 Mountain Rd 05672

(See map & index p. 169.)

TRAPP FAMILY LODGE   802-253-8511   [9]
♥♥♥ Resort Hotel. **Address:** 700 Trapp Hill Rd 05672

WHERE TO EAT

CLIFF HOUSE RESTAURANT   802/253-3558   [2]
♥♥♥ New American. Casual Dining. **Address:** 5781
Mountain Rd 05672

DEPOT STREET MALT SHOP   802/253-4269   [10]
♥♥ American. Casual Dining. **Address:** 57 Depot St 05672

FLANNEL   802/253-9263   [4]
♥♥♥ New American. Fine Dining. **Address:** 4000 Mountain
Rd 05672

HARRISON'S RESTAURANT & BAR   802/253-7773   [8]
♥♥ New American. Casual Dining. **Address:** 25 Main St (SR
100) 05672

PIECASSO PIZZERIA & LOUNGE   802/253-4411   [7]
♥♥ Pizza Sandwiches. Casual Dining. **Address:** 1899
Mountain Rd 05672

SOLSTICE   802/760-4735   [1]
♥♥♥ American. Fine Dining. **Address:** 7412 Mountain Rd
05672

SUNSET GRILLE & TAP ROOM   802/253-9281   [6]
♥ Barbecue. Casual Dining. **Address:** 140 Cottage Club Rd
05672

SUSHI YOSHI   802/253-4135   [5]
♥♥ Asian. Casual Dining. **Address:** 1128 Mountain Rd 05672

TRATTORIA LA FESTA   802/253-8480   [3]
♥♥ Italian. Casual Dining. **Address:** 4080 Mountain Rd
05672

THE WHIP BAR & GRILL   802/253-7301   [9]
♥♥ Regional American. Casual Dining. **Address:** 18 Main St
05672

SWANTON (A-2) pop. 2,386, elev. 148'

In the past, smuggling was one of Swanton's more lucrative businesses. This town near the Vermont-Québec border was the scene of controversy when enterprising Vermonters drove cattle across the border into Canada, where the livestock was sold to British soldiers during the War of 1812. Twentieth-century smugglers followed in their predecessors' footsteps during Prohibition when they ran liquor into the state by automobile.

Before 1700 the St. Francis Indians, guided by French Jesuits, built the first chapel in the Vermont territory at Swanton. After France lost the land to the English, the Native Americans moved the chapel stone by stone to St. Hyacinthe, Québec.

Missisquoi National Wildlife Refuge, 3 miles northwest off SR 78, covers 6,792 acres along the Missisquoi River delta and Lake Champlain. Waterfowl and other wildlife can be seen along a 1.5-mile interpretive trail. Several other refuge trails are open for wildlife observation. Hunting is allowed in season with a permit. Phone (802) 868-4781.

SWANTON MOTEL   802-868-4284
♥♥♥
Motel
Rates not provided

Address: 112 Grand Ave (US 7) 05488 **Location:** I-89 exit 21, 0.8 mi w on SR 78, then 0.5 mi s. **Facility:** 13 units, some two bedrooms and kitchens. 1 story, exterior corridors. **Parking:** winter plug-ins. **Pool:** outdoor. **Activities:** picnic facilities.

VERGENNES (C-1) pop. 2,588, elev. 176'

Settled in 1766 and incorporated in 1788, Vergennes is one of America's oldest incorporated cities and one of the smallest, at less than 2 square miles. During the War of 1812, 177 tons of cannon balls were cast in the city. The restored, 300-seat 1897 Vergennes Opera House, 120 Main St., is open weekdays for self-guiding tours; phone (802) 877-6737.

Bixby Memorial Free Library displays a collection of Abenaki Indian artifacts and items from other tribes; phone (802) 877-2211.

LAKE CHAMPLAIN MARITIME MUSEUM, on the eastern shore of Lake Champlain at 4472 Basin Harbor Rd., has over a dozen exhibit buildings chronicling the maritime history and nautical archeology of the Champlain Valley through interactive learning stations, video and audio displays, historical artifacts, and images. One of the most popular deciphers the stories of some unusual and dramatic shipwrecks in the lake. Also of interest is a full-size replica of a Revolutionary War gunboat from Lake Champlain's fleet.

Summer workshops on boat-building, blacksmithing and maritime skills are available, along with on-water ecology and historical excursions. **Time:** Allow 2 hours minimum. **Hours:** Daily 10-5, late May to mid-Oct. **Cost:** $14; $12 (ages 62+); $8 (ages 6-18). **Phone:** (802) 475-2022.

STRONG HOUSE INN   (802)877-3337
♥♥♥
**Historic
Country Inn**
$145-$345

Address: 94 W Main St 05491 **Location:** 0.6 mi s on SR 22A. **Facility:** This lovely, 1834 Federal-style inn has historic guest rooms ranging from cozy to luxurious. The great room has a full bar and comfy chairs; it's a superb place to unwind after exploring the trails. 13 units. 1-2 stories (no elevator), interior corridors. **Terms:** 2 night minimum stay – seasonal and/or weekends, 14 day cancellation notice, 30 day in season-fee imposed. **Activities:** trails, massage. **Guest Services:** valet laundry. **Featured Amenity:** full hot breakfast.

WAITSFIELD (C-2) pop. 164, elev. 712'
• Hotels p. 172 • Restaurants p. 172

Founded by Gen. Benjamin Wait in 1782 in a region known as Mad River Valley—which also comprises the towns of Warren, Fayston and

Moretown—this former dairying and lumbering center is now in the heart of a premier winter sports region. Hiking, road and mountain biking, fishing, swimming, and downhill and cross-country skiing are popular activities. The Village Bridge, Vermont's oldest covered bridge in continuous use, is in the middle of town. It was built in 1833.

Mad River Valley Chamber of Commerce: 4403 Main St., P.O. Box 173, Waitsfield, VT 05673. **Phone:** (802) 496-3409 or (800) 828-4748.

THE INN AT ROUND BARN FARM   802/496-2276
♥♥♥ Historic Bed & Breakfast. **Address:** 1661 E Warren Rd 05673

TUCKER HILL INN   802/496-3983
♥♥♥ Classic Country Inn. **Address:** 65 Marble Hill Rd 05673

WHERE TO EAT

AMERICAN FLATBREAD   802/496-8856
♥♥ Pizza. Casual Dining. **Address:** 46 Lareau Rd 05673

THE MAD TACO WAITSFIELD   802/496-3832
♥ Southwestern. Quick Serve. **Address:** 2 Village Square 05673

WARREN (C-2) elev. 915'

Named for physician and General Joseph Warren, who died in action at Bunker Hill, Warren is one of the trio of Mad River Valley communities.

THE PITCHER INN   802/496-6350
♥♥ ♥♥ Country Inn. **Address:** 275 Main St 05674

WHERE TO EAT

275 MAIN   802/496-6350
♥♥♥ ♥♥♥ Regional American. Fine Dining. **Address:** 275 Main St 05674

WATERBURY (C-2) pop. 1,763, elev. 427'

For a town with only two traffic lights, Waterbury sure has a lot going on. It's near some of the east's major ski resorts—Mad River Glen, Stowe Mountain Resort and Sugarbush Resort are all close by. It's a quintessentially quaint and charming New England village with an impressive historic district. You'll also find interesting 19th-century architecture, a restored train station and even a covered bridge or two nearby.

In addition to the aforementioned skiing—cross country as well as downhill—there's plenty to keep you outside enjoying the fresh air and beautiful scenery. There are trails to hike and mountain biking adventures to experience. You can fish in lakes or catch a trout in the Winooski River, launch a boat or canoe, or go for a swim or a picnic. Nearby Green Mountain National Forest and Mount Mansfield *(see place listings p. 155 and p. 162)* and Waterbury Reservoir provide opportunities for many of these endeavors.

Take a break from recreational activities and enjoy a sample of Cherry Garcia or Chunky Monkey

at hometown favorite Ben & Jerry's Ice Cream Factory Tours, or try a cup of the house blend at Waterbury's own Green Mountain Coffee Roasters Visitor Center.

Self-guiding tours: A brochure detailing a historical walking tour of Waterbury Village is available at local convenience stores.

BEST WESTERN PLUS WATERBURY-STOWE
                                        (802)244-7822

♥♥♥
Hotel
$125-$300

Best Western PLUS   **AAA Benefit:** Members save up to 15% and earn bonus points!

Address: 45 Blush Hill Rd 05676 **Location:** I-89 exit 10, just nw on SR 100. **Facility:** 83 units. 2 stories, interior corridors. **Terms:** cancellation fee imposed. **Amenities:** *Some:* safes. **Pool:** heated indoor. **Activities:** hot tub, playground, game room, exercise room. **Guest Services:** valet and coin laundry.

[SAVE] [🍴] [🍷] [🏊] [💪] [BIZ] [📶]
[✕] [🛏] [🖥] [/SOME UNITS] [HS] [🖨]

FAIRFIELD INN & SUITES BY MARRIOTT WATERBURY-STOWE   (802)241-1600
♥♥ Contemporary Hotel. **Address:** 1017 Waterbury-Stowe Rd 05676

AAA Benefit: Members save 5% or more!

WHERE TO EAT

THE BLUE STONE WATERBURY   802/882-8185
♥♥ American. Casual Dining. **Address:** 15 Stowe St 05676

PROHIBITION PIG   802/244-4120
♥♥ Comfort Food Barbecue. Casual Dining. **Address:** 23 S Main St 05676

THE RESERVOIR RESTAURANT & TAP ROOM   802/244-7827
♥♥ American. Sports Bar. **Address:** 1 S Main St 05676

WEST DOVER

BIG BEAR'S LODGE   802/464-5591
♥♥ Motel. **Address:** 344 Rt 100 N 05356

GRAND SUMMIT RESORT HOTEL & CONFERENCE CENTER
                                        802/464-6600
♥♥♥ Resort Hotel. **Address:** 89 Grand Summit Way 05356

WESTON (F-2) elev. 1,300'

Weston nestles in a valley below the source of the West River. Its many restored buildings help to preserve the atmosphere of a 19th-century Vermont village. The Weston Priory, 3 miles north of the village at 58 Priory Hill Rd., is a Benedictine monastery that welcomes the public; phone (802) 824-5409.

WESTON PLAYHOUSE, on the village green at 12 Park St., is Vermont's oldest professional theater company. The building's white-columned, Greek Revival facade was restored after a fire in 1962. Following the final curtain during the summer season the Act IV Cabaret, in the downstairs lounge, presents a music and comedy revue.

Hours: Performances are offered Tues.-Sat. at 7:30 p.m. (also Wed. and Sat. at 2, Sun. at 3), late June-early Sept. **Cost:** $30-$58. **Phone:** (802) 824-5288.

WEST TOWNSHEND

WINDHAM HILL INN   802/874-4080
▼▼▼▼ Historic Country Inn. **Address:** 311 Lawrence Dr 05359

WHERE TO EAT

WINDHAM HILL RESTAURANT   802/874-4080
▼▼▼▼ Regional American. Fine Dining. **Address:** 311 Lawrence Dr 05359

WHITE RIVER JUNCTION pop. 2,286

FAIRFIELD INN & SUITES BY MARRIOTT   (802)291-9911

▼▼▼
Hotel
$89-$335

 Fairfield

AAA Benefit: Members save 5% or more!

Address: 102 Ballardvale Dr 05001 **Location:** I-91 exit 11, just s. **Facility:** 67 units. 3 stories, interior corridors. **Parking:** winter plug-ins. **Terms:** cancellation fee imposed. **Activities:** exercise room. **Guest Services:** coin laundry. **Featured Amenity:** full hot breakfast.

HAMPTON INN BY HILTON WHITE RIVER JUNCTION
(802)296-2800

▼▼▼
Hotel
$123-$349

 Hampton by HILTON

AAA Benefit: Members save 5% or more!

Address: 104 Ballardvale Dr 05001 **Location:** I-91 exit 11, just s on US 5. **Facility:** 93 units. 3 stories, interior corridors. **Parking:** winter plug-ins. **Terms:** check-in 4 pm, 1-7 night minimum stay, cancellation fee imposed. **Pool:** heated indoor. **Activities:** exercise room. **Guest Services:** coin laundry. **Featured Amenity:** breakfast buffet.

HOLIDAY INN EXPRESS HOTEL & SUITES   802/299-2700
▼▼▼ Hotel. **Address:** 121 Ballardvale Dr 05001

WHERE TO EAT

BIG FATTY'S BBQ   802/295-5513
▼ Barbecue. Quick Serve. **Address:** 186 S Main St 05001

ELIXIR RESTAURANT   802/281-7009
▼▼▼ American. Fine Dining. **Address:** 188 S Main St 05001

THYME   802/295-3312
▼▼▼ New American. Fine Dining. **Address:** 85 N Main St 05001

TIP TOP CAFE   802/295-3312
▼▼▼ American. Casual Dining. **Address:** 85 N Main St 05001

TUCKERBOX TURKISH & MEDITERRANEAN CUISINE
802/359-4041
▼▼ Turkish. Casual Dining. **Address:** 1 S Main St 05001

WILLISTON

COURTYARD BY MARRIOTT BURLINGTON/WILLISTON
(802)879-0100
▼▼▼ Hotel. **Address:** 177 Hurricane Ln 05495

AAA Benefit: Members save 5% or more!

FAIRFIELD INN BY MARRIOTT BURLINGTON/WILLISTON
(802)879-8999

▼▼
Hotel
$55-$245

Fairfield

AAA Benefit: Members save 5% or more!

Address: 2844 St George Rd 05495 **Location:** I-89 exit 12, just n on SR 2A. **Facility:** 102 units. 3 stories, interior corridors. **Parking:** winter plug-ins. **Terms:** cancellation fee imposed. **Pool:** outdoor. **Activities:** exercise room. **Guest Services:** valet and coin laundry, boarding pass kiosk, area transportation.

SONESTA ES SUITES BURLINGTON VT   802/878-2001

▼▼▼
Extended Stay Hotel
Rates not provided

Address: 35 Hurricane Ln 05495 **Location:** I-89 exit 12, just s on SR 2A, then just e. **Facility:** 96 kitchen units, some two bedrooms. 2 stories (no elevator), exterior corridors. **Pool:** heated indoor. **Activities:** hot tub, picnic facilities, exercise room. **Guest Services:** valet and coin laundry. **Featured Amenity:** breakfast buffet.

WHERE TO EAT

CHEF'S CORNER CAFE & BAKERY   802/878-5524
▼▼ American. Quick Serve. **Address:** 300 Cornerstone Dr 05495

MCGILLICUDDY'S IRISH ALE HOUSE   802/857-5908
▼▼ Irish. Casual Dining. **Address:** 28 Walnut St 05495

VERMONT TAP HOUSE WILLISTON   802/879-7060
▼▼ Small Plates Pizza. Brewpub. **Address:** 22 Merchants Row 05495

WOODSTOCK (E-3) pop. 900, elev. 700'
• Hotels p. 174 • Restaurants p. 175

A resort and residential community, Woodstock is noted for its historic Federal-style homes and charming village green. Four local church bells were cast in Boston by either Paul Revere or a worker at his foundry.

Three covered bridges can be seen along scenic US 4. The Middle Bridge stands on Union Street; the Taftsville Bridge stands 3 miles east of the village;

and the Lincoln Bridge is in West Woodstock, 4 miles west.

Although it is best known for skiing, Woodstock also offers summer recreation, including golf, horseback riding and hiking. Holiday decorations and lights create a magical atmosphere during Woodstock's well-known Wassail Weekend the second weekend in December; the festivities include caroling, carriage rides and a parade with horseback riders in 19th-century garb.

Woodstock Area Chamber of Commerce: 34 Mechanic St., P.O. Box 486, Woodstock, VT 05091. **Phone:** (802) 457-3555 or (888) 496-6378.

 BILLINGS FARM & MUSEUM is .5 mi. n. on SR 12 across the Elm Street Bridge to 69 Old River Rd. It encompasses both a modern working dairy farm with one of the finest Jersey cattle herds in the nation and a museum depicting rural Vermont farm life in the late 19th century. In 1871 Vermont native Frederick Billings purchased the Woodstock farm where early conservationist George Perkins Marsh had grown up nurturing his love of nature. The restored farmhouse is now a living-history center offering a look at Billings Farm's farming and forestry operations circa the 1890s.

The museum, housed in four renovated 19th-century barns, portrays daily chores such as butter and cheese-making in addition to seasonal activities like ice cutting and sugaring. Tools, home furnishings, machinery and a re-created workshop, kitchen and country store are displayed. Visitors also can observe the daily activities of the modern dairy operation, including the afternoon milking, and participate in special activities. Nominated for an Academy Award, the film "A Place in the Land," which traces the history of the farm from the Marsh years through its Rockefeller ownership, is shown daily in the 96-seat theater.

Self-guiding tours of the farmhouse are available. **Time:** Allow 2 hours minimum. **Hours:** Daily 10-5, Apr.-Oct.; Sat.-Sun. 10-4, Nov.-Feb. (also daily 10-4, Christmas week and school break weeks in Feb.). **Cost:** $16; $14 (ages 62+); $8 (ages 5-15); $4 (ages 3-4). **Phone:** (802) 457-2355.

SUGARBUSH FARM is at 591 Sugarbush Farm Rd. The farm produces maple syrup and cheeses. Exhibits and a video presentation about farm life and syrup making detail production processes, and free samples are provided. Visitors can walk through the woods and see some of the equipment used in collecting maple sap and making syrup.

Time: Allow 1 hour minimum. **Hours:** Daily 9-5. Phone for winter hours and road conditions. Closed Thanksgiving and Christmas. **Cost:** Free. **Phone:** (802) 457-1757 or (800) 281-1757.

506 ON THE RIVER INN   802/457-5000
🔻🔻🔻 Boutique Hotel. **Address:** 1653 W Woodstock Rd (US 4) 05091

BRAESIDE LODGING   802/457-1366
🔻🔻 Motel. **Address:** 908 US 4 E (Woodstock Rd) 05091

THE JACKSON HOUSE INN   (802)457-2065
🔻🔻🔻🔻 Historic Bed & Breakfast. **Address:** 43 Senior Ln 05091

THE LINCOLN INN & RESTAURANT AT THE COVERED BRIDGE   802/457-7052
🔻🔻🔻 Country Inn. **Address:** 2709 W Woodstock Rd 05091

THE SHIRE WOODSTOCK   802/457-2211
🔻🔻 Motel. **Address:** 46 Pleasant St 05091

VILLAGE INN OF WOODSTOCK   (802)457-1255
🔻🔻🔻 Historic Bed & Breakfast. **Address:** 41 Pleasant St (US 4) 05091

THE WOODSTOCKER B&B   (802)457-3896

🔻🔻🔻
Historic Bed & Breakfast
$159-$399

Address: 61 River St 05091 **Location:** 0.5 mi w on US 4. Located in a residential area. **Facility:** An 1830 Cape Dutch-style house, this B&B is in a picturesque area within walking distance of the village green. Guest rooms feature modern farmhouse décor; plush robes are provided. 9 units. 2 stories (no elevator), interior corridors. **Terms:** 2 night minimum stay - seasonal, 14 day cancellation notice-fee imposed. **Featured Amenity:** full hot breakfast.

🖼 SAVE ECO 🍴 📶 ✖ ☎

WOODSTOCK INN & RESORT   (802)457-1100

🔻🔻🔻
Resort Hotel
$179-$1819

Address: 14 The Green 05091 **Location:** On US 4; center. Located on village green. **Facility:** Combining New England history and charm, this inn is close to boutiques and restaurants. Room highlights include luxurious bedding, handcrafted furniture, a marble vanity counter and a makeup mirror. 142 units. 4 stories, interior corridors. **Parking:** on-site and valet. **Terms:** check-in 4 pm, 2-3 night minimum stay - seasonal and/or weekends, 14 day cancellation notice-fee imposed, resort fee. **Amenities:** video games, safes. **Dining:** 2 restaurants, also, The Red Rooster, see separate listing. **Pool:** heated outdoor, heated indoor. **Activities:** sauna, hot tub, steamroom, fishing, regulation golf, tennis, recreation programs, bicycles, game room, health club, spa. **Guest Services:** valet laundry, area transportation.

SAVE ECO 🚭 🍴 🛁 / CALL 🦽 🐾 👤 BIZ 📶 ✖ 📷 📱 💻 / SOME UNITS 🐾 HS

WHERE TO EAT

MELAZA CARIBBEAN BISTRO   802/457-7110
♦♦ Caribbean. Casual Dining. **Address:** 71 Central St 05091

MOUNTAIN CREAMERY   802/457-1715
♦ American. Casual Dining. **Address:** 33 Central St 05091

PI BRICK OVEN TRATTORIA   802/457-9277
♦♦ Pizza. Casual Dining. **Address:** 49 Central St 05091

THE PRINCE & THE PAUPER   802/457-1818
♦♦♦ Continental. Fine Dining. **Address:** 24 Elm St 05091

THE RED ROOSTER   802/457-6671

♦♦♦ Regional American Fine Dining $15-$38

AAA Inspector Notes: The contemporary décor includes light hardwood surfaces, an atrium skylight and a view of the gardens. The chef focuses on using local ingredients, such as Vermont cheeses and heirloom varieties of vegetables. Dishes are expertly seasoned and simply delicious. Some seasonal favorites include beef carpaccio, blue crab cakes, lemon salted scallops and Cornish game hen. Top off your meal with one of the pastry chef's delectable delights. **Features:** full bar. **Reservations:** suggested. **Address:** 14 The Green 05091 **Location:** On US 4; center; in Woodstock Inn & Resort. **Parking:** on-site and valet. B L D CALL ♿

WORTHY KITCHEN   802/457-7281
♦♦ Comfort Food. Casual Dining. **Address:** 442 Woodstock Rd 05091

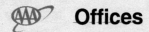

Offices

Main office listings are shown in **BOLD TYPE** and toll-free member service numbers appear in *ITALIC TYPE*.
All are closed Saturdays, Sundays and holidays unless otherwise indicated.
The addresses, phone numbers and hours for any AAA/CAA office are subject to change.
The type of service provided is designated below the name of the city where the office is located:

+ Auto travel services, including books and maps, and on-demand TripTik ® routings.
● Auto travel services, including selected books and maps, and on-demand TripTik ® routings.
■ Books/maps only, no marked maps or on-demand TripTik ® routings.
▲ Travel Agency Services, cruise, tour, air, car and rail reservations; domestic and international hotel reservations; passport photo services; international and domestic travel guides and maps; travel money products; and International Driving Permits. In addition, assistance with travel related insurance products including trip cancellation, travel accident, lost luggage, trip delay and assistance products.
✪ Insurance services provided. If only this icon appears, only insurance services are provided at that office.
◖ Car Care Plus Facility provides car care services.
◨ Electric vehicle charging station on premises.

AAA NATIONAL OFFICE: 1000 AAA DRIVE, HEATHROW, FLORIDA 32746-5063, (407) 444-7000

MAINE

AUBURN—AAA NORTHERN NEW ENGLAND, 600 CENTER ST SHAWS PLZ, 04210. WEEKDAYS (M-F) 8:30-5:00, SAT 9:00-1:00. (207) 786-0664, *(800) 310-1222.* + ▲ ✪

AUGUSTA—AAA NORTHERN NEW ENGLAND, 20 WHITTEN RD STE 11, 04330. WEEKDAYS (M-F) 8:30-5:00, SAT 9:00-1:00. (207) 622-2221, *(800) 640-5608.* + ▲ ✪

BANGOR—AAA NORTHERN NEW ENGLAND, 339 GRIFFIN RD, 04401. WEEKDAYS (M-F) 8:30-5:00, SAT 9:00-1:00. (207) 942-8287, *(800) 223-3700.* + ▲ ✪

BIDDEFORD—AAA NORTHERN NEW ENGLAND, 472 ALFRED ST STE 102, 04005. WEEKDAYS (M-F) 8:30-5:00, SAT 9:00-1:00. (207) 282-5212, *(866) 485-8812.* + ▲ ✪

BRUNSWICK—AAA NORTHERN NEW ENGLAND, 147 BATH RD STE A130, 04011. WEEKDAYS (M-F) 8:30-5:00, SAT 9:00-1:00. (207) 729-3300, *(800) 499-3111.* + ▲ ✪

ELLSWORTH—AAA NORTHERN NEW ENGLAND, 130 OAK ST STE 3, 04605. WEEKDAYS (M-F) 8:30-5:00, SAT 9:00-1:00. (207) 667-6260, *(800) 437-0281.* + ▲ ✪

PORTLAND—AAA NORTHERN NEW ENGLAND, 68 MARGINAL WAY, 04101. WEEKDAYS (M-F) 8:30-5:00, SAT 9:00-1:00. (207) 780-6950, *(800) 482-7497.* + ▲ ✪

SOUTH PORTLAND—AAA NORTHERN NEW ENGLAND, 401 WESTERN AVE, 04106. WEEKDAYS (M-F) 8:30-5:00, SAT 9:00-1:00. (207) 775-6211, *(800) 336-6211.* + ▲ ✪

WATERVILLE—AAA NORTHERN NEW ENGLAND, 13 WASHINGTON ST, 04901. WEEKDAYS (M-F) 8:30-5:00, SAT 9:00-1:00. (207) 873-0692, *(800) 359-2106.* + ▲ ✪

NEW HAMPSHIRE

CONCORD—AAA NORTHERN NEW ENGLAND, 48 FT EDDY RD, 03301. WEEKDAYS (M-F) 8:30-5:00, SAT 9:00-1:00. (603) 228-0301, *(800) 222-3422.* + ▲ ✪

KEENE—AAA NORTHERN NEW ENGLAND, 429 WEST ST, 03431. WEEKDAYS (M-F) 8:30-5:00, SAT 9:00-1:00. (603) 358-0460, *(800) 222-3407.* + ▲ ✪

MANCHESTER—AAA NORTHERN NEW ENGLAND, 560 S WILLOW ST, 03103. WEEKDAYS (M-F) 8:30-5:00, SAT 9:00-1:00. (603) 669-0101, *(800) 222-3445.* + ▲ ✪

NASHUA—AAA NORTHERN NEW ENGLAND, 379 AMHERST ST UNIT 6B, 03063. WEEKDAYS (M-F) 8:30-5:00, SAT 9:00-1:00. (603) 889-0165, *(800) 222-3750.* + ▲ ✪

PORTSMOUTH—AAA NORTHERN NEW ENGLAND, 599 LAFAYETTE RD #15, 03801. WEEKDAYS (M-F) 8:30-5:00, SAT 9:00-1:00. (603) 436-8610, *(800) 222-3420.* + ▲ ✪

SALEM—AAA NORTHEAST, 489 S BROADWAY, 03079. WEEKDAYS (M-F) 9:00-5:00, SAT 9:00-1:00. (603) 898-9953 + ▲ ✪

SOMERSWORTH—AAA NORTHERN NEW ENGLAND, 452 HIGH STREET, 03878. WEEKDAYS (M-F) 8:30-5:00, SAT 9:00-1:00. (603) 750-3080, *(866) 484-5681.* + ▲ ✪

WEST LEBANON—AAA NORTHERN NEW ENGLAND, 267 PLAINFIELD RD UNIT 2, 03784. WEEKDAYS (M-F) 8:30-5:00, SAT 9:00-1:00. (844) 291-7121. + ▲ ✪

VERMONT

MONTPELIER—AAA NORTHERN NEW ENGLAND, 384 RIVER ST, 05602. WEEKDAYS (M-F) 8:30-5:00, SAT 9:00-1:00. (802) 229-0505, *(800) 717-0222.* + ▲ ✪

RUTLAND—AAA NORTHERN NEW ENGLAND, 302 US RT 7 S, 05701. WEEKDAYS (M-F) 8:30-5:00, SAT 9:00-1:00. (802) 775-1558, *(800) 388-1558.* + ▲ ✪

WILLISTON—AAA NORTHERN NEW ENGLAND, 28 WALNUT ST STE 160, 05495. WEEKDAYS (M-F) 8:30-5:00, SAT 9:00-1:00. (802) 878-8233, *(800) 477-1323.* + ▲ ✪

Border Information

U.S. Residents Traveling to Canada

Border crossing requirements: Travelers are required to present proper travel documents in order to enter Canada and return to the U.S.

Air travel: A U.S. passport is required.

Land or sea travel: Proof of citizenship and proof of identity are required. Approved documents include a passport or passport card, Enhanced Driver's License or NEXUS trusted traveler program card. Visit the U.S. Department of State website travel.state.gov for the most current information on these requirements. Canadian citizens should refer to the Canada Border Services Agency website www.cbsa-asfc.gc.ca.

U.S. resident aliens: An Alien Registration Receipt Card (Green Card) as well as a passport from the country of citizenship is required.

Children: All children must provide their own travel documents. In lieu of a U.S. passport or passport card, children under 16 traveling to Canada by land or sea may present an original or copy of their birth certificate, a Report of Birth Abroad obtained from a U.S. Consulate or a Naturalization Certificate. Minors must be accompanied by both parents; if one parent is absent, a notarized

letter of consent from the absent parent giving permission to go on the trip is required.

Legal Issues: Persons with felony convictions, DUI convictions or other offenses may be denied entry into Canada.

Firearms: Canada has strict laws regarding the importing, exporting, possession, use, storage, display and transportation of firearms. These are federal laws that apply across the country. Firearms are divided into classes: non-restricted (most ordinary rifles and shotguns); restricted (mainly handguns) and prohibited (full and converted automatics and certain handguns, among others).

To bring a non-restricted or restricted firearm into Canada you must:
- Be 18 years of age or older
- Declare firearm(s) in writing at the first point of entry
- Obtain an Authorization to Transport (ATT) from a provincial or territorial Chief Firearms Officer prior to arrival at the point of entry; contact the Canadian Firearms Centre at (800) 731-4000 for additional details.

Hunters may bring in, duty-free, 200 rounds of ammunition; a valid license or declaration to purchase ammunition is required. Those planning to hunt in multiple provinces or territories must obtain a hunting license from each one.

Firearms are forbidden in many of Canada's national and provincial parks, game reserves and adjacent areas. For additional information regarding the temporary importation and use of firearms consult the Canada Border Services Agency website.

Personal items: Clothing, personal items, sports and recreational equipment, automobiles, snowmobiles, cameras, personal computers and food products appropriate for the purpose and duration of the visit may be brought into Canada duty and tax-free. Customs may require a refundable security deposit at the time of entry.

Tobacco products: Those meeting age requirements (18 years in Alberta, Manitoba, Northwest Territories, Nunavut, Saskatchewan, Quebec and Yukon; 19 years in other provinces) may bring in up to 50 cigars, 200 cigarettes, 200 grams of tobacco and 200 tobacco sticks.

Alcohol: Those meeting age requirements (18 years in Alberta, Manitoba and Quebec; 19 years in other provinces and territories) may bring in limited alcoholic beverages: 40 fluid ounces (1.14 litres) of liquor, 53 fluid ounces (1.5 litres) of wine (about two 750-ml bottles) or 287 fluid ounces (8.5 litres) of beer or ale (the equivalent of 24 12-ounce bottles or cans).

- Amounts exceeding the allowable quantities are subject to federal duty and taxes, and provincial/territorial liquor fees.
- Provincial fees are paid at customs at the time of entry in all provinces and Yukon.
- It is illegal to bring more than the allowable alcohol quantity into the Northwest Territories or Nunavut.

Purchases: Articles purchased at Canadian duty-free shops are subject to U.S. Customs exemptions and restrictions; those purchased at U.S. duty-free shops before entering Canada are subject to duty if brought back into the United States.

Prescription drugs: Persons requiring medication while visiting Canada are permitted to bring it for their own use. Medication should be in the original packaging with a label listing the drug and its intended use. Bring a copy of the prescription and the prescribing doctor's phone number.

Gifts: Items not exceeding $60 (CAN) in value (excluding tobacco, alcoholic beverages and advertising matter) taken into or mailed to Canada are allowed free entry. Gifts valued at more than $60 are subject to regular duty and taxes on the excess amount.

Pets: You must have a certificate for a dog or cat 3 months and older. It must clearly describe the animal, declare that the animal is currently vaccinated against rabies and include a licensed veterinarian signature.

- Collar tags are not sufficient proof of immunization.
- Be sure the vaccination does not expire while traveling in Canada.
- The certificate is also required to bring the animal back into the U.S.

Exemptions: Service animals; healthy puppies and kittens under 3 months old with a health certificate signed by a licensed

veterinarian indicating that the animal is too young to vaccinate.

Vehicles

- Vehicles entering Canada for leisure travel, including trailers not exceeding 8 feet 6 inches (2.6 m) in width, are generally subject to quick and routine entry procedures.
- To temporarily leave or store a car, trailer or other goods in Canada if you must leave the country, you must pay an import duty and taxes or present a valid permit. Canadian Customs officials issue vehicle permits at the point of entry.
- You are required to carry your vehicle registration document when traveling in Canada.
- If driving a car other than your own, you must have written permission from the owner.
- If driving a rented car, you must provide a copy of the rental contract.
- A valid U.S. driver's license is valid in Canada.
- In all Canadian provinces and territories except Alberta, British Columbia and Saskatchewan, it is illegal to use radar detectors, even if unplugged.
- Seat belt use is required for the driver and all passengers.

Financial Responsibility Laws in Canada: When an accident involves death, injury or property damage, Canadian provinces and territories require evidence of financial responsibility.

U.S. motorists should check with their insurance company regarding whether they are required to obtain and carry a yellow Non-Resident Inter-Province Motor Vehicle Liability Insurance Card (accepted as evidence of financial responsibility throughout Canada). Those not carrying proper proof may be subject to a substantial fine. If renting a vehicle, check with the rental car company.

U.S. Residents Returning to the U.S.

U.S. citizens returning to the U.S. from Canada by air must have a valid passport. Those returning by land or sea are required to present the appropriate travel documents outlined above.

Every individual seeking entry into the United States—foreign visitors, U.S. citizens or lawful permanent residents—must be inspected at the point of entry and each family (persons living in the same household related by blood, marriage, domestic partnership or adoption) must complete a declarations form. Random searches may be conducted by U.S. Customs and Border Protection agents.

U.S. Exemptions for a Stay in Canada of 48 Hours or More
- Each individual may bring back tax- and duty-free articles not exceeding $800 in retail value.
- Any amount over the $800 exemption is subject to duty.
- The exemption is allowed once every 31 days.
- A family may combine purchases to avoid exceeding individual exemption limits.
- Exemptions are based on fair retail value (keep receipts of all purchases as proof).
- Exemptions apply to articles acquired only for personal or household use or as gifts and not intended for sale.
- The exemption may include 100 cigars, 200 cigarettes and 1 litre (33.8 fluid ounces) of liquor per person over age 21. Customs enforces state liquor laws.
- All articles must accompany you on your return.

U.S. Exemptions for a Stay in Canada Less Than 48 Hours
- Each individual may bring back tax- and duty-free articles not exceeding $200 in retail value.
- The exemption may include no more than 10 cigars, 50 cigarettes, 150 millilitres (5 fluid ounces) of alcohol or 150 millilitres of perfume containing alcohol.
- A family may not combine purchases.
- If purchases exceed the $200 exemption, you forfeit the exemption and all purchases become subject to duty.
- All articles must be declared and accompany you upon return.

Gifts
- Gifts up to $100 fair retail value may be sent to friends or relatives in the United States provided no recipient receives more than one gift per day (gifts do not have to be included in the $800 exemption).
- Gifts of tobacco products, alcoholic beverages or perfume containing alcohol valued at more than $5 retail are excluded from this provision.

- Mark the contents, retail value and "Unsolicited Gift" on the outside of the package.

Prohibited: Narcotics and dangerous drugs, drug paraphernalia, obscene articles and publications, seditious or treasonable matter, lottery tickets, hazardous items (fireworks, dangerous toys, toxic or poisonous substances) citrus products and switchblade knives. Also prohibited are any goods originating in embargoed countries.

Canadian Residents Traveling to the U.S.

Canadian citizens entering the U.S. by air must have a valid passport. Canadian citizens entering the U.S. by land or sea are required to present the appropriate travel documents; refer to the Canada Border Services Agency website www.cbsa-asfc.gc.ca or travel.state.gov for the most current information on these requirements.

If traveling to the United States with a minor 15 years or younger, carry documentation proving your custodial rights. A person under age 18 traveling to the United States alone or with only one parent or another adult must carry certified documentation proving that the trip is permitted by both parents.

U.S. Customs permits Canadian residents to bring—duty-free for personal use and not intended for sale—the following: clothing, personal items and equipment appropriate to

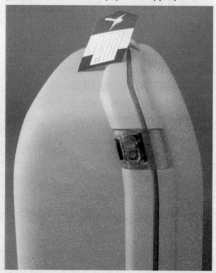

the trip, up to 200 cigarettes, 50 cigars or 2 kilograms of tobacco, and 1 litre of liquor.

Canadian Residents Returning to Canada

There are no exemptions for same-day cross-border shoppers.

Canadian residents may claim a $200 (CAN) exemption on goods, excluding alcoholic beverages and tobacco products, if returning after less than 48 hours and not using any other exemption. This exemption may apply any number of times in a year. No tobacco or alcohol may be brought back if returning from a visit of less than 48 hours.

For each absence of 48 hours or more (but fewer than seven days), residents may bring back, free of duty and taxes, goods valued up to $800 (CAN) any number of times a year, provided the visit to the United States is 48 hours or more and all goods accompany the purchaser (a written declaration may be required).

If returning after 7 days or more (not counting the departure day from Canada) you may claim up to a $800 (CAN) exemption, but goods other than alcohol and tobacco products need not accompany you (a written declaration may be required).

Permitted within the $200 and $800 exemptions: up to 50 cigars, 200 cigarettes, 200 tobacco sticks and 200 grams of tobacco; and up to 1.14 litres (40 fluid ounces) of liquor, 1.5 litres (53 fluid ounces) of wine (about two 750-ml bottles) or 8.5 litres (287 fluid ounces) of beer or ale (the equivalent of 24 12-ounce bottles or cans). You must meet the minimum age requirement of the province or territory entered to claim alcohol or tobacco products.

While AAA makes every effort to provide accurate and complete information, AAA makes no warranty, express or implied, and assumes no legal liability or responsibility for the accuracy or completeness of any information contained herein.

Photo Credits

Page numbers are in bold type. Picture credit abbreviations are as follows:
■ (i) numeric sequence from top to bottom, left to right ■ (AAA) AAA Travel library.

■ (Cover) Portsmouth, NH / © iStockphoto.com / Sean Pavone

■ **2** (i) © iStockphoto.com / DenisTangneyJr

■ **2** (ii) Arcaid Images / Alamy Stock Photo

■ **2** (iii) Sandra Foyt / Alamy Stock Photo

■ **8** (i) © iStockphoto.com / Mak_photo

■ **8** (ii) © iStockphoto.com / Ron and Patty Thomas

■ **9** © iStockphoto.com / sara_winter

■ **10** (i) © iStockphoto.com / GMVozd

■ **10** (ii) Courtesy of Wikimedia Commons

■ **13** (i) © iStockphoto.com / ArtMarie

■ **13** (ii) © iStockphoto.com / Vladone

■ **13** (iii) Hemis / Alamy Stock Photo

■ **13** (iv) © iStockphoto.com / PictureLake

■ **13** (v) Sean Pavone / Alamy Stock Photo

■ **14** (i) eye35 / Alamy Stock Photo

■ **14** (ii) imageBROKER / Alamy Stock Photo

■ **14** (iii) © iStockphoto.com / schnuddel

■ **14** (iv) Arcaid Images / Alamy Stock Photo

■ **90** (i) © iStockphoto.com / DenisTangneyJr

■ **90** (ii) © iStockphoto.com / littleny

■ **91** Jon Bilous / Alamy Stock Photo

■ **92** (i) © Mathew Brady / Wikimedia Commons

■ **92** (ii) Courtesy of Wikimedia Commons

■ **95** (i) © iStockphoto.com / simonmayer

■ **95** (ii) Brad Mitchell / Alamy Stock Photo

■ **95** (iii) Ellen McKnight / Alamy Stock Photo

■ **95** (iv) © iStockphoto.com / DenisTangneyJr

■ **95** (v) © iStockphoto.com / sjlayne

■ **96** (i) Frank Vetere / Alamy Stock Photo

■ **96** (ii) John Elk III / Alamy Stock Photo

■ **96** (iii) © Terrance Klassen / age fotostock

■ **96** (iv) Andre Jenny / Alamy Stock Photo

■ **136** (i) © iStockphoto.com / Songquan Deng

■ **136** (ii) © iStockphoto.com / Kirkikis

■ **137** © iStockphoto.com / VisualCommunications

■ **138** (i) © Arminnius / Wikimedia Commons / CC BY SA

■ **138** (ii) © George Grantham Bain / Wikimedia Commons

■ **141** (i) © iStockphoto.com / nautilus_shell_studios

■ **141** (ii) H. Mark Weidman Photography / Alamy Stock Photo

■ **141** (iii) © iStockphoto.com / Ron_Thomas

■ **141** (iv) MiraMira / Alamy Stock Photo

■ **141** (v) David Lyons / Alamy Stock Photo

■ **142** (i) Sandra Foyt / Alamy Stock Photo

■ **142** (ii) © FOTOSEARCH RM / age fotostock

■ **142** (iii) nik wheeler / Alamy Stock Photo

■ **142** (iv) David Lyons / Alamy Stock Photo

■ **177** © Garry Gay / Alamy Stock Photo

■ **179** © image100 / age fotostock

Make the Connction

For trip planning and local activities, AAA guidebooks are just the beginning.

Open the door to a whole lot more on **AAA.com**. Get extra travel insight, more information and online booking.

Find this symbol for places to look, book and save on AAA.com.

Experience the DIAMOND Difference

With so many hotel and restaurant rating systems, it's hard to know who to trust. That's why AAA uses professional inspectors to conduct in-person evaluations using guidelines based on member priorities.

 FIVE REASONS TO TRUST AAA

1 - Inspection visits are unscheduled
2 - Our guidelines are an open book
3 - We're in it for members
4 - We know travel inside out
5 - We're picky

Every AAA Inspected & Approved establishment is good for the kind of experience it offers. So the only question is, how many Diamonds are right for your needs?

Inspected & Approved

Visit AAA.com/Diamonds

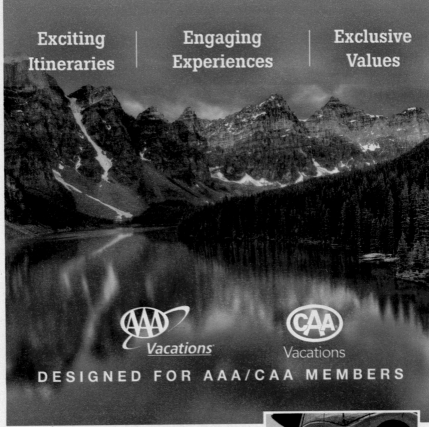

We're here to get you there.

AAA members get more with Hertz.*

- Up to 20% savings on the base rate of all rentals
- Additional driver fee waived for AAA members
- Complimentary use of one child safety seat
- Young Renter fee waived for AAA members ages 20-24
- Free Hertz Gold Plus Rewards® membership with exclusive bonus points
- Discounted NeverLost® navigation system and satellite radio
- 10% off prepay fuel option

Click: AAA.com/hertz
Call: 1-800-654-3080
Visit: Your local AAA branch or Hertz neighborhood location.

*Discount applies to pay later base rates only. Taxes and Fees excluded. Discount will vary depending on location, date length, car class & other factors. Benefits available at participating locations in the U.S. and Canada. Terms apply. © 2018 Hertz System, Inc. All rights reserved. CS 518009.